VARIORUM COLLECTED STUDIES SERIES

# Popes and Church Reform
# in the 11th Century

H.E.J. Cowdrey

# Popes and Church Reform
# in the 11th Century

VARIORUM

Aldershot · Burlington USA · Singapore · Sydney

This edition copyright © 2000 by H.E.J. Cowdrey

**Published in the Variorum Collected Studies Series by**

Ashgate Publishing Limited
Gower House, Croft Road,
Aldershot, Hampshire GU11 3HR
Great Britain

Ashgate Publishing Company
131 Main Street
Burlington, Vermont 05401
USA

Ashgate website: http://www.ashgate.com

ISBN 0–86078–797–4

**British Library Cataloguing-in-Publication Data**
Cowdrey, H.E.J. (Herbert Edward John), 1926–
     Popes and Church Reform in the 11th Century.
     (Variorum Collected Studies Series; CS674).
     1. Gregory, VII, Pope, ca. 1015–1085. 2. Catholic Church.
     3. Church renewal –Catholic Church. 4. Church history–
     11th century.
     I. Title.
     282

**US Library of Congress Cataloging-in-Publication Data**
Library of Congress Card Number: 00–100178

Printed by St Edmundsbury Press Ltd., Bury St Edmunds, Suffolk.

VARIORUM COLLECTED STUDIES SERIES CS674

# CONTENTS

This volume contains vii + 310 pages

## PUBLISHER'S NOTE

*The articles in this volume, as in all others in the Variorum Collected Studies Series, have not been given a new, continuous pagination. In order to avoid confusion, and to facilitate their use where these same studies have been referred to elsewhere, the original pagination has been maintained wherever possible.*

*Each article has been given a Roman number in order of appearance, as listed in the Contents. This number is repeated on each page and is quoted in the index entries.*

# PREFACE

This is the second volume in the Variorum Collected Studies series of articles that were preparatory to and illustrative of my book *Pope Gregory VII, 1073–1085* (Oxford, 1998). A principal conclusion that I hoped to establish in this book was that Gregory was a pope of deeper spirituality than has been generally allowed and that, consciously following the tradition of Pope Gregory the Great, a major concern was the moralization of the western church and society. At the same time, he was a profoundly Roman pope who was steeped in the traditions of the Roman church. He was also deeply concerned in the life of regional churches, both those of central Italy which were directly subject to the jurisdiction of the pope as bishop of Rome, and those of the periphery of Latin Christendom, such as the Anglo-Norman lands and Scandinavia. His attempts to promote the reform of the church provoked mixed reactions. The coolness of Archbishop Lanfranc of Canterbury is a significant case-study of a major figure of the highest ability and integrity who viewed Gregory with considerable reservations, not least, perhaps, because of their different approaches to the problems raised by the eucharistic teachings of Berengar of Tours.

*St Edmund Hall,*                                                    H.E.J. COWDREY
*Oxford.*

# ACKNOWLEDGEMENTS

Grateful acknowledgement is made to the following publishers, journals, and editors for their kind permission to reproduce the ten articles included in this volume: Dr W. Kos, on behalf of Adolf M. Hakkert (I); Dr James Hogg and *Analecta Cartusiana* (II); Dr C. Puccino, on behalf of Garland Publishing Inc. (III); Dr Richard Barber, on behalf of The Boydell Press (IV, XI); Dr Stefano Miccichié on behalf of Rubbettino Editore (V); Dr Oswald Schönberg, on behalf of Herzog August Bibliothek Wolfenbüttel and Verlag Harrassowitz (VI); Dr Giuseppe Zucchelli, on behalf of the Pontificio Ateneo Salesiano (VII); Professor Claudio Leonardi, on behalf of *Studi Medievali* (VIII): Dr W. Setz, on behalf of *Monumenta Germaniae Historica* (IX); Professor Rigon, on behalf of Herder Editrice e Libreria (X).

# ELEVENTH-CENTURY REFORMERS' VIEWS OF CONSTANTINE

In the seventeenth century, John Milton had no difficulty in marshalling later medieval testimony, notably that of Dante, Petrarch, and Ariosto, for his contention that "Constantine marred all in the church". It was an opinion that had been gaining ground since Bernard of Clairvaux had inveighed against the laws that daily resounded in the Lateran palace as being those of Justinian not Christ, and against the trappings of papal power which made the pope the successor not of Peter but of Constantine.[1] The popes of the reforming days of the second half of the eleventh century had thought differently, as had those at Rome and elsewhere who propagated their cause. For them, Constantine was *vir religiosissimus Constantinus primus*, and his age was epitomised as the *pii Constantini tempora*. Two periods were looked back to as golden ages of the early church. One was that of the early church of Jerusalem in the Acts of the Apostles, chapters 2: 42–47 and 4: 32–35, in which the company of those who believed was of one heart and soul. The other was the age of Christian emperors of whom Constantine was the first and towering exemplar; it was ended by the miseries of the Lombard invasion of Italy, although Pope Gregory the Great harvested its spiritual and ecclesiastical fruit for the benefit of a future age that might aspire to renovate its pristine excellence. In this paper I aim to do two things: first, to give some account of the image of Constantine which was transmitted from his own age to that of popes like Gregory VII and Urban II and their supporters, and secondly to consider how, as a consequence, the later eleventh–century reformers presented an emperor who seemed to meet their standard of what an emperor should be and do.

A legend of the most religious Constantine was quick to begin. In the East, it was encouraged by Bishop Eusebius of Caesarea's *Vita Constantini*,

---

[1]    J. MILTON, *Of Reformation in England*, in *The Works of John Milton*, 3/1, New York 1931, pp. 26–27; St. BERNARD, *De consideratione*, 1, 4, 5; 4, 3, 6, in: *Sancti Bernardi Opera*, 3: *Tractatus et opuscula*, ed. J. LECLERCQ & H.M. ROCHAIS, Rome 1963, pp. 399, 453. For further discussion, see H.E.J. COWDREY, "The Gregorian Papacy, Byzantium, and the First Crusade," in J.D. HOWARD-JOHNSTON (ed.), *Byzantium and the West c.850–c.1200*, Amsterdam 1988, pp. 145–169, esp. 145–147.

or, better, his Εἰς Κωνσταντῖνον τὸν βασιλέα, for he was selective, declaring it to be his intention to record only the pious acts of the emperor.[2] This he did. However, there was no Latin translation until the sixteenth century; in the West, Eusebius' *Life* remained virtually unknown. The disregard may have helped the legend which Eusebius initiated to grow there. For, according to Eusebius, Constantine sought baptism only at the end of his life; he received it in Asia Minor, near Nicomedia and, in fact, at the hand of its bishop, another Eusebius, who was not free from the taint of Arianism.[3] The West was not hampered by this record from developing the tradition that Constantine was baptised at Rome, after his conversion, and by the hand of Pope Silvester I. In his addition to his Latin translation of Eusebius' *Ecclesiastical History*, Rufinus of Aquileia adapted Eusebius' story of Constantine's having a vision of a cross in the sky with the angelic commentary: "Constantine, τούτῳ νίκα, quod est, in hoc vince", and added that it was a conversion experience like that of Saul on the Damascus road.[4] He did not mention Constantine's baptism, but the way was prepared for it to become associated with his conversion.

In the Latin West, the two centuries between the time of Rufinus (died 410) and that of Pope Gregory the Great (590–604) saw two lines of development in the record of Constantine.[5] First, a number of Latin authors, especially in historical works, made brief but memorable reference to him. They sometimes drew upon the traditions of the Greek East where, from the late fourth century, he was venerated both in the church's liturgical and homiletic activity and also in court ceremony and state propaganda. But whereas the East tended towards hagiography in the strict sense of regarding him as a saint and as Ἰσαπόστολος, unlike his mother Helena he was never canonised in the West. There, he was built up as an ideal secular ruler who knew his place before God and the clergy, behaving with exemplary piety and humility. The tied epithets and phrases which gathered about him and which were to reverberate to the central middle ages had nothing to do with words like *sanctus* or *beatus*; rather, they expressed his sense of what was due from

---

2     F. WINKELMANN, *Über das Leben des Kaisers Konstantin*, in *Eusebius Werke*, 1/1, *Griechischen christlichen Schriftsteller der ersten drei Jahrhunderte*, Berlin 1975, 1.11, 1–2, p. 20.

3     Ibid. 4, 24–26, pp. 145–164.

4     *Ecclesiastical History*, 9, 8, 15, ed. E. SCHWARTZ & T. MOMMSEN, GCS 9, Leipzig 1903–08, pp. 827–829; cf. *Vita Const.* 1, 28–30, ed. WINKELMANN, pp. 29–30.

5     For a fuller discussion, to which I am much indebted, see A. LINDER, "The Myth of Constantine the Great in the West: Sources and Hagiographical Commemoration," *StMed*, 3rd ser., 16, 1975, pp. 43–95.

the secular to the spiritual: he was *religiosissimus, piissimus, piae memoriae princeps*, and the like. As Rufinus commented of his victories, "the more religiously and humbly he submitted himself to God, the more widely God subdued all things to him".[6] Constantine reciprocated as a Christian prince should. As Gregory the Great wrote to King Ethelbert of Kent, he recalled the Roman republic from the wicked cults of idols and subjected it, along with himself, to Christ, to whom he altogether converted himself with all peoples subject to him.[7]

His particular deeds and dispositions flowed from this kingly religion and humility. He was credited with building the seven major churches of Rome. According to the *Liber pontificalis* of the early sixth century, he began with the Lateran which it named the *basilica Constantiniana*, and proceeded to the churches of St Peter and St Paul, then to the others and to churches at Ostia and Albano.[8] Another important work was the *Historia ecclesiastica tripartita* which, under the name of Cassiodorus, assembled excerpts from the Greek historians Socrates, Sozomen, and Theodoret, and circulated in the medieval West. It referred approvingly to Constantine as the emperor who gave freedom of worship to Christians and who passed laws in their favour.[9] Most praiseworthy of all for the *Historia* and for other Latin sources was Constantine's deportment at the council of Nicaea (325). According to Eusebius of Caesarea, Constantine had there asserted his position, saying that he was also a bishop, ordained by God to oversee whatever is external to the church.[10] But for the *Historia*, he was an exemplar of humility who sat modestly in the bishops' midst, and did so only with their leave.[11] Rufinus had described his humility more graphically and in words upon which the eleventh century would seize. He had been compelled to compose the bickering and strife of the assembled bishops, yet in doing so he addressed them as follows:

> God has appointed you as bishops (*sacerdotes*) and has given you power over us as well; we are therefore rightly judged by you. You, however, cannot

---

6    RUFINUS, *Historia ecclesiastica*, 1, 8, (PL 21, 478).

7    *S. Gregorii Magni Registrum epistularum*, 11, 37, 18–25, ed. D. NORBERG, 2 vols., *Corpus Christianorum, Series Latina*, 140, 140A, Turnholt 1982, II, p. 930.

8    *Le Liber pontificalis*, ed. L. DUCHESNE, 3 vols., Paris 1886–1957, I, pp. 172–184.

9    *Cassiodori-Epiphanii Historia ecclesiastica tripartita*, 1, 9, ed. W. JACOB & R. HANSLIK, *CSEL*, 71, Vienna 1952, pp. 24–29.

10   *Vita Const.* 4, 24, ed. WINKELMANN, p. 128.

11   *Hist. eccles. trip.* 2, 5, ed. JACOB & HANSLIK, pp. 89–92.

rightly be judged by men. Look, then, to God alone as your judge, for whatever your disputes, they are reserved for his divine hearing. You are appointed by God to be gods on our behalf; it is not right that a man should judge gods but only he of whom it is written, "God stands in the assembly of gods; he judges gods in their midst" (cf. Ps 81: 1 Vg.).[12]

The biblical text was one that Gregory the Great would borrow from Rufinus, with approval for his eulogy of Constantine, when he sought to persuade the Emperor Maurice at Constantinople that emperors should not countenance accusations against bishops, who were to be received with honour, not with judgement.[13] Constantine was an exemplar of something very like what eleventh-century reformers would call the liberty of the church.

The second line of development in the record of Constantine up to the time of Gregory the Great is constituted by the legends which developed about him, about the pope, Silvester I, who was in office at the time of his conversion, and about his mother Helena. This development, in its Latin form, can now only be illustrated, not fully described or discussed. It was manifest in the writings of the historians. Rufinus propagated the story of Constantine's vision of the cross,[14] which the *Historia ecclesiastica tripartita* also retailed, although in a variant version that set it, not at Rome before the battle of the Milvian Bridge, but on the Danube frontier.[15] Rufinus further wrote of Helena's visit to Jerusalem, the outcome of which was the legend of the invention of the cross. After a diligent search there, Helena located three crosses, one of which was miraculously disclosed to be that of Christ. She founded a church at Jerusalem on the site where the cross was found; and she sent Constantine not only part of the cross but also nails which were found with it and which her son utilised for bridles for his horses and to decorate a helmet suitable for battle.[16]

More potent than such passages in the historians were longer hagiographical compositions. One of the most influential texts that the post-Constantinian church bequeathed to the middle ages was the *Actus Silvestri*.[17] Originating at Rome between the late fourth and the late fifth

---

[12]   *Hist. eccles.* 1, 2 (PL 21, 468).
[13]   *Reg. epist.* 5, 36, 50–64, ed. NORBERG, 1, pp. 305–306.
[14]   See p. 64 above.
[15]   *Hist. eccles. trip.* 1, 4, 4–9, ed. JACOB & HANSLIK, pp. 16–17.
[16]   *Hist eccles.* 1, 7–8 (PL 21, 475–478).
[17]   The only printed text remains that in B. MOMBRITIUS, *Sanctuarium seu Vitae sanctorum*, new ed., 2 vols., Paris 1910, II, pp. 508–531; Mombritius' compilation of saints' Lives was made c. 1480. The earliest form of the *Actus Silvestri* is often best approached through the citations of

centuries but probably under Pope Siricius (384–99), it circulated very widely in several recensions; with good reason it has been presented as an embodiment of "the Constantinian foundation-legend of Christian Rome".[18] Its main features were as follows. It began by exhibiting Silvester in pagan times as a Christian confessor. Then, pre-dating his becoming pope, it turned to his part in Constantine's conversion. It featured him, not as the holy emperor, so much as the pious and right-minded establisher of the Christian empire.[19] Having been the church's persecutor, he became its protector; once the enemy of Christians, he became their friend.

According to the *Actus Silvestri*, his part in slaughtering Christians had caused his leprosy, to cure which the pagan priests of Rome (*pontifices Capitolii*) told him to bathe in the blood of infants. Moved by their mothers' tears, Constantine drew back, thereby winning a victory over himself which was greater than his victories on the battlefield: "vicit crudelitatem pontificum pietas Romani imperii." A vision of St Peter and St Paul, who were in effect the Christian Dioscori, led him to recall Pope Silvester from exile in hope of another way of cleansing, in return for which he was to restore all churches in the Roman empire and himself to worship the true God. After Silvester explained the Christian faith to him, he did penance and confessed his sins; then the pope baptised him in the baths of the Lateran palace. Thus his soul was cleansed from the filth of sin and his body from leprosy. Henceforth the pagan Capitol gave way to the Christian Lateran as the centre of Roman religion.

---

manuscript sources in the secondary literature. See esp. W. LEVISON, "Konstantinische Schenkung und Silvester-Legende," and "Kirchenrechtliches in den Actus Silvestri," repr. in idem, *Aus Rheinischer und Fränkischer Frühzeit*, Dusseldorf 1948, pp. 390–465, 466–473; E. EWIG, "Das Bild Constantins des Grossen in den ersten Jahrhunderten des abendländischen Mittelalters," *HistJb* 75, 1956, pp. 1–46; R.J. LOENERTZ, "Actus Sylvestri. Genèse d'une légende," *RHE* 70, 1975, pp. 426–439; A. LINDER, "The Myth of Constantine the Great in the West," and idem, "Constantine's 'Ten Laws' Series," in *Fälschungen im Mittelalter, 2: Gefälschte Rechtstexte. Der bestrafte Fälscher, Monumenta Germaniae Historica, Schriften*, 33/2, Hanover 1988, pp. 491–507; W. POHLKAMP, "Tradition und Topographie: Papst Silvester I. (314–335) und der Drache vom Forum Romanum," *RQ* 78, 1983, pp. 38–100; idem, "Kaiser Konstantin, der heidnische und der christliche Kult in den Actus Silvestri," *Frühmittelalterliche Studien* 18, 1984, pp. 357–400; idem, "*Privilegium ecclesiae Romanae pontifici contulit*: Zur Vorgeschichte der Konstantinischen Schenkung," in *Fälschungen im Mittelalter*, II, pp. 413–490.

[18]  POHLKAMP, "*Privilegium ecclesiae Romanae pontifici contulit*," p. 425.
[19]  Ibid, p. 436.

In the octave of his baptism, which was represented as occurring at Easter, Constantine each day issued a law in the church's favour and they were followed by two others. Most were fictitious but all were programmatic for later ages; thus, for example, the law of the fourth day conferred upon the pontiff of the Roman church the privilege that, throughout the Roman world, he was the head of the bishops as the emperor was the head of the judges.[20] It was a recognition by the emperor of the universal jurisdiction of the pope over the bishops. Constantine thereafter founded the basilicas of St Peter's and the Lateran. Some 7,000 people followed Constantine's example by then being baptised. At a meeting with the reluctant senate in the Basilica Ulpia, Constantine discussed the cult of idols. The upshot was that Christian bishops would henceforth enjoy the same privileges as pagan priests, although no religious compulsion was to be applied and conversion was to be voluntary.

In 315, Constantine went on to stage a dispute with Jews about Christ's divinity. The account begins with a fictitious exchange of letters with his allegedly Judaising mother Helena who was in the East and who was urging her son to convert from his new Christianity to Judaism. Constantine set up a debate at Rome between Silvester and twelve rabbis under the presidency of two pagan *iudices dati*. The dispute was settled by a miracle in which Silvester restored to life an animal which the rabbis had slaughtered. It was construed as a victory for the Catholic faith in the city and the world.

In an appendix, the *Actus Silvestri* retailed a story of the subduing of the dragon of the Forum Romanum which, having been accustomed during pagan times to be pacified by monthly feeding by the vestal virgins, was wrathful at its discontinuance since Christianity was recognised. Silvester urged Constantine to stand fast against the pagan custom of appeasing the dragon, and himself successfully bound its mouth after fortifying himself by the name of Christ. Constantine recognised this victory by confirming his own worship of the true God and by proclaiming an age of reconciliation and peace.

Thus, Constantine was celebrated in the West as the founder of a Christian city and empire in which the centre of religion had been transferred from the pagan Capitol to the Christian Lateran, in which a dutiful emperor was committed to the reign of peace, and in which the universal prerogative

---

[20] The most satisfactory available version of the laws is LINDER, "Constantine's 'Ten Laws'," pp. 493–497. The law of the fourth day runs, in its original words: "Quarta die privilegium ecclesie Romane pontifici contulit, ut in toto orbe Romano sacerdotes ita hunc caput habeant sicut omnes iudices regem" (p. 494).

of the pope as the true Roman pontiff was recognised to be one of the laws of an emperor who knew the difference between the spiritual and the temporal jurisdictions in the Roman world.

A further expansion of the legends centring upon Constantine may be briefly noticed. It was concerned with the rehabilitation of his mother Helena by means of stories about the invention of the holy cross. It is well illustrated by the so-called *Acts of Judas-Cyriacus* which, having been developed in the East, appear to have been translated into Latin by the end of the sixth century. They later also passed into the Western vernacular languages.[21] Helena's determination to recover the cross of Christ's passion brought her into dispute with the Jews and especially with a certain Judas who, despite the chronological impossibility, was thought to be a brother to the first martyr St Stephen. A combination of threats by burning or starvation and of encouragement by miracle led him to number himself with Stephen and to discover three crosses, one of which was established through a miracle of healing to be that of Christ. Helena resolved to put the cross in a casing of jewels and to set it in a new church on the site of Calvary. Judas was baptised and in due course ordained bishop of Jerusalem. Thereafter, the nails of the passion were also discovered; Helena caused a bridle to be made from them which she sent to Constantine as a pledge of victory and peace.[22] Such legends of the invention of the holy cross and of the dispatch of relics to Constantine reinforced his image as a Christian and victorious ruler; they associated with him the most precious and efficacious of Christian relics.

With regard to the legends of Constantine, the transition from the ancient to the early medieval world marked no break. There was continuity at Rome as in the Latin world at large. Only a few examples can now be given. Perhaps most important of all is one that illustrates continuity at Rome: the so-called *Constitutum Constantini* or the "Donation of Constantine".[23]

---

21    The *Acts* are printed, in an uncritical text, in MOMBRITIUS, *Sanctuarium*, I, pp. 376–379, whence *Acta Sanctorum: May* I, 445–448; for a better text, see J. STRAUBINGER, *Die Kreuzabfindungslegende: Untersuchungen über ihr altchristlichen Fassung mit besonderen Berücksichtigung der syrischen Texte*, Paderborn 1912, pp. 15–49.

22    "Erit autem arma inexpugnabilis contra omnes adversarios. Victoria enim erit regis et pax belli": ed. STRAUBINGER, p. 46.

23    For the text, see *Das Constitutum Constantini (Konstantinische Schenkung): Text*, H. FUHRMANN (ed.), *MGH Fontes iuris Germanici antiqui*, 10, Hanover 1968. Among the enormous secondary literature, I am especially indebted to FUHRMANN, *Einfluss und Verbreitung der pseudoisidorischen Fälschungen*, *MGH Schriften*, 24/1–3, Stuttgart 1972–74, II, pp. 354–385; also to N. HUYGHEBAERT, "La Donation de Constantin ramenée à ses véritables dimensions," *RHE* 71, 1976, pp. 45–

About this most controversial of documents it must suffice to make a few remarks about the direction of recent study. It was written between the mid-eighth and the mid-ninth century but probably near the earlier date, almost certainly at Rome and by a minor clerk of the Lateran *patriarchium*. In form, it is a privilege from Constantine to Pope Silvester I. However, it lacks a firm structure of *narratio* and *dispositio*. It has more the character of an allocution by Constantine with a single flow of narrative to which dispositive elements are incidental. Whatever its connection with the inception of the papal states, its dispositions about the endowment of Roman churches are grandiose and vague.[24]

It has been well described as not a false diploma but a pseudo-diploma.[25] When read as a whole, its central concern was not the endowment of the papacy but the prerogatives of the Roman church and of the Lateran within that church. From beginning to end, it was a pronouncement of Constantine the right-thinking emperor which expressed in most thoroughgoing terms the Roman church's image of what it was and of what, in the providence of God, it would always be to the end of time.

In the first half, or *confessio*, of the *Constitutum Constantini*,[26] an emperor who was both well disposed — *fidelis, mansuetus, maximus, beneficus* — and prosperous — *pius, felix, victor ac triumphator, semper augustus*[27] — described a conversion experience in terms which followed the relevant part of the *Actus Silvestri*. Having confessed the true faith in which Silvester instructed him, Constantine told of his leprosy, his compunction when advised by the *sacerdotes Capitolii* to bathe in the blood of slaughtered infants, his vision of St Peter and St Paul, his recall of Silvester from exile, his time of penance at the Lateran palace, his baptism there which cleansed his leprosy, and his full grasp of the faith which he had now adopted. The *Constitutum Constantini* emphasised his recognition of the authority of St Peter according to Christ's commission in St Matthew's Gospel.

In the spirit of Constantine's ten laws in the *Actus Silvestri*, according to the *Constitutum Constantini* he went on to exalt the prerogatives of the Roman church and its superiority to his own earthly empire:

> And when I acknowledged what blessed Silvester proclaimed and found myself
> entirely healed by blessed Peter, with all my governors and the whole senate,

---

69, and idem, "Une légende de fondation: le *Constitutum Constantini*," *Le Moyen Age*, 85, 1979, pp. 177–209.

24  Ed. FUHRMANN, lines 202–209, 261–270, pp. 85–86, 93–94.
25  HUYGHEBAERT, "La Donation de Constantin," p. 52.
26  To line 155, p. 80, in Fuhrmann's edition.
27  Ed. FUHRMANN, lines 4–6, p. 56.

with the nobility and the whole Roman people subject to the majesty of our empire, I thought fit that, as Peter was manifestly appointed vicar of the Son of God upon earth, so also the bishops (*pontifices*) who succeed to (*gerunt vices*) the chief of the apostles should secure from us and from our empire a power and supremacy which rise superior to what seemed to be granted to the earthly clemency of our imperial majesty. For ourselves, we preferred that the chief of the apostles and his vicars should be our powerful advocates (*patronos*) before God. And as our own imperial power is earthly, we determined to venerate and honour his [Peter's] holy Roman church and that the most holy see of blessed Peter should be gloriously exalted above our empire and earthly throne, ascribing to him power, the rank and capacity of majesty, and imperial dignity.[28]

After this pronouncement, which is arguably the key passage of the *Constitutum Constantini*, Constantine ratified Rome's primacy over the other patriarchal sees of all churches in the world, as well as the pope's supreme jurisdiction over Christian worship and the integrity of the faith.[29]

After Constantine thus followed the *Actus Silvestri* in affirming the superiority of the Roman church over all other churches, he went further by affirming that of the Lateran basilica, as well. It was Constantine's own foundation and, in token of the twelve apostles, he had carried on his shoulders twelve baskets of earth when its foundations were laid. It was to be honoured as the head and apex of all churches upon earth.[30] It was dedicated to Christ the Saviour, and the word *salvator* occurs thirteen times in the *Constitutum Constantini*. The insistence upon the Saviour and upon the living and immediate power of St Peter as his vicar served further to reinforce the Lateran's precedence over the pilgrimage basilicas of St Peter and St Paul which Constantine also built; while they sheltered the apostles' dead bodies, the Lateran stood for Peter's living power, in himself and in his vicar the reigning pope.

Constantine went still further in demonstrating his *pietas* to the apostles when, in gratitude for his baptism and cleansing, he transferred the Lateran palace, which he declared to excel all palaces upon earth, to the popes, together with the imperial insignia. Appropriate dignities were transferred from the Roman senate to the Roman clergy. To complete his exhibition of honour to the pope he transferred the centre of his own earthly power to Byzantium, "because," he said, "it was not right that an earthly empire

---

28     Ibid., lines 156–170, pp. 80–82.
29     Ibid., lines 171–187, pp. 82–84.
30     Ibid., lines 188–203, pp. 84–85.

should hold sway where the government (*principatus*) of the bishops and the head of the Christian religion were established by the heavenly emperor".[31]

When read as an allocution placed upon the lips of Constantine which built upon the legends of the *Actus Silvestri* to confirm the prerogatives of the Roman church and to assert the superiority of the spiritual power and its autonomy in religious matters, it is not hard to understand how, far into the middle ages, the *Constitutum Constantini* sustained the image of Constantine as a pious and exemplary emperor.

Legends of Constantine and Helena proliferated in Carolingian times. A critical event for Northern France and the Rhineland was the bringing c. 840 to the abbey of Hautvilliers (dioc. Reims) of the Roman relics of Helena. Within the next ten years, a monk of the abbey named Altmann wrote a *Vita sanctae Helenae* which well illustrates the early medieval picture of Helena and her son.[32] The *Life* begins by comparing the twelve persecutions of Christians between Nero and Diocletian with the twelve plagues in Egypt. Constantine was introduced as the emperor who delivered Christians from such straits. "By the mercy of God," Altmann proclaimed, "he turned the destruction and malice of earlier emperors into peace and goodness; he changed their persecution of Christians into his defence."[33] After his conversion, Constantine resolved to build the church of Christ among all peoples. After his vision of the cross with the accompanying words "O Constantine, in hoc vince", he sent his mother to find the cross. Having found it in Jerusalem, she sent him part of the wood and the nails of the passion.[34] The differences between mother and son which had been a feature of, for example, the *Actus Silvestri* had no place in the *Life*, which stressed the perfect harmony that always prevailed between them while tending to focus the glory upon Constantine.[35] But Helena's sanctity was vindicated.

Legends of Constantine the most pious emperor spread widely in the Latin West. Its hymnody took up the theme of St Helena, sometimes taking in the legend of Judas Cyriacus.[36] Devotion to the holy cross, and the commemoration of its invention, spread across Europe by the early eleventh

---

[31]  Ibid., lines 274–276, pp. 94–95.
[32]  *Acta Sanctorum: August* 3, 580–599.
[33]  *Vita*, cap. 2, 19, p. 586.
[34]  *Vita*, cap. 2, 27–30, p. 588.
[35]  *Vita*, caps 3, 33; 5, 50–52, pp. 590, 595–596.
[36]  For example, the Spanish examples in G.M. DREVES, *Analecta hymnica medii aevi*, 55 vols., Leipzig 1886–1922, XVI, 144–145, nos 238, 241; XXVII, 74–75, no. 38.

century.[37] In sculpture, copies of the equestrian statue of Marcus Aurelius in the Capitol at Rome, which was believed to be of Constantine, spread the image of Constantine the warrior-emperor through wide areas of Europe; at Parthenay-le-Vieux, for example, his bridle with its legendary associations was a prominent feature.[38] No work of art better sums up the perception of Constantine by Romanesque artists than the Stavelot Triptych in the Pierpont Morgan Library, New York. At the centre is a reliquary of the true cross. Its left wing is devoted to Constantine, and depicts his vision of the cross, his victory at the Milvian Bridge, and his baptism by Pope Silvester. Its right wing balances it with the Helena of the *Acts of Judas Cyriacus*, interrogating the Jews, supervising with Judas' aid the finding of the three crosses, and the miraculous authentication of the cross of Christ.[39] With its equal treatment of mother and son, the Triptych epitomises the legend of the pious emperor as it came down to the age of the Gregorian reform and after.

While the image of Constantine the most pious and Christian emperor was thus permeating Latin Europe by way of legend and devotion, it was also finding its way into the sources of the church's law. It was of the utmost importance for the dissemination of the *Constitutum Constantini*, and ultimately for its interpretation, that, at about the time that Altmann of Hautvilliers was writing his *Vita sanctae Helenae*, it was included in the Pseudo-Isidorian Decrees, in some texts fully but sometimes only the *confessio* without the *donatio* that followed.[40] It was given its apposite place amongst documents allegedly relating to the council of Nicaea (325). It was prefaced by a letter attributed to Pope Miltiades (310–14) which, in some manuscripts, has the inscription *De primitiva ecclesia et sinodo Nicena*.[41] The letter referred to Constantine as *vir religiosissimus*; it praised him for recognising the Christian religion and for instituting the building and endowment of churches. He duly honoured St Peter. By an anachronism,

---

[37]  See esp. A. FROLOW, *La Relique de la vraie croix: recherches sur le développement d'un culte*, Paris 1961; idem, *Les Reliquaires de la vraie croix*, Paris 1965.

[38]  See esp. J. ADHÉMAR, *Influences antiques dans l'art du moyen âge français*, London 1939, pp. 207–16 and plate 63; C. BROOKE, *The Twelfth Century Renaissance*, London 1969, p. 15 and illustrations 2–4.

[39]  FROLOW, *La Relique*, pp. 335–336 no. 347; W VOELKLE, in the exhibition catalogue *The Stavelot Triptych: Mosan Art and the Legend of the True Cross*, New York 1980, pp. 9–25 and illustrations 1–9.

[40]  *Decretales Pseudo-Isidorianae et Capitula Angilramni*, ed. P. HINSCHIUS, Leipzig 1863, pp. 249–254; cf. Fuhrmann's comments, *Einfluss und Verbreitung*, II, pp. 365–374.

[41]  Ed. HINSCHIUS, pp. 274–279.

Miltiades was made to praise Constantine's pronouncement at the council of Nicaea as reported by Rufinus, in which he declared the bishops to stand superior to all human jurisdiction.[42] When introducing the canons of Nicaea, Pseudo-Isidore cited Isidore of Seville's comment that the canons of general councils began from the time of Constantine who had given Christians the opportunity of free assembly. Pseudo-Isidore commented that the decision of the episcopal council about Arius was brought to Constantine, who honoured it as if brought from God himself.[43]

The eleventh-century reform papacy and its advocates inherited this eulogistic estimate of Constantine which, through the massive legendary tradition that gathered around him, was formed over some seven hundred years. Pope Leo IX (1049-54) and his circle made much of it in their dealings with Constantinople in the years 1053 and 1054. It was a useful propaganda point that the reigning Byzantine emperor, Constantine IX Monomachus (1042-54) bore the name of the great Constantine himself. The letter which, early in 1054, Leo's legate Cardinal Humbert of Moyenmoutier, who had probably drafted it, took to the emperor addressed him as the successor of great Constantine in blood, name and empire. Constantine was *ille primus et religiosissimus imperator*, and *ille mirabilis vir*. The present inheritor of his name was exhorted to manifest the constancy which it signified by upholding all that his forebear had done to establish and defend what rightfully belonged to the apostolic see of Rome.[44] When Humbert sought to refute the customs of the Greeks about fasting, he referred to Pope Silvester I as the "spiritual father" of the great Emperor Constantine who had ordered matters as was right.[45] It was in line with this

---

[42]  See pp. 65–66 above; Pseudo-Isidore's use of RUFINUS, *Hist. eccles.* at HINSCHIUS, p. 256, should also be noticed.

[43]  Ed. HINSCHIUS, pp. 254, 257; cf. ISIDORE of SEVILLE, *Etymologiarum libri XX*, 6, 16, 2–6, ed. W.M. LINDSAY, 2 vols., Oxford 1911, not paginated. Pseudo-Isidore also placed at the head of his collection of papal decretals a forged *Excerpta quaedam ex synodalibus gestis sancti Silvestri papae* which began with an account of the council of Nicaea held "temporibus sancti Silvestri papae et Constantini piissimi Augusti" (ed. HINSCHIUS, p. 449).

[44]  C. WILL, *Acta et scripta quae de controversiis ecclesiae Graecae et Latinae saeculo undecimo composita extant*, Leipzig & Marburg 1861, pp. 85–89, no. 3, esp. pp. 86a, 88a (= PL 143, 777–781, no. 103, esp. cols 778AB, 779D–780A).

[45]  *Dialogus*, cap. 6 (WILL, *Acta et scripta*, pp. 93–126 no. 5, at p. 97ab = PL 143, 929–974, at col. 957A). For Silvester and the Saturday fast, see *Actus Silvestri*, MOMBRITIUS, *Sanctuarium*, II, 510, lines 1–15, but I have not been able to trace a source for Humbert's citation.

heightening of the prerogatives of Rome that, in Leo IX's days, there began to be used at Rome a lightly but pointedly revised version of the *Constitutum Constantini*.[46] According to it, Constantine did not, as in earlier versions, distinguish the four patriarchal sees of the East as being special (*precipuas*); moreover, Constantinople was relegated to the fourth place below Alexandria, Antioch, and even Jerusalem.[47]

The most important document of this period is a long letter of Pope Leo IX, in which Humbert's hand is probably to be detected, to Patriarch Michael Cerularius of Constantinople and Archbishop Leo of Ochrida.[48] In form, it was the pope's reply to a letter which the archbishop had addressed to the Apulian bishop John of Trani about the errors of Latin Christians. It is more than unlikely that the pope's letter, commonly referred to as his *Libellus*, reached Constantinople in either 1053 or 1054; but it was of fundamental and lasting significance in the West, not least for Western perceptions of Constantine and his legacy to the church of which it was eulogistic. It offered a sharp and searching, if somewhat unstructured, examination of where authority in Christendom resided. According to H.G. Krause's analysis, the *Libellus* comprises two main sections: first, a rebuttal as themselves heretical of the arguments which Leo ascribed to the two Eastern archbishops (caps 5–22); and secondly, a vindication of the relationship of Rome and Constantinople as being that of mother and daughter (caps 23–36). The overriding concern was to vindicate the *regale sacerdotium* of the apostolic see.[49] In Krause's words, "the nature of the papal power was such that it had both a priestly and a kingly character. The supreme priestly power (*summi sacerdotii privilegium*) was derived from Peter's power of the keys (*celestis regni gubernacula*) and from his power to bind and loose (as in Matt. 16: 19); the supreme earthly power was derived from the *Constitutum Constantini*. The Emperor Constantine the Great had conferred upon St Silvester and upon all Peter's successors to the end of the world not only imperial power and dignity (*imperialis potestas et dignitas*) but also the imperial insignia and entourage (*infule et ministri imperiales*)".[50]

---

[46]  FUHRMANN, *Einfluss und Verbreitung*, II, pp. 283–285; idem, *Das Constitutum Constantini*, pp. 15–17, 30–32.

[47]  Ed. FUHRMANN, lines 171–173, p. 82.

[48]  WILL, *Acta et scripta*, pp. 65–85, no. 2 (= PL 143, 744–769, no. 100). For this letter, see esp. H.-G. KRAUSE, "Das Constitutum Constantini im Schisma vom 1054," in *Aus Kirche und Reich: Studien zu Theologie, Politik und Recht im Mittelalter. Festschrift für Friedrich Kempf*, ed. H. MORDEK, Sigmaringen 1983, pp. 131–158.

[49]  Cap. 13, WILL, *Acta et scripta*, p. 72a (= PL 143, 752D).

[50]  "Das Constitutum Constantini," p. 138.

In the second section of the *Libellus*, Constantine had demonstrated that Constantinople was Rome's daughter church when he was the agent of the Roman and apostolic see in reviewing both the customs and the very physical walls of the Eastern city.[51] It was, however, in the first section that the *Libellus* made most of Constantine. There was much discussion of how heresy had been resisted in the early church, and of the active and critical role of St Peter and his successors in upholding the faith. In its light, the archbishops were castigated for their violation of the principle that no one should pass judgement upon the apostolic see.[52] The *Libellus* called in testimony Silvester's decree as recorded in Pseudo-Isidore, where it was said to be passed "with the approval of his spiritual son and most religious Emperor Constantine with the whole Nicene synod", that the supreme see of Rome should be judged by no one; then it cited from the *Actus Silvestri* Constantine's law of the fourth day after his baptism, that bishops should everywhere have the pope for their head as judges had the king for theirs.[53]

Constantine thus met with approval for upholding the pope's spiritual and judicial power. He did so, as well, by making proper provision for the pope's temporal power. The *Libellus* was concerned to establish a duality of the powers of pope and emperor, and to vindicate the superiority of the former. In so doing, it safeguarded two principles of which Constantine was claimed to be the praiseworthy upholder. In line with his law of the fourth day it allowed that bishops and kings each had their proper sphere, and it cited with approval a reply of Constantine to his mother Helena to the effect that it was by lay princes that God gave his laws to the world.[54] Secondly, the

---

51    "... nunquid enim Romana et apostolica sedes, quae per evangelium genuit Latinam ecclesiam in occidente, mater non est Constantinopolitanae ecclesiae in oriente, quam per gloriosum filium suum Constantinum et nobiles sapientesque Romanos non tantum moribus sed et muris studuit reparare?": cap. 23, cf. cap. 28; WILL, *Acta et scripta*, pp. 78ab, 80b (= PL 143, 760D–761A, 763B–D).

52    Cap. 7, WILL, *Acta et scripta*, p. 68b (= PL 143, 748CD).

53    Cap. 10, WILL, *Acta et scripta*, p. 70b (= PL 143, 551AB); cf. HINSCHIUS, *Decretales Pseudo-Isidorianae*, p. 248; LINDER, "Constantine's 'Ten Laws'," p. 494.

54    After citing Rom. 13: 1–2 and Prov. 8: 15, Humbert continued: "Quod etiam saepe dictus Augustus Constantinus perspicacis animae vivacitate deprehendit, et matri suae religiosae Helenae inter nonnulla sic rescripsit: 'Qui moderatur saecula, et disponit totius mundi suffragia, quibus alimur et sustentamur, per se quidem spirantia vivificat, sed per pectora principum sua iura saeculis dictat'": cap. 12, WILL, *Acta et scripta*, pp. 71b–72a (= PL 143, 772CD). Humbert cited the *Actus Silvestri:* MOMBRITIUS, *Sanctuarium*, II, p. 515, lines 22–25.

*Libellus* took care to rule out any suggestion that popes derived even their temporal power from an absolute imperial gift: Constantine had dutifully restored to God's ministers in the West a trust that he had himself only temporarily received.[55] With these two caveats, the *Libellus* cited at length the *Constitutum Constantini* in order to warrant the pope's temporal power in the West which complemented his spiritual power. After referring to Christ's commission to St Peter, it invoked the general purport of Constantine's privilege in order to exhibit how, as *prudentissimus terrenae monarchiae princeps*, he had conceded to the popes to the end of time not only a prestigious imperial power and dignity but also the specific reality of the imperial insignia and entourage; for he deemed it inappropriate that those whom the divine majesty had set over a heavenly empire should be subject to any earthly one.[56] Later on, the *Libellus* reproduced verbatim extensive portions, in the newly revised version, of the dispositive part, or *donatio*, of the *Constitutum Constantini* which, it was pointed out, Constantine had himself deposited upon the body of St Peter.[57] The purpose of the citation was to show that Constantine had humbly and gladly recognised the special dignity of the Roman church. He had furnished the popes with abundant buildings, with ample endowments, with human agents, and with the eloquent symbols of empire.[58]

By thus appealing to the *Constitutum Constantini*, Pope Leo sought to vindicate the temporal lordship of the apostolic see as an integral part of its *regale sacerdotium*. Negatively, it established its immunity from any temporal *dominium*; positively, it established its claim to lordship over Rome and the *patrimonium Petri*. There is much to warrant Krause's conclusion that, in the context of events in 1054, Leo sought not only to refute the errors of the eastern archbishops but also to secure the help of the Eastern emperor Constantine IX Monomachus in recovering from the Normans in South Italy the lands that his eponymous ancestor had conferred upon the church.[59] However this may be, by citing only the dispositive section of the *Constitutum Constantini* and by making it the Magna Carta of

---

[55]  "Et tamen imperialis celsitudo hoc totum quod potuit effecit, quando tota devotione quidquid a Domino acceperat, eidem in ministris suis reddidit": cap. 12, WILL, *Acta et scripta*, p. 71b (= PL 143, 742C).

[56]  Cap. 12, WILL, *Acta et scripta*, p. 71b (= PL 143, 752B).

[57]  Cap. 13, WILL, *Acta et scripta*, p. 72a (= PL 143, 757A); cf. *Const.*, ed. FUHRMANN, lines 293–295, p. 97.

[58]  Caps 13–15, WILL, *Acta et scripta*, pp. 72a–14b, = PL 143, 753B–756A, citing *Const.*, ed. FUHRMANN, lines 157–187, 214–300, pp. 80–84, 86–96.

[59]  "Das Constitutum Constantini," pp. 138–141.

the pope's claim to temporal lordship, Leo was beginning to depict the document as the title deed of the Roman church to its property. But it formed only part of an as yet tightly knit complex of respects in which Constantine had duly provided for the spiritual and temporal welfare of the apostolic see as the head of the Christian church in a Christian empire.

The propagandists of the early reform papacy continued to express in the West the praise for Constantine that Leo and Humbert had directed to the East. This is true of Humbert himself. In his *Adversus simoniacos*, he repeatedly praised *maximus Constantinus* for his measures on behalf of the Christian church at the time of the council of Nicaea. He had wrested away the privileges that earlier emperors had given to pagan priests and shrines, and he had zealously diverted them from superstition to religion and to the benefit of Christian churches and clergy. He thereby set an example to future emperors in so far as they were right-minded.[60] In a remarkable chapter, Humbert recalled his own talks at Constantinople with the Emperor Constantine Monomachus. They established that, for all the errors that fraught the Constantinopolitan empire, neither its emperor nor its laymen presumed to meddle with the disposal of churches or with ecclesiastical ordinations or resources; these had been at the disposal of metropolitans and other churchmen ever since the days of Constantine. In effect, he was a pattern anti-simoniac who had made pronouncements of which catholics should ever be mindful. Humbert cited at length from Pseudo-Isidore the second letter attributed to Pope Melchiades about the exemption of bishops from human jurisdiction, about the freedom of Christians to build and endow churches, about his own church-building at Rome, and about his own vacation of Rome in order that it might be under the unfettered rule of Peter and his successors.[61] As presented to the West no less than to the East, Humbert's Constantine was a pattern emperor, especially in his recognition that the church should enjoy freedom from lay control.

Humbert's contemporary at Rome, Cardinal Peter Damiani, was similarly laudatory in his two substantial references to Constantine. Peter was an admirer of the Emperor Henry III (1039–56) for his campaign against simony. In his *Liber gratissimus* (1052), he said that Henry had won a victory over the enemies of the catholic church which was like that of Constantine, who had crushed the dogma of the Arian sect by the arms of the orthodox faith, and had championed that faith against an Arian assault upon

---

[60] *Humberti cardinalis Libri III adversus simoniacos*, 1, 1; 2, 37, ed. F. THANER, *MGH Libelli de Lite*, 1, pp. 104, 185. The first two books were written by 1057, and the third by 1060.

[61] *Adv. sim.* 3, 8, pp. 206–209.

the church's unity.[62] In his *Disceptatio synodalis* (1062), Peter Damiani made his spokesman for the Roman church appeal to the *Constitutum Constantini*, by which Constantine accorded to the apostolic see a primacy (*principatus*) over all the churches of the world. He referred to Constantine's building of the basilica of St Peter and the patriarchate of the Lateran, to his resigning his imperial insignia to Silvester and his successors, and to his granting Silvester a perpetual right to the Lateran palace and jurisdiction over the Italian kingdom. He cited the express words of the *Constitutum Constantini* about Constantine's transfer of his empire and royal power to Constantinople. The conclusion that he drew was that the earthly emperor has no power over the Roman church.[63] For Peter Damiani as for Humbert, Constantine was above all the upholder of the prerogatives and the freedom of the apostolic see.

The incidental character of the references to Constantine by Humbert and Peter Damiani should not create the impression that he was little regarded in later eleventh-century Rome. That this was far from the case is apparent from an anonymous pilgrim-guide to the Lateran, usually known as the *Descriptio basilicae Lateranensis*. Like many such guides, it passed through several editions; but, in its original form, it dates from between 1073 and 1118 but probably from soon after 1073; its survival in seven manuscripts indicates that it was widely known.[64]

---

62    *Die Briefe des Petrus Damiani*, no. 40, ed. K. REINDEL, *MGH Die Briefe der Deutschen Kaiserzeit*, 4/1–4, Munich 1983–93, I, p. 503. Peter Damiani's eulogy of Henry III stands in contrast to the denigration of him as *imperator ille nequissimus*, because of his intervention at Rome in 1046, in the anonymous tract *De ordinando pontifice* of 1047/8. Constantine was the first right-thinking witness whom the author summoned to testify against Henry that "he should not have set his hand upon a bishop". Constantine was addressed as "the most religious Emperor Constantine, who obeyed the blessed Pope Silvester and bowed your head for his blessing"; he repeated the words of the Pseudo-Isidorian second letter of Pope Melchiades, that bishops should not be judged by human judgement: lines 183–189, H.H. ANTON, *Der sogenannte Traktat 'De ordinando pontifice'. Ein Rechtsgutachten in Zusammenhang mit der Synode von Sutri (1046)*, Bonn 1982, p. 80; cf. *Decretales Pseudo-Isidorianae*, ed. HINSCHIUS, p. 248, cap. 11.

63    *Die Briefe*, no. 89, ed. REINDEL, II, 546–547. *Const.* lines 271–276, ed. FUHRMANN, pp. 94–95, are cited verbatim.

64    The edition of the *Descriptio* in *Codice topografico della città di Roma*, ed. R. VALENTINI & G. ZUCCHETTI, *Fonti per la storia d'Italia*, 81, 88–91, 4 vols., Rome 1940–53, III, pp. 319–373, is based upon its late twelfth-century form. The only printed text in its original form is in D. GEORGI, *De liturgia Romani pontificis in solemni celebratione missarum libri duo*, 3

After advancing the claim of the Lateran to hold dominion and rule over all other churches (*super omnes ecclesias totius orbis terrarum obtinet dominatum et principatum*) and before listing the relics of the Lateran basilica and the chapel of St Lawrence, it gave a brief history of the Lateran which centred upon Constantine. It began with the martyrdoms of Peter and Paul, whose doctrine illuminated a church which the devil attacked through Nero and successive emperors "for three centuries and more", but could not prevail. After this time of testing the faithful by the fire of suffering, God was pleased to raise up Constantine. The story of his conversion is expressly taken from the *Actus Silvestri*, with references to Constantine's initial persecution of Christians, the divine penalty of his leprosy, his humane refusal to shed the blood of innocent babes, his vision of Peter and Paul,[65] his instruction by Pope Silvester, and his baptism and cleansing from leprosy. In return, Constantine granted the pontiff of the Roman church the privilege expressed in his law of the fourth day, that bishops everywhere should have the Roman pontiff for their head and chief as judges had the emperor for theirs. Thus, in Constantine the Roman emperor turned from being the persecutor of Christians to being their peace and protection. Constantine brought greater benefits still: the account of him next turned to the invention of the holy cross, relics of which formed a major part of the Lateran treasure. Citing the historian Sozomen, the author brought in a reference to Constantine's vision of the cross before his battle with Maxentius at the Milvian Bridge and to the angels' words, "Constantine, in hoc vinces".[66] Preoccupied by wars, Constantine charged his mother Helena to seek the true cross at Jerusalem. The account of him ends with a summary, not clearly based upon a specific source, of how Helena discovered the cross and then sent part of its wood, together with the nails of the passion and other Old and New Testament relics, to form the basis of the

---

vols., Rome 1731–44, III, pp. 542–555, no. 14. For the various recensions and a stemma of MSS, see C. VOGEL, "La *Descriptio ecclesiae Lateranensis* du diacre Jean," *Mélanges en l'honneur de Monseigneur Michel Andrieu*, Strasbourg 1956, pp. 457–476; also further comment by H.E.J. COWDREY, "Pope Urban II and the Idea of the Crusade," in *Festschrift für Bernhard Töpfer*, forthcoming.

[65] The *Descriptio* claimed that paintings on wood of Peter and Paul in the treasure of the Lateran basilica were those from which Constantine recognised them, and noted other items for which *Constantinus imperator Dei servus* was responsible: GEORGI, *De liturgia*, III, p. 548.

[66] The author perhaps adapted the citation of Sozomen in *Hist. eccles. trip.* 1, 4, 7–8, ed. JACOB & HANSLIK, p. 17; see p. 66 above. But he may have used a Latin translation of SOZOMEN, *Ecclesiastical History*, 1, 3, ed. J. BIDEZ, *GCS* 40, Berlin 1960, p. 11.

Lateran treasure. Such was the prevailing view of Constantine at the Lateran basilica which went by his name;[67] no pilgrim to it was left in doubt of the admiration which was deemed to be Constantine's due. One may notice how little it appears to have been derived from the *Constitutum Constantini*, to which the pilgrim guide does not allude.

The greatest of the reforming popes, Gregory VII (1073–85), always remembered that, from boyhood, he had been associated with the household of St Peter and with the Lateran.[68] The references in his letters to Constantine and Silvester are in line with the tradition of the most religious emperor which had come down from antiquity and was recognised during his earlier years by Cardinals Humbert and Peter Damiani. His most revealing references are in the two letters to Bishop Hermann of Metz which he wrote in justification of his sentences of excommunication and deposition of King Henry IV of Germany in 1076 and 1080.[69] In his letter of 1076, Gregory was concerned to refute the suggestion that the royal dignity exceeded the episcopal. Basing himself on the account of Constantine's due modesty at the council of Nicaea in the *Historia ecclesiastica tripartita*,[70] Gregory noticed that Constantine took the lowest place among the bishops and approvingly cited the text that "God resists the proud and gives grace to the humble" (James 4: 6). In his letter of 1081, he reverted to this incident at greater length, now by way of Pope Gregory I's letter to the Emperor Maurice.[71] This time, he placed the emphasis upon Constantine's recognition that the emperor should not pass judgement upon bishops but be judged by them. Gregory made the same point in 1083 to King William I of England who had imprisoned his half-brother Bishop Odo of Bayeux, and held up Constantine as a model whom he should imitate.[72] Later in his second letter to Hermann of Metz, Gregory made clear the limit of the excellence of even the best temporal rulers. He listed the emperors whom the church praised and honoured: first among them was Constantine *pię memorię imperatoris*; they were lovers of righteousness, propagators of the Christian religion, and defenders of churches, yet they had performed no miracles and, unlike most popes, were not numbered among the saints. Within this limitation, Constantine was a model ruler. A further indication was his supposed

---

[67]  *Gregorii VII Registrum*, 3, 10a, ed. E. CASPAR, *MGH Epistolae selectae*, 2, Berlin 1920–23, p. 268.

[68]  *Reg.* 3, 21; 4, 11; 7.14a, pp. 288, 311, 483.

[69]  *Reg.* 4, 2; 8, 21, pp. 295–296, 553, 559.

[70]  See pp. 65–66 above. There seems to be no ground for Caspar's reference to the letters of Gregory I.

[71]  See p. 66 above.

[72]  *Reg.* 9, 37, p. 631.

material support for the papacy from his realms at large. Gregory adduced evidence for this in 1081 when, in his model oath for a German king, he included a promise to safeguard the rent (*census*) which Constantine and Charlemagne had assigned to St Peter.[73] Above all, it met with Gregory's approval that the empire of Constantine and the papacy of Silvester I had marked an end to the machinations of the devil against the apostolic see and had ushered in a stability for the church which had lasted until the tempests of his own pontificate.[74] The same model period had heralded the great church councils which had for ever confirmed the catholic church in the true faith.[75]

In all his letters, Gregory made no citation from or express reference to the *Constitutum Constantini*; indeed, apart from canon-law collections which will be noticed later, it attracted very little notice in sources from his pontificate.[76] Gregory may have had it in mind when formulating the eighth clause of his *Dictatus papae*, "Quod solus possit uti imperialibus insigniis".[77] While he would no doubt have invoked the *Constitutum Constantini* to warrant his claims to special concern for islands like Corsica and Sardinia,[78] he never did so explicitly.

Until and including the pontificate of Gregory VII, Latin sources whether at Rome or elsewhere were virtually unanimous in perpetuating the eulogy of Constantine the most religious emperor and champion of the rights of the church and papacy that ecclesiastical writers had sustained during ancient and

---

73  *Reg.* 9, 3, p. 576. For the *census*, cf. *Reg.* 8, 23, pp. 565–566, and see G. MEYER von KNONAU, *Jahrbücher des Deutschen Reiches unter Heinrich IV. und Heinrich V.*, 7 vols., Leipzig 1890–1909, III, p. 366 n. 34.

74  *Reg.* 2, 45, p. 183; *The Epistolae vagantes of Pope Gregory VII*, ed. and trans. H.E.J. COWDREY, Oxford 1972, p. 132, no. 45.

75  *Reg.* 8, 1, p. 511.

76  For medieval use of the *Const.*, see G. LAEHR, *Die Konstantinische Schenkung in der abendländischen Literatur des Mittelalters bis zur Mitte des 14. Jahrhunderts*, Berlin 1926, pp. 24–50. The reference in a German letter of perhaps 1076/9 in the Hanover Letter-collection to a "privilegium Romane ecclesie ... a Constantino imperatore et beato Silvestro compositum" is justifiably regarded by Erdmann as being to the *Constitutum Constantini* because it was confirmed "sub terribili anathemate"; cf. *Const.* lines 287–292, ed. FUHRMANN, p. 96; but it may also be coloured by the law of the fourth day in the *Actus Silvestri* (above, n. 20): *Die Hannoversche Briefsammlung (1. Hildesheimer Briefe), no. 34, Briefsammlungen der Zeit Heinrichs IV.*, ed. C. ERDMANN & N. FICKERMANN, *MGH Die Briefe der Deutschen Kaiserzeit*, 5, Weimar 1950, p. 74.

77  *Reg.* 2, 55a, p. 204.

78  *Const.*, ed. FUHRMANN, lines 203–206, pp. 85–86; cf. *Reg.* 1, 29; 5, 4; 6, 12, pp. 46–47, 351–352, 413–415.

early medieval times. From the mid-1080s, while popes and papalist writers did not qualify their praise until the time of St Bernard, the presentation of him became more complex. Broadly speaking, three strands may be distinguished in their utterances. First and foremost, Constantine continued to be spoken of in traditional terms, both at Rome and elsewhere. Successive versions of the *Descriptio basilicae Lateranensis* illustrate the persistence at Rome of the praise that the original text expressed.[79] In his *Libellus contra invasores et symoniacos*, which in its final version dates from c. 1097, the Roman cardinal-priest Deusdedit placed Constantine first in his lists of *christianissimi imperatores* who preserved good customs handed down from apostolic times by seeing to the building and endowment of churches, by claiming no dominion or jurisdiction over the clergy or the church's property and by forbidding others to make such claims, and by ensuring that bishops were canonically elected.[80] At the council of Nicaea, Constantine upheld the freedom of clergy and monks from lay accusation, however blatant their crimes; he approvingly cited Rufinus's record of Constantine's speech at the council which expressed the principle that bishops could not be judged by men but were reserved for divine judgement.[81] Constantine was applauded as well for his insistence that the goods of schismatics should be forfeited.[82]

In Italy, too, the Gregorian publicist Bonizo, bishop of Sutri (1075–76) and Piacenza (1086–89), drew extensively upon the *Actus Silvestri*, rather than upon the *Constitutum Constantini*, in praising Constantine as an epoch-making figure in Christian history and as a paragon of right custom in the church. He did so in his *Liber ad amicum* (1085/6) and in his mature work, the *Liber de vita christiana*, of a few years later.[83] He reiterated the familiar view that, from the time of St Peter to that of *pius Constantinus*, the church was subject through persecuting emperors to a continuous warfare with the devil which had its roll of honour in the succession of martyr-popes. Then Constantine, the leader (*dux*) of the Roman empire, made himself

---

[79]    See pp. 79–81 above.
[80]    *Deusdedit presbyteri cardinalis Libellus contra invasores et symoniacos et reliquos scismaticos*, 1, 8, 17; 3, 10, 12 (ed. E. SACKUR, *MGH Libelli de Lite*, II, pp. 302, 316, 350–351, 353).
[81]    *Libellus*, 3, 6, 10, pp. 347, 351–352, citing RUFINUS, *Hist. eccles.* 1, 2, as above, n. 12.
[82]    *Libellus*, 2, 16, p. 334.
[83]    *Bonizonis episcopi Sutrini Liber ad amicum*, ed. E. DÜMMLER, *MGH Libelli de Lite*, I, pp. 568–620; BONIZO of SUTRI, *Liber de vita christiana*, ed. E. PERELS, Berlin 1930.

subject to the Christian religion.[84] Thereafter until the cruel regimes of the Lombards (*a pii Constantini usque ad Longobardorum crudelia regna*) Roman emperors habitually ruled in fear of God and obediently to the advice of their bishops and especially of the bishops of Rome; they favoured the churches, loved the clergy, and honoured the bishops, creating public peace during their lives and winning an eternal crown upon their deaths. The few wicked emperors came to a bad end.[85] As for Constantine himself, Bonizo dwelt upon his baptism by Silvester. He reviewed critically the various traditions about the date of the baptism, insisting against the *Historia ecclesiastica tripartita*, which "mirabiliter aborret a vero", that it took place early.[86] Its results were, according to Bonizo, that the temples were closed and the churches opened, the image of the Saviour replaced that of Jupiter, and peace was restored to all the churches of the world. It was, indeed, quickly broken by Arius and other heretics, but Bonizo was concerned to sound the praises of Constantine (*Constantini laudes*). He especially applauded his laws as rehearsed in the *Actus Silvestri*, citing not only that of the fourth day constituting the Roman pontiff head of all bishops as the emperor was head of all judges,[87] but also that of the first day according to which Christ should be freely worshipped by the whole Roman world.[88] In pursuit of this law, Constantine was responsible for the invention of Christ's cross; he was also the greatest propagator of the name of Christ, the founder of New Rome, and an outstanding founder of Christian basilicas. He had built the Lateran basilica and baptistery; on the day after his baptism, he had founded St Peter's and had himself carried twelve baskets of earth in honour of the twelve apostles.[89] In face of the Arian heresy that so quickly threatened the peace of the church, he convened the council of Nicaea. But he properly set himself below the bishops, deeming it improper that his throne should be placed among those who would judge the twelve tribes of Israel.[90] Across the Alps in Swabia, Bernold of St Blasien likewise continued the praise of the conduct at Nicaea of the *piissimus imperator Constantinus*.[91]

---

[84] *Lib. ad amic.* 1, p. 573; *Lib. de vita christ.* 3, 110; 4, 98, pp. 109, 165.
[85] *Lib. ad amic.* 2, pp. 575–577.
[86] *Lib. de vita christ.* 4, 33, pp. 123–124.
[87] *Lib. ad amic.* 2, p. 573, *Lib. de vita christ.* 4, 33, pp. 123–124.
[88] *Lib. de vita christ.* 4, 98, p. 164.
[89] *Lib. ad amic.* 2, pp. 573–574, *Lib. de vita christ.* 4, 34, 98; 8, 1; pp. 124, 164, 253.
[90] *Lib. ad amic.* 2, p. 574, citing *Hist. eccles. trip.* (see pp. 65–66 above).
[91] *Apologeticus*, cap. 3, *Libelli Bernaldi presbyteri monachi*, ed. F. THANER, *MGH Libelli de Lite*, II, pp. 62–63.

A second strand in the more complex presentation of Constantine from c. 1085 tended to reinforce his high reputation.  Hitherto, eleventh-century sources had said relatively little of Constantine the Christian warrior whose victorious warfare was heralded by his vision of the cross in the heavens and by the words, "Constantine, in hoc vince".  The *Descriptio basilicae Lateranensis* kept it alive,[92] but it seems to have been through Gregory VII's posthumous supporters that it began to strike home with renewed force. After mid-1075, the elderly Bernard, *scholasticus* of Constance and Hildesheim and a perfervid Gregorian, compiled a book of canons against the Emperor Henry IV, adding a commentary in the course of which he listed kings and princes who, to repress the madness of subversive men, had very frequently taken arms as the Lord prompted them, fought as he inspired them, and so triumphed that he crowned them.  First among such kings was the Emperor Constantine: converted from persecutor of Christians to champion of Christianity, he took arms against Maxentius, "tyrant of the city of Rome"; when, in hope of victory, he called upon the name of Jesus, there was displayed to him in the heavens a fiery cross, in the power of which he triumphed to the glory of the Crucified.[93]

Such language in the mid-1080s foreshadowed the Crusade preaching of ten years afterwards.  It comes as no surprise that, in the first recension of his Chronicle which dates from 1105/6, Ekkehard, who had visited the Holy Land during the ill-fated Crusade of 1101 and became a monk at Tegernsee c. 1102/3 and abbot of Aura in 1108, should relate the taking of the cross by the crusading armies of 1095–99 to the vision of Constantine.  He wrote that "this truly cross-bearing army displayed upon its garments the sign of the cross in token of death, believing that, according to the vision long ago revealed to Constantine the Great, the army would triumph in this sign over the enemies of the cross of Christ".[94]  This confidence in the cross of victory which Constantine saw in the sky appears to have been deliberately fostered in 1095–96 during the progress through Southern and Central France by Pope Urban II (1088–99).  He set out from Rome, where, especially in the

---

[92]   See pp. 80–81 above.

[93]   *Liber canonum contra Heinricum Quartum*, cap. 9, ed. F. THANER, *MGH Libelli de Lite*, I, p. 482.

[94]   "Crucis signaculum in vestibus idem vere crucifer exercitus ob mortificationis preferebat commonitorium, credens in hoc iuxta visionem Magno quondam Constantino revelatam ab inimicis crucis Christi se triumphaturum": *Ekkehardi Chronica, a.1099*, in *Frutolfi et Ekkehardi Chronica necnon Anonymi Chronica imperatorum*, ed. F.-J. SCHMALE & I. SCHMALE-OTT, Darmstadt 1972, p. 138; for Ekkehard's career and for the date of the first recension, see pp. 19–31, 33–34.

papal treasuries of the Lateran, relics of the holy cross seen as part of the legacy of Constantine formed part of everyday human consciousness; he came to parts of France where the equestrian statue of a warrior identified with Constantine was familiar.[95] After his sermon in November 1095 at the council of Clermont, Urban's journey was marked by dedications of churches and altars to the holy cross.[96] At la Trinité, Vendôme, he dedicated an altar "in honore victoriosissimae crucis".[97] At Marmoutier, near Tours, he dedicated the abbey church to the Holy Cross, St Mary, the apostles Peter and Paul, and St Martin; the principal relic which he placed in the main altar was a fragment of the true cross (*particula ... victoriosissimae crucis*). While Urban was at Tours, many knights sowed upon their garments the *vexillum* of the holy cross.[98] The pope kept Easter at Saintes; while he was there, the sign of the cross appeared in the sky.[99] Such evidence suggests that the cross of Christ which the knights of the West assumed was the cross of victory which Constantine had seen in his vision and which would find a prominent place in works of art such as the Stavelot Triptych.[100] The First Crusade appears to have made its contribution to Constantine's high reputation.

A third strand in the presentation of Constantine after the mid-1080s was ambivalent and ultimately damaging so far as his medieval reputation was concerned. It arises from how his reign was interpreted in canon law, especially in view of a revived concern with the *Constitutum Constantini*. For reasons which are far from clear, it received very little attention during most of the pontificate of Gregory VII. This can scarcely be because it seemed to concede too much to the decree of an emperor in establishing the prerogatives of the apostolic see,[101] for the same objection would apply to the *Actus Silvestri*, especially to its record of Constantine's "ten laws",

---

[95]  See pp. 73, 80–81 above.

[96]  For Urban's journey, see A. BECKER, *Papst Urban II. (1088–1099), MGH Schriften*, 19/1–, Stuttgart 1964–, II, pp. 435–457; also T. RUINART, "Beati Urbani papae II vita," *Ouvrages posthumes de D. Jean Mabillon et de D. Thierri Ruinart*, ed. V. THUILLIER, 3 vols., Paris 1724, III, pp. 1–410, whence PL 151, 9–266.

[97]  26 Feb. 1096: BECKER, *Papst Urban II.*, II, pp. 445–446; RUINART, "Beati Urbani," pp. 245, 386.

[98]  3–c. 25 Mar. 1096: BECKER, *Papst Urban II.*, II, pp. 446–447; RUINART, "Beati Urbani," pp. 246–248, 387–390; *Gesta Ambaziensium dominorum*, in *Chroniques des comtes d'Anjou et des seigneurs d'Amboise*, ed. L. HALPHEN & R. POUPARDIN, Paris 1913, pp. 100–101.

[99]  Charter of Saint-Maixent in *Analecta juris pontificii*, X$^e$ sér., Rome 1869, col. 551, no. 93.

[100]  See p. 73 above.

[101]  For example, lines 156–164, ed. FUHRMANN, pp. 80–81, 82–83.

overall picture of the *regale sacerdotium* of the Roman pontiff. Some two and a half centuries after its probable date of drafting, the *Constitutum Constantini* was becoming the "Donation of Constantine". *Donatio Constantini* gradually found its way into the titles that appear in manuscripts.[109]

The post-Gregorian canonists also kept alive in their collections the traditions about Constantine the *vir religiosissimus* who had recognised the Christian religion and instituted the building and endowing of churches which had been established by Pseudo-Isidore in the second letter ascribed to Pope Miltiades.[110] In so doing, they perpetuated the reputation of the good Emperor Constantine while also accentuating the tendency to highlight his material enrichment of the church. Thus, Ivo of Chartres more than once applauded him as the emperor who acknowledged the pope's principate over the whole world and who, having himself embraced Christianity, allowed churches everywhere to be built.[111] In his *Decretum* of c. 1140 which ushered in the *ius novum* of the later middle ages, Gratian of Bologna in a chapter with the disarming heading "Quare in primitiva ecclesia praedia vendebantur" so excerpted Melchiades as to show how, thanks to *vir religiosissimus Constantinus*, the church had everywhere become propertied in head and members. Gratian himself studiously avoided reference to the *Constitutum Constantini*. It was left to his first glossator, Paucapalea, to introduce into his treatment of *sacerdotium* and *regnum* a text of the *donatio* half of the *Constitutum Constantini* which closely followed that in Anselm of Lucca and Deusdedit.[112] Gratian, too, was made to exhibit Constantine as the promoter of a propertied church.

---

[109]    London, British Library, MS Royal 1 A XVI; see FUHRMANN, pp. 21, 55.
[110]    See p. 73 above.
[111]    "Quod Constantinus primus imperatorum fidem Christianorum patenter adeptus, fabricandi ecclesias omnibus potestatem dedit": *Decretum*, 3, 7, cf. *Panormia*, 2, 3 (PL 161, 201, 1083).
[112]    *Decretum* C. 12, qn 1, c.15, *Corpus iuris canonici*, ed. E. FRIEDBERG, 2 vols., Leipzig 1879–81, I, p. 682. The *paleae* P. 1, D.96, cc. 13–14, ed. FRIEDBERG, 1, pp. 342–345, which begin with a reference to Constantine's law of the fourth day, are best studied in PETERSMANN, "Die kanonistische Überlieferung," pp. 406–13, 416–417, 428–445; see also D. MAFFEI, *La Donazione di Costantino nei giuristi medievali*, Milan 1964, pp. 26–29.

But by Gratian's time, disenchantment with the failure to accomplish the moral reform that the eleventh-century church leaders initiated made Western Christians look ever more intently to the model of the primitive church "when all who believed were together and had all things in common; and they sold their possessions and goods and distributed them to all, as any had need" (Acts 2: 44–5).[113] The incompatibility between the two models of the church which the Pseudo-Isidorian account of Constantine proposed — those of the life of the disciples *in principio nascentis ecclesiae* when goods were sold and distributed, and of the triumphant and endowed church under the Christian emperors who began with Constantine — became increasingly apparent.[114] It could no longer be disregarded, as it was in Gratian's chapter. Constantine continued to enjoy a reputation as *pius imperator*, but from Bernard of Clairvaux onwards there was always ambivalence about him. The "Donation of Constantine" as now understood pointed the way to Dante's idea of a fatal dower:

*Ah* Constantine, *of how much ill was cause*
*Not thy Conversion, but those rich demaines*
*That the first wealthy* Pope *received of thee.*[115]

In its repeated critiques of the Pseudo-Isidorian Decrees, made without the benefit of reference to the parent text the *Actus Silvestri*, the *Defensor pacis* went further and questioned whether the words of *devotus Constantinus* really meant that other bishops were subject in jurisdiction to the Roman bishop.[116]

As the Stavelot Diptych illustrates, the reputation of Constantine as the most religious emperor survived the developments that have been the subject of the latter part of this paper. But, from the late eleventh century onwards, there were more sides than one to the picture that was presented. The

---

[113]  See esp. G. MICCOLI, "Ecclesiae primitivae forma," in *Chiesa gregoriana: Ricerche sulla Riforma del secolo XI*, Florence 1966, pp. 225–299.

[114]  For twelfth century developments, see LAEHR, *Die Konstantinische Schenkung*, pp. 44–73, and MAFFEI, *La Donazione di Costantino*, pp. 23–101.

[115]  *Inferno*, 19, 115–117 (Milton's translation).

[116]  1, 19, 8; 2, 11, 8; 16, 9; 18, 5–7; 20, 13; 21, 2; 22, 10; 22, 19–20; 25, 4–5; 27, 3; 28, 19; *The Defensor Pacis of Marsilius of Padua*, ed. C.W. PREVITÉ-ORTON, Cambridge 1928, pp. 104–105, 212, 279–280, 307–309, 325–326, 328, 349–350, 356–357, 383–384, 426–427, 451–452.

canonists' emphasis upon material endowment gave rise to doubts and contrasts which were already preparing the way for the English Independent John Milton summarily to conclude that "Constantine marred all in the church".[117]

---

[117]    As above, n. 1.

I am grateful to the British Academy for a generous contribution towards the cost of attending the Conference at which this paper was given. My thanks are also due to Katherine Scargill for her expertise in word-processing the paper.

# II

## THE SPIRITUALITY OF POPE GREGORY VII

In 1079, Pope Gregory VII (1073-85) wrote to the monks of Saint-Victor at Marseilles a letter in which he expressed his gratitude for the services of their abbot, Bernard, and offered them spiritual encouragement. His letter ended with a characteristic prayer which will serve to introduce his spirituality:

> May Almighty God, from whom all good things come, by the merits and intercession of the Virgin Mother of God and through the authority of Blessed Peter and Paul, the princes of the apostles, look with favour upon you, may he continually renew and keep you, may he reveal to you what is the 'new song' (Rev. 14: 3), and may he inflame you in holy jubilation; so that you may fully know how to weep for human frailty and how to experience the unspeakable goodness of God; and so that, by growing continually in his love, you may, with the Mother of Heaven as guide, deserve to come to the true knowledge of him and to his marvellous joy.[1]

Such a passage discloses a fervent and deep spirituality with characteristics of its own which was coloured by Gregory's sense of a pope's pastoral mission towards monks as towards other sorts and conditions of men and women. Yet his spirituality has seldom been discussed.[2] This is partly because he wrote no spiritual works of his own, and no sermons or prayers of his survive; most of the evidence must be gleaned from his letters. Fuller discussion is called for because, as is increasingly appreciated, Gregory was a figure of profound religious conviction and awareness. Moreover, he was of outstanding calibre among

---

[1] *Reg.* 6.15, to the monks of Saint-Victor at Marseilles, 2 Jan. 1079, p. 420.

[2] The fullest discussion is by H.-X. Arquillière, *Saint Grégoire VII: essai sur sa conception du pouvoir pontifical* (Paris, 1934), pp. 222-48; see also A. Fliche, *La réforme grégorienne et la reconquête chrétienne*, Histoire de l'Église, edd. A. Fliche and V. Martin 8 (Paris, 1946), pp. 61-2; G. Hofmann, 'La vie de prière dans les lettres de Grégoire VII', *Revue d'ascetique et de mystique*, 25 (1949), 225-33; G. Fornasari, 'Conscienza ecclesiale e storia della spiritualità. Per un redefinizione della Riforma di Gregorio VII', *Benedictina*, 33 (1986), 25-50; ibid., 'Verità, tradimento della verità e falsità nell'epistolario di Gregorio VII: un abbozzo di recerca', in: *Fälschungen im Mittelalter. Internationaler Kongreß der Monumenta Germaniae Historica, München, 16.-19. September 1986*, MGH Schriften, 33/1-6 (Hanover, 1988-90), 2.217-40.

medieval popes, and he played an epoch-making part in the ecclesiastical and political life of his time. Also, he was a monk-pope with deep roots in the Benedictine tradition, while his lifetime and the decades immediately after witnessed the foundation of new religious orders such as the Carthusians (1084) and the Cistercians (1098). It is worth asking whether there were features of Gregory's spirituality which looked forward to the newer orders as well as back to the older Benedictinism.

There can be no serious doubt about Gregory's monastic profession, which he probably made before 1046 as the young clerk Hildebrand in the Roman monastery of St Mary-on-the-Aventine.[3] It was always a guiding reality in his life. As pope, he urged a newly elected abbot to 'bind himself in the depth of his being to the holy Rule' of St Benedict (*sancte regule medullitus te astringas*),[4] and it has been convincingly argued that Gregory's prominent concern to secure obedience in ecclesiastical as in all human affairs sprang from his understanding of monastic obedience as enjoined by the Rule.[5] Such obedience is inward and spiritual, even more than outward and physical. It is itself an aspect of spirituality, and points to other respects in which Gregory's view of the Christian life and its obligations drew upon monastic sources. So far as the older monasticism with which he was associated is concerned, four respects suggest themselves for comment.

First and foremost, Gregory's letters suggest that his spirituality rested upon a broad and deep familiarity with the holy scriptures such as was cultivated in monastic circles. Gregory certainly pressed such a familiarity upon monks and

---

[3] For Gregory as a monk, see H.E.J. Cowdrey, *The Cluniacs and the Gregorian Reform* (Oxford, 1970), pp. 137-8, 148 n. 4.

[4] *Reg.* 7.7, to Cardinal Richard of Marseilles, 2 Nov. 1079, p. 468.

[5] K.J. Benz, 'Die Regula Benedicti in den Briefen Gregors VII.', in: *Itinera Domini. Gesammelte Aufsätze aus Liturgie und Mönchstum. Emmanuel von Severus OSB zur Vollendung des 70. Lebensjahres an 24. August 1988 dargeboten* (Münster, 1988), pp. 263-79; ibid. 'Kirche und Gehorsam bei Papst Gregor VII. Neue Überlegungen zu einem alten Thema', in: *Papsttum und Kirchenreform: historische Beiträge. Festschrift für Georg Schwaiger zum 65. Geburtstag*, edd. M. Weitlauff and K. Hausberger (St Ottolien, 1990), pp. 97-150.

their associates: 'Let your mind meditate daily upon the lessons of the holy scriptures', he wrote to the community at Vallombrosa, 'by which the assertions of heretics are confuted and the faith of holy church is defended.'[6] He expected of others, and seems himself to have practised, the scriptural study and the self-cultivation based upon it which were at the heart of the monastic culture of his day.[7] Like the Rule of St Benedict, the holy scriptures were to be digested *medullitus* - in the depth of one's being, by a process sometimes known as rumination. A glimpse at the - in fact, far from complete - index of biblical references in Caspar's edition of Gregory's Register reveals how often Gregory made, not only verbatim citations of biblical passages, but also borrowings, adaptations, and echoes of biblical language. The presence in a letter of a number of such biblical references indicates that Gregory himself dictated it.

Two subjects which he developed often and firmly in his letters, with a wealth of biblical citation, may be instanced as suggesting themes of his own spirituality. One is that of seeking to imitate the love of Christ by being prepared to lay down one's life for one's friends. In 1073, Gregory developed this subject at length to the clergy and people of Carthage, whom he reproved for not supporting their archbishop when he was under persecution by the Moslem emir; he similarly encouraged the archbishop to bear faithful witness when under persecution.[8] In 1074, when seeking to recruit knights for the defence of Constantinople against devastation and slaughter at the hands of the Seljuk Turks, he cited the example of the Redeemer and pleaded that, as he laid down his life for men, so they should lay down their lives for their brothers.[9] In the same year, he brought the subject home to himself, when he told Countess Matilda of Tuscany and her mother Beatrice of his own commitment: 'I would most gladly cross the sea, if

---

[6] *Epp. vag.* no. 2, after 12 July 1073, p. 6.
[7] J. Leclercq, *The Love of Learning and the Desire for God: a Study of Monastic Culture*, trans. C. Misrahi (London, 1978), esp. pp. 13-21, 87-105.
[8] *Reg.* 1.22-3, to the clergy and Christian people of Carthage, and to Archbishop Cyriacus of Carthage, 15 Sept. 1073, pp. 36-40.
[9] Reg. 1.49, to all Christians, 1 Mar. 1074, pp. 75-6; cf. 2.31, to King Henry IV of Germany, 7 Dec. 1074, pp. 165-8, and 2.37, to all the faithful of St Peter, 16 Dec. 1074, pp. 172-3.

need be to lay down my life for Christ.'[10] Meditation upon the New Testament nourished Gregory's concern with the imitation of Christ in his sufferings and death and with charity as ultimately proven in a willingness to lay down one's life for others.

Another theme in Gregory's spirituality which may be discerned in his reflective use of holy scripture is that expressed in the liturgical collect for the third Sunday after Pentecost which he cited: 'that we should so pass through things temporal that we do not finally lose things eternal.'[11] Gregory repeatedly developed this theme, with a wealth of biblical citation, in pastoral letters to kings and lay magnates. In 1077, for example, such persons in Spain received a lengthy exposition of it; the following passage illustrates the density of scriptural references:

> Therefore, do not mind high things (cf. 1 Tim. 6: 17) or be forgetful, on account of the loftiness of your present glory, of the human condition which is the same for kings and paupers; but, as the apostle warns, 'Humble yourselves under the mighty hand of God, that he may exalt you in the time of tribulation' (cf. 1 Pet. 5: 6). Do not set your hope in the uncertain riches of this world (cf. 1 Tim. 6: 17), but in him of whom it is written, 'For by me kings reign' (cf. Prov. 8: 15), and elsewhere, 'For power is given to you from the Lord and virtue from the Most High, who will question your works and examine your thoughts' (Wisd. 6: 4). In him also you should treasure up for yourselves the riches of good works (cf. Matt. 6: 20), building a firm foundation (cf. 1 Tim. 6: 19) and a possession of a better and an unfailing substance (cf. Heb. 10: 34), where you may live eternal life. For here we have no abiding city, but we seek one to come (Heb. 13: 14), whose builder and founder is God (Heb. 11: 10).[12]

The most famous of all Gregory's letters, his justification in 1081 to Bishop Hermann of Metz of his second excommunication and deposition of King Henry IV of Germany, ended with a like thought, based upon the imitation of Christ:

---

[10] *Epp. vag.* no. 5, (to Countess Matilda of Tuscany), (1074, after 16 Dec.), pp. 10-13.

[11] Cited in *Reg.* 2.71, to Duke Wratislav II of Bohemia, 17 Apr. 1075, p. 232/3-4. The collect takes up 2 Cor. 4: 18.

[12] *Reg.* 4.28, to the kings and lay magnates of Spain, 28 June 1077, pp. 343-7.

If this virtue of charity is neglected, whatever good a man may do will lack any fruit of salvation. But if men act humbly and continue as they should in love of God and their neighbour, they may rely on the mercy of him who said, 'Learn of me, for I am meek and humble in heart' (Matt. 11: 29). If they have been his humble imitators, they will pass from a servile and transient kingdom to one of true liberty and of eternity.[13]

Gregory's concern for his own passage from time to eternity is manifest in letters to Abbot Hugh of Cluny about the state of his own soul. Thus, echoing the Wisdom literature of the Old Testament, Gregory could lament that 'praise is not of value, nor is prayer that entreats hastily holy, in the mouth of a sinner (cf. Ecclus 15: 9) whose life is [not] praiseworthy and whose business is this-worldly'; to compensate, he besought the prayers for himself of the monks 'who for the merits of their life deserve to be heard'.[14]

Gregory's drawing upon the holy scriptures, the evidences for which are manifest throughout his letters, provides evidence of a spirituality with deeply monastic roots.

A second respect in which Gregory's spirituality has affinities with the older monasticism is his sense of the necessity and the centrality of intercessory prayer.[15] Gregory earnestly sought for himself the intercessions of all Christians, but above all of monks, and especially of the monks of great abbeys like Montecassino, La Cava, and Cluny: 'We have received a heavy burden to carry', he told Bishop Hermann of Metz, 'and we can in no wise bear it unless we are supported by you and all the faithful of Christendom.'[16] In return, intercessory prayer manifestly had a major part in his own spirituality. His letters contain a number of promises to intercede for others. For example, in reassuring the Empress-mother Agnes of Germany about her daughter Matilda's welfare, he said

---

[13] *Reg.* 8.21, to Bishop Hermann of Metz, 15 Mar. 1081, p. 562/18-25.
[14] *Reg.* 2.49, to Abbot Hugh of Cluny, 22 Jan. 1075, pp. 188-90.
[15] See Cowdrey, *The Cluniacs*, pp. 124-5.
[16] e. g. *Reg.* 1.1-2, to Abbot Desiderius of Montecassino, and to Prince Gisulf of Salerno, 23 Apr. 1073, pp. 3-4, 1.6, to Cardinal-bishop Gerald of Ostia and the subdeacon Rainbald, 30 Apr. 1073, p. 10, 1.53, to Bishop Hermann of Metz, 14 Mar. 1074, p. 80, 5.21, to Abbot Hugh of Cluny, 7 May 1078, pp. 384-5.

that 'we, too, gladly pray for her; and although our own merits do little to commend our prayers to God, the holiness of St Peter whose servant we are assists us, and we trust that they are not altogether vain in the sight of the Lord.'[17] When her son King Henry IV of Germany seemed to be well disposed and amenable, Gregory told him that he daily remembered him when saying mass.[18] He also prayed regularly for Henry's sister, Queen Judith of Hungary, in view of the tribulations of her life.[19] He asked his legates in Germany, Cardinal-bishop Peter of Albano and Bishop Ulrich of Padua, to pray for him as he prayed for them.[20]

The clearest insight that is available into Gregory's intercessory prayer is afforded by thirty-seven concluding wishes that are added to letters written in almost all years of his pontificate. They open with the words *Omnipotens Deus* or closely similar words; an example is the excerpt from a letter to the monks of Saint-Victor at Marseilles with which this paper opened.[21] The wishes are transparently of Gregory's own dictation, and are adapted to the situation of each person or group concerned. Most are addressed to leading lay, but sometimes ecclesiastical, figures who, at least for the time, stood high in Gregory's favour; some, however, envisaged large groups of Gregory's supporters. In Gregory's eyes, they were probably more than wishes, but brought grace and objective blessing. Similar to liturgical collects in form and sometimes in phrase, they were rich in biblical allusion. Only occasionally did they refer positively to the fortunes

---

[17] Reg. 1.85, to the Empress Agnes, 15 June 1074, pp. 122-3; see also his assurance of daily prayers for Countesses Beatrice and Matilda of Tuscany: 2.9, 16 Oct. 1074, p. 139, and of regular prayers for Matilda's late estranged husband Duke Godfrey of Lorraine: 4.2, to Bishop Hermann of Metz, 25 Aug. 1076, p. 297.

[18] Reg. 2.30, to King Henry IV of Germany, 7 Dec. 1074, p. 164; see also his reference to prayers for the late King Sweyn Esthrithson nf Denmark: 5.10, to King Harold Hein of Denmark, 6 Nov. 1077, pp. 361-2.

[19] Reg. 2.44, to Queen Judith of Hungary, 10 Jan. 1075, p. 181.

[20] Epp. vag. no. 31, (1079, July/Oct.), p. 84.

[21] On Gregory's so-called Schlußwünschen, see 0. Blaul, 'Studien zum Register Gregors VII.', *Archiv für Urkundenforschung*, 4 (1912), 113-228, at pp. 121-2. A full list is given in the Appendix to this paper. For the use of this epistolary form by other eleventh-century writers, see *Briefsammlungen der Zeit Heinrichs IV.*, edd. C. Erdmann and N. Fickermann, MGH *Briefe*, 5 (Weimar, 1950), p. 17 n. 1.

of this life, such as victory for the Patarene cause at Milan; like much of Gregory's meditation upon scripture, they commonly had the theme of so passing through this life that those prayed for might attain eternal salvation and glory in the world to come. They repay detailed study; overall, they provide a salutary reminder of how profoundly Gregory remained a monk in aspiration and outlook, and of how misleading it can be to regard his aims as this-worldly and in contrast with a monastic view of life.

A third affinity between Gregory's spirituality and that of the monastic order was his profound devotion to the Blessed Virgin Mary. The twelfth century was to witness an increase in such devotion, particularly among the Cistercians whose monastic churches were dedicated to the Virgin; but, in the eleventh century, the Cluniacs, too, strongly promoted it.[22] Gregory's devotion to the Virgin was remembered after his lifetime; Paul of Bernried, who completed his *Vita Gregorii VII* in 1128, wrote of his special devotion while still Archdeacon Hildebrand to a picture of her in St Peter's basilica. On one occasion when, having vindicated a bishop against false accusers, he returned to Rome, he prostrated himself before it. As a sign to him that he would in his turn be falsely accused, the Virgin wept and moved Hildebrand himself to tears. But when he had been cleared before the pope of the charge that he had accepted bribes, the Virgin smiled upon him.[23] In his letters as pope, Gregory's Marian devotion found its fullest expression when he wrote to devout noble women. In 1081, he sent to Queen Adelaide of Hungary the one letter which he is known certainly to have written with his own hand. He gave the queen his familiar advice to despise all

---

[22] For Cluniac devotion to the Virgin, see P. Cousin, 'La dévotion mariale chez les grands abbés de Cluny', in: *A Cluny: Congrès scientifique. Fêtes et cérémonies en l'honneur des saints Abbés Odon et Odilon* (Dijon, 1950), pp. 210-18; for its further development, R.W. Southern, *The Making of the Middle Ages* (London, 1953), pp. 105, 159-60, 201, 232, 238-40, 246-56.
[23] Paul of Bernried, *Vita Gregorii VII*, cap. 23, in: *Pontificum Romanorum qui fuerunt inde ab exeunte saeculo IX usque ad finem saeculi XIII vitae ab aequalibus scriptae*, ed. J.B.M. Watterich, 2 vols. (Leipzig, 1862), 1.482-3.

Songs, not least in the letters in which he advised frequent communion, sets him apart from Gregory, who never referred to it in surviving writings.[30] Nevertheless, Gregory's advice about frequent communion has a closer parallel in Peter's letters of the mid-eleventh century than in Carthusian or Cistercian sources of the early twelfth century.[31]

It was in the letter to Countess Matilda of Tuscany in which he urged upon her the honouring of the Mother of God that Gregory also recommended frequent communion: 'We should, my daughter, take refuge in this unique sacrament and seek after this unique medicament'; he wrote to increase her faith and confidence in receiving the Lord's body.[32] When Gregory wrote to Matilda, she was subject to twofold stress: her marriage to Duke Godfrey of Lorraine had ended in their estrangement, and she wished to take the veil·- a step from which Gregory earnestly dissuaded her.[33] These circumstances must be remembered; nevertheless, some comment is possible upon Gregory's own thoughts about the eucharist.[34] It is to be observed that he supported his advice about frequent communion, not by reasons expressed in his own words, but by a catena of five passages on the eucharist from three ancient writers - Ambrose, Gregory the Great, and John Chrysostom. His reliance upon such writers and his reluctance to

---

[30] I hope to write further about Peter Damiani and Hildebrand/Gregory in my forthcoming biography of Gregory.

[31] For early rules about communion among the Carthusians, see Guigo I, *Coutumes de Chartreuse*, 4.27, 29-30, 8.4-5, ed. by a Carthusian, Sources chrétiennes 313 (Paris, 1984), pp. 168-71, 180-3; for the Cistercians, see J.-B. Auberger, *L'Unanimité cistercienne primitive: mythe ou réalité?* (Achel, 1986), p. 383.

[32] *Reg.* 1.47, to Countess Matilda of Tuscany, 16 Feb. 1074, pp. 72/1-73/22.

[33] For Matilda's circumstances, see, besides the opening sentences of *Reg.* 1.47, 1.50, to Countesses Beatrice and Matilda of Tuscany, 4 Mar. 1074, pp. 76-7.

[34] There is some anecdotal evidence of Gregory's devotion while saying mass, esp. the story of the dove which perched on his shoulder as a symbol of the Holy Spirit, which occurs (in different contexts) in *Chronica monasterii Casinensis*, 3.54, ed. H. Hoffmann, *MGH SS* 34 (1980), 435-6, and in Paul of Bernried, *Vita Gregorii VII*, caps 30-1, pp. 486-7; also the story that, when saying mass, Gregory had the grace of tears which, whenever it failed, the recollection of John Gualbertus, first abbot of Vallombrosa, served to renew: *Vita sancti Iohannis Gualberti*, cap. 85, ed. F. Baethgen, *MGH SS* 30/2, 1102. Gregory's tears while saying mass were also observed at first hand by Guy of Ferrara: *De scismate Hildebrandi* (as n. 27).

formulate thoughts of his own have a parallel in his reserve, which he maintained over some thirty years until his Lent synod of 1079, in dealing with dogmatic aspects of the Berengarian controversy.[35] But his choice of excerpts from the Christian fathers was rich in thought and feeling. From Ambrose and Gregory the Great, he left it to be inferred that frequent communion was to be best understood as daily communion. From Ambrose, Gregory presented the eucharist as being conducive to the remission of sins and as a remedy for the faults of fallen human nature. From Gregory, he explained how it was a sacrifice, in which the risen Christ, who had been slain once and for all and was now glorified, was nevertheless daily immolated upon earth for men, and how the eucharistic action daily joined earth to heaven. From John Chrysostom, he declared the eucharist to be the food of Christians which raised human nature from its fallen state. By such citations as he made for the edification of Matilda, he sought to perpetuate what was most spiritually helpful in ancient authors without raising the problems and uncertainties of later eleventh-century controversy.

Some aspects of Gregory's spirituality as his letters reveal it arose from his experience of bearing the burden of the papal office. The deepest and most characteristic disclosure of his petitionary prayer for his own condition comes in a letter of 1078 to Abbot Hugh of Cluny.[36] His self-disclosure begins with his frequent metaphor of his being subject to tempests as though he were at sea and far from the harbour that he aspired to reach. Exceptionally, however, he proceeded to an expression of personal isolation while bearing the intolerable burden of the papal office: 'We are oppressed by such constraints and wearied by such great labours, that those who are with us are not only unable to sustain them

---

[35] For Gregory and the Berengarian controversy, see H.E.J. Cowdrey, 'The Papacy and the Berengarian Controversy', in: *Auctoritas und Ratio: Studien zu Berengar von Tours*, edd. P. Ganz, R.B.C. Huygens, and F. Niewöhner (Wiesbaden, 1990), pp. 109-38, esp. pp. 122-36. For Gregory's use of a series of texts on the eucharist which may have been that upon which he drew when writing to Countess Matilda, see pp. 122, 127.

[36] *Reg.* 5.21, to Abbot Hugh of Cluny, 7 May 1078, pp. 384/30-385/20 (the continuity of thought in the *Omnipotens Deus* passage with which the letter ends should be observed); cf. 2.49, to Abbot Hugh of Cluny, 22 Jan. 1075, pp. 189/28-190/11.

he had himself observed, Gregory shed daily at mass, so that he offered a double sacrifice to God - that of the eucharist, and that of his own contrition.[42]

Guy of Ferrara's description of Gregory's life-style and makes it easy to understand why, in his Life of Bishop Hugh of Grenoble (1080-1132) whom Gregory consecrated bishop, Prior Guigo I of Chartreuse showed evident admiration for Gregory as pastor and spiritual counsellor. After Hugh's election to his bishopric, he was subject to grave temptation and consulted Gregory at Rome. According to Guigo, Gregory helped Hugh to come to terms with his temptation and to make it a matter not for despair but for rejoicing - one recalls Gregory's own self-disclosure of 1078 to Abbot Hugh of Cluny.[43] Gregory advised Hugh of Grenoble in the light of the scriptural text that the Lord both disciplines those whom he loves and chastises every son whom he receives (cf. Heb. 12: 6); therefore, the more severely God laid the discipline upon Hugh's soul, the more manifest was the proof that he loved him as a father.[44] There was a kinship between Gregory's spiritual values and Guigo's.

Secondly, Gregory foreshadowed and prepared the way for twelfth-century developments both inside and outside the monastic order by his endeavours to base penance more largely upon personal contrition and penitence. In his prayer for the monks of Saint-Victor with which this paper opened, he asked that they might 'fully know how to weep for human frailty and how to experience the unspeakable goodness of God'.[45] In letters to the countesses of Tuscany, Gregory referred to the *Miserere* when he hoped that a *cor contritum et humiliatum* (Ps. 50: 19) would lead to prayer prostrate before the Virgin on the part of those who

---

[42] Guy of Ferrara, De scismate Hildebrandi, 1.2 , pp. 534-6; see also Wenric of Trier, *Epistola sub Theoderici episcopi Virdunensis nomine composita*, cap. 1, ed. K. Francke, *MGH Libelli*, 1.285-6.
[43] See above, p. 12
[44] Guigo, *Vita sancti Hugonis episcopi Gratianopolitani*, cap. 2.7-8, PL 153.767.
[45] See above, p. 1.

sought to extinguish all sin, just as it would serve to soften the rigour of human judgement.[46]

Such an increasingly inward and personal understanding of penitence seems to have guided Gregory in his measures of 1078 to 1080 for the better administration of penance. At his November synod of 1078, consideration of false and true penances seems to have mainly concerned the external conditions of penances. False penances were defined as those which did not conform to the tariff of penances set out by the best ecclesiastical authorities according to the gravity of the offences (*pro qualitate criminum*).[47] The synod had rather more to say about the awarding of true penance. If a knight, merchant, or official, none of whom could avoid sin in the pursuit of his avocation, sought penance for some grave matter, he could not do true penance unless he withdrew from his avocation (with some mitigation for the knight, who might bear arms with the permission of godly bishops in order to defend lawfulness). The synod seems to have recognized that further consideration of penances was called for, because, lest a man under penance on these terms should despair, in the meanwhile (*interim*) it exhorted him to do such good as he could, 'so that Almighty God might illumine his heart to penitence (*ut omnipotens Deus cor illius illustret ad penitentiam*)'.[48] It was an evident recognition of the need for inner contrition.

That Gregory was concerned to elicit such contrition and so to deepen the spirituality of Christians at large as he sought to deepen that of favoured persons

---

[46] See the citation above, p. 8, and *Reg.* 1.77, to Countesses Beatrice and Matilda of Tuscany, 15 Apr. 1074, p. 109/17-21.

[47] Gregory probably had mainly in mind lenient and merely formal penances: cf. *Reg.* 7.10, to the clergy and laity of Brittany, 25 Nov. 1079, pp. 471-2, esp. pp. 471/29-35, 472/6-15; but he may also have had in mind penances which were excessively burdensome so that they left no room for sufficient penance for other sins. See the massive penance imposed in 1073 by the Roman cardinals on Peter Raymundi, son of the count of Barcelona, for the murder of his stepmother: P. F. Kehr, 'Das Papsttum und das katalanische Prinzipat bis zur Vereinigung mit Aragon', *Abhandlungen der Akademie der Wissenschaften zu Berlin* (1926), pp. 80-1, no. 7.

[48] *Reg.* 6. 5b, 19 Nov. 1078, pp. 401/23-4, 404/4-17. It should be borne in mind that the Latin word *penitentia* means both 'penance' and 'penitence'. For further discussion of Gregory and penance, see H.E.J. Cowdrey, 'The Reform Papacy and the Origin of the Crusades' forthcoming

and ibid., 'Pope Gregory VII and the Bearing of Arms', forthcoming

like Matilda of Tuscany is suggested by a letter of November 1079 to the clergy and laity of Brittany. Gregory urged them to attend a synod to be presided over by his legate, Bishop Amatus of Oloron, which would remedy an ingrained custom of false penance. He said that those who persisted either in grave sins like homicide, adultery, or perjury, or else in inherently sinful ways of life like those of the merchant and armed man, 'could not perform the fruit of true penance'. He defined an unfruitful penance as one that was accepted while persisting either in the sin for which it was awarded or in one of comparable gravity. To do penance worthily, a person must return to the starting-point of faith (*necesse est, ut ad fidei recurrat originem*); he must watchfully and carefully keep what he promised in baptism - to renounce the devil and his pomps and to believe in God; by thinking rightly about God he must obey his commandments.[49] True penance must be attended by an inner conversion which activated the springs of religion.

Gregory returned to the subject with renewed fervour at his Lent synod of 1080. The decree of 1080 which deals with penance has a definition and a depth of explanation which are in sharp contrast to the decree of 1078. Unlike that decree, it reads as though it were based upon an allocution by Gregory himself. In warning against false penances, the decree of 1080, like the letter to the Bretons, referred to baptism: as false baptism does not wash away original sin, so after baptism false penance does not cancel a wrong that has been committed. Turning to true penance, the decree for the first time separated heinous sins like murder and perjury from the 'vocational' sins of merchants, armed men, and officials. It was upon heinous sins that Gregory concentrated. The decree first required conversion: let each man turn to God. It then required that a man should so turn to God that he abandoned all his iniquities and henceforth continued in the fruits of good works. The operative word was 'all'; the point was driven home by a text from the prophet Ezekiel which spoke of turning from all sins and of keeping all the commandments of God: 'If the unrighteous shall be converted from all his sins

---

[49] *Reg.* 7.10.

and shall keep the whole of my commandments, he shall surely live and not die' (cf. Ezek. 18: 21). In what reads like an explanatory gloss rather than Gregory's own words,[50] it is affirmed that warriors, merchants, and. officials who continue in their sinful ways cannot be held to have turned to God or to have done true penance. The decree ends with an exhortation which again reads like part of Gregory's allocution: all who seek penance should avoid blind guides and resort to those well instructed in religion and scriptural teaching who can therefore point out the path of truth and salvation.[51]

The contrast between the decrees of 1078 and 1080 suggests that, at this time, Gregory attempted to change and to deepen the general understanding of penance. He insisted upon inner conversion, upon due contrition for all sins, and upon a purpose of general amendment of life. Under competent direction, Christians were called upon to seek the spiritual renewal in which Gregory had counselled Matilda of Tuscany. In the new departures of his decree of 1080, Gregory began to prepare the way for the twelfth-century developments in penitential teaching and practice that are associated with Peter Abelard and the Victorines, and in the refinement of the spiritual life of the individual that marked the Carthusians and the Cistercians.[52]

Thirdly, Gregory's spiritual legacy to the twelfth century was apparent in the links, indirect but effectual, which joined him to the Carthusians. It is most apparent in the lives and influence of a number of monk-bishops who, while maintaining close contact with the Carthusian Order, also served as role-models for the episcopate. An example is Bishop Hugh I of Grenoble who, although not himself a Carthusian, was bishop of the diocese in which la Grande Chartreuse was situated and lived in close association with it; his *Life* was written by Prior

---

[50] The new sentence is introduced by the words 'In quibus verbis manifeste datur intellegi, quoniam ...', which suggest a gloss by the drafter of the decree.
[51] *Reg.* 7.15a (5), 7 Mar. 1080, pp. 481-2.
[52] For the history of penance, see C. Vogel, *Le Pécheur et la pénitence au moyen âge* (Paris, 1967); see also K. Müller, 'Der Umschwung in der Lehre von der Buße während des 12. Jahrhunderts', in: *Theologische Abhandlungen Carl von Weizsäcker zu seinem siebzigsten Geburtstage* (Freiburg, 1892), pp. 287-320.

Guigo I.[53] It has already been noticed that Gregory's spiritual and pastoral care for Hugh when newly a bishop and when assailed by severe temptation was a matter for comment by Guigo.[54] Guigo also exhibited Hugh as seeking in a disordered diocese to implement Gregory's most cherished aspirations for reform - to secure the celibacy of the clergy, to put an end to simony, and to free churches and church property from lay misappropriation and control.[55] But Guigo was far more concerned to exhibit Hugh as a model of private and public episcopal virtue. In his own spiritual life, Hugh remained reminded of his early counsel from Gregory about his inner life, for he was always subject to two afflictions - the undisclosed temptation that Gregory had taught him to live with, and sickness of the head and stomach which his austerities of life had brought on.[56] His custody of his senses was strict, and he possessed in abundance the grace of tears which had been a mainstay of Gregory's own spiritual life.[57] Like Gregory, too, he practised frugality in his manner of life.[58] Such were the private virtues which made possible Hugh's public virtues. These consisted especially in his assiduity in hearing confessions, giving penance, preaching for the conversion of sinners, and offering spiritual advice.[59] His formation as a bishop well suited him to be the religious and instructed spiritual mentor whom, in his decrees about penance in 1078 and especially in 1080, Gregory called for in order to administer penance prudently and with respect to the whole of a man's life. As Guigo presented Hugh, he understood, conformed to, and implemented Gregory's requirements. He did so in his diocese, and he did so in collaboration with a

---

[53] Guigo, *Vita sancti Hugonis episcopi Gratianopolitani*, PL 153.761-84; for a fuller discussion, see H.E.J. Cowdrey, 'The Carthusians and their Contemporary World: the Evidence of Twelfth-Century Bishops' Vitae', in: *Die Kartäuser und ihre Welt - Kontakte und gegenseitige Einflüsse*, ed. J. Hogg, Analecta Cartusiana 62, 2 vols (Salzburg, 1993), 1.26-43.
[54] Above, p. 14.
[55] *Vita Hugonis*, 2.9, col. 768A-C.
[56] *Vita Hugonis*, 3.13, col. 770CD.
[57] For Hugh's custody of the senses, *Vita Hugonis*, 4.15-18, cols 772-5; for his grace of tears, ibid. 2.9, 3.13-14, cols 768C, 771BC.
[58] *Vita Hugonis*, 2.9, 3.13, 5.19, cols 768BC, 770CD, 775B-D.
[59] *Vita Hugonis*, 3.14, 3.15, 5.19, 20, 22, cols 771CD, 773B, 775D, 776B, 777B-D.

monastic figure who was fully in sympathy. Guigo's *Life* of Hugh shows Gregorian spirituality coming to its fruition.

It may be concluded that the spiritual and pastoral aspects of Gregory VII's pontificate deserve profound attention. He was rooted in the spirituality of the monasticism of the eleventh century, especially Benedictine but also Italian. His understanding of the papal office elicited a powerful spirituality with a character of its own. It directed him towards a reconsideration of current practice, especially regarding penance, which anticipated and prepared the way for the monastic and general spirituality of the twelfth century.

## APPENDIX

The following is a list of the passages at the end of Gregory's letters which begin with the *Omnipotens Deus* (or similar) formula: see above, p. 6.

| Reference | | Pages | Date | Addressees |
|---|---|---|---|---|
| 1. *Reg.* 1.15 | | 24-5 | 1 July 1073 | All the faithful, esp. in Lombardy |
| 2. " | 1.38 | 61 | 17 Dec. 1073 | Duke Wratislav II of Bohemia |
| 3. " | 1.40 | 63 | 3 Jan. 1074 | Countess Matilda of Tuscany |
| 4. " | 1.50 | 77 | 4 Mar. 1074 | Countesses Beatrice and Matilda of Tuscany |
| 5. " | 1.62 | 91 | 19 Mar. 1074 | Abbot Hugh of Cluny |
| 6. " | 1.77 | 111 | 15 Apr. 1074 | Countesses Beatrice and Matilda of Tuscany |
| 7. " | 1.83 | 119 | 9 May 1074 | King Alphonso VI of León-Castile |
| 8. " | 2.7 | 136 | 22 Sept. 1074 | Duke Wratislav II of Bohemia |
| 9. " | 2.8 | 138 | 22 Sept. 1074 | Bishop John of Olmütz |
| 10. " | 2.31 | 168 | 7 Dec. 1074 | King Henry IV of Germany |
| 11. " | 2.37 | 173 | 16 Dec. 1074 | All the faithful of St Peter |
| 12. *Epp. vag.* 5 | | 12 | 1074, after 16 Dec. | Countess Matilda of Tuscany |
| 13. *Reg.* 2.44 | | 182 | 10 Jan. 1075 | Queen Judith of Hungary |
| 14. " | 2.70 | 230 | 17 Apr. 1075 | Duke Geisa of Hungary and his subjects |
| 15. " | 2.71 | 232 | 17 Apr. 1075 | Duke Wratislav II of Bohemia |
| 16. " | 2.74 | 237 | 17 Apr. 1075 | Prince Demetrius of Russia and his wife |
| 17. " | 3.7 | 259 | 1075, early Sept. | King Henry IV of Germany |
| 18. " | 3.15 | 277 | 1076 (Apr.) | The Milanese knight Wifred |
| 19. " | 4.1 | 292 | 25 July 1076 | All the faithful in Germany |
| 20. " | 4.2 | 297 | 25 Aug. 1076 | Bishop Hermann of Metz and all the faithful in Germany |
| 21. " | 4.17 | 323 | 31 Mar. 1077 | King William I of England, Queen Matilda, and their children |
| 22. " | 5.10 | 363 | 6 Nov. 1077 | King Harold Hein of Denmark |
| 23." | 5.21 | 385 | 7 May 1078 | Abbot Hugh of Cluny and all his monks |

| | | | | |
|---|---|---|---|---|
| 24. *Reg.* 6.1 | | 391 | 1 July 1078 | All in Germany who were not excommunicated |
| 25. " | 6.3 | 396 | 22 Aug. 1078 | Bishop Hugh of Die and Abbot Hugh of Cluny |
| 26. " | 6.13 | 417-18 | 15 Dec. 1078 | King Olav III of Norway and his subjects |
| 27. " | 6.14 | 419 | 30 Dec. 1078 | Duke Welf IV of Bavaria and his followers |
| 28. " | 6.15 | 420 | 3 Jan. 1079 | The monks of Saint-Victor at Marseilles |
| 29. " | 6.29 | 422 | 21 Mar. 1079 | King Ladislaus I of Hungary |
| 30. " | 6.35 | 452 | 20 Apr. 1079 | The archbishops of Rouen, Tours, and Sens |
| 31. *Epp. vag.* | 31 | 84 | 1079, July/Oct. | Cardinal-bishop Peter of Albano and Bishop Ulrich of Padua |
| 32. *Reg.* 7.23 | | 502-3 | 24 Apr. 1080 | King William I of England |
| 33. " | 8.1 | 513-14 | 6 June 1080 | Archbishop Gregory of Tsamandus |
| 34. " | 8.22 | 565 | (1081) | Queen Adelaide of Hungary |
| 35. " | 9.2 | 572 | (1081) | King Alphonso VI of León-Castile and his subjects |
| 36. *Epp. vag.* | 47 | 114 | (1082/3) | Count Robert I of Flanders |
| 37. " | 54 | 134 | (1084, July/Nov) | All the faithful |

## ABBREVIATIONS

The following abbreviations are used in the Appendix and footnotes to this paper:

| | |
|---|---|
| *Epp. vag.* | *The Epistolae vagantes of Pope Gregory VII*, ed. and trans. H.E.J. Cowdrey (Oxford, 1972) |
| *MGH* | *Monumenta Germaniae Historica* |
| -----, *Briefe* | -----, *Die Briefe der deutschen Kaiserzeit* |
| -----, *Epp. sel.* | -----, *Epistolae selectae* |
| -----, *Libelli* | -----, *Libelli de lite pontificum et imperatorum* |
| -----, *Schriften* | -----, *Schriften der MGH* |
| -----, *SS* | -----, *Scriptores* |
| *PL* | *Patrologia Latina*, ed. J.P. Migne |
| *Reg.* | *Gregorii VII Registrum*, ed. E. Caspar, *MGH Epp. sel.* 2 (Berlin, 1920-2) |

# Pope Gregory VII and the Chastity of the Clergy

Throughout the eleventh century, church reformers from all backgrounds whether laymen, monks, or members of the secular clergy agreed with Pope Gregory VII (1073-1085) in aspiring to extirpate the two "heresies" of simony—the trafficking through money, flattery, or services in ecclesiastical orders and offices, and clerical unchastity—active sexual relationships, whether involving a form of matrimony or not, as engaged in by those in the major orders (including bishops), deacons, or subdeacons.[1] So far as the popes were concerned, measures against them were taken with fresh zeal between the Emperor Henry III's reforming expedition to Rome in 1046 and Archdeacon Hildebrand's succession to the chair of St. Peter as Gregory VII over a quarter of a century later. For example, Pope Leo IX (1049-54) at his Roman synod after Easter 1049 forbade those in major orders to have sexual relations with their wives; a year later, he went so far as to command all clergy and laity to abstain from communion with priests and deacons who were guilty of fornication. At one or other of these synods, he further decreed that priests' harlots within the walls of Rome should be made serfs (*ancillae*) of the Lateran palace. Away from Rome, at his synod of Mainz in October 1049, Leo proscribed "the simoniac heresy and the detestable marriage of priests."[2] Writing in 1051 to the cathedral canons at Lucca, Leo asserted the value of a canonical life with the community of property as a salutary alternative to the moral scandal and material wastefulness of a married clergy.[3] Pope Nicholas II (1059-61) also legislated vigorously at his Roman synod in April 1059. No one might hear the mass of a priest who was known to have a concubine or a woman improperly living with him (*subintroductam mulierem*).[4] All in major orders who had taken or retained a concubine since Leo IX's ruling were banished from the sanctuary, while to those who duly obeyed Leo's injunction to chastity, Leo commended an apostolic common life both as a daily practice and as a spiritual ideal. Nicholas included his requirements about clerical chastity in an encyclical, *Vigilantia universalis regiminis*, which his successor Alexander II (1061-73) reissued, probably after his own Roman synod in 1063.[5]

Hildebrand witnessed this papal campaign at first hand;[6] he will also have been familiar with such arguments for clerical chastity as were propagated by two cardinal-bishops: Humbert, formerly a monk of the Lotharingian monastery of Moyenmoutier who from 1050 to 1061 was cardinal-bishop of Silva Candida, and the hermit-monk of Fonteavellana, Peter Damiani, who from 1057 to 1072 was cardinal-bishop of Ostia. Humbert wrote in connection with his legatine journey of 1054 to Constantinople; he replied to a tract by a Studite monk, Nicetas, who attacked the western practice of prohibiting and, if necessary, dissolving the marriages of priests. Humbert's furious onslaught affirmed that, in the Roman church, marriage was permitted to those in minor orders, but those promoted to the subdiaconate or above must thereafter observe perpetual continence. He deprecated the eastern custom of ordaining to the generality of the priesthood only those who were married; it was unseemly that new husbands made weak by recent sexual delight should handle the immaculate body of Christ and that they should quickly return their consecrated hands to caressing the bodies of women. The bull of excommunication that Humbert left on the altar of Sancta Sophia included a reference to the error of the Byzantines in permitting and defending the carnal marriages of those who minister at the holy altar.[7]

In a number of his letters, Peter Damiani concerned himself with the need for absolute continence in all who were in major orders in the west and especially Italy.[8] He did not spare the bishops from his strictures;[9] all in authority—popes, bishops, and lay rulers like Countess Adelaide of Turin—were to eradicate fornication. All sexual activity was included in this term; for the women of the clergy could not legally marry and were, therefore, concubines or whores. No one might hear the mass of a priest, the gospel read by a deacon, or the epistle read by a subdeacon whom he knew to consort with women. Peter repeatedly gave reasons of cultic purity for such a prohibition: because Christ's natural body was formed in the temple of a virgin's womb, he looks to his ministers nowadays to be continent and clean in the presence of his sacramental body; with regard to bishops in particular, hands that confer the Holy Spirit should not touch the genitals of harlots. Peter looked for moral, as well as cultic, purity in the clergy but this tended to be the subject of separate letters to those of exemplary life.[10]

If Hildebrand lived in the midst of such zeal for clerical chastity at Rome, he was also acquainted at first hand with the popular movement of the Patarenes which, from the mid-1050s, gathered strength in Lombardy and especially at Milan.[11] At first resisting clerical incontinence and soon also simony, the Patarene leaders proclaimed that only clerks of pure and humble life were true ministers of Christ. The sacraments of the rest were without benefit: one spokesman said that their sacrifices were like dogs' dung while their churches were stables for horses.[12] The Patarenes, therefore, proclaimed a kind of lay strike against offending clergy. The faithful were to boycott their churches; Milanese clerks were forced to sign a bond promising chastity; if they were impenitent, their houses were ransacked; access to the altar was barred; those who tried to approach the altar were dragged away.[13] The Patarene leader Ariald also established a *canonica* or center of common life and worship, where exemplary clergy might minister.[14] Both before and after he became pope, Hildebrand was a strong supporter of the Patarenes and, especially, of the knight Erlembald, their most militant leader.[15]

In view of both of this support for the Patarenes and of the concern at Rome on the part of the popes and others between 1046 and 1073 to commend and to enforce clerical chastity, the distribution by date of reference to it in surviving letters of Gregory VII is surprising. It is as follows:[16]

| Year | Reg. | Epp. vag. | Total |
|------|------|-----------|-------|
| 1073 | 1.27, 28, 30 | - | 3 |
| 1074 | 1.77, 2.10, 11, 25, 29, 30 | - | 6 |
| 1075 | 2.45, 47, 55, 61, 62, 66, 67, 68, 3.3, 4 | 6, 7, 8, 9, 10, 11 | 16 |

272

| | | | |
|---|---|---|---|
| 1076 | 4.10, 11 | 16 | 3 |
| 1077 | 4.20 | - | 1 |
| 1078 | 5.18 | - | 1 |
| 1079 | - | 32 | 1 |
| 1080 | - | 41 | 1 |
| 1081 | 9.5 | - | 1 |

No less remarkable is the distribution of regions with which Gregory's letters were concerned:

| Region | Reg. | Epp. vag. | Total |
|---|---|---|---|
| Germany | 1.30, 2.10,11, 25, 29, 30, 45, 61, 66, 67, 68, 3.3, 4, 5.18 | 6, 7, 8, 9, 10, 11, 58 | 21 |
| Germany and the kingdom of Italy | - | 32 | 1 |
| The kingdom of Italy | 1.27, 28, 77, 2.47, 55, 62 | - | 6 |
| France (excluding Normandy) | 4.10, 11, 20, 9.5 | 41 | 5 |
| The Anglo-Norman kingdom | - | 16 | 1 |

Even when allowance is made for possible gaps in the registration or survival of letters, it is apparent that, so far as his own *acta* are concerned, Gregory concentrated heavily on the German and Italian kingdoms of Henry IV. Even so, most of his surviving letters date from the rather less than two years between his Lent synod at Rome in early March 1074 and the worsening of relations between pope and king which led, in February 1076, to Gregory's first sentence of deposition and excommunication. Otherwise put, the promotion of clerical chastity was at the forefront of Gregory's direct personal attention only during the short period that his attention was not diverted by the struggle of pope and king in Germany or by matters related to it. Thus, his campaign against clerical celibacy was slow to start. For almost the first year of his pontificate, he referred to it only in two letters of the same date to Italian bishops, Albert, bishop-elect of Acqui and Bishop William of Pavia, whom he urged to support his own long-standing ally, Erlembald of Milan.[17] Otherwise, his sole reference was in a letter to one of Gebhard's clerks having come to Gregory in Capua.[18] Gregory's letters leave no doubt of his profound and sustained commitment to strive against clerical fornication. But he spent most of the second half of 1073 in South Italy in an endeavor to compose the affairs of the papacy's Norman allies whose loyalty mattered when Henry IV's disposition was uncertain. From 1076, Gregory was usually too much preoccupied by his contest with Henry IV for him to give his mind strenuously to the enforcement of clerical chastity; after his second excommunication and deposition of Henry in 1080, the subject almost completely vanished from his letters.

Gregory passed decrees about clerical chastity at his Lent synods of 1074 and 1075. His campaign in these years was his major endeavor to enforce it. It built up gradually. The sole report of the synod of 1074 is, significantly, from Germany: the Mainz recluse, Marianus Scottus, recorded that Gregory forbade priests, deacons, and all clerks to have wives or at all to live with women, save those "whom the Rule or the Nicene synod allowed."[19] Marianus wrote of no sanctions that Gregory may have imposed. In 1074, Gregory dispatched to Germany as legates the cardinal-bishops Gerald of Ostia and Hubert of Palestrina. After Easter, they released Henry IV from the excommunication that he had incurred by associating with excommunicated counselors. They were also commissioned to teach obedience to the strict rule of clerical chastity.[20] The legates encountered resistance from the German bishops and were unable to hold a synod. But upon returning to Rome, they added their testimony to that of the Empress-mother Agnes that Henry was minded to cooperate in eradicating simony and in remedying "the chronic disease of the fornication of the clergy."[21]

Hitherto in 1074, Gregory's letters to Germany about clerical fornication had been occasional. There were none before October. Then he ordered Archbishop Udo of Trier to investigate the charges of the cathedral clergy of Toul that their bishop, Pibo, had a record of simony and of living with a woman in fornication. Archbishop Udo and his colleagues found the charges to be groundless, and Udo pleaded with Gregory never again to be given a similar commission.[22] The matter did nothing to commend papal intervention to the German bishops. Also in October, a German count and his wife, almost certainly Count Albert of Calw and his wife Wiltrud, received a letter from Gregory in which he complained of the slackness of the German bishops in enforcing the laws of God; as a consequence, the clergy were guilty of many transgressions, including sexual uncleanness. Gregory exhorted his lay correspondents to stand fast in the truth and constancy of faith; they were to cleave to what the apostolic see had decreed about bishops and priests who were simoniacal or who lay in fornication.[23] Gregory named no sanctions, but, if he was referring to the decree of Leo IX, Nicholas II, and Alexander II, the implication was that godly laity should avoid the ministrations of sinful clergy. In November, Gregory wrote to Archbishop Anno of Cologne about a tithe dispute. He added an exhortation to Anno to proclaim in his own diocese and in those of his suffragans the duty of all priests, deacons, and subdeacons to live chastely.[24] Once again, he added no sanctions against offending clergy, but his sense of the regency of the matter was clear.

During the twelve months or so that followed, three reasons can be suggested to explain why Gregory should have directed a much more sustained campaign in Germany and, to a lesser extent, in the kingdom of Italy,[25] against simony and clerical fornication. First, it should be remembered that Gregory enjoyed the one period of, as he supposed, good relations with Henry IV that occurred during his pontificate. He was increasingly persuaded of Henry's goodwill and cooperation. The exigencies of the Saxon war in Germany compelled Henry to profess docility. Gregory, for his part, hoped soon to welcome Henry to Rome for imperial coronation and to find him willing to deserve coronation by furthering his purposes.[26] Secondly, Gregory could not afford to leave unheeded the failure of his legates of 1074 to make headway with the reform of the besetting evils of the German church.[27] Thirdly, as a consequence, Gregory was determined to call to active obedience the German episcopate which, in the latter months of 1074, was showing resistance to his aspirations and methods for the reform of the church.[28] Except that, in 1075, he sent no more legates, he now sought to use every means at his disposal to strive against simony and clerical fornication.

Even so, the terms of Gregory's decree against clerical unchastity at his Lent synod of 1075 are far from certain. The brief record of the synod in the Register does not give them,[29] and they seem to have been differently formulated for Italian and German destinations. The principal sources are Gregory's letters. Writing on 23 March to the Italian metropolitan Sigehard of Aquileia, Gregory expressed himself relatively mildly. A priest, deacon, or subdeacon who had a wife or concubine (*uxorem vel concubinam*—this is one of only two instances in Gregory's letters of the word *uxor* being unequivocally conceded to a clerk's partner) must altogether put her away and do penance; the refractory must cease from ministering at that altar, and henceforth they might not receive or enjoy the fruits of an ecclesiastical benefice. Such ecclesiastical sanctions as brought to bear by the metropolitan or his suffragans were the only ones invoked. There was no word of coercive action on the part of the laity.[30] But in undated but probably almost contemporary letters to the German archbishops Siegfried of Mainz and Werner of Magdeburg, Gregory required, without distinguishing wives from other women, that "all who were guilty of the crime of fornication" must cease from service at the altar. As his prime sanction against those who disobeyed, Gregory prescribed that the people should in no way accept their ministrations, "so that those who are not corrected from the love of God and the honor of their office may be brought to their senses by the shame of the world and the reproof of the people (*verecundia saeculi et obiurgatione populi resipiscant*)." The archbishops were also to exercise their own pastoral zeal.[31] On 29 May, and so six days after his mild letter to the archbishop of Aquileia, Gregory wrote of his measures against offending German clergy in similar terms; if, after episcopal admonitions, they did not repent, the laity should altogether shun their ministrations.[32] To Germany, Gregory wrote as though his synod had, like those of Nicholas II and Alexander II, called for at least a passive boycott by the laity of the ministrations of incontinent clergy.

Following his letter to Anno of Cologne in November 1074,[33] it was principally to German archbishops—Sigehard of Aquileia is the only known exception—that Gregory looked for support, both in their dioceses and in their provinces, against the "heresies" of simony and clerical fornication. First and foremost, he looked to the senior German metropolitan, Archbishop Siegfried of Mainz. At the beginning of December 1074, he summoned him with his suffragans urgently to come to Rome for his next Lent synod. By way of preparation, he was searchingly to investigate how his suffragans had come by their bishoprics and how they had lived since acquiring them (*introitum et conversationem predictorum episcoporum diligentissime inquiras*), and he was to send an advance report to Gregory; for Gregory knew that some of their reputations were not praiseworthy.[34] Siegfried excused his own attendance on grounds of ill-health. He promised obedience to God and to Gregory in the matters of clerical chastity and simony, but he pleaded with Gregory to exercise mildness and discretion.[35] But, after the Lent synod, Gregory wrote to Siegfried that the Roman decree (*hoc decretum*), of which he seems to have circulated a copy, must be zealously taught to the whole clergy and inviolably obeyed by them.[36] Archbishop Werner of Magdeburg, and perhaps other archbishops, received an identical letter.[37] On 29 March, Gregory again wrote to Archbishop Werner, exhorting him to emulate Joshua of old:

> By apostolic authority we enjoin and command
> you that, in order to preach and the more zealously
> inculcate the chastity of the clergy, you strenuously
> and urgently sound upon the priestly trumpet, until
> you shatter and raze the wall of Jericho, that is, the
> works of rebellion and the pollution of filthy lust.[38]

On the same day, he wrote again to Archbishop Anno of Cologne, calling upon him and his suffragans to gird themselves more strongly to secure the chastity of the clergy; Anno should summon a provincial synod at which he should resolutely preach it.[39]

It was not only to the German metropolitans that Gregory in 1075 addressed his letters about clerical unchastity. Again on 29 March, he wrote to Bishop Burchard II of Halberstadt with a view to confirming the bishop's assiduousness in favoring chaste and religious clerks as fellow-workers in his task. As for the lewd and incontinent, they should either be offered fatherly correction or, if they were incorrigible, they should be excluded from the holy altars; unless they duly repented, the laity should in no wise hear their ministrations.[40] If Gregory showed in the case of Burchard how he encouraged a bishop whom he thought to be properly active, his dealings with the diocese of Constance reveal his approach to one whom he deemed recalcitrant. Its bishop, Otto, did not come to the Lent synod of 1075; Gregory was quick to send him individual notice of his measure against simony and clerical fornication, which he was urged to uproot from his diocese. Later in the year, Gregory sent Otto a letter of stern rebuke for not only conniving at the retention by clerks of their women (*mulierculae*) but also for allowing them to begin new relationships. Gregory summoned Otto to account for himself at the Lent synod of 1076. He also wrote to the clergy and laity of his diocese; he explained his own position and instructed them, if the bishop persisted in his obduracy, to show him neither respect nor obedience.[41]

So far as the German laity are concerned, Gregory sought to incite all ranks to resist unchaste clerks by words and by actions. For much of 1075, Gregory was persuaded of King Henry IV's willing cooperation. He rejoiced about it in December 1074;[42] in July 1075, he included amongst Henry's supposed virtues his willing purpose effectively to promote the chastity that became the clergy as servants of God.[43] At the beginning of the year, he had addressed the South German dukes, Rudolf of Swabia, Berthold of Carinthia, and Welf of Bavaria, with a view to stimulating all-out lay action. He castigated the weakness of the German archbishops and bishops in allowing the ministrations of clerks guilty of simony and fornication and in disregarding the sanctions imposed by successive popes since Leo IX. Whatever the bishops might or might not say, Gregory therefore looked to the dukes as to other reliable laity on no account to accept the ministrations of offending clerks. Their resistance was to go further than merely boycotting them. Under the sanction of obedience, they were to strive to publish and to argue for papal measures both in the king's court and in other places and assemblies in the German kingdom. They were to exclude offending clerks from participating in the holy mysteries, "even by force should it prove necessary (*etiam vi si opportuerit*)." This phrase was an incitement to the laity to use such active force as was familiar in Italy but as had not hitherto been called for in Germany. Gregory laid down that, should this new departure meet with the objection that it was not the laity's business to act in such a way, the reply should be that the objectors should not obstruct the dukes' and the people's salvation; let the objectors come and dispute with Gregory at Rome about the obedience that he was imposing upon the laity.[44]

By early in 1075, Gregory was thus seeking to mount a two-pronged attack in Germany upon simony and clerical unchastity—an attack by the archbishops and bishops acting through their synods, and an attack by the laity both great and small acting through the king's court and their own assemblies. At much the same time, Gregory was also seizing his opportunities to enlist Italian laity in the same cause. The laity of the county of Chiusi were to take all necessary steps to expel from the cathedral a provost guilty of perjury and notorious fornication and to do what was necessary to renew the pristine state of their church.[45] The people of Lodi, on the other hand, were to help their exemplary bishop, Opizo, to extirpate simony and clerical fornication from his diocese and to do so with all their strength (*totis viribus*).[46]

By the end of 1075, Gregory was urging the clergy and laity of the kingdom of Germany not to obey bishops who continued to condone or to ignore clerical fornication. The faithful were told neither to obey such bishops or to follow their precepts.[47] In the same year, the Augsburg Annals, a source unfriendly to Gregory, commented on the wandering preachers who were everywhere sowing discord as well as on the preposterous papal decree that clerical continence should be enforced through laymen.[48] A letter such as Gregory's to all clergy and laity reads like his sanction for such a campaign.

The events of the winter of 1075-76, which included the German and Lombard bishops' renunciation of obedience to Gregory followed by Gregory's deposition and excommunication of King Henry IV, brought to an abrupt end Gregory's writing of letters to Germany and Italy about clerical chastity. In letters to these kingdoms, the subject reappears only in a brief letter, probably early in 1079. It is addressed to "all who show due obedience to St. Peter throughout the whole kingdom of Italy and of the Germans"; it forbade all priests, deacons, and subdeacons who were guilty of the crime of fornication entry to the church until they repented and mended their ways, while the laity were not to hear their offices.[49] The letter seems to have been associated with Gregory's endeavor at his Lateran synods of 1078-80 to promote the moral improvement of the Christian life; in November of 1078, a decree required that a bishop who connived at clerical fornication or who failed to punish it should himself be suspended.[50] At this stage, Gregory seems to have demanded of the laity only abstention from the ministration of offending clergy, not the active and forcible resistance which he countenanced in his letter to the South German dukes. His restraint may have been deliberate, for after the election of Rudolf of Swabia in 1077 as anti-king, he was disturbed by the ravages and the perils of civil strife in Germany.[51] He may have recoiled from adding to it by fomenting aggressive action against offending clergy.

Not until November 1076 did Gregory refer in letters relating to France to the subject of clerical fornication; it was brought to his attention by reports of controversy in Flanders about whether or not clerks who persisted in fornication might celebrate mass. Gregory wrote letters on the same day to Countess Adela and to her son Count Robert I le Frison in which he insisted that they might not do so but that they should be expelled from the sanctuary until they had duly repented; where possible, they should be replaced by priests who lived chastely. Gregory called upon the count to be diligent in resisting clerical fornication and simony, but he employed no phrases that implied the use of physical violence.[52] A letter of 1080 to Bishop Hubert of Thérouanne shows Gregory reacting to a report of a Flemish bishop's consenting to clerical fornication.[53]

As concerns France more widely, only once do Gregory's letters record a general initiative against clerical fornication. In March 1077, and so just before the full deployment of the authority of Gregory's papal vicars in France, Bishops Hugh of Die and Amatus of Oloron, Gregory entrusted Bishop Josfred of Paris with a number of commissions on his behalf. At the end of this letter, he urgently called upon Josfred to urge bishops throughout France to act as he had required German bishops to act after his Lent synod of 1075. The bishops were altogether to prohibit from ministering at the altar priests who would not desist from fornication, while Josfred himself was not to desist from publishing this prohibition in every place and assembly. If Josfred found the bishops to be lukewarm or if errant clerks were rebellious, he was to forbid the whole people from receiving their ministrations until they were shamed into amendment of life or compelled to return to a life of chastity (*ad castitatem religiose continentie redire cogantur*).[54] This phrase carries more than a hint that the laity should not only boycott their ministrations but should proceed to physical coercion. It is surprising that, two months later when Gregory sent Bishop Hugh of Die his first major agenda in French affairs, he made no mention of clerical fornication.[55]

In letters involving the Anglo-Norman kingdom, Gregory's references were occasional and in reaction to circumstances. In 1076, Gregory sought the cooperation of King William I to secure the expulsion from the Breton see of Dol of Bishop Juhel, whose offenses included marriage and the alienation of church property in order to provide his daughters with dowries.[56] In 1081, Gregory instructed his legates Hugh of Die and Amatus of Oloron to be restrained in their dealings with the king whom Gregory praised, amongst other things, for compelling priests under oath to separate from their wives (*uxores*); Gregory may have had in mind the canons of the council of Lillebonne (1080) which William had held.[57]

The limits of time and place within which Gregory wrote in his surviving letters about clerical chastity are thus surprisingly narrow. But the concern about it amongst reformers everywhere and Gregory's own zeal to enforce it, not least in his letter of 1077 to Bishop Josfred of Paris, make it more than unlikely that he ceased to work for it. The contest between *sacerdotium* and *regnum* of which his dealings with the German monarchy were an expression brought other business to the forefront of Gregory's own attention. But the legates and papal vicars of whom he made increasing use had a responsibility for ensuring that the momentum of Gregory's drive was maintained. Three examples may be given by way of illustration.

First, between 1077 and 1079, the Roman subdeacon Bernard and Abbot Bernard of Saint-Victor of Marseilles served as Gregory's legates in Germany. Their principal concern was with the high matter of the German kingdom, and Gregory's letters to them said nothing of clerical chastity. Yet they were concerned to promote it. In 1077, they held an assembly at Constance to which Bishop Otto had returned and had exceeded the limited powers that were allowed him. The legates took the opportunity to condemn the simony and the clerical fornication that were rampant in the diocese according to the terms of Gregory's synodal ruling. They insisted that no Christian should receive the ministrations of clerks who had been condemned for incontinence.[58]

Secondly, in France and northern Spain, Bishops Hugh of Die and Amatus of Oloron became widely active as papal vicars from this time and they held a number of legatine councils. The few records of the canons that were enacted make clear their zeal to enforce clerical chastity. At Poitiers in 1078, Hugh decreed that sons of priests and others born in fornication might not be admitted to holy orders or become monks and regular canons. No deacon, priest, or subdeacon was to have a concubine or to have under his roof any woman who might give rise to suspicion of evil; whoever knowingly heard the mass of an offending priest was to be deemed excommunicate.[59] At Gerona in the same year, Amatus ruled that, if any clerk henceforth married or took a concubine, both his orders and his office would be in jeopardy; he must withdraw from the clergy until he had done canonical satisfaction.[60] A letter of 1081 from Gregory to the two legates referred to "many knights" who had won their favor by coercing fornicating and simoniacal clergy.[61] The letter confirms the indication in Gregory's letter to Bishop Josfred of Paris that, whatever restraint he may have adopted in Germany, in France Gregory continued to countenance, if not call for, the bringing to bear of lay violence against offending clergy, and that his papal vicars undertook a militant campaign.

Thirdly, one of Gregory's staunchest supporters in south Germany was Bishop Altmann of Passau (1065-91) who, by 1081, was Gregory's papal vicar in that region. He was greatly concerned to implement Gregory's requirements of the clergy, especially their chastity.[62] He loyally, and in face of bitter opposition, proclaimed in his diocese Gregory's decree of 1075.[63] He wrote to Gregory for advice about the ecclesiastical position of clerks who had offended.[64] But he was remembered as one whose approach was by no means only negative; it was said of him that as in some places he destroyed the service of the devil, so in others he established the service of Christ.[65] Throughout his episcopate, he did so by establishing houses of regular canons which at once set a standard of clerical life for others to follow and provided places of refuge and society for those who came under persecution. During and after Gregory's pontificate, such houses bore continual witness to his demands on the clergy. It was a Bavarian regular canon, Paul of Bernried, who c. 1128 wrote a Life of Gregory which testified to and applauded his measures in Germany against simony and clerical fornication.[66]

These three examples show how, when Gregory himself was diverted by events from interventions to promote the chastity of the clergy, his legates and papal vicars, as well as other agents, maintained the impetus that he began in 1074 and 1075.

A final aspect of Gregory's concern for clerical chastity calls for comment. By contrast with the writings of Cardinal Humbert,[67] Gregory made no reference whatsoever to the custom of marriage amongst the parish clergy of the eastern churches. He did not mention it when writing about points of difference between Latins and Greeks; in view of his tolerance, though not approval, of the Greeks' use of leavened bread in the Eucharist as well as of his genuine desire to promote better relations, it is probably that his silence is a deliberate one.[68] Certainly, in this as in other matters, he was far from being a disciple of Cardinal Humbert.

Such, in summary, was the course of Gregory's actions, on his own part and through papal legates and vicars, to promote the chastity of the clergy. In the light of this evidence, it is possible to investigate Gregory's reasons for so strenuously acting to achieve it.

Undoubtedly, one of his reasons was his conception of the need for cultic purity in those who ministered at the altar. He said as much in 1076 in his letter to Count Robert of Flanders after he received reports of priests in his county who engaged in fornication but nevertheless when singing mass handled the body and blood of Christ. He said that such priests paid no heed to the great insanity and crime of at one and the same time handling the body of a harlot and the body of Christ.[69] Yet, by contrast with the emphasis laid upon this argument by Cardinals Humbert and Peter Damiani, this is the sole occurrence of it in Gregory's letters. Characteristically, he used emotive phrases of a general kind, such as "a base manner of life (*turpis vite conversatio*)," "the pollutions of filthy lust (*sordide libidinis pollutiones*)," or "the foul pollution of lustful contagion (*feda libidinosae contagionis pollutio*)."[70] Gregory also applied such language to simony. It, too, was a "contagion (*contagium*)."[71] He bracketed together "these detestable plagues—the simoniac heresy and the fornication of ministers of the sacred altar."[72] Gregory usually did not dwell upon the cultic inappropriateness of clerks having intercourse with women but sought to set up an overall emotive barrier against both fornication and simony which, by deterring clerks from these "heresies," would free them as an order of the church to cultivate the moral character that befitted their ministrations.

Gregory distanced himself from the polemic of Humbert and Peter Damiani in another respect. They, like some other late eleventh-century and twelfth-century reformers, campaigned against clerical unchastity by branding it as "Nicolaitism." The word was derived from references in the book of Revelation, 2.6, 14-15, to a sect of the Nicolaitans which the Lord, and all right-thinking Christians, abhored; its offences included fornication. From the second century, the name was thought to be derived from that of Nicholas, the last-named of the seven original deacons of the apostolic church (Acts 6.1-6). Despite his blameless character as described in scripture, he acquired the reputation of having been the first fornicator among the clergy. The revival of the term "Nicolaitans" in the eleventh century was owing to Cardinal Humbert in his polemic of 1053 against the Studite monk Nicetas. The learned cardinal consulted the compendium of ancient heresies which was compiled by the fourth-century Greek author Epiphanius of Constantia (Salamis). It enabled him to remind Nicetas of "the accursed deacon Nicholas, the leader of this heresy [what he called adultery, rather than marriage, of priests] whom we thing came forth from hell"; according to Epiphanius, Humbert pointed out, Nicholas had taught that priests should both have and sexually enjoy wives as laymen did.[73] Peter Damiani eagerly followed Humbert by writing against *Nicolaitae*.[74] In 1059, he saw to it that Archdeacon Hildebrand was familiar with the term; he wrote to him:

> Now, clerks are called Nicolaites when they have intercourse with women against the law of ecclesiastical chastity. Obviously, they become fornicators when they couple together in this foul commerce; they are rightly called Nicolaites when they defend their death-bringing plague as though by authority. For a vice is turned into a heresy when it is confirmed by the defense of misguided teaching.[75]

Despite such instruction, Gregory as pope never used the word "Nicholaite" in letters in his Register, and it occurs only once outside; in 1076, Bishop Juhel of Dol was stigmatized as a simoniac and a Nicolaite (*Nicolaita*) on account of his publicly notorious marriage.[76] Gregory was similarly reticent about the legends of Simon Magus, the father of all simoniacs.[77] It is probable that Gregory deliberately played down such legends and that, despite the prominence of the Nicolaitans in the writings of Humbert and Peter Damiani, he preferred to campaign against clerical unchastity by using other arguments.

Characteristically, the other arguments that Gregory advanced were moral or tended in the direction of seeing chastity as a virtue. While Gregory would certainly not have distinguished so sharply as would the present-day commentator between cultic and moral considerations, he showed a tendency to stress the latter, as being appropriate to the nature of the church in relation to Christ. He did so with regard to the clergy whom he was trying to win for a life of chastity. Especially in his letters to Archbishop Anno of Cologne, he turned from the state of the individual clerk day by day as he ministered at the altar to focus upon the corporate, moral purity which befitted the church as the bride of Christ. St. Paul declared that, as bride, the church should "know no stain or wrinkle (Eph. 5.27)." Its clergy should bring to such a church the gracious service of a spotless and unstained household. Within the ministering household, chastity was, for the clergy, a virtue of the chamberlains of Christ as the virgin husband and of the church as the virgin spouse. Chastity became more than simply the suitability to handle the sacrament; it was conformity to Christ and his bride the church in the completeness of their union. Such conformity presented moral demands of the widest kind; as Gregory commented to Anno, "the other virtues are of no value before God without chastity, neither is chastity of value without the other virtue."[78] Chastity took its place as part of the overall vision for the church that Gregory, in 1084, declared to have always been his concern: "that the holy church, the bride of Christ, our lady and mother, should return to her former glory and stand free, chaste and catholic."[79]

Gregory set clerical chastity in a moral context yet more decisively in the arguments that he directed, not towards offending clerks themselves but to all in authority, clerical and lay, great and small, through whom he wished to discipline them by whatever means. He appealed insistently to their duty of obedience to the directions of the church and especially of the apostolic see. Gregory's conception of obedience was not mainly one of outward conformity to the positive laws of the church but rather an inner commitment to the injunctions of a personal superior as within the monastic context.[80] Thus, he grounded his requirement of obedience in the Bible and in the comment upon it of his predecessor Pope Gregory the Great. In letters about clerical chastity, he five times urged his correspondents to be obedient in promoting it by citing part or the whole of one of his favorite biblical citations. It was from the prophet Samuel's rebuke of the disobedient King Saul when he had wrongly spared the king and the spoil of the Amalekites: "To obey is better than sacrifices and to hearken than to offer the fat of rams. For rebellion is as the sin of witchcraft, and stubbornness is as iniquity and idolatry (1 Sam. 15.22-23)." With this text, Gregory associated the comment of Pope Gregory the Great, that obedience constitutes true sacrifice, and that it carries the reward of faith.[81]

To the South German dukes in 1074, Gregory used Samuel's rebuke of disobedience in order to condemn the German bishops' slackness against sinful clergy, so that sacred ministrations were unworthily performed and the people were led astray. To the clergy and people of Constance in 1075, Gregory cited at length Gregory the Great's homily on obedience. In the same year, he communicated Samuel's rebuke and Gregory I's comment to Bishop Burchard of Halberstadt. In 1076, he used the same combination of text and explanation to comment to Count Robert of Flanders upon the indivisibility of obedience among all Christians: if bishops did not obey the admonitions of the church by enforcing clerical chastity, lay princes were absolved from obedience to their bishops. In his encyclical of 1079 to all the faithful in Italy and Germany, Samuel's words and Gregory I's commentary were again cited, this time to extend the duty of obedience in opposing clerical fornication to all true Christians.[82] By thus setting the campaign against clerical unchastity in a context of obedience to the church and its authorities, Gregory directed it from cultic considerations towards obedience and the gaining of human salvation. "I beseech you," Gregory ended his encyclical of 1079, "obey your apostolic precepts that you may attain to your inheritance in the heavenly kingdom."

Compatibly with these considerations about the chastity of the clergy, Gregory in his letter of 1075 to Bishop Otto of Constance presented it as simply part of the right constitution of things as manifested in the church. He stated as an evident fact that there were three orders in the church, so that men were either virgins, or continent, or married (*aut virgines sunt aut continentes aut coniuges*). Whoever stood outside these three orders was not numbered among the sons of the church or within the boundaries of the Christian religion.[83] Gregory argued from the inherent duties and constraints that arose for each order. He ruled out the possibility of clerical marriage by a characteristic *a fortiori* argument. If the least of laymen were known to keep a mistress, he transgressed the law of his order and was debarred from the sacraments of the altar until he repented as a member severed from the Lord's body. That being so, no one could dispense or minister the holy sacraments when, by having transgressed the bounds of his order, he could not even be a partaker of them. Clerical chastity was part of the necessity of things.

Gregory's argument from the three orders of society makes clear why he normally subsumed all relationships of clerks with women under the term "fornication."[84] Only the laity could be *coniuges* and so enter into marriages. Thus, all clerical relationships with women, including their apparent marriages, were contrary to the right ordering of society and therefore not what they purported to be. The argument from the three orders also makes clear why, unlike Cardinal Humbert, Gregory did not seek warrant in the Bible for his demands upon the clergy, nor was he concerned to establish that clerical continence was the rule from the earliest days of the church.[85] For him, it was enough that it was required by the nature of the orders of men in the church; to warrant it, he appealed to rulings by the greatest rather than by the earliest of the popes of antiquity—Leo the Great (440-61) and Gregory the Great (590-604).[86]

Gregory's reasons for requiring the chastity of the clergy may be summarized as follows. He was at one with his contemporaries in demanding it for the cultic reason that it was not fitting for hands that ministered at the altar also to handle the bodies of women. Yet he was reticent about this reason and almost always expressed the cultic aspect by using emotive language of a general character about the polluting effect of lust upon the clerk's manner of life. He made very little use indeed of language and arguments of a legendary nature which were based on New Testament texts about the Nicolaitans. In this as in other respects, he was not the disciple of

Cardinal Humbert or Cardinal Peter Damiani. Instead, he showed a clear tendency to move from cultic arguments towards moral ones. With an eye to the final perfection of the church, he demanded that the clergy should cultivate chastity as a virtue together with the other virtues that befitted the household servants of Christ and his bride, the church. All those, clerical or lay, great or small, who could in any way enforce it were to do so as an exercise of their own Christian obedience within the church. The pattern to be followed was that of the three orders of the church—the virgins, the continent, and the married, each of which had its separate manner of life; this manner of life must not be infringed or confused with that of the others.

Gregory's energetically promoted campaign to enforce clerical chastity, especially in the years 1074 and 1075, added to the resistance that clerks were already offering to the endeavors of reforming churchmen to make them abandon their wives and companions.[87] Thus, probably at a council of Paris in 1074, Abbot Walter of Saint-Martin of Pontoise resisted the overwhelming majority of those present who declared that Hildebrand's decree about married priests was unsupportable and unreasonable, so that it should not be obeyed. Significantly in view of Gregory's own arguments, Walter urged the duty of obedience to papal authority. The upshot of the debate was that Walter was seized and carried off to the king's palace.[88]

A sharp picture of similar happenings in Germany is presented by the monastic annalist Lampert of Hersfeld. According to him, the whole company of the clergy (*tota factio clericorum*) was incensed by Gregory's demands. For them, he was a man who was palpably heretical and a proclaimer of insensate teaching. By his violent demands, he was trying to make men live after the manner of angels; if he denied them the use of nature to which they were habituated, he would loosen the reins of fornication and all uncleanness. Anyhow, the clergy would rather desert their priesthood than their marriage; it would remain to be seen how Gregory, in whose eyes men were unclean, would summon up enough angels to staff the parishes of the church. Lampert wrote of the dilemma of Archbishop Siegfried of Mainz, caught between the mandate of the pope rigorously to enforce a rule of chastity and the fury of a recalcitrant clergy.[89] Probably in October 1074, Siegfried held a synod at Erfurt at which he found no support among the bishops.[90] A year later, he convened another synod at Mainz at which Bishop Henry of Chur produced Gregory's latest stern letter to Siegfried.[91] When Siegfried declared himself minded to implement Gregory's demands, the reaction was so violent that, according to Lampert, he barely escaped with his life.

Lampert's picture is complemented by other evidence. At about the time of the synod of Mainz, Siegfried's suffragan, Bishop Otto of Constance, held a diocesan synod at which the clergy rejected the canon of the council of Nicaea about clerical chastity.[92] Gregory's anger at Otto's acquiescence in his clergy's rejection elicited Gregory's three forceful letters to Constance of late 1075.[93] Bishop Altmann of Passau, on the other hand, behaved as Gregory would have wished. At a synod almost certainly held late in 1075, he resolutely upheld Gregory's position. On St. Stephen's Day (26 December), he reiterated it in a sermon at the cathedral, thereby provoking a tumult from which he, like Siegfried of Mainz, had difficulty in escaping.[94]

Such incidents were of more than local and temporary significance. They served to make Gregory's demands for clerical chastity a subject of widespread debate and therefore notoriety. The debate was conducted through polemical writings which further fueled concern. A full consideration of them would exceed the scope of the present study,[95] but some of the literature both for and against Gregory's demands may be noticed by way of example.

Against Gregory, between 1074 and 1079, there was written in Germany an *Epistola de continentia clericorum* which purported to be addressed by the saintly Bishop Ulrich of Augsburg (923-73) to a Pope Nicholas.[96] In Ulrich's lifetime, there was no pope of this name. The reference was clearly to Pope Nicholas II in view of the measures of 1059-60 concerning clerical continence, with regard to which the pope was said to have dealt "not legitimately but wrongfully, not canonically but injudiciously (*non iuste, sed impie, non canonice, sed indiscrete*)." Pseudo-Ulrich argued that the duty of the pope was to commend but not to command continence. Compulsion was alien to scripture and to the canonical tradition; the author deployed arguments such as Lampert of Hersfeld recorded amongst the clergy that enforced continence was fraught with moral perils for the clergy and raised the danger of scandal in the church at large. A detail of the letter was its reference to the supposed intervention at the council of Nicaea of the martyr-figure and bishop of Upper Thebes, Paphnutius, who persuaded the council to permit married clergy the liberty of abstaining from their wives or not.[97] According to the chronicler Bernold of St. Blasien, at his Lent synod of 1079, Gregory VII condemned the so-called rescript of Ulrich to Pope Nicholas about the marriage of priests and especially the precedent allegedly set by Paphnutius' intervention at Nicaea.[98]

A further illustration of opposition to Gregory's measures is provided by two letters, evidently of 1078, which survive from what seems to have been a widespread riposte in northern France to Bishop Hugh of Die's legatine action against married clergy.[99] The first is addressed by a circle of clergy at Cambrai to the church of the province of Rheims. The senders expressed an intention of defending the public liberty of the clergy. One respect in which they sought to do this was by protecting their liberty to marry. They strongly resisted any attempt to prohibit marriage to all ranks of the clergy in major orders; clerks who had not vowed themselves to continence had the right to be the husband of one wife. Probably under the influence of Pseudo-Ulrich, the letter cited in justification the supposed intervention of Paphnutius at the council of Nicaea. The reply of the clergy of Noyon to those of Cambrai survives. It is couched in cautious terms; while it defended the ordination of the sons of clergy, it did not go so far as to justify clerical marriage as such but pleaded for further consideration. The points that stand out from this exchange of letters are, first, the resistance of the clergy as expressed by the clerks of Cambrai to the rigor of Gregory's demands as transmitted by his legates, second, the rapid dissemination of such a supposed precedent for questioning it as the incident of Paphnutius' swaying the council of Nicaea, but, third, the reluctance of the clergy of Noyon to commit themselves to the resistance canvassed by their brothers at Cambrai. There was genuine debate, and minds were not closed against such reform as Hugh of Die was seeking.

On the side of Gregory VII, particular significance attaches to the writings of Bernold of St. Blasien and his circle.[100] Bernold's career adds to the interest of his writings. He was born c. 1050 the son of a priest; this circumstance made him, like others of his time, sensitive as to the propriety of clerical marriage. By 1075, he was a canon of Constance. The attitudes of the bishop and clergy of the diocese concentrated his mind so that he became a dedicated advocate of a strictly Gregorian persuasion, not least in matters of clerical discipline. In the cathedral school at Constance, he had been well educated in biblical and canonical studies and in the skills of literary presentation, and his education was reinforced by good personal character. In 1084, he was ordained priest by Cardinal Odo of Ostia, and he became the close associate of Bishop Gebhard III of Constance whom Odo also ordained. By the time of Gregory VII's death, he had become a monk of the reformed house of St. Blasien. The polemical tracts that he wrote while at Constance included his *De incontinentia sacerdotum* of 1075-76, which had the form of an exchange of letters with a priest named Alboin.[101] Whereas Bernold defended canon three of the council of Nicaea, Alboin took his stand upon the intervention of Paphnutius. It was, in effect, a scholarly answer to Pseudo-Ulrich. Soon afterwards, Bernold wrote his *Apologeticus*;[102] in it, he defended Gregory's synodal decrees against simoniacs and incontinent ministers at the altar and sought to demonstrate with a wealth of detail and argument their complete compatibility with the sacred canons of holy scripture. Bernold took as his starting point the letter of "our pope" Gregory VII to Bishop Otto of Constance in the spring of 1075.[103] Bernold's apologetic was important not only for its inherent qualities of learning and presentation but through his connections with the networks provided by the cathedral school at Constance and then by south German reformed monasticism. It was enhanced by his visit to Gregory at Rome in 1079 and by his contact in Germany with Cardinal Odo of Ostia, the future Pope Urban II.[104] Bernold illustrates the force and freedom with which Gregory's demand for clerical chastity, along with other demands that he made, could circulate and find commendation in Germany. Further afield, similar channels of long-term communication opened up; for example, the spiritual force of such newer orders as the Carthusians was effective in gradually commending Gregory's objectives, particularly clerical chastity, in France.[105]

Posterity has ascribed to Gregory VII an epoch-making role in demanding and enforcing the chastity of the clergy and in thereby establishing in the Latin church the closest possible association between priesthood and celibacy. There are some grounds for considering such a claim to be excessive. As regards his synodal decrees and the methods by which he sought to procure their enforcement, it is impossible to point to any element that was not present in the work of his papal predecessors from Leo IX to Alexander II or in the activities of groups like the Patarenes which were well established before he became pope. Moreover, after his death, the problem of clerical chastity remained an endemic one. Yet it is probably correct to regard Gregory's pontificate as a turning point. His stringent requirement of chastity was advanced, particularly in 1075, with a force and insistence that were new. Compared with the enthusiastic crudeness of Peter Damiani's advocacy of it and the heavy and legendary vehemence of Humbert's, Gregory's tendency to shift the emphasis from the cultic to the moral in arguing for continence and his close association between the chastity of the individual clerk and the quest for a church which was truly the bride of Christ, without stain or wrinkle, added fresh depth to the concept of chastity as proposed to the clergy. Far more than before 1073, the networks of communication by which papal aims and aspirations were disseminated caused them to strike home with the clergy and laity. The developments of Gregory's pontificate challenged the life-style of every clerk, both in respect of his relationship with women and also in respect of the standards by which his ministry should be governed. No one who reads Gregory's letters can fail to grasp the unprecedented impact that was made by the spiritual and moral demands that they conveyed.

This impact was not lost upon the world of the later reform papacy. When, in 1139, Pope Innocent II sought to consolidate its work in the canons of the Second Lateran Council, the canon on clerical chastity was said to have been drawn up "following in the footsteps or our predecessors Gregory VII, Urban [II], and Paschal [II]," without mention of Gregory's predecessors. It forbade anyone to hear the masses of those whom he knew to have wives or concubines. In order that the law of continence and the cleanness that was pleasing to God might be spread abroad among ecclesiastical persons and holy orders, all clergy and others who had presumed to take wives in transgression of their sacred purpose were to separate from them. Innocent took the step of stating definitively that unions of this kind, which were manifestly contracted against the rule of the church, could not be regarded as marriages at all. Those who rightly separated from their partners must perform due penance for such great sins.[106] If the canon lacked the moral force of Gregory's own pronouncements, it confirmed the actions that he had taken and took them to their conclusion by definitively stating that marriages of clerks were null and void. Celibacy was the rule to which all in major orders were expected to conform in purpose and in actuality.

## NOTES

1. For a general survey of the history of clerical celibacy, see Georg Denzler, *Das Papsttum der Amtszölibat*, Päpste und Papsttum 5, 2 vols. (Stuttgart, 1973-76). For Gregory VII and his age, Carl Mirbt, *Die Publizistik im Zeitalter Gregors VII.* (Leipzig, 1894), remains fundamental. For Gregory's letters, the most recent editions are *Das Register Gregors VII.*, ed. Erich Caspar, *MGH Epistolae selectae* 2 (Berlin, 1920-23) [hereafter *Reg.*], and *The Epistolae vagantes of Pope Gregory VII*, ed. Herbert Edward John Cowdrey (Oxford, 1972) [hereafter *Epp. vag.*].

2. Bonizo of Sutri, *Liber ad amicum* 5, ed. Ernest Dümmler, *MGH Libelli de lite imperatorum et pontificum* 1: 588-89, *Die Briefe des Petrus Damiani* no. 112, ed. Kurt Reindel, *MGH* Die Briefe der Deutschen Kaiserzeit 4, 3:280-81, Adam of Bremen, *Gesta Hammaburgensis ecclesiae pontificum* 3.30, ed. Werner Trillmich, in *Quellen des 9. und 11. Jahrhunderts zur Geschichte der Hamburgischen Kirche und des Reiches*, ed. Werner Trillmich and Rudolf Buchner, Ausgewählte Quellen zur Deutschen Geschichte des Mittelatlers 11 (Darmstadt, 1961), 364.

3. *Ep.* 55, *PL* 143:671-72.

4. In the early church, the term *mulieres subintroductae* had originally been used of women who lived with men in spiritual marriage. In this context, however, the reference was to a canon of the council of Nicaea (325) which forbade clerks to dwell with any *subintroducta mulier*, unless perhaps a mother, sister, or aunt, or other such person as was above suspicion: canon 3, *Conciliorum oecumenicorum decreta*, ed. Guiseppe Alberigo et al. (3rd edn., Bologna, 1973), 7.

5. The best text of the encyclicals is in Rudolf Schieffer, *Die Entstehung des päpstlichen Investiturverbots für den Deutschen König*, Schriften der *MGH* 28 (Stuttgart, 1981), 208-25; see caps 3-4, pp. 218-21.

6. At the synod of 1059, he made an impassioned plea for the adoption at Rome of a strict form of canonical life, although his concern was to exclude private property and he is not recorded as having mentioned the subject of chastity; Albert Werminghoff, "Die Beschlüsse des Aachener Concils im Jahre 816," *Neues Archiv der Gesellschaft für altere Deutsche Geschichtskunde* 27 (1902), 605-75, at 669-71.

7. Nicetas' *Libellus contra Latinos*, caps. 15-16, Humbert's *Responsio sive contradictio adversus Nicetae Pectorati libellum*, caps. 25-34, and the bull of excommunication are edited in Cornelius Will, *Acta et scripta quae de controversiis ecclesiae Graecae et Latinae saeculo undecimo composita extant* (Leipzig and Marburg, 1861), pp. 133-35, 147-50, 153-54. Leo IX drew upon Humbert's reply in a letter of his own to Nicetas, fragments of which survive as his *Ep.* 105 *bis*, *PL* 143:781-82.

8. See esp. *Die Briefe des Petrus Damiani* no. 61, 2:206-18, no. 65, 2:228-47, no. 112, 3:258-88, no. 114, 3:295-306, no. 141, 3:488-502, no. 162, 4:145-62.

9. Thus, in 1059, he told Pope Nicholas II that "Nuper habens cum nonnullis episcopis ex vestrae maiestatis auctoritate colloquium, sanctis eorum femoribus volui seras apponere, temptavi genitalibus sacerdotum, ut ita loquar, continentiae fibulas adhibere": *Ep.* 61, 2:207. Their lack of response led him to write the tract that followed.

10. e.g. *Die Briefe des Petrus Damiani* no. 59, 2:195-202.

11. Of the various sources for the Patarenes, see esp. Arnulf of Milan, *Liber gestorum recentium*, ed. Claudia Zey, *MGH Scriptores rerum Germanicarum in usum scholarum separatim editi* 67 (Hanover, 1994), Andrew of Sturmi, *Vita sancti Arialdi*, ed. Friedrich Baethgen, *MGH SS*, 30/2 (1929), 1049-75, and (for Peter Damiani's report to Hildebrand on his visit in 1059) *Die Briefe des Petrus Damiani* no. 65, 2:228-47. For a brief

account of the Patarenes, see H. E. J. Cowdrey, "The Papacy, the Patarenes and the Church of Milan," *Transactions of the Royal Historical Society*, 5th ser. 18 (1968), 25-48, repr. H. E. J. Cowdrey, *Popes, Monks and Crusaders* (London, 1984), no. V.

12. Arnulf, *Liber gestorum recentium*, 3.9, p. 177.

13. Arnulf, *Liber gestorum recentium*, 3.10, pp. 178-79.

14. Andrew of Sturmi, *Vita sancti Arialdi*, caps. 11-12, pp. 1057-58.

15. Hildebrand's support is disapprovingly traced by Arnulf, *Liber gestorum recentium*.

16. This table is based upon the list in Mirbt, *Die Publizistik*, 268, n. 4. In records of Gregory's Lateran synods, the matter is expressly referred to only in *Reg.* 6.5*b* (Nov. 1078). There are no references to it in letters of or after 1082. *Epp. vag.* no. 58 is omitted from this table because it is a fragment and undatable.

17. *Reg.* 1.27-28, 13 Oct. 1073, pp. 44-45; in each case, Gregory replied to messages that came to him.

18. *Reg.* 1.30, 15 Nov. 1073, pp. 50-51.

19. Marianus Scottus, *Chronicon a.* 1096 (1074), ed. Georg Waitz, *MGH SS* 5 (1844), 560. For the legislation at Nicaea, see above n. 3; it was incorporated by Carolingian reformers into the documents of their day, e. g., *Institutio canonicorum Aquisgranense* (816) cap. 39, *MGH Conc.* 2,1:360.

20. *Reg.* 2.66, p. 221, cf. 2.12, pp. 143-44 for the lack of response to the legates in the German church.

21. *Reg.* 2.30, p. 163.

22. *Reg.* 2.10, pp. 140-42, *Die Hannoversche Briefsammlung (1. Hildesheimer Briefe)* no. 17, *Briefsammlungen der Zeit Heinrichs IV.*, ed. Carl

Erdmann and Norbert Fickermann, *MGH* Die Briefe der Deutschen Kaiserzeit 5 (1950), 38-41.

23. *Reg.* 2.11, pp. 142-43.

24. *Reg.* 2.25, p. 157.

25. In Lombardy, the vicissitudes of the Patarenes should be borne in mind: as n. 11.

26. See esp. 3.7, pp. 256-58.

27. As n. 20.

28. See, e. g., Archbishop Liemar of Bremen's letter to Bishop Hezilo of Hildesheim, with its protest against Gregory, "Periculosus homo vult iubere, que vult, episcopis ut villicis suis": *Die Hanoversche Briefsammlung*, no. 15, pp. 33-35.

29. *Reg.* 2.25*a*, pp. 196-97.

30. *Reg.* 2.62, p. 217. For further comment upon it, see Giusepp Fornasari, "La riforma gregoriana nel 'regnum Italiae'," *Studi Gregoriani* 12 (1989): 314-16. The word *uxor* also occurs in *Reg.* 9.5, p. 580.

31. *Epp. vag.* nos. 6-7, pp. 14-17. The case for dating *Epp. vag.* nos. 6-11, pp. 14-27, to 1075 is presented by Cowdrey, *Epp. vag.* pp. 160-61. For the Lent synod of 1075, see also Berthold, *Annales a.* 1075, ed. Georg. H. Pertz, *MGH SS* 5 (1844), 277-78.

32. *Reg.* 2.66, pp. 221-22.

33. *Reg.* 2.25.

34. *Reg.* 2.29, pp. 161-62.

35. *Codex Udalrici* no. 42 *Monumenta Bambergensia*, Bibliotheca rerum Germanicarum, ed. Philipp Jaffé, 6 vols. (Berlin, 1864-73), 5:88-91. See also

62. The principal source for Altmann's work is *Vita Altmanni episcopi Pataviensis*, ed. Wilhlem Wattenbach, *MGH SS* 12 (1856), 226-43.

63. *Vita Altmanni*, caps. 11, 17, pp. 232-33, 234.

64. *Epp, vag.* no. 58, pp. 140-41.

65. *Vita Altmanni*, cap. 8. P. 231.

66. Paul of Bernried, *Vita Gregorii VII*, in Johann M. Watterich, *Pontificum Romanorum . . .vitae* 2 vols. (Leipzig, 1862), 1:476-546. See esp. caps. 26, 36-42, pp. 484, 489-96.

67. See above, p. 270.

68. Gregory's most important letter about the eastern churches is *Reg.* 8.1, pp. 510-14, where Gregory admittedly did not cover all aspects of the *Graecorum temeritas*.

69. *Reg.* 4.11, p. 310.

70. *Reg.* 1.27, 28, 2.68, pp. 45, 226, *Epp. vag.* nos. 6, p. 14, 9, p. 20; in the last letter, Gregory invoked St. Paul's prohibition of even eating with vicious men (1 Cor. 5.11).

71. *Reg.* 3.4, p. 249. Gregory seems to have regarded simony as the graver sin, e.g. the penalty for simony as Gregory prescribed it to Archbishop Sigehard of Aquileia was deposition, while that for disobedient fornicators was suspension from their office: *Reg.* 2.62, p. 217.

72. *Reg.* 2.55, p. 200.

73. *Responsio* caps. 25-26, 34, pp. 147-50. For Epiphanius, see his *Panarion* 25.1.1-6.6, esp. 1,4-5, in *Epiphanius von Constantia, Ancoratus, Panarion, De fide*, ed. Karl Holl, GCS 25, 31, 37, 3 vols. (Leipzig, 1915-33), 1:267-74, esp. 267-68.

74. *Die Briefe des Petrus Damiani* nos. 61, 65, 112, 129, 2: 216-18, 230-31, 235, 242-45, 3:286, 432-33.

75. *Die Briefe des Petrus Damiani* no. 65, pp. 230-31.

76. *Epp. vag.* no. 16, pp. 44-45.

77. See H. E. J. Cowdrey, "Simon Magus in South Italy," *Anglo-Norman Studies* 15 (1992-93): 77-90.

78. *Reg.* 2.25, 67, pp. 157-223-24. For the bridal imagery, see also 2.55, p. 200. In the citation, Gregory was following Pope Gregory the Great, *Moralia in Iob* 21.3, ed. Marc Adriaen, CC 143, 143A, 143B, 3 vols. (Turnhout, 1979-85), 2:1068.

79. *Epp vag.* no. 54, pp. 132-33.

80. For such an interpretation of Gregory's concept of obedience, see Karl J. Benz, "Kirche und Gehorsam bei Papst Gregor VII. Neue Überlegungen zu einem alten Thema," in *Papsttum und Kirchenreform. Historische Beiträge. Festschrift für Georg Schwaiger zum 65. Geburtstag*, ed. Manfred Weitlauff and Karl Hausberger (St. Ottilien, 1990), 97-150.

81. *Moralia in Iob*, 35.14, 3:1792-93.

82. The five letters are *Reg.* 2.45, p. 184, 2.66, p. 222, 4.11, pp. 310-11, *Epp. vag.* nos. 10, pp. 24-25, 32, pp. 86-87.

83. *Epp. vag.* no. 9, pp. 20-21. For the three orders, see Giles Constable, *Three Studies in Medieval Religious and Social Thought* (Cambridge, 1995), 305-13.

84. Gregory used the word *uxor* of clerical partners only twice: *Reg.* 2.62, p. 217, p. 5, p. 580. On the other hand, he used the more unfavorable language only when bishops were involved; Juhel of Dol "nuptiis publice celebraris scortum potius quam sponsam ducere non erubuit, ex qua et filios

procreavit": *Epp. vag.* no. 16, pp. 44-45; cf. his comments on Bishop Pibo of Toul: *Reg.* 2.10, pp. 140-41.

85. See Humbert, *Responsio* caps. 25-27, pp. 147-48.

86. The principal references to clerical chastity in the writings of these popes are: Leo I, *Epp.* 14.4, 167.3, *PL* 54:672-73, 1204; *S. Gregorii Magni, Registrum epsitularum* 1.52, ed. Dag Norberg, CC 140, 140A, 2 vols. (Turnhout, 1982), 1:54-55.

87. e.g. the violence that Archbishop John of Avranches is said to have experienced as a synod at Rouen had as its background earlier Norman synodal legislation against clerical marriage; whatever the date of the synod, which may have been 1072 or 1074, it is unlikely to have been a reaction against Gregory's decrees: Orderic Vitalis, *Ecclesiastical History* 4, 2:200-1 and n. 5.

88. The source for Walter's intervention is his twelfth-century *Lives,* which present considerable critical difficulties: *Vita Galteri longior* and the later *Vita Galteri brevior,* in Joseph Depoin, *Cartulaire de l'abbaye de Saint-Martin de Pontoise* (Pontoise, 1895-1901), 185-201, 174-184, at 193, 179. The evidence of these Lives indicates that the incident should be dated to the council of Paris in 1074 rather than that in 1092: Ienje van 't Spijker, *Als door een speciaal stempel. Traditie en vernieuwing in heiligenlevens uit Noordwest-Frankrijk (1050-1150)* (Hilversum, 1990), 42-44. (I am grateful to Dr. van 't Spijker for advice and information about Abbot Walter.)

89. *Lamperti monachi Hersfeldensis Annals aa.* 1074-75, ed. Oswald Holder-Egger, revised by Wolfgang D. Fritz, Ausgewählte Quellen zur Deutschen Geschichte des Mittelalters 13 (Berlin, n.d.), pp. 256-61, 302-3. Lampert may have confused events of these two years.

90. Siegfried's problems with his clergy are further illustrated by his letters to Gregory: *Codex Udalrici* nos. 42, 45, 5:88-91, 97-100, and by his letter to the leading clergy of his province: *Mainzer Urkundenbuch,* 1: *bis 1137,* ed. Manfred Stimming (Darmstadt, 1932), no. 343, p. 239.

91. *Reg.* 3.4, pp. 248-50.

92. *De damnatio scismaticorum* 2.2, ed. Friedrich Thaner, *MGH Libelli de lite* 2:45; for the canon of Nicaea, see above, n. 4.

93. *Epp. vag.* nos. 9-11, pp. 18-27.

94. *Vita Altmanni* caps. 11, 17, 12:232-34.

95. For fuller discussion, see Mirbt, *Die Publizistik*, 12-16, 36-44. 270-342; Ian S. Robinson, *Authority and Resistance in the Investiture Contest: the Polemical Literature of the Late Eleventh Century* (Manchester and New York, 1978), 165-68.

96. *Pseudo-Udalrici Epistola de continentia clericorum*, ed. Lothar von Heinemann, *MGH Libelli de lite* 1: 244-60.

97. Pseudo-Ulrich owed his knowledge of this matter to Cassiodorus, *Historia ecclesiastica tripartita* 2.14, ed. Walther Jacob and Rudolf Hanslik, CSEL 71 (Vienna, 1952), 107-8. The Greek sources that lie behind Cassiodorus are Socrates, *Historia ecclesiastica* 1.11, *PG* 67:101-4, and Sozomen, *Historia ecclesiastica* 1.23.1, ed. Joseph Bidez and Günther C. Hansen, GCS 50 (Berlin, 1960), 44-45.

98. Bernold, *Chronicon a.* 1079, p. 436. Bernold was present at the synod.

99. *Cameracensium et Noviomensium clericorum epistolae*, ed. Heinrich Böhmer, *MGH Libelli de lite* 3:573-78. The diocese of Cambrai at this time was subject ecclesiastically to the metropolitan see of Rheims, but it was divided politically between Germany and France.

100. See esp. *Libelli Bernoldi presbyteri monachi* ed. Frederick Thaner, *MGH Libelli de lite* 2:1-168.

101. *Libelli* 1, pp. 7-26.

102. *Libelli* 3, pp. 59-88.

103. *Epp. vag.* no. 8, pp. 16-19.

104. For a survey of the Gregorian networks and friendships, see I. S. Robinson, "The Friendship Network of Gregory VII," *History* 62 (1978): 1-22, and I. S. Robinson, "The Dissemination of the Letters of Pope Gregory VII During the Investiture Contest," *Journal of Ecclesiastical History* 34 (1983): 175-93.

105. See H. E. J. Cowdrey, "The Carthusians and their Contemporary World: the Evidence of Twelfth-Century Bishops' *Vitae*," in *Die Kartäuser und ihre Welt Kontakte und gegenseitige Einflüsse*, ed. James Hogg, Analecta Carthusiana 62, 2 vols. (Salzburg, 1993), 1: 26-43.

106. Canon 7, *Conciliorum oecumenicorum decreta*, p. 198.

# IV

## Simon Magus in South Italy

Amongst the mosaics of the Cappella Palatina at Palermo, there are, in the southern and northern aisles, series which depict scenes from the lives of St Peter and St Paul, who are first shown separately and then as a pair. The mosaics are hard to date, but they probably belong to the third quarter of the twelfth century. Apart from the priority in time that they imply for Paul's missionary activities, the sequences of the apostles taken separately follow events recorded in the Acts of the Apostles. But when they are taken together, history dissolves into fiction. The fiction is located at Rome, and has three episodes. First, and so far historically according to Acts 28: 14–15, Paul journeyed there, having been accompanied from the Forum of Appius and Three Taverns by a party which came down from Rome to meet him; when Paul saw it, he thanked God and took courage. Unhistorically, Peter is shown as leader of the party from Rome; upon meeting, the apostles embraced, watched by one of Peter's companions. A second episode, wholly fictitious, introduces Simon Magus, the father of all simoniacs who appeared in Acts at Samaria as a sometime practitioner of magic whose marvels had won him a following there; although he was baptised, Peter roundly rebuked him when he offered silver in return for the power of being himself able to confer the Holy Spirit (Acts 8: 9–24). The mosaic shows Peter and Paul in dispute with Simon Magus before the Emperor Nero. *Nero rex* sits crowned and enthroned with Simon Magus at his right hand, while Peter and Paul earnestly engage him. In the third mosaic, nemesis strikes: the caption runs that 'Here, by Peter's command and by Paul's prayer, Simon Magus falls to the ground.' Simon had caused Nero to erect a scaffold upon high ground so that he could demonstrate a miraculous power of flight. Icarus-like, he fell from the sky; he is shown plummeting down, escorted by two winged demons. The apostles have triumphed. There is no reference to their subsequent martyrdom by Nero's command, but Peter's victory is reinforced by a painting on the roof-timbers over the third mosaic, where he stands with three deacons and, in his hand, the keys of heaven.[1] The threefold sequence recurs in mosaics of Monreale cathedral which probaby date from the late 1180s.[2]

These and related fictitious scenes relating to Peter's dealings with Simon Magus have a familiar place in art history; they are exemplified over a wide area of place and time. In the east, the death of Simon Magus had a recognized place

[1] O. Demus, *The Mosaics of Norman Sicily*, London 1950, 46 and nn., 299, Plates 43AB (Demus indicates the extent and nature of restoration); E. Borsook, *Messages in Mosaic: the Royal Programmes of Norman Sicily (1130–1187)*, Oxford 1990, 29–31, 39–41, Fig. 4, Plates 16, 54–6.
[2] They are in the side-chapel at the south-east corner of the cathedral: Demus (as n.1), 119, 123–48, Plate 83; Borsook (as n.1), 53, 60–1, Plates 57, 76.

in the Painter's Manual which was the repository of age-long Byzantine artistic traditions.[3] In the west, the earliest known examples were the mosaics of the disputation before Nero and of Simon's fall and death in the Lady Chapel built at St Peter's in Rome under Pope John VII (705–7), and which are known from early seventeenth-century copies.[4] They were probably the inspiration of paintings including the same subjects in the north apse of the abbey of St John at Müstair, in Switzerland; originally dating from Carolingian times, they were partly repainted in the third quarter of the twelfth century according to ideas then current.[5] In the last decade of the tenth century, similar themes occur in the illuminations of a book, the Antiphonary of Prüm, north of Trier.[6] Early in the next century, the embroideries of the pluviale known as the mantle of St Kunigunde, wife of the German emperor Henry II, which is now at Bamberg, included four panels concerning Simon Magus.[7] The same theme occurs in the mosaics of St Mark's at Venice, which survive only in early seventeenth-century replacements which probably preserve the subjects, though not necessarily the inscriptions, of their twelfth-century predecessors.[8] It is within this broad context of artistic interest in the legends of Simon Magus that the mosaics of the Cappella Palatina and Monreale must be set.

This distribution of artistic representations of the legends of Simon Magus is the tip of an iceberg whose bulk is to be found in a proliferation from the earliest Christian times of literary versions which became no less widespread in the early and central middle ages. Upon this material, a large and important book urgently needs to be written; only a few, tentative comments can be offered now. By and large, two distinct, and to a surprising degree separate, lines of tradition developed about the Simon Magus of the Acts of the Apostles who, it should be remembered, was not there said to have done further evil, whether himself or through his followers; on the contrary, he answered Peter's rebuke by beseeching the apostle to pray for him to the Lord, that nothing of what Peter had said might come upon him. The line of subsequent tradition that is most familiar to historians was relatively late in developing. It was first presented in a sophisticated form by Pope Gregory the Great (590–604).[9] It built upon Simon as the mercenary figure who, when he saw Peter conferring the Holy Spirit, offered silver that he might

---

[3]  P. Hetherington, *The 'Painter's Manual' of Dionysius of Fourna: an English Translation, with Commentary, of cod. gr. 708 in the Saltykov-Schedrin State Public Library, Leningrad*, London 1974, 66. Although Dionysius wrote in 1730/4, the purpose of the Manual was to co-ordinate and regulate Byzantine artistic traditions.

[4]  J. Wilpert, *Die römischen Mosaiken und Malereien der kirchlichen Bauten von 4–13 Jahrhundert*, 4 vols, 2nd edn, Freiburg-im-Breisgau 1917, i.399–400, Fig. 136. Sketches by G. Grimaldi survive in Rome, Vatican Library, MSS Barb. lat. 2732, fo. 75v, and 2733, fo. 89.

[5]  L. Birchler, 'Zur karolingischen Architektur und Malerei in Münster-Müstair', in *Frühmittelalterliche Kunst in den Alpenländern*, Olten/Lausanne 1954, 167–252 at 221–4, Fig. 96; B. Brenk, *Die romanische Wandmalerei in der Schweiz*, Berne 1963, 28–61, esp. 44–7, Fig. 3ab, Plates 20–1, 23.

[6]  Paris, BN, MS lat. 9448, fo. 55v. See P. Lauer, *Les Enluminures romanes des manuscrits de la Bibliothèque nationale*, Paris 1927, 116–21; A. Goldschmidt, *German Illumination*, 2 vols, Munich/Florence 1928, Plate 68.

[7]  W. Messerer, *Der Bamberger Domschatz in seinem Bestande bis zum Ende der Hohenstaufen-Zeit*, Munich 1952, 15–16, 27, 57–61, Plates 49, 51. The pluviale is of Bavarian origin.

[8]  O. Demus, *The Mosaics of San Marco in Venice*, 2 vols in 4 parts, Chicago/London 1984, i.219–27.

[9]  *Homiliae XL in Evangelio*, 1.4.4, 17.3, *PL* lxxvi. 1091–2, 1145–6; *Epp.* 9.216, 219, 12.9,

receive a like gift. According to the Acts of the Apostles, Peter rebuked him: 'Your silver perish with you, because you thought you could obtain the gift of God with money!' Simon became the prototype of all who, by proffering service, money, or promises sought to traffic in sacred orders and offices. A second line of tradition largely left aside this aspect of the Simon Magus story. In it, Simon was built up as the figure who, at Samaria, said that he was himself someone great, and who while still unbaptised had induced a following to take him at his word, saying that 'This man is the power of God who is called Great.' It was by magic arts that Simon had so amazed the crowds. According to the legends, there ensued a contest, to the death on both sides, between Simon the counterfeit power of God and Peter who exercised God's true power. It was a contest partly of words and partly of wonders: Simon with his magic was opposed by Peter with the Holy Spirit of God. Its climax was the encounter before Nero as depicted in the Cappella Palatina mosaics. Its outcome, which they do not depict, was the apostles' martyrdom by Nero's command – Peter by crucifixion head-downwards, and Paul by beheading.

This luxuriant growth of legends involving Simon Magus, not as trafficker in orders and offices but as, literally, magician, is already exemplified in such Christian fathers as the Apologist Justin Martyr (c.100–c.165) and Hippolytus of Rome (c.170–c.236).[10] Simon Magus was deemed to be a founder of Gnostic heresy and the first and father of all heretics. Of the literature about him that proliferated in the post-Constantinian church, it must suffice to cite two examples which, in Latin translation, circulated widely into the central middle ages. The 'Clementine Recognitions' were so called after St Clement, the bishop of Rome whom, according to some traditions, Peter himself ordained to be his successor there. The Recognitions took their present form in the late fourth century, and survive in a Latin version by Rufinus of Aquileia (345–410). It survives in many manuscripts from Germany, Italy, France, and England, and gave wide currency to a prolonged rivalry between Peter and Simon Magus with the eastern cities of Caesarea, Tripolis, and Antioch as its locations.[11] The rivalry in its climax at Rome was the subject of a large literature on the martyrdoms there of Peter and Paul which made a major contribution to the medieval cult of the princes of the apostles and to the image of Christian Rome. It is well exemplified by the *Passio sanctorum Petri et Pauli auctore Marcello* (usually referred to as Pseudo-

*S. Gregorii Magni Registrum epistularum*, ed. D. Norberg, 2 vols, Corpus Christianorum, Series Latina CXL, CXLA, Turnhout 1982, ii. 776–9, 782–5, 980–2.

[10] Saint Justin, *Apologies*, ed. A. Wartelle, Paris 1987, 1.26, 56, pp. 131–2, 177; Hippolytus, *Refutatio omnium haeresium*, 6.20, ed. M. Marcovitch, Patristiche Texte und Studien 25, Berlin/New York 1986, 228–9.

[11] For the text of the Clementine Recognitions, see *Die Pseudoklementinen*, ii: *Rekognitionen in Rufins Übersetzung*, ed. B. Rehm, Die Griechischen christlichen Schriftsteller der ersten Jahrhunderte 51, Berlin 1965, 118–77; the MSS are listed at xvii–cvii; for a discussion, Rehm, 'Clemens Romanus II. (Ps. Clementinen)', *Reallexikon für Antike und Christentum* iii (1957), 197–206. Despite its age, there is invaluable material in G. Salmon, 'Clementine Literature', *A Dictionary of Christian Biography, Literature, Sects and Doctrines*, edd. W. Smith and H. Wace, 4 vols, London 1877–87, i.567–78 (summary of the Recognitions at 568–70). Salmon's articles 'Linus', 'Marcellus (11)', and 'Simon Magus', in the same *Dictionary* iii. 726–9, 813, iv. 681–8, also repay reading. Also useful are É. Amann, 'Simon le Magicien', and A. Bride, 'Simonie', *Dictionnaire de Théologie Catholique* xiv (1941), 2130–40, 2141–60; V.I.J. Flint, *The Rise of Magic in Early Medieval Europe*, Oxford 1991, esp. 19, 46, 81, 338–44.

who was also the author of a history of the Norman conquest of South Italy. The full title of the poem in the sole surviving manuscript, now Bologna, Biblioteca Universitaria, MS 2843, is *Liber Amati monachi Casinensis destinatus ad domnum Gregorium papam in honore beati Petri apostoli*.[23] Its four books bring together as does no other medieval source, literary or otherwise, all facets of the apostle's biblical and legendary biography. Books I and II are about the biblical Peter, and respectively follow closely, with only occasional accretions, the accounts of him in the Gospels and in the Acts of the Apostles. Books III and IV show a wide acquaintance with the legendary sources for his subsequent life and martyrdom. Book III tells the story from his time at Caesarea to his time at Antioch; it depends largely, but by no means only, upon Gauderic's *Vita sancti Clementis*. Book IV is entitled *De passione apostolorum Petri et Pauli*, and has Pseudo-Marcellus as the principal of its various sources.[24]

As a result of its layout and sources, Amatus's poem was unusual in that it brought out both lines of tradition about Simon Magus – the would-be trafficker in sacred things, and the magician and life-long opponent of the greater wonder-worker, St Peter. On the biblical evidence of Acts 8, Amatus devoted a powerful section to Peter's rebuking of Simon when he asked to purchase the Holy Spirit and to Peter's consequent expulsion of the 'plague of Simon' (*Symonis haec pestis*).[25] The poem placarded Simon as the exemplar of those who, in the eleventh century, traded in ecclesiastical offices and orders. The legendary evidence for Simon was then fully deployed to exhibit him as the lethal rival of Peter during the rest of his life, who eventually suffered the débâcle of his own magical powers at Rome, but who also brought about the martyrdom of Peter and Paul at the hands of a wicked Nero.

As constituting the poem a tract for the times, its dedication to Pope Gregory VII is important. Unfortunately, almost the whole of Amatus's dedicatory epistle to him is lost through damage to the manuscript. However, his regard for Gregory, whose abhorrence of simony as a current ecclesiastical offence he shared, led Amatus to conclude his account of Peter's rebuking of Simon at Samaria with a eulogy of Gregory's zeal against simony.[26] Elsewhere, Amatus referred with enthusiasm to Gregory's authority as pope, with undertones of his distance from everything simoniacal. In comment upon Christ's commission to Peter at Caesarea Philippi (Matt. 16: 13–19), he reflected that Peter's power had now passed freely (*gratis*) to Gregory who was thus the pattern of rightly-acquired authority.[27] In comment upon Christ's promise to Peter that his faith would not fail and that, when he had turned again, he would strengthen his brethren (Luke 22: 31–2), Amatus referred to Peter's *pura fides* and to his freedom from stains of evil (*pravorum . . . macula*). Christ's gifts to Peter had devolved upon Gregory, at whose feet kings prostrated themselves, whose laws they obeyed, and by whom they governed their kingdoms.[28] A reference here to the penance at Canossa in January 1077 of King Henry IV of Germany before Gregory is possible but not

---

[23] Lentini (as n.22), i.60. For Amatus, see Cowdrey (as n.19), xx, 25–6, 75–9, 83–5, 88.
[24] Amatus's sources are analysed by Lentini (as n.22), ii.45–98.
[25] 2.7, ed. Lentini, i.83–4.
[26] 2.7, lines 8–14, ed. Lentini, i.84.
[27] 1.6, lines 20–2, ed. Lentini, i.65.
[28] 1.18, ed. Lentini, i.72–3.

certain. Of greater moment is Amatus's identification of Gregory as currently the representative of Peter who embodied the purity and freedom of his authority. The question arises whether, since Gregory was thus identified with Peter, in the remainder of the poem the king who opposed him, Henry IV of Germany, was to be identified with the Emperor Nero who wickedly opposed the martyred Peter. Amatus did not make the identification, and the political sensitivity of Monte-cassino's position would have made it rash for him to do so.[29] Yet the tendency of Amatus's poem was towards such an identification, which others were soon to make.[30] Amatus's depiction of Peter's triumph in his contest with Simon Magus at least pointed in this direction and suggested a line of telling propaganda as the struggle between Gregory and Henry intensified.

In his poem, Amatus makes clear his active interest while a monk of Monte-cassino in the whole gamut of history and legend about Simon Magus. He combined it with ardent zeal against simony as an ecclesiastical abuse, and for Gregory VII in his determination to eradicate it. The next part of this paper will be concerned with the questions of where Amatus stands in the long history of the dissemination of the legends of Simon Magus, and of whether he provides evidence that these legends were especially disseminated in and from South Italy.

Amatus was certainly a pioneer in his extensive use of the legends for polemi-cal purposes in connection with ecclesiastical reform. Widespread though the legends had for centuries been in art, in hymnody, and in manuscript diffusion, until the mid-1070s they were largely ignored in polemical literature and in the writings of reformers. Despite the propaganda opportunities presented by the story of Simon Magus's débâcle and death at Rome, there is, surprisingly, no trace of the legends in Cardinal Humbert's *Adversus simoniacos* (1057/8).[31] Peter Damiani referred to them only once – in a rhyming colophon at the conclusion of his *Liber gratissimus*, addressed in 1062 to Bishop Cadalus of Parma (the anti-pope Honorius II); Peter warned Cadalus that he was like Simon Magus in aspiring to the stars and that the jaws of hell would likewise swallow him.[32] The almost entire disregard of the legends by the early Roman reforming cardinals is the more remarkable since they cannot have been unaware of the mosaics of John VII at St Peter's.

From the mid-1070s and into the twelfth century, references to the Simon Magus legends of the kind that occur in Amatus's fourth book appeared sporadi-cally but quite widely in polemical literature against simony. German writers of Gregorian stamp occasionally drew upon them. An early example is the Reiche-nau chronicler Berthold, who wrote the second recension of his chronicle during the late 1070s. When Bishop Henry of Speyer, whom Gregory had deposed and excommunicated for simony at his Lent council of 1075, on the very day of his sentence died by choking as he rose from an overladen meal-table, Berthold saw a wielding of St Peter's sword by which he had cast down the heresiarch Simon as

---

[29] This sensitivity is illustrated by the Chronicle of Montecassino, e.g. *Chronica monasterii Casinensis*, 3.18, 50, ed. H. Hoffmann, *MGH Scriptores*, xxxiv.385, 430–3.
[30] See below, p. 84.
[31] *Humberti cardinalis Libri III. adversus simoniacos*, ed. F. Thaner, *MGH Libelli de lite*, i. 95–253.
[32] *Die Briefe des Petrus Damiani*, no. 89, ed. K. Reindel, *MGH Die Briefe der deutschen Kaiser-zeit* 4, ii. 531–72, at 572.

he made his would-be ascent to heaven. Falling to earth he was rent asunder into four pieces and dispatched to hell for eternal damnation. Let all simoniacs beware of a like fate![33] In 1081, another supporter of Gregory VII, Archbishop Gebhard of Salzburg, rounded on episcopal supporters of King Henry of Germany who in 1080 at the synod of Brixen had proclaimed Gregory's deposition and called for his supersession by Archbishop Guibert of Ravenna. Gebhard pressed them as to whether it was compatible with their office to assist a Christian king in his purpose 'after the example of Nero to make Peter and Paul once more suffer in their members, and again set Simon Magus against Simon Peter.'[34] Henry was thus the new Nero and Guibert the new Simon.

The legends of Simon Magus also found currency in popular songs and rhymes. In the domains of Countess Matilda of Tuscany, a lively poem *Adversus simoniacos* praised Gregory VII who was embattled with a wrathful Caesar. After referring to Simon Magus's building a tower against Peter and to his being struck by Peter's irresistable blow, the poem described the division of society into two camps,

> Quorum rex est alter Christus, alter est Leviathan;
> Ille vitae, iste mortis regnat super agmina;
> Ergo quorum quis sit victor, nemo sanus ambigit.[35]

In a poem by Alfanus, the friend of Abbot Desiderius of Montecassino who was archbishop of Salerno from 1058 to 1085, Nero was said to have avenged the death of his 'friend' Simon Magus by having St Peter crucified.[36] In 1095, a monk of Saint-Laurent at Liège composed a series of poems about the afflictions of his abbot and monastery at the hands of the Henrician bishop, Otbert. He had strong words to say about the plight of Rome in view of the Wibertine schism, which he depicted as directly the work of Nero and Simon Magus:

> Vel quis afflictę poterit mederi
> Cum Nero Romam teneat Symonque
> Papa vocetur?

With an eye to the struggle at Liège, the poet invoked Simon Magus's proud flight towards heaven and urged St Peter to renew his victory over him.[37] Another poem about simony, evidently written by an author in England, attacked the simony of Herbert of Losinga, abbot of Ramsey (1087–91) and bishop of Thetford (1091–1119). This simony is mocked and challenged in terms derived from the legends

---

[33] *Bertholdi Annales, a*.1075, *MGH Scriptores*, v. 278.
[34] *Gebehardi Salisburgensis archiepiscopi Epistola ad Herimannum Mettensem episcopum data*, cap. 32, ed. K. Francke, *MGH Libelli de lite*, i. 278.
[35] M. Lokrantz, *L'opera poetica di S. Pier Damiani*, Stockholm/Göteborg/Uppsala 1964, 153–5, no. D 7. It is preserved in a Polirone MS; for its date and background, see Lokrantz, 21–2, 206–8.
[36] A. Lentini and F. Avagliano, *I carmi di Alfano I, arcivescovo di Salerno*, Miscellanea Cassinese 38, Montecassino 1974, 183–4, no. 37.
[37] *Monachi cuiusdam exulis S. Laurentii De calamitatibus ecclesiae Leodiensis opusculum*, ed. H. Boehmer, *MGH Libelli de lite*, iii. 622–41, esp. 625, 627, 639, 640. For the circumstances, see G. Meyer von Knonau, *Jahrbücher des deutschen Reiches unter Heinrich IV. und Heinrich V.*, 7 vols, Leipzig 1898–1909, iv. 463–8.

of Simon Magus's flight and downfall.[38] It was, however, only with the volu-
minous writings of the Augustinian canon Gerhoh of Reichersberg (1093–1169)
that the castigation of simoniacs in such imagery occurs north of the Alps with
such great intensity.[39]

There is evidently no overall pattern to the use of material from the legends of
Simon Magus in the reformers' struggle against simony. Much, at least, of the
evidence is best interpreted as the local and independent use of material already
to hand in artistic and manuscript forms to promote a widely-shared objective
which became more sharply focused with the Wibertine schism. There is nothing
to suggest that even so remarkable an anti-Simoniac composition as Amatus's
poem circulated at all widely, or that it directly influenced any other writer. (For
comparison, it should, however, be remembered that even Cardinal Humbert's
*Adversus simoniacos* appears to have had only a small circulation and cannot be
shown to have had much influence.[40]) It is not even certain that Amatus's poem
reached Gregory VII: it is not likely that he saw the surviving manuscript which
is in Beneventan script; there are also numerous points of textual correction and
revision which would be hard to explain if this manuscript had reached Gregory.[41]
He may have seen another, earlier manuscript, perhaps not in Beneventan script,
but there is no unambiguous indication that he did so.

There is, nevertheless, some evidence, in addition to the Cassinese sources that
have already been noticed,[42] that interest in the Simon Magus legends was particularly a feature of South Italy. This is strongly suggested by Gregory VII
himself. For all his zeal against simony, he only twice·referred to these legends in
his letters – once obliquely and once expressly. Whether or not he knew the
legends from Amatus, and the circumstances suggest that he did, both letters were
written in the midsummer of 1080, and in a South Italian environment. His
oblique reference was in a letter of 27 June, which he addressed to Abbot Hugh of
Cluny from Ceprano, a town in the marches between the lands of St Peter and the
principality of Capua; on 29 June, Robert Guiscard, duke of Apulia, took there an
oath of fealty to Pope Gregory VII. Abbot Desiderius of Montecassino had taken
a leading part in negotiations that led to the *rapprochement* between the pope and
the duke. In his letter to Abbot Hugh, Gregory exploded with wrath about a
report, freshly received, that a Cluniac monk named Robert, who was in the
Spanish kingdom of León-Castile, had been complicit in resisting the supersession of the Hispanic rite by the Latin:

> This Robert, having become an imitator of Simon Magus, has not feared
> with all the crafty malignity that he could muster to rise up against the
> authority of St Peter (*Symonis magi imitator factus, quanta potuit maligni-*
> *tatis astutia, adversus beati P. auctoritatem non timuit insurgere*), and by

38 *De simoniaca haeresi carmen*, ed. H. Boehmer, *MGH Libelli de lite*, iii. 615–17; cf. William of
Malmesbury, *De gestis regum*, ii. 385–6.
39 e.g. *Opusculum de edificio Dei* (1128/9), cap. 66, *Liber de novitatibus huius temporis* (1156),
caps 2, 4, *De investigatione Antichristi* (1160/2), 1.63, edd. E. Sackur, *MGH Libelli de lite*, iii.173,
290, 293, 378–9.
40 R. Schieffer, *Die Entstehung des päpstlichen Investiturverbots für den deutschen König*, Schriften der MGH 28, Stuttgart 1981, 36–47.
41 Lentini (as n.22), i. 29–39.
42 See above, pp. 81–3.

his prompting to lead back into their former error a hundred thousand men who had begun through our own diligent labour to return to the way of truth.

Gregory's reference to Simon Magus's 'crafty malignity' and his contrast between error and truth appear to allude to Simon's confrontation with Peter at Rome rather than to his mercenary request at Samaria. There is no doubt about Gregory's reference to the Roman legends when, on 21 July, he dispatched an encyclical letter from Ceccano, a little to the west of Ceprano, about Henry IV of Germany's putting forward of Archbishop Guibert of Ravenna to be anti-pope. He addressed it to the bishops 'of the Principates, Apulia, and Calabria', that is, of all Italy to the south of the lands of St Peter and the duchy of Spoleto. Once again, he wrote to express a furious reaction: this time, on the day after he heard about Henry's synod of Brixen. The reference in his condemnation of the Wibertines to the legend of the contest at Rome between Peter and Simon Magus is loud and clear:

As for these men who have no reasons to justify them, but are utterly reprobate through a conscience burdened with every kind of crime, we with the greater confidence reckon them to be of no account because they believe that they have risen to great heights. By the mercy of God, and by the prayers of St Peter which wonderfully cast down Simon Magus, their master, when he set out for such heights, we hope that their ruin will not be for long delayed.

Whatever may have been the source from which Gregory knew this legend, he thought that a reference to it was appropriate in a letter for general circulation in South Italy.[43]

Certainly there appears to have been fertile soil in South Italy for such legends to grow, for there is evidence to suggest an interplay of ideas between Rome and Montecassino and a utilization of the legends in the abbey's historical tradition. From 1059, Abbot Desiderius of Montecassino was also an 'external cardinal' of the Roman church in his capacity as cardinal-priest of Santa Cecilia.[44] A contemporary as cardinal-priest was Deusdedit of San Pietro in Vincoli, who demonstrated his attachment to Desiderius in 1087 when he dedicated his *Liber canonum* to him as Pope Victor III.[45] In his *Libellus contra invasores et symoniacos*, the longer and definitive version of which dated from c.1097, Deusdedit at some length presented the genesis of the Wibertine schism in terms of Archbishop Guibert of Ravenna as the new Simon Magus. As such, he was the evil genius of his Nero, King Henry IV of Germany. He had dragged Henry more deeply than ever into the simoniac heresy, in the usual sense of selling ecclesiastical offices. Seduced by the new Simon Magus, he considered himself to be exempt from

---

[43] For the letters, see *Gregorii VII Registrum*, 8.2,5, ed. E. Caspar, *MGH Epistolae selectae*, 2, Berlin 1920–3, 517–18, 521–3. For events in Italy, see Cowdrey (as n.19), 138–43; for those in Spain, H.E.J. Cowdrey, *The Cluniacs and the Gregorian Reform*, Oxford 1970, 230–9.

[44] K. Ganzer, *Die Entwicklung des auswärtigen Kardinalats im hohen Mittelalter*, Tübingen 1963, 17–23.

[45] V. Wulf von Glanvell, *Die Kanonessammlung des Kardinals Deusdedit*, Paderborn 1905, 1–5. For Deusdedit, see R. Hüls, *Kardinäle, Klerus und Kirchen Roms, 1049–1130*, Tübingen 1977, 194.

papal justice as though he were not of St Peter's flock. In 1084, the new Simon Magus enthroned Henry at Rome and crowned him emperor 'more by bribery than by force'. When Henry intruded schismatic bishops and abbots into offices from which catholics had been driven, he did so 'by the commerce of his master Simon', and still acted as Simon's Nero.

Deusdedit went on to make play of a setback for the anti-pope Clement III (Guibert of Ravenna) in 1097/8. Clement had recently established his forces at Argenta, a place strategically situated on the River Po to the north-west of Ravenna, and provided for its defence by building a high tower. The loss of this fortification prompted Deusdedit to draw an analogy with the fall of Simon Magus from his tower at Rome:

> Guibert . . as if for his own defence built a high tower at a township called Argenta and awaited simoniac angels, but flying with them he fell into the foulest of Stygian marshes. His legs were broken – that is, by God's favour to us, his goods are now as good as destroyed and reduced to nothing. No one showed him the reverence and obedience due to a pope except his Nero and his criminal accomplices, and those who sold themselves to him by permanent or temporary oaths on account of their avarice, which is the service of idols.[46]

This polemic of Deusdedit was quickly borrowed by the compiler of the middle section of the Chronicle of Montecassino. This great Chronicle is of composite authorship. It was begun by a master chronicler, Leo Marsicanus, to whom reference has already been made in connection with the Cassinese tradition of the Clementine Recognitions;[47] but his contribution effectively ends with the year 1075. From 1127, the Chronicle was the responsibility of another archivist and librarian of the abbey, the notorious forger Peter the Deacon. For the long intervening period, 1075 to 1127, the material in the Chronicle as it now stands raises formidable problems of sources and authorship. They are particularly acute in the critical years of the 1080s, for which a number of disparate traditions seem to have been drawn upon in an uncritical manner.[48] However, in one constituent part of the account of Abbot Desiderius's months as Pope Victor III, despite manifest chronological absurdity Deusdedit's polemical chapters about the anti-pope Clement as Simon Magus were lightly and crudely adapted to present Victor's pontificate as a triumphant struggle between him and his rival. Clement was a new Simon Magus who during the struggle shared, at least morally, the heresiarch's fate.[49]

A comparable view found expression in the allocution which the Chronicle placed upon Victor's lips at his synod of Benevento in late August 1087. Like all such speeches, it is likely to be a free composition made at a later date; it nevertheless represents a Cassinese viewpoint. In rehearsing the crimes of *Guibertus eresiarcha* against his predecessor Gregory VII, Victor was depicted as

[46] 2.11–12, ed. E. Sackur, *MGH Libelli de lite*, ii. 328–30. For the building and loss of Argenta, see Meyer von Knonau (as n.37), v.13–14.
[47] See above, p. 81.
[48] For the Chronicle, see Cowdrey (as n.19), xvii–xix, 101–2, 194–206, 239–44, 251–62.
[49] *Chron. Cas.* 3.70, *MGH Scriptores*, xxxiv.452–3. For a comparison of the texts, see Cowdrey (as n.19), 257–60.

saying that Guibert incited conspiracies and plots against him; perjured and simoniacal, so far as in him lay he deprived Gregory of his priestly office, stirring up against him the Roman empire, peoples, and kingdoms. Moved by the perfidy of Simon Magus whose officer (*officina*) he had become, he had used the emperor's army to invade the apostolic see and to make himself the head in the Roman church of all evil, wickedness, and perdition. Victor concluded by citing St Paul's saying that there could be no accord between Christ and Belial and nothing in common between believer and unbeliever (2 Cor. 6:15): 'every heretic is an unbeliever', he said; 'because a simoniac is a heretic, he is therefore an unbeliever.'[50] Here, again, the tone is taken from Simon Magus's legendary doings at Rome. The Montecassino Chronicle's presentation of Victor III and his vindication of the Gregorian papacy points to a continuing strand of thought at the abbey, already apparent in the poem of Amatus, that the full weight of the legends of Simon Magus should be brought to bear in support of Gregory VII and his cause. The Wibertine schism and the struggle against the anti-pope Clement III served to intensify this conviction. The interest of the South Italian abbey of Montecassino in the legends of Simon Magus was strong, and perhaps uniquely strong.

This study of the history and use of the legends of Simon Magus points to conclusions both particular and general. In particular, the legends were in process of formation from the earliest days of Christianity. Long before the eleventh century, they were highly developed and widely disseminated; they were known both through many manuscripts and in the visual arts. Their use in eleventh- and twelfth-century polemics was, nevertheless, sporadic and occasional; it appears in widely dispersed localities. Yet the evidence from and centring upon Montecassino suggests that South Italy was of especial importance in harnessing the legends to the cause of the Gregorian papacy, and that there was significant interplay with Roman circles in propagating them. Gregory himself seems to have thought them appropriate for citation in writing encyclically to the bishops of South Italy. The mosaics of the Cappella Palatina and at Monreale may, therefore, serve as late reminders of an interest in the fate of Simon Magus which was characteristically South Italian.

A general conclusion to which the use of the legends of Simon Magus points is that, energetic and universally promoted amongst eleventh- and twelfth-century reformers though the campaign against simony was, it cannot be regarded as having been well orchestrated from above, certainly not by the Gregorian papacy. Much depended upon individuals and upon localities; there was little pattern or co-ordination; themes so apparently promising as the fall and death of Simon Magus were developed surprisingly seldom. It was much the same with the reforming campaign against clerical marriage and fornication which was concurrently waged. This campaign affords an instructive comparison. The zeal in promoting it of the papacy as of other reforming circles is, of course, beyond question. Yet, as in the case of simony, the forms taken by propaganda were various and unco-ordinated. This is illustrated by the term 'nicolaitism' which was sometimes applied to clerical marriage and concubinage. Like simony, it was derived from the Bible and developed by legend. In the book of Revelation (2:6,

[50] *Chron. Cas.* 3.72, 453–5.

14–15), there are references to 'Nicolaitans' as a sect that the Lord, like all right-thinking Christians, abominated; its offences included fornication. St Irenaeus of Lyons (c.130–c.200) believed that the Nicolaitans, 'qui indiscrete vivunt', originated with Nicolaus, last-named of the seven initial deacons of the Christian church (Acts 6:1–6).[51] He had been a proselyte of Antioch, and the very little that is on record about him indicates that he was an entirely blameless and sincere young man. But the association of his name with that of the Nicolaitans was sufficient to condemn him. A sixth-century writer placed Nicholas second only to Simon Magus in his list of heresiarchs,[52] while in the twelfth century Gerhoh of Reichersberg, having branded Simon Magus as 'the leading trafficker', dubbed Nicholas 'the first fornicator among the clergy' (*Symonem magum, precipuum negociatorem, Nycolaum primum in clero fornicatorem*).[53]

It was Cardinal Humbert of Silva Candida, who was surprisingly silent about the legends of Simon Magus, by whom the word 'nicolaitism' found currency in the central medieval west. In his learned, fiery writings against the Greeks, he drew upon the work of the fourth-century refuter of heretics, Bishop Epiphanius of Salamis. In a letter of 1053 to the Studite monk Nicetas, Humbert's condemnation of the marriage of priests declared that 'the prince of this heresy, Nicholas, came forth from hell.'[54] It was, perhaps, under Humbert's tutelage that, in 1059, Pope Nicholas II prefaced his synodical letter that followed his Roman council in April by a reference to its decisions 'concerning the heresy of the Nicolaitans, that is, concerning married priests, deacons, and all appointed to be among the clergy.'[55] Cardinal Peter Damiani borrowed Humbert's language, and declared that 'married priests are called Nicolaitans, inheriting such a name from one Nicholas who propounded this heresy.'[56] Given the currency of this usage amongst the leading reformers at Rome, it is surprising that it occurs but rarely in papal letters, and only once in those of Gregory VII.[57] He appears to have had little use for the legends of Simon Magus, and next to none for that of the deacon Nicholas; it is not the only respect in which he was far from being a disciple of

---

[51] *Adversus haereses*, 1.26.3, edd. A. Rousseau and L. Doutreleau, 5 vols in 8 pts, Sources chrétiennes 100, 152–3, 210–11, 263–4, 293, Paris 1965–82, i.348.
[52] *Decretale de recipiendis et non recipiendis libris*, 5.9, in E. von Dobschütz, *Das Decretum Gelasianum de libris recipiendis et non recipiendis*, Texte und Untersuchungen zur Geschichte der altchristlichen Literatur 38/4, Leipzig 1912, 13. It is not now attributed to Pope Gelasius I (492–6).
[53] *Epistola ad Innocentium papam* (1131), cap. 7, *MGH Libelli de lite*, iii. 205.
[54] *Contra Nicetam*, cap. 25, *PL* cxliii.996–7.
[55] *MGH Constitutiones et acta publica imperatorum et regum*, i.548–9, no. 385; cf. D. Jasper, *Das Papstwahldekret von 1059: Überlieferung und Textgestalt*, Sigmaringen 1986, 21.
[56] *Ep*. 112, (as n.32), iii. 286, cf. *Ep*. 61, ii. 216–17.
[57] *The Epistolae vagantes of Pope Gregory VII*, ed. and trans. H.E.J. Cowdrey, Oxford 1972, no. 16, p. 44. Writing to King William I of England in late 1076, Gregory complained that Bishop Juhel of Dol, in Brittany, 'quasi simoniacum esse parum et pro nihilo deputaret, nicolaita quoque fieri festinavit.'

---

ADDITIONAL NOTE. Since this paper was completed, Dr Lindy Grant has kindly drawn to my attention the sculptures of the Flight and Death of Simon Magus upon two nave capitals of the cathedral of Saint-Lazare at Autun: A. Kingsley Porter, *Romanesque Sculpture of the Pilgrimage Roads*, 10 vols, Boston 1923, i.112, ii. Plates 73, 75; D. Grivot and G. Zarnecki, *Gislebertus, sculpteur d'Autun*, Paris 1960, p. 68 and Plates 35, 38. The sculptures date from between 1119 and 1132, and demonstrate the currency of the legends of Simon Magus in Burgundy at that time.

Cardinal Humbert. Indeed, the word 'nicolaitism' that Humbert sent upon its medieval travels never secured the currency of the word 'simony'.

There can be no doubt of the determination of the reform popes from Leo IX (1049–54) to extirpate the practices that both nouns signify. Yet the propaganda by which they were resisted was little orchestrated from above, least of all by the popes. The legends of Simon Magus and of the deacon Nicholas occur separately and sporadically. Until Gerhoh of Reichersberg, they seldom both appear prominently in the same publicist. And although regions where they were especially current may be suggested, like South Italy and Montecassino for the legends of Simon Magus, the evidence for the use of what might seem effective propaganda themes is less extensive than might be expected. One possible reason for this is the moral earnestness of the major reforming popes, especially Gregory VII, which was not easily distracted into fantasy. A second reason is the extent to which pressures for reform were arising widely in the church, whose leaders had to make the best of them that they could. They by no means settled the agenda; they had to do what they could to give direction, order, and refinement to demands and methods that came to them from below.

# V

# The Gregorian Papacy
# and Eremitical Monasticism

The purpose of this paper is to consider the attitude of the reform popes during the last quarter of the eleventh century to eremitical forms of monasticism and the contribution of this monasticism to the reform of the church which the papacy was concerned to promote. Thus, a background may be provided for the study of St Bruno (c. 1030-1101), founder in 1084 of la Grande Chartreuse in what was later Dauphiné and in 1091 of Santa Maria della Torre near Squillace in Calabria.

Unlike the reform popes since 1046 who had preceded them but like their successors up to 1119, Gregory VII (1073-85), Victor III (1086-7), and Urban II (1088-99) all had a prolonged and substantial commitment to monasticism, but in its older, Benedictine or Cluniac form. The circumstances of Gregory's monasticism remain uncertain though the fact does not; he probably made his profession early in life at the Roman monastery of St Mary-on-the-Aventine, and contemporaries always recognized him as a monk-pope. Victor entered Montecassino in 1055 after several years of residence in other houses, and from 1058 he was its abbot. Urban was a Cluniac, who became a monk between 1067 and 1070, and was grand prior of Cluny by 1076; he remained such until, probably in 1079, he became cardinal-bishop of Ostia. The relationship between the Gregorian papacy and the older black monasticism from which these three popes came has been much discussed, and it remains a matter of debate; arguably, it was close and basically sympathetic, so that it was not for nothing that, in 1080, Gregory could say of his friend abbot Hugh of Cluny that «we walk by the same way, by the same mind, and by the same spirit»[1]. Less thought has been given to papal relationships with the newer, more austere eremitical monasticism which, during the eleventh and early twelfth centuries, was spreading both in Italy and to the north of the Alps. Yet the popes' relations with it were significant and sometimes close and fruitful.

Gregory's relations were more so than has been appreciated. Even during his pre-papal years at Rome as Archdeacon Hildebrand, it seems to have exercised a certain fascination upon him. This is not the occasion to seek to penetrate the problem of how he interacted with Peter Damiani, the hermit-monk of Fonteavellana and disciple and biographer of St Romuald, who from 1057 to 1072 was cardinal-bishop of Ostia. No word survives from Hildebrand's side to suggest how he regarded Peter. But Peter's reiterated description of Hildebrand as «my holy Satan» (the personal adjective *my* is to be observed) seems to cast him in the role of the Satan of the book of Job, who was concerned to test the holy man to the limit in respect of his manner of life[2]. Hildebrand was, however, also prepared to learn from Peter, whose counsels on fasting led him to abstain from leeks and onions because of his excessive fondness for them[3]. This tendency towards rigorous asceticism was repeatedly attested. In 1059, at Pope Nicholas II 's Lateran council, Hildebrand was the spokesman of observant religious superiors in Rome and of their followers in recalling clerks from the laxity about personal property of the *Institutio canonum* of 816/17 to the absolute standard of the primitive church; in the ensuing discussion, there was condemnation of the lavish quotas of food and drink which the Carolingian legislation provided. They matched the excesses of the Cyclopes rather than Christian temperance, and they smacked of Gallic *gourmandise*[4]. When later publicists who were not well disposed to Gregory, like Wenric of Trier and Guy of Ferrara, sought to balance the light and shade of Greg-

---

[1] For the Cluniacs, see H.E.J. COWDREY, *The Cluniacs and the Gregorian Reform*, Oxford 1970, and *St Hugh and Gregory VII*, in *Le Gouvernement d'Hugues de Semur à Cluny*. Actes du Colloque scientifique internationale, Cluny, September 1988, ed. B. Maurice, Cluny 1990, pp. 173-90; and for Montecassino, *ibid., The Age of Abbot Desiderius. Montecassino, the Papacy, and the Normans in the Eleventh and Early Twelfth Centuries*, Oxford 1983. For the citation, *Reg.* 8.3, p. 520.

[2] *Die Briefe des Petrus Damiani*, nos 57, 107, ed. K. REINDEL, *MGH Briefe*, 4, 2.167, 3. 186.

[3] *Ibid.* no. 160, 4 (forthcoming).

[4] A. WERMINGHOFF, *Die Beschlüsse des Aachener Concils im Jahre* 816, pt. 4, «Neues Archiv der Gesellschaft für ältere deutsche Geschichtskunde», 27, 1902, pp. 669-75.

ory's whole career, they were in agreement in noticing and praising his parsimony of diet and of life-style in a Roman environment which favoured high living. According to Guy, Gregory ate only once a day and prolonged his fast until evening; although his table was well provided, he himself partook only of wild herbs and vegetables [5].

If his life-style was so austere, it is not surprising that Hildebrand should have established a bond with the monks of Vallombrosa under their founding abbot, John Gualbertus. They combined a strict Benedictine observance with a zeal by preaching and other external activity to extirpate the spiritual and moral abuses of surrounding clergy and laity; simony was an especial object of their attention. There is a conflict of evidence about whether Hildebrand ever met John Gualbertus. When the latter died in 1073, Hildebrand had just become pope; in a letter of condolence and eulogy to his monks, he said that they had never met [6]. But John's first biographer, Andrew of Strumi, said, though at second hand, that they had done so: beforehand, Hildebrand had tested John's patience by sharp reproofs (this calls to mind «my holy Satan» who assailed Peter Damiani); but when Hildebrand met John (*ad eius intuitu*), he was so impressed that he forgot what he had intended to say and henceforth they were joined in unshakeable brotherly love [7]. About Hildebrand's attachment to John and his monks, there can be no doubt. When, in 1068, a Vallombrosan monk named Peter proved through an ordeal by fire the simoniacal guilt of Bishop Peter Mezzabarba of Florence, Hildebrand, like Abbot Desiderius of Montecassino, was warm in his support, while Pope Alexander II and Cardinal Peter Damiani were cautious [8]. From 1072 until his death in 1089, the hero of this episode, which earned him the nickname *Petrus Igneus*, was cardinal-bishop of Albano, and a staunch supporter of the three reform popes of these years. Andrew of Strumi recorded his testimony to Gregory's continuing spiritual debt to John Gualbertus: whenever he celebrated mass and was

---

[5] *Wenrici scolastici Trevirensis Epistola sub Theoderici episcopi Virdunensis nomine composita*, cap. 1, ed. K. FRANCKE, *MGH LdeL*, 1.285-6; *Wido episcopus Ferrarienis De scismate Hildebrandi*, 1.2, edd. R. Wilmans and E. Dümmler, *MGH LdeL*, 1.534-6; cfr. *Benzonis episcopi Albensis Ad Heinricum IV imperatorem libri VII*, 6.6, *MGH SS*, 13.666, lines 11-13.

[6] *Epp. vag*. pp. 4-7, no. 2.

[7] *Vita sancti Iohannis Gualberti*, cap. 61, ed. F. Baethgen, *MGH SS* 30/2.1092.

[8] G. MICCOLI, *Pietro Igneo. Studi sull'età Gregoriana*, Istituto storico Italiano per il medio evo, Studi storici fasc. 40-1, Rome 1960, pp. 1-45, 139-57.

denied the gift of tears, the recollection of John served to renew it [9]. Gregory's letter of condolence to the Vallombrosan monks upon John's death is a testimony to his appreciation alike of the prayers and of the activities of their style of strict monasticism:

> ... his spotless faith shone wonderfully abroad throughout all Tuscany. ... We send you words of fatherly exhortation that the zeal of your right-eousness may watch the more diligently and burn the more keenly to root out the tares from the Lord's field. ... Let your mind meditate daily upon the lessons of the holy scriptures by which the assertions of the heretics are confuted and the faith of holy church is defended against the members of the devil who are trying to overthrow the Christian religion by their manifold devices; let your mind stand upright to the confusion of evil men in the liberty wherein it is wont to stand [10].

As archdeacon, Hildebrand once showed evidence of admiration for the more austere elements in the life of St Benedict of Nursia. In 1069, Pope Alexander II dispatched him to the monastery of Subiaco to put an end to the vexations of neighbouring lay lords and to restore its internal discipline. A tradition at Subiaco recalled that, having restored security and order, Hildebrand ascended to the Sacro Speco whither St Benedict had first withdrawn from the world [11].

The documents of Gregory's pontificate provide little evidence for his further dealings with Italian centres of eremitical monasticism. At an unknown date he gave Vallombrosa a privilege which is lost, and in 1074 he renewed his predecessor's privilege of 1072 for Camaldoli [12]. Perhaps in 1081, he declined a request from the abbot of Fucecchio and the prior of Camaldoli that he should absolve a noble, Ughiccio, son of Count William of Bulgarelli, because he was not satisfied of his penitence; but he concluded his letter with a request that the monks should pray daily for the noble's

---

[9] *Vita s. Ioh. Gual.* cap. 85, p. 1102; Guy of Ferrara referred to Gregory's gift of tears (as n. 5).

[10] As n. 6.

[11] *Chronicon Sublacense*, ed. R. Morghen, Rerum Italicarum Scriptores, new ser. 24/6, Bologna 1927, pp. 10-12.

[12] *QF* pp. 2, 46-9, nos. *7, 70.

repentance, because such intercession was the proper and valuable service of the monks [13].

Gregory's dealings with monks and hermits in France and neighbouring parts of the kingdom of Burgundy are more instructive. The strict Benedictine monastery of la Chaise-Dieu (dioc. Clermont) is an example [14]. The three abbots, Durand, Adelelme, and Seguin, who ruled during Gregory's pontificate were strenuous opponents of simony. Gregory demonstrated his favour most signally in a privilege of 1080, in which he referred to it as *monasterium sancti Roberti*, thereby acknowledging the sanctity of its founder in 1043, Robert of Turlande. Gregory safeguarded it from outside interference, especially on the part of the canons of Clermont, and his confirmation of its widespread possessions implied a realization of its reforming work, not least in south-west France [15]. Gregory entrusted to Seguin's oversight the monastery of Frossinoro (dioc. Modena), a foundation of Countess Matilda of Tuscany which she had given to the apostolic see in 1077 [16]. With regard to the secular church, Abbot Durand became an active and reforming bishop of Clermont, a diocese for which Gregory was solicitous [17]. In 1080, Gregory regarded la Chaise-Dieu, with Cluny, as a place to which Archbishop Manasses of Reims, who was under sentence of deposition by the council of Lyons (1080), might temporarily retire to consider his position [18]. In 1081, Abbot Seguin was with Gregory's legates, Bishops Hugh of Die and Amatus of Oloron, at their council of Saintes [19]. Apart from its abbots, Jarento, a monk at la Chaise-Dieu from *c*. 1074, became a leading Gregorian in the latter decades of the eleventh century. In 1075, he received holy orders from Bishop Hugh of Die. After he had become prior of his monastery, Hugh chose him to be abbot of Saint-Bénigne at Dijon

---

[13] *Epp. vag.* pp. 104-7, no. 43. One of Gregory's last privileges from Salerno, in May 1085, was for Fucecchio: *QF* pp. 265-7, no. 218.

[14] For a fuller account, see H.E.J. COWDREY, *Pope Gregory VII and la Chaise-Dieu*, in *Maisons de Dieu et hommes d'église. Florilège en l'honneur de Pierre-Roger Gaussin*, Saint-Etienne 1992, pp. 25-35.

[15] *QF* pp. 210-12, no. 181.

[16] HUGH OF FLAVIGNY, *Chronicon*, 2, *MGH SS* 8. 417.

[17] RALPH, *Vita s. Adelelmi*, cap. 8, *España Sagrada*, ed. H. Flórez, Madrid 1747- 27. 852-4; cfr. *Reg.* 4. 22, p. 333.

[18] *Reg.* 7.20, pp. 495-6.

[19] *Recueil des actes de l'abbaye de Cluny*, edd. A. Bernard and A. Bruel, 6 vols, Paris 1876-1903, 4. 715-16 no. 3580.

during his council of Autun (1077)[20]. The network of Gregorian legates and other agents with which la Chaise-Dieu had an association is an indication that it had its modest but genuine part in disseminating Gregory's reforming aspirations.

Its relations with bishops tended in the same direction. Apart from Durand's work at Clermont, which continued until his death just after welcoming Urban II to Clermont for his council of 1095, particular significance attaches to relations between la Chaise-Dieu and Bishop Hugh of Grenoble (1080-1132). Hugh was to be deeply concerned with the foundation of la Grande Chartreuse, and his *Life* was written by prior Guigo I[21]. According to it, Hugh was chosen to be bishop at a council held by Bishop Hugh of Die at Avignon. He refused consecration by his metropolitan, deeming him to be a simoniac, and travelled to Rome where Gregory not only consecrated him but bestowed pastoral case upon him when he was afflicted by grave temptations. Upon returning to Grenoble, Hugh found a clergy and people immersed in the evils that Gregory was concerned to eradicate-clerical marriage and concubinage, simony, and the wasting of church lands; but his efforts to counter them were in vain. After less than two years, he entered la Chaise-Dieu as a monk, completing his noviciate before returning to his diocese at Gregory's behest. Apart from the command to return, there is no evidence for Gregory's view of so long an absence from his diocese. But Gregory's memory of Hugh's spiritual crisis at Rome and his understanding of the magnitude of Hugh's task as bishop of so difficult a diocese are as likely to have made him approve as to condemn a temporary retreat into strict monastic discipline. At least, the result was beneficial, for Prior Guigo was able to exhibit Hugh, whom Pope Innocent II had canonized, as a paradigm reforming bishop whose long reign on balance showed the benefit of interaction between a pastoral bishop and such strict monastic centres as la Chaise-Dieu and la Grande Chartreuse. Dimly though they can be

---

[20] For Jarento, see HUGH OF FLAVIGNY, *Chron.* 2, pp. 413, 415-17, 462-3; *Annales sancti Benigni Divionesis, a*. 1077, *MGH SS* 5. 42.

[21] GUIGO, *Vita sancti Hugonis Gratianopolitani episcopi, PL* 153.761-84. For fuller accounts of Hugh, with references, see H.E.J. COWDREY, *Hugh of Avalon, Carthusian and Bishop*, in *De Cella in Seculum. Religious and Secular Life and Devotion in Later Medieval England*. An Interdisciplinary Conference in Celebration of the Eighth Centenary of the Consecration of St Hugh of Avalon, Bishop of Lincoln, 20-22 July 1986, ed. M.G. Sargent, Cambridge 1989, pp. 41-57, esp. pp. 48-9; and *ibid.* (as n. 14).

preceived through the scanty evidence, Gregory's dealings with la Chaise-Dieu suggest that he was aware of the benefits of such interaction.

Gregory showed himself well disposed towards individuals who adopted strict or eremitical forms of the religious life as well as towards a major community like la Chaise-Dieu. They were particularly welcome when they settled within the city of Rome. Three, in themselves very different, examples may be cited. Until her death in December 1077, the Empress-mother Agnes of Poitou was established in Rome as a penitent and head of a small community of pious women. Gregory's letters demonstrate the high regard in which he held her, both for her devotion and for her services as an intermediary with her son, King Henry IV of Germany. After giving a long account of her personal austerities, the Reichenau annalist Berthold recorded how, in the first days of 1078, Gregory himself buried her at a concourse of the whole Roman church by the side of St Petronilla in her church on the Vatican hill[22]. Robert of Tombelaine spent many years as a hermit upon the rock after which he is named in the bay of Mont Saint-Michel, where he wrote a commentary upon the Song of Songs. When Bishop Odo of Bayeux established monks in the church of Saint-Vigor outside that city, he appointed Robert as their superior. In 1082, when Odo fell out of favour with his half-brother, King William I of England, the community of Saint-Vigor was dispersed. Robert made a pilgrimage to Rome where, according to Orderic Vitalis, Pope Gregory received him honourably and retained him there, so that he served the Roman church for the remainder of his life[23].

The most instructive example of a hermit with whom Gregory had mutually favourable dealings is Count Simon of Crépy[24]. He was a leading feud-

[22] For Agnes as a penitent at Rome and for her services to the papacy, see *Die Briefe des Petrus Damiani*, nos. 124, 130, 144, (as n. 2), 3. 408-11, 434-6, 5257; *Reg.* 1.1, 19-21, 85, 2.3, 30, 44, 4.3, pp. 4, 32-5, 121-3, 126-7, 163-4, 180-2, 297-9. For her life at Rome with a small community of women dedicated to prayer and almsgiving, see Abbot John of Fécamp's letter to her in: J. LECLERCQ and J.P. BONNES, *Un Maître de la vie spirituelle au xi^e siècle: Jean de Fécamp*, Paris 1946, pp. 211-17, esp. lines 33-5. For her austere life and her burial, BERTHOLD, *Annales, a.* 1077, *MGH SS* 5. 303-4.

[23] For Robert, see *The Ecclesiastical History of Orderic Vitalis*, 8.1, 25, ed. M. Chibnall, 6 vol, Oxford 1969-80, 4. 116-17, 304-6. For his *Commentarium in Cantica canticorum* and other writings, see *PL* 150. 1359-78.

[24] For Simon, see the *Vita Simonis Crespeiensis auctore synchrono*, *PL* 156.1211-24, and for a fuller discussion with references, H.E.J. COWDREY, *Count Simon of Crépy's Monastic Conversion*, forthcoming *Mélanges M. Pacaut*.

atory of the Capetian king who inherited a vast principality between the Rivers Seine and Somme. In 1077, he astonished his contemporaries by becoming a monk at the strict monastery of Saint-Oyend in the Jura, where he intensified the personal austerities that he had for long practised while in the world. It must always be remembered that, in the first chapter of his *Rule*, St Benedict had envisaged that, after long service as coenobites under a Rule and an abbot, an élite of monks would advance to a solitary life as anchorites; in long-established black-monk houses like Cluny, this was an acceptable progression. But, in the eleventh century, some especially devout people, with the approval of their spiritual mentors, were abbreviating the coenobitical stage of their profession, or even dispensing with it, so that they passed quickly to an eremitical life. Simon of Crépy soon left Saint-Oyend for the forest, whence Gregory, who knew him from earlier visits to Rome, summoned him and established him, with a small group of companions, in a hermitage near the church of St Thecla on the Ostian Way. Somewhat reluctantly, Simon remained in Rome under Gregory's personal direction until he died, probably in 1081/2. By Gregory's command his way of life was given the signal mark of approval of burial in St Peter's basilica amongst the papal tombs. There could be no more emphatic witness that Gregory approved of the eremitical life, even in one who had once inherited a great feudal principality.

Two aspects of the manifold significance of Simon's course of life may now be emphasized. First, for all the tensions and contrasts, it points to an area of understanding and complementarity between the older monasticism and the new. One of Simon's mentors was Abbot Hugh of Cluny. In 1077, Count Simon gave his parents' bodies fresh burial in the church of Saint-Arnoul at Crépy, which he gave to Abbot Hugh to become a Cluniac priory. He described himself as the abbot's *servulus* who held him in outstanding love[25]. Yet within months, he took the habit at Saint-Oyend, not at Cluny. There is insufficient direct evidence to warrant an analysis of his reasons. But there is no need to suppose that he saw any clash or contradiction of loyalties. He may have recognized what each was good for: Cluny was appropriate for his father's liturgical commemoration, but for his own acclerated vocation to the eremitical life which he desired Saint-Oyend was to be preferred. Nor need it be supposed that he acted against Abbot Hugh's advice or wishes. Relations remained good, and as a monk of Saint-Oyend, Simon served Hugh well during a visit to the Capetian court. Hugh may

---

[25] *Recueil* (as n. 19), 4.613-14, no. 3499.

have perceived that Simon's spiritual home was not Cluny but Saint-Oyend. Both showed flexibility, and a grasp of the strengths of differing monastic options.

Secondly, Simon's career suggests that Gregory was no less flexibile and pragmatic when it came to the conversion to the religious life of prominent lay and feudal figures. Perhaps too much has been made of Gregory's querulous response to Abbot Hugh of Cluny when, in 1078, he admitted to Cluny Duke Hugh of Burgundy [26]. The incident must be put into its context, for according to Simon's *Vita* it was Simon's entry into Saint-Oyend that prompted the duke of Burgundy to leave the world, as well as Count Guy of Mâcon and many others. This poses the question why Gregory should have welcomed Simon's conversion, which led to the political disintegration of his principality, and should also have invited him to lead an eremitical life at Rome [27], but why he should have deprecated the conversion of the duke of Burgundy which Simon's example prompted. The answer appears to be that, whereas according to what Gregory expected of a lay prince Simon duly prepared the way for his conversion, under papal guidance, by establishing peace and concord in his lands, Hugh made no such preparation. Gregory could, therefore, castigate Abbot Hugh «because you have taken or received the duke into rest at Cluny, and you have brought it about that a hundred thousand Christians lack a guardian.» In any case, Abbot Hugh seems to have known very well how to appease Gregory's anger. Gregory's letters of 1079 make it virtually certain that Abbot Hugh visited Rome and agreed to allow his grand prior, Odo, the future Pope Urban II, to become the cardinal-bishop of Ostia [28]. With such a present, Gregory quickly forgot his wrath at the loss into the cloister of the duke of Burgundy, and made such eulogies of Abbot Hugh as have been noticed — «we walk by the same way, by the same mind, and by the same spirit». However this may have been, Simon of Crépy's case shows how firmly established a place the eremitical life had in Gregory's mind, not least when it was lived at Rome. When Gregory thought that different forms of monasti-

---

[26] *Reg.* 6.17, pp. 423-4.

[27] Simon's *Vita* recorded that, when Simon in 1080 negotiated on Gregory's behalf with Robert Guiscard, duke of Apulia, about the rehabilitation of the alliance between the Normans and the papacy, his preaching led to the conversion of some sixty Norman knights to monasticism.

[28] COWDREY, *St Hugh and Gregory VII* (as n. 1), esp. pp. 180-3.

cism, new as well as old, were working for the good of the church, he was forward to accommodate them. As for older and newer ways, at least upon occasion they were seen to complement rather than to contradict each other.

About Victor III, it needs only be noticed that, at the outset of his monastic life, this outstanding figure in eleventh-century Benedictine history had personal experience of the eremitical life [29]. His successor, the Cluniac Urban II, showed himself remarkably open to newer, as well as to older, forms of the religious life. If he indeed composed the epitaph upon Simon of Crépy's tomb, praising him as «of famous lineage and a leading figure of the French nobility who, from love of poverty, left his country and the world because he set the Spirit of God above all riches», he shared to the full Gregory's personal regard for Simon and his approval of his eremitical way of life [30]. According to the Cistercian *Exordium parvum*, Urban brought a sympathetic and moderating hand to bear upon relations between the abbey of Molesme and the *novum monasterium* of Cîteaux. His letter of 1099 about Abbot Robert's return from Cîteaux to Molesme suggests that he envisaged the relationship between the two houses in terms of the first chapter of St Benedict's Rule: Molesme was a *monasterium* for those who sought coenobitic service under the discipline of a Rule, while Cîteaux was an *eremus* for those who sought solitude. The two ways of life complemented each other, and both were to be fostered [31]. The high esteem that this black-monk pope accorded to regular canons is well known [32]. Most remarkable of all is his support for the wandering preacher Robert of Arbrissel, founder in 1101 of the double monastery of Fontevraud. According to his *Vita prima*, when Urban came to Angers in February 1096, he summoned him from his hermitage in the forest of Craon where he was living an austere life with a group of companions. Urban caused Robert to preach before

[29] *Chronica monasterii Casinensis*, 3.6, MGH SS 34.367.

[30] PL 156.1223-4.

[31] caps 5-6, 11, in: *Les Plus Anciens Textes de Cîteaux*, edd. J. de la C. Bouton and J.B. van Damme, Cîteaux, Commentarii Cistercienses Studia et Documenta 2, Achel 1985, pp. 62-3, 71.

[32] See esp. H. FUHRMANN, *Papst Urban II und der Stand der Regularkanoniker, Bayerische Akademie der Wissenschaften, ph. hist. K1.,SB, Jg. 1984, Heft 2*, München, 1984, and ibid., *Das Papsttum zwischen Frömmigkeit und Politik — Urban II. (1088-1099) und die Frage der Selbstheiligung*, in *Deus qui mutat tempora. Menschen und Institutionen im Wandel des Mittelalters. Festschrift für Alfons Becker*, Sigmaringen 1987, pp. 157-72.

him, and afterwards gave him a general licence to preach, charging him to become an itinerant preacher[33].

To summarize. The monastic popes of the last quarter of the eleventh century came into contact with a variety of strict monastic and eremitical movements and persons, differing and even contrasting widely among themselves. In the shaping of the ideals and practices of these movements and persons, the popes and their predecessors had little if any direct part. They had to accept and to use them as they presented themselves. By and large, the popes showed themselves remarkably well disposed towards them as to the older monasticism. As the example of Simon of Crépy shows, provided that even a great feudatory made what a pope regarded as appropriate preparation for the peace and security of his people, his conversion was not only acceptable but to be welcomed. Papal dealings with Vallombrosa and la Chaise-Dieu indicate that the popes valued such communities both for their austere religion and for their part in the struggle against simony, clerical marriage and concubinage, and other matters of reform. If a black-monk house like Cluny could provide the papacy with a Cardinal Odo of Ostia, Vallombrosa could supply a Cardinal Peter of Albano. Though the case of Count Hugh of Burgundy involved the black-monk house of Cluny, it showed how the taking from the world of a major figure might involve any monastic group intension and at least temporary papal disapproval; Simon of Crépy, however, shows the impossibility of generalizing because such conversions could meet with a papal welcome. The popes sometimes reacted with enthusiasm, and usually with a benevolent pragmatism. Thus, Urban II sought to be an impartial though well-disposed referee between what he saw as the claims of coenobitism at Molesme and those of eremitism at Cîteaux. Guided by genuine sympathy and by their desire to secure the spiritual and reforming benefits that different groups of monks and hermits who lived by ways of their own devising had to offer, the popes were concerned to guide and to use them in whatever ways opportunity might offer.

Thus much, at least, can be said of the attitude of the reform papacy of St Bruno's day to eremitical monasticism. It remains to consider some aspects of Bruno's career in the light of it[34].

---

[33] BAUDRY OF DOL, *Vita B. Roberti de Arbrisello*, 2.13-15, PL 162.1050-1.

[34] Bruno's surviving letters are edited, with a valuable introduction, in *Lettres des premiers Chartreux*, 1: *S. Bruno - Guigues - S. Anthelme*, ed. by a Carthusian, SC 88, 2nd edn, Paris 1988. Recent studies include *Maestro Bruno, padre de monjes* por un Cartujo, Madrid 1980, German trans. G. POSADA, *Der heilige Bruno, Vater der Kartäuser*, Cologne 1987, and

Bruno was born at Cologne a little before 1030. Thus, by the time of his entry in 1081/3 into the religious life, briefly at Sèche-Fontaine near Troyes and then, in 1084, at la Grande-Chartreuse, he was well into his fifties. Hitherto, he was a secular clerk, not a monk. Most of his life had been spent at Reims, whither he may have come in time for Pope Leo IX's reforming council of September 1049; if not, he must have heard of it from some who were present. He was thus early aware of the new papal reforms. For most of his thirty years at Reims, he was a member of the cathedral chapter; from *c*. 1056 he was *scolasticus* or master of the cathedral school, and in the mid-1070s he was briefly chancellor. The scandalous and eventful career of Archbishop Manasses I (1068/9-1081) ensured that, as a canon of the cathedral, Bruno would become involved in the struggle to reform the French church. He came to the notice of Gregory VII and of his zealous legate in France, Hugh, bishop of Die and (from 1082) archbishop of Lyons, who remained a central figure in papal and ecclesiastical affairs until his death in 1109.

In the eyes of the reformers, Manasses was deeply tainted by simony, and he ruled oppressively and autocratically, increasingly using his position to augment his temporal power and possessions [35]. Opposition within his cathedral chapter became active from the summer of 1076 when, at the council of Clermont, the provost, also named Manasses, confessed to simony and placed his office in Hugh of Die's hand. He further laid a complaint against the archbishop. Bruno was prominent amongst a group of canons that henceforth opposed Manasses strongly. In the autumn, they were compelled to take refuge at Roucy with Count Ebolus, who supported Gregory VII. In September 1077, Archbishop Manasses was cited to Hugh of Die's council of Autun but did not come; he was suspended upon the accusation of his clergy. When the legate reported to the pope, his letter commended to him both Provost Manasses, now a sincere defender of the catholic faith, and Bruno, whom he commended as an uncompromised master at Reims (*Remensis ecclesiae in omni honestate magistrum*). Both men deserved to be backed by Gregory's authority, for they had been counted worthy to suffer shame for the name of Jesus and could be relied upon to promote

---

French trans. Un Chartreux, *Maître Bruno, père des Chartreux*, Analecta Cartusiana 115, Salzburg 1990; B. BLIGNY, *Saint Bruno, le premier chartreux*, Rennes 1984.

[35] The fullest account of Archbishop Manasses remains that of A. FLICHE, *Le Règne de Philip I<sup>e</sup>, roi de France (1060-1108)*, Paris 1912, pp. 360, 367-8, 391, 417-23.

God's cause in France [36]. Thus, while a secular canon at Reims, Bruno commended himself to Gregory's dedicated and hyper-zealous standing legate in France, who brought to Gregory's notice his usefulness as an active papal supporter.

In the spring and summer of 1078, Archbishop Manasses was able adroitly to secure from Gregory a lifting of the sanctions against himself; he wrote a letter to the pope accusing Provost Manasses and his party of being the agents of Count Ebolus in warfare against the churches of Rome and of Reims [37]. He also presented his case in person at Rome. In 1080, he was summoned to Hugh of Die's council of Lyons but declined to appear; however, he submitted to the legate and to the council a lengthy apologia in which he attacked Bruno. He claimed that he himself and Provost Manasses, who acted on behalf of all his colleagues, had reached an agreement to which only two of the canons demurred. One of the two was Bruno who, the archbishop alleged, was no clerk of his, for he had been neither born nor baptized at Reims; he was a canon of St Cunibert at Cologne in Germany. Manasses had never much cultivated Bruno, and knew little about his life and status (*libertas*). Moreover, Bruno had been ungrateful for many benefits that he had conferred [38]. Bruno was evidently the archbishop's uncompromising opponent on the grounds of his simony and unsuitability for his office. The verdict of the council of Lyons was that Manasses should be deposed; Gregory confirmed it while giving him a last chance of rehabilitation which he refused. One of Gregory's conditions was that he should completely restore to Provost Manasses, Bruno, and others «who have manifestly spoken up for righteousness against you» (*qui pro iustitia contra te locuti fuisse videntur*) the goods of which they had been despoiled [39]. The

---

[36] «Digni sunt enim ambo a vobis, et in his quae Dei sunt, vestra auctoritate confirmari, quoniam digni habiti sunt pro nomine Iesu contumeliam pati; et ideo consultores profuturos causae Dei et cooperatores in partibus Franciae adhibeatis»: *Ep*. 29, *RHGE* 14.613-14; cfr. HUGH OF FLAVIGNY, *Chron*. 2, p. 415.

[37] *Ep*. 76, *RHGF* 14. 611-12.

[38] *Ep*. 9, *RHGF* 14. 781-6, esp. 783AB,D. This is the only statement that Bruno was a canon of St Cunibert, and it remains obscure. Either it refers to a canonry received, perhaps through family influence, in early youth, and is intended to cast a slur upon his reforming credentials, or, more probably, it is ironical: Bruno was foreign to the diocese and, if a canon, it must be of his native city where the archbishop was the imperialist Sigewin (1079-89).

[39] *Reg*. 7.20, pp. 495-6.

archbishop was impenitent, and in 1081 he ceased to hold office; Bruno's active opposition to him continued until the end.

Little is known of events during the next two years in the history either of the church of Reims or of Bruno. An entry in Bruno's mortuary roll offers a hint, but no more, that there was a desire at Reims that he should be the next archbishop [40]. If so, he resisted it, for the next step in his life was his entry upon the religious life.

In a letter written after 1096 while at La Torre to his fellow-canon of Reims Ralph *le Verd*, who became provost of Reims in 1096 as successor to Manasses when the latter became archbishop, and in his turn archbishop from 1106 to 1124, Bruno made clear the commitment to the religious life that he had already formed by 1083. At a time unspecified, he, Ralph'and a certain Fulcuius Monoculus had been together in a garden near the house of one Adam with whom Bruno was lodging. Since Bruno was a guest, the meeting was probably not in Reims; perhaps it occurred during the canons' exile in 1076. All three had promised, vowed, and arranged to take the monastic habit. Fulcuius's departure for Rome led them to defer until his return, but he was delayed there and other business supervened; thus, their ardour had cooled. In 1096, Bruno wrote urging Ralph no longer to delay the fulfilment of his vow [41].

For his part, he had fulfilled his own vow long ago. It had led him first to enter the eremitical life with two companions, Peter and Lambert, at Sèche-Fontaine, where they built a church and cells with the approval of the monks of Molesme [42]. Unlike Simon of Crépy, he seems to have experienced no period of coenobitic monasticism, nor is there evidence as to whether he took a vow of stability, and if so upon what terms [43]. Bruno's companions quickly decided for a coenobitic life, setting up a monastery

---

[40] Bruno's mortuary roll is printed in *PL* 152.553-606; the titulus in question is no. 52, inscribed at the cathedral of Sainte-Marie at Reims: «Cumque faveret ei fortuna per omnia, iamque / Hunc praeferremus omnibus et merito, / Namque benignus erat omnique peritus in arte, / Facundusque satis divitiis potens». There is no other direct evidence that Bruno was proposed for, or that he refused, the see. The next archbishop, Raynald I (1083-96) was treasurer of the church of Saint-Martin at Tours, and proved to be a capable and successful archbishop.

[41] cap. 13, *Letters* (as n. 34), pp. 74-7. For Fulcuius's identity, see *ibid.* pp. 256-7.

[42] The only reference to Bruno's stay at Sèche-Fontaine is in a charter in J. LAURENT, *Cartulaire de l'abbaye de Molesme (916-1250)*, 2 vols, Paris 1907-11, 2.134-6, no. 138.

[43] In the earliest Carthusian Customs, those of Prior Guigo I, compiled 1121-8, the term *stabilitas* does not appear with the addition *loci*, and the emphasis is upon stability in

which, by 1086, had become a priory depending upon Molesme. Bruno moved away, and by mid-1084 he had arrived with six companions at la Grande Chartreuse. There, he established an eremitical community.

The mid-1080s, which saw Gregory VII's departure from Rome to Salerno, Victor III's brief and uneasy pontificate, and the election of Urban II, were not propitious for papal interest in the new foundation, although it was made under the direction of Bishop Hugh of Grenoble whom Gregory had ordained and befriended[44]. But Bruno had been Urban II's teacher (*praeceptor*) when the pope had been a clerk at Reims. Probably in 1090, he ordered Bruno to travel to the Roman curia «to assist the pope with help and advice in ecclesiastical business» (*eundem papam solatio et consilio iuvaturus*)[45]. Bruno's prompt obedience led to a situation at la Grande Chartreuse that elicited Urban's close concern, for as he expressed it, «it was right that those who are wearied by their travails on behalf of the Roman church should find relief by its aid»[46]. When Bruno first accepted the summons, his companions had dispersed, and Bruno had retroceded the lands upon which la Grande Chartreuse was established to the donors — effectively to la Chaise-Dieu, which had a priory nearby at Saint-Robert-de-Cornillon. But before departing for Rome, Bruno had reassembled the community and had appointed one of them, Landuin, to be their prior. Urban intervened on their behalf by actions which were, first of all, practically effective. In 1090 he wrote to Abbot Seguin of la Chaise-Dieu, charging him to restore the community to its lands and to return Bruno's act of retrocession. He further instructed Archbishop Hugh of Lyons and Bishop Hugh of Grenoble to ensure Seguin's compliance. By a charter of 17 September 1090, Seguin confirmed to Landuin and his companions and to their successors the free and entire possession of la Grande Chartreuse. In March 1091, Urban completed its rehabilitation by addressing a privilege to both

---

character and of profession: *Guigues 1ᵉʳ, Coutumes de Chartreuse*, ed. by a Carthusian, SC 313, Paris 1984, 15.2, 23.1, 73.3, pp. 198, 214, 278.

[44] Guigo, *Vita S. Hugonis*, 3.11-12, PL 153.769-70; *Recueil des plus anciens actes de la Grande-Chartreuse (1086-1196)*, ed. B. Bligny, Grenoble 1958, pp. 1-8, no. 1.

[45] Notice of Bruno from: A. WILMART, *La Chronique des premiers Chartreux*, «Revue Mabillon», 16, 1926, pp. 77-142, at pp. 119-22; *Letters* (as n. 34), p. 242. The noun *solatium* means the ready and practical help which should be brought to holders of office, great and small, as in the Rule of St Benedict, 1.4, 31.17, 35.3-4, 53.3-4, 53.18.20, 66.5; *consilium* is the advice that abbots and rulers should take and their qualified subjects should offer, as in the Rule, 3.1-4, 12-13, 65.15.

[46] *Recueil* (as n. 44), pp. 9-10, no. 2.

Bruno and Landuin by which he placed it under the protection of the apostolic see and approved Landuin's election as prior [47].

Secondly, Urban's provisions are noteworthy for the stamp of approval which he set upon the eremitical life as the Carthusians practised it. In his letter to the archbishop of Lyons and the bishop of Grenoble, he declared that «it belongs to our pastoral office to defend this Shunammite girl» — the new Carthusian plantation — «who has been found in this disorder». He referred to the biblical Abishag, the beautiful Shunammite maiden who, when King David was old and unable to get warm, chastely nursed him in her bosom (1 Kgs. 1:1-4). Urban employed an image of the contemplative life which Bruno would also use in his letter to Ralph *le Verd* to urge it upon him as that which alone could warm a man in the love of God by his total turning away from the glories and pleasures of the world [48]. When Urban took la Grande Chartreuse into papal protection, he praised the eremitical life of the first Carthusians more openly:

> It is written: «Let his followers dwell in his tabernacle» (Job 18:15), and, «Let joy and gladness be found in it, the giving of thanks and the voice of praise» (Isa. 51:3). Wherefore, dearly beloved and called by the Lord to the tabernacle which he has prepared for you to inhabit upon the Carthusian mountain in the diocese of Grenoble, may you possess in it joy and gladness through the contemplation of heavenly things, so that you may continually lift up your hearts to God and enjoy the Lord. May the voice of praise and thanksgiving resound in you, because once you were in the shadows of this world, but now by God's mercy you are light in the Lord (Eph. 5:8) [49].

There can be no doubt about Urban's cordial approval of the eremitical life as Bruno established it at la Grande Chartreuse. His obedience in answering Urban's summons to Rome was no less admirable in his eyes, and his new foundation must not suffer harm on his account [50].

Bruno's migration to the curia did not bring Urban the help and counsel that he sought; Bruno quickly found its bustle and way of life insupportable. As the Carthusian biographical memoir of him put it, because he burned with love for the solitude and spiritual repose that he had abandoned,

---

[47] *Ibid.*, pp. 9-16, nos. 2-5.
[48] *Ibid.*, pp. 11-12, no. 3; Letter to Ralph, cap. 7, *Lettres* (as n. 34), p. 72.
[49] *Recueil*, pp. 15-16, no. 5.
[50] *Ibid.*, pp. 9-10, no. 2.

he left the curia and even spurned the archbishopric of Reggio Calabria to which he was elected with Urban's goodwill. Instead, he withdrew, in the company of numerous laity and clerks, to the Calabrian *eremus* of La Torre [51]. He established himself there at some time in 1091. He did not forfeit Urban's goodwill. In 1092, the pope acceded to the request of Bruno and his companion Lanuin that he confirm the complete freedom of La Torre from outside interference as conceded by Count Roger I of Sicily and confirmed by Bishop Theodore of Squillace, and in 1098 he renewed his confirmation. Urban's language was more formal and restrained than in the case of la Grande Chartreuse, but it expressed the pope's duty «to provide for the repose (*quies*) of God's servants, as the Lord shall give us power» [52].

Three features of Bruno's ten years at La Torre, when placed in relation to his six years at la Grande Chartreuse, call for comment in connection with papal attitudes to his style of religious life. First, if somewhat paradoxically, Bruno exhibited, and was acknowledged at Rome to have exhibited to a pre-eminent degree, the virtue of stability in his religious profession. The point was strongly made in November 1101, when Pope Paschal II wrote to Lanuin who, after some contention within the community, had succeeded Bruno as its head. Upon returning to Rome from La Torre, Cardinal Richard of Albano had reported upon the return of peace and concord to the *eremus*, and that harmony had returned *in locum sanctae memoriae magni Brunonis*, whom Paschal urged Lanuin to imitate:

> May there be in you the spirit of this man, and his vigour of ecclesiastical discipline and constancy of character and strictness (*gravitas*). For by God's help, whatever this master's praiseworthy reputation and religion may have won for him, we grant to you, for the same spirit guides you. We earnestly desire you to visit us soon, so that we may tell you face to face the secrets of our heart [53].

The stability that Paschal saw in Bruno's «vigour of ecclesiastical discipline and constancy of character and strictness» arose from a greater unity and consistency in his years of eremitism than appear at first sight. His transfer from the climatic severities of la Grande Chartreuse to the political dangers of the Calabrian frontier area surrounding La Torre, as occasioned by his

---

[51] As n. 45.
[52] *PL* 151.353, 509, nos. 67, 241. For papal dealings with La Torre, see *IP* 10.63-75.
[53] *PL* 163.78, no. 55, = *IP* 10.69, no. 5.

obedience to Urban II 's summons to Rome, did not mean that he turned his back upon his earlier community; his concern for la Grande Chartreuse persisted to the end of his life. It is to be noticed that his followers and others predominantly referred to him by the personal title of *magister* rather than by the official title of *prior*. Moreover, at both places after 1091 he was commonly named together with his leading associate at either place — Landuin at la Grande Chartreuse and Lanuin at La Torre [54]. He thus maintained a degree of superiority over both; even to the end of his life, he maintained his association with, and at least his moral authority over, la Grande Chartreuse. Therefore towards the end of Bruno's life, Prior Landuin of la Grande Chartreuse travelled to him at La Torre but died upon his return journey, a prisoner in the hand of partisans of the antipope Clement III whom he strongly opposed and whose impenitent death he bewailed [55]. A letter of encouragement that Bruno dispatched in 1099/1100 to his brethren at la Grande Chartreuse has survived. It was written in tones of fatherly

[54] The titles by which Bruno and his principal followers, Landuin at la Grande Chartreuse and Lanuin at La Torre, were known was as follows: *frater*. Used of Bruno by Abbot Seguin of la Chaise-Dieu: *Recueil* (as n. 44), pp. 13-14, no. 4. Used of himself by Bruno from La Torre when addressing his *fratres* at la Grande Chartreuse: *Letters* (as n. 34), p. 82, no. 2.1. Used by Bruno at La Torre when writing of Landuin of la Grande Chartreuse: *Lettres*, pp. 84, 86, no. 2.3,5. *magister*. Used of Bruno in relation to la Grande Chartreuse by Bishop Hugh of Grenoble, Pope Urban II, and Abbot Seguin of la Chaise-Dieu: *Recueil*, pp. 3, 12, 14, nos. 1, 3, 4. Used of Bruno by the monks of la Grande Chartreuse in their Chronicle: *Lettres*, p. 232. Used at La Torre in Prior Lambert's Statutes: C. LE COUTEULX, *Annales ordinis Cartusiensis ab anno 1084 usque ad annum 1429*, 8 vols, Montreuil-sur Mer 1887-8, 1.237-49. Used of Bruno by Pope Paschal II: *Ep*. 55, *PL* 163.78B. Used by Prior Guigo of Bruno in his *Vita S. Hugonis*, 3.11-12, *PL* 153.769C, 770BC, and of Landuin, 3.11, col. 769C. *pater*. Used by the monks of la Grande Chartreuse to introduce Bruno's letter to them from La Torre: *Lettres*, p. 82, no. 2, Incipit. Used of Bruno by the monks of La Torre in their letter about his mortuary roll: *PL* 152.553A. Used of Landuin by Bruno: *Lettres*, pp. 84, 86, no. 2.3, 5. *prior*. Used of Bruno at la Grande Chartreuse by Abbot Seguin of la Chaise-Dieu: *Recueil*, p. 14, no. 4. According to Guigo I, Landuin succeeded Bruno as prior: *Vita S. Hugonis*, 3.11, col. 769C. Bruno at La Torre spoke of Landuin as prior of la Grande Chartreuse: *Lettres* pp. 84, 86, no. 2.3,5. Used of Landuin by Pope Urban II: *Recueil*, p. 16, no. 5. Bruno and Landuin were associated at la Grande Chartreuse by Urban II: *Recueil*, p. 15, no. 5. Bruno and Lanuin were associated at La Torre by Pope Urban II: *Epp* 67, 241, *PL* 151.353A, 509AB, and by Count Roger I of Sicily: F. UGHELLI, *Italia sacra*, new edn. by N. Coleti, 10 vols, Venice 1717-22, 9.426C, cfr. B. TROMBY, *Storia critico-cronologica diplomatica del patriarcha S. Brunone e del suo ordine cartusiano*, 10 vols, Naples 1773-9, 2, App. pp. 301-2 (... *domini Brunonis, et fratris nostri Lanuini eremitarum virorum sanctissimorum consiliis*).

[55] WILMART, *Chronique* (as n. 45), pp. 123-4.

authority, and ended by saying that his principal desire was to come to them and see them [56]. Bruno is not known to have drawn up a Rule or body of Customs for either of his communities. But there is enough in common between the Customs of la Grande Chartreuse as written by Prior Guigo I and those of La Torre as written after Bruno's death by Prior Lambert, a confrère of Bruno who succeeded Lanuin as prior in 1116/20, as well as in the shared characteristic of an eremitical way of life prudently tempered by a little coenobitism, to indicate that Bruno left a similar stamp upon both places [57]. Bruno appears to have been in a real sense their common superior, with an equal and similar commitment to the spiritual welfare of them both.

Secondly, Bruno's sense of stability manifested itself in his insistence, for others as for himself, upon the inviolabilty of a vocation to the religious life, once it had been accepted and sealed by a vow. This is the theme of the long letter that he wrote from La Torre to Ralph *le Verd* [58]. It had been preceded by other communications, both by letter and through personal intermediaries. After praising the superiority of the contemplative to the active life, Bruno urged Ralph, provost though he was of the cathedral of Reims where the cause of reform had been hard-fought, to flee the vexations and miseries of his present employment. Let him transfer from the tempest of this world to the safe and quiet anchorage of the monastic harbour. Bruno pressed to the limit the arguments that were leading contemporary reformers to establish a separation of the sacred from the profane, and so, for example, to rid the church of simony, clerical marriage, and lay investiture. To be a reformer in the world was not enough: Bruno attacked every tie that held Ralph to the world. On the one hand, he should not be attached to his present office, with its deceitful riches and with the status of a provostship whose duties could not be performed without great danger to the soul; on the other hand, he should not be held back from the cloister or the cell from consideration for his archbishop, even though he was the reformed and reforming Manasses II who greatly trusted in and leaned upon his provost's counsels. For it was not easy always to offer counsel that was just or needful; it was better to turn away and to pursue the highest good. Bruno therefore urged Ralph to use a pilgrimage to St Nicholas at Bari as an opportunity to visit La Torre so that they could talk face to face; it was Bruno's hope that

[56] *Lettres*, pp. 82-9, no. 2.

[57] For Guigo, see n. 43, and for Lambert, n. 54. Le Couteulx compares points of similarity and difference.

[58] *Lettres*, pp. 66-81, no. 1.

such a journey might be the means of renewing their common commitment to the monastic life.

There is much in this letter that might serve to call from active service in churches in desperate need of reforming clergy the very clerks upon whom the papacy depended for the implementation of its most cherished aims. Yet the common commitment of Bruno and Ralph must not be forgotten. Bruno was recalling Ralph to a vow of monastic conversion which he had long ago taken in the garden next to the house of a certain Adam. In Bruno's eyes, such a vow was permanently binding under the gravest penalties of divine anger:

> What, then, remains, dearest brother, save for you to free yourself as quickly as you can from bonds of such an obligation, lest you incur the Almighty's wrath for so great and long-standing a reproach of falsehood, and are therefore punished everlastingly?

Bruno's pleas were not addressed to all and sundry, but to a man thus committed; it cannot be presumed that they would have been disowned by Urban II, who had himself transferred by way of a monastic vow from being a canon of Reims to seek the quiet of Cluny, in spite of the needs of Reims in the days of Manasses I.

For, thirdly, both at la Grande Chartreuse and at La Torre, Bruno showed himself responsive in word and deed to the needs of the church at large, as did the Carthusian tradition of the twelfth century that he established[59]. According to Prior Guigo, at la Grande Chartreuse as ruled by Bruno, the diocesan bishop, Hugh of Grenoble, liked to spend prolonged periods of spiritual refreshment. Despite the bishop's earlier monastic interlude at la Chaise-Dieu, Bruno made no attempt to recall him to the religious life but insisted that he return to his troubled and difficult diocese, saying: «Go, go to your own sheep, and pay to them the debt that you owe them»[60]. Bruno's *eremus* of La Torre was established upon the lands of the Norman Count Roger I of Sicily, upon whose political support and goodwill Urban II depended; Bruno's cultivation of good relations with the Norman princes and their followers was to the pope's great advantage[61]. Bruno and

---

[59] See COWDREY (as n. 21).

[60] *Vita S. Hugonis*, 3.12, PL 153.770.

[61] The part played by Count Roger in establishing La Torre is made clear in Urban II, *Epp.* 67, 241, PL 151.353, 409. The many charters for La Torre of both Count Roger I of

Lanuin collaborated in the conversion of the diocese of Squillace from Greek to Latin usages. A charter of Count Roger I expressed the count's regret that, in so famous a city where many Normans were now established, there was as yet no papal and Latin church (*pontificalis et Latina nondum extiterat ecclesia*). With the aid of a papal legate and others who included Bruno and Lanuin, he installed a Latin bishop [62]. From their side, the honour and obligation which the hermits of La Torre felt that they owed to the apostolic see found expression in the opening paragraph of their covering letter to Bruno's mortuary roll:

> To the first place, which we believe and confess to have primacy and headship in the church, and to its whole ruling curia, we, the humble hermits of the Calabrian monastery of St Mary the Mother of God, whose founder and ruler while he was alive in the body was brother Bruno, send honour and greeting in due subjection [63].

A bond of active loyalty and service manifestly persisted between both the communities that Bruno founded and the apostolic see, which the popes acknowledged [64].

It may be concluded that, like eremitical monasticism in general, Bruno's two foundations and the life that was lived in them were not spiritually distant from or incompatible with the aspirations and policies of the reform papacy. As was the case with all new orders at the time, the popes had no part in founding or in shaping Carthusian life; they had to take it as it was presented to them. But by and large they accepted it, and they were eloquent in genuine praise of its founder and of his vision of monastic peace. It was an expression, if an extreme one, of the holy with which the reformers were concerned, that is, of the separateness of true Christians from the

Sicily and Duke Roger I of Apulia which are discussed in Tromby (as n. 54) raise serious and complex problems of authenticity, and they are not used as evidence in this paper. For a summary of the problems, see F. CHALANDON, *Histoire de la domination normande en Italie et en Sicile*, 2 vols, Paris 1907 1.304 n. 2. For Urban II 's dealings in Calabria, and especially for his journey there in 1091 upon which Bruno may have accompanied him and secured his approval for the foundation of La Torre, see H.W. KLEWITZ, *Studien über die Wiederherstellung der römischen Kirche in Süditalien durch das Reformpapsttum*, «Quellen und Forschungen aus italienischen Archiven und Bibliotheken», 25, 1934/5, pp. 105-57, at pp. 121, 123, 136-40, repr. *Reformpapsttum und Kardinalkolleg*, Darmstadt 1957, pp. 157- 8, 160, 177-83.

[62] UGHELLI and TROMBY, (as n. 54).

[63] *PL* 152.553.

[64] Esp. Paschal II (as n. 53).

Probably not long afterwards, Berengar complained in a postscript to a letter that he wrote for Eusebius-Bruno and Count Geoffrey *Martel* of Anjou that he was altogether clear of error and blame, having been defamed most unjustly and unworthily of the apostolic see through the lord pope's intemperance (*immoderantia*).[19].

After the council of Brionne in late 1050, Berengar's complaints against Leo became ever more shrill and sharp[20]. Stung by Leo's statement that he was a heretic, he wrote a tract, subsequently lost, against the pope upon whose name he played as 'by no means holy and by no means a lion from the tribe of Judah.'[21] He extended his strictures to include the pope's personal imprudence at Vercelli in lodging with its bishop, Gregory, who was compromised morally[22], and – repeating a theme of his letter to Eusebius-Bruno – also his readiness, under Cardinal Humbert's influence, to proceed to the 'reordination' of bishops and abbots who had been simoniacally ordained.[23]. In 1050 Berengar had not been personally present at the papal councils of Rome and Vercelli. He was left with a bitter grievance against Leo that he had been condemned unheard and peremptorily[24]. He did not shrink from referring to Leo's judgement at Vercelli as sacrilegious[25]. Even someone who, like Paulinus, *primicerius* of Metz, approved of Berengar's eucharistic teaching reproved him for using this adjective of the pope[26]. As time went by polemical writers hostile to him became increasingly censorious. Durandus of Troarn took exception to Berengar's having branded Leo a heretic[27]. Bernold of St Blasien reported still more extravagant slanders that Berengar uttered against the pope and the apostolic see, dubbing the holy pope Leo not *pontifex* but *pompifex* (pomp-maker) and *pulpifex* (flesh-maker); in words and writing he did not fear to call the holy Roman church a council of vanity and a church of the malignant, and the Roman see not apostolic but the seat of Satan[28].

It is clear that observers extended Leo's own positive and consistent rejection of Berengar's eucharistic teaching to the Roman see in

---

19  EF no. 85, p. 147/12-14.
20  See Montclos, pp. 94-103.
21  *RCL* i. 205-11, p. 41.
22  *RCL* i. 340-64, p. 45.
23  *RCL* i. 365-86, pp. 45-6.
24  *RCL* i. 274-90, 393-426, 462-6, pp. 43, 46-7, 48.
25  *RCL* i. 412-14, p. 47.
26  Huygens, 'Textes latins', p. 467, n. 16.
27  *Liber de corpore et sanguine Christi*, ix, PL cxlix. 1422B.
28  *De veritate corporis et sanguinis Domini*, PL cxlviii. 1456AB = Huygens, 'Bérenger', pp. 381/85-382/96; cf. Berengar's comments as cited by Lanfranc, *DC* 426AB, 430AB.

its corporate capacity, particularly as afforced in councils by bishops, abbots, and others from the church at large. According to Lanfranc, the reading out of Berengar's letter to him that had given rise to suspicion that he sympathized with his former master's teaching led to Berengar's case being raised with the apostolic see[29]; in council it was not only the pope but the whole body present that officially if provisionally condemned him[30].

There can be no mistaking the dominance of Cardinal Humbert in the Rome of Leo IX, or the decisiveness of his views on the eucharist as on reordinations[31]. This was already clear in his letter of 1050/1 to Bishop Eusebius–Bruno of Angers, which he began by stating that he wrote on behalf of the pope who was absent, and continued by blaming the bishop for his eucharistic views as for his murmuring against Leo's 'reordinations'. Humbert brushed aside his complaints with masterful authority and insisted upon the teaching magisterium of the Roman see[32]. Lanfranc confirms Humbert's standing and authority[33]. He further illuminates how matters stood at Rome by lamenting that the 'leaking' of Berengar's letter to himself[34] falsely caused many at the Roman council of 1050 to think that he favoured Berengar's teaching[35]. When expounding his true position, Lanfranc claimed that 'it pleased all and displeased no one'[36]. One other key figure of the Roman church is known by name to have opposed Berengar. At Vercelli, Peter, a member of a Roman family who was a deacon of the Roman church and since 1044 its *bibliothecarius* and *cancellarius*[37], sharply criticized a figurative understanding of the eucharist: 'si adhuc in figura sumus', he asked, 'quando rem tenebimus?'[38]

---

29  Montclos, p. 54, n. 1 = Huygens, 'Textes latins', p. 456; *DC* 413AB = Huygens, 'Bérenger', p. 375/160 – 75.
30  *DC* 413A–C = Huygens, 'Bérenger', pp. 375/160 – 376/185; EF no. 85, p. 147/12 – 14; cf. *EA* 68D for the council of Vercelli.
31  Humbert was certainly present at the Roman council of 1050: Leo IX, *Ep.* 38, PL cxliii. 646D.
32  *EH* pp. 614/9 – 615/7.
33  *DC* 410A–C = Huygens, 'Bérenger', p. 372/77 – 9 (partly).
34  Above, n. 29.
35  *DC* 413AB = Huygens, 'Bérenger', pp. 375/160 – 376/180.
36  *DC* 413B = Huygens, 'Bérenger', p. 376/183 – 5.
37  For Peter, see L. Santifaller, 'Saggio di un elenco dei funzionari, impiegati e scrittori della cancellaria pontificia dall'inizio all'anno 1099', *Bullettino dell'Istituto storico Italiano per il medio evo e Archivio Muratoriano*, lvi (1940), pp. 140 – 2, and R. Hüls, *Kardinäle, Klerus und Kirchen Roms, 1049 – 1130* (Tübingen, 1977), pp. 252 – 3.
38  *RCL* i. 438 – 40, p. 48.

How did Berengar at this time regard the authority of the pope and of the apostolic see? He shared the general preparedness to look to Rome, and even hoped for a vindication there of his teachings. He could express reverence for the Roman church and its pontiff[39]. Before the council of Vercelli, he hoped, in a political context, to enlist Leo IX's aid in securing his freedom from imprisonment by King Henry I of France[40]. At Tours in 1054 he referred unequivocally to Hildebrand's authority as legate on the pope's behalf[41]. In the letter that, early in 1059, he wrote to Hildebrand in the name of Count Geoffrey of Anjou, he recalled the hopes that he had placed in Hildebrand, although they had been disappointed[42]. Nevertheless he felt scandalized at having been condemned unforewarned and unheard in 1050[43]. Before writing of Leo IX's intemperateness towards himself, he remarked in the body of the letter that he wrote for Bishop Eusebius–Bruno and the count of Anjou that an appeal lay open to Christ as a higher judge than the pope[44]. For himself, Berengar seized upon what pretexts he could to evade judgement when an adverse result seemed likely. In face of Leo's condemnation at Vercelli he claimed that he could not be compelled to appear even before the pope at a tribunal meeting neither at Rome nor in his own ecclesiastical province[45]. Whatever his hopes of Hildebrand at Tours, he was glad of the pretext of Leo IX's death and so of the extinction of Hildebrand's legatine authority for not accompanying Hildebrand back to Rome[46]. If Berengar appreciated the advantages of a Roman judgement when it might be in his favour, he was wary when the outcome might be in doubt.

So far as Pope Victor II (1054–7) is concerned, the sole evidence is Lanfranc's observation, made after proclaiming Leo IX's steadfastness, that he measured up to it[47]. So far as is known, it was only with Pope Nicholas II's council at Rome in April 1059 that the Berengarian controversy was again on the papal agenda. This council saw the apogee of Humbert's anti–Berengarian zeal. He drew up the forceful but crudely formulated profession of faith that was forced upon Ber-

---

39  *RCL* i. 398–400, 417–24, pp. 46, 47.
40  *RCL* i. 405–11, 515–26, pp. 47, 50.
41  *RCL* i. 590–3, 603–6, pp. 52–3.
42  EF no. 87, p. 149/8–19.
43  *RCL* i. 405–26, 456–69, pp. 47, 48–9.
44  EF no. 85, pp. 146/1–9, 147/10–11.
45  *RCL* i. 393–405, pp. 46–7.
46  *RCL* i. 661–70, p. 54.
47  *DC* 413D = Huygens, 'Bérenger', pp. 376/199–377/203.

engar, who was present[48]. An understanding of Nicholas's own role is made difficult by the presentation of proceedings in the later writings of Berengar and Lanfranc. Berengar wrote his *Scriptum contra synodum* soon after he returned to France; it survives only in twenty-three fragments that Lanfranc included in his *De corpore et sanguine Domini* of the middle 1060s. Berengar's purpose was to discredit the pope and the council, but above all to concentrate upon Humbert's alleged self-contradictions and undermining of the Catholic faith[49]. In reply, Lanfranc, who was not present at the council but who was of one mind with Humbert, was at pains to set its authority on the broadest possible base. He said that Humbert was the servant and spokesman of the church. His formulation of eucharistic orthodoxy had the sanction of the pope and of the council, and also of subsequent acceptance throughout Latin Christendom:

> You asked [Lanfranc told Berengar] Pope Nicholas and his council to hand you verbally the statement of faith that should be maintained and to confirm it in writing. Responsibility for doing this was placed upon Bishop Humbert. He therefore wrote the statement of faith that is given above, and with general approval he handed it to you to read and profess. ... Pope Nicholas, rejoicing in your change of mind (*conversio*), dispatched your sworn statement in writing throughout the cities of Italy, France, and Germany, and to whatever places the rumour of your depravity might hitherto have come ...[50].

Had matters been as neat and definitive as Lanfranc claimed, it would be hard to account for the uncertainties that remained at Rome and elsewhere into the 1060s and 1070s,[51] or for the refinements upon Humbert's formulation that were required before Berengar could be effectively silenced. Nevertheless, Berengar's writings corroborate Lanfranc's implication of firm papal leadership when he presented the council of 1059 as Nicholas's council, his depiction of

48  *DC* 410C – 412A = Huygens, 'Bérenger', pp. 372/73 – 107, 374/132 – 375/155.

49  Berengar's view of the limits of papal authority is further apparent in his assertion that, after his death on 14 Nov. 1060, Count Geoffrey Martel was saved despite excommunication by Pope Leo IX: EF no.103, pp. 171 – 2.

50  *DC* 411D – 412A = Huygens, 'Bérenger', pp. 374/132 – 175/144.

51  E.g. the position of Archbishop Alfanus I of Salerno as indicated by the letter of a friend or pupil to Berengar edited in the Appendix to R.W. Southern, 'Lanfranc of Bec and Berengar of Tours', in: *Studies in Medieval History presented to Frederick Maurice Powicke*, edd. R.W. Hunt, W.A. Pantin, and R.W. Southern (Oxford, 1948), pp. 47 – 8. Southern's date for the letter is probably to be accepted: H.E.J. Cowdrey, *The Age of Abbot Desiderius. Montecassino, the Papacy and the Normans in the Eleventh and Early Twelfth Centuries* (Oxford, 1983), p. 91, n. 158.

the pope's rejoicing at Berengar's alleged *conversio*, and his impression of the council as an occasion when the pope and the assembled clergy possessed and exercised effective authority. As for Lanfranc[52], so for Berengar the pope was an active chairman. Berengar was cheated of his hopes. He had come by Hildebrand's courteous invitation[53], and he had done so willingly[54]. He had kept silent for most of the proceedings; after this restraint, he reproved the pope for having, as it were, thrown him to the wild beasts in the arena. He requested another kind of hearing, whether privately with the pope or with a small circle of theologically competent bishops; the pope merely and perhaps ironically suggested that he confide in Hildebrand[55]. Nicholas's decisive position and hostile stance are also suggested by Berengar's outraged aspersions upon him as a man whose lack of learning and moral worthiness he could, if he chose, enlarge upon[56]. Although Berengar also hinted at sympathy from some[57], he confirmed that his reception from the council as a whole was hostile. When his opinions were put to it, its members stopped their ears and rejected them[58]. It may be concluded that, under Nicholas II as under Leo IX, Berengar's teachings were repugnant to the pope himself. In the Roman councils of 1050 and 1059, the prevailing, although perhaps not quite the universal, reaction was likewise adverse.

Under Pope Alexander II (1061–73), both at Rome and in Anjou circumstances changed so far as Berengar and his cause were concerned. At Rome, his most determined adversaries were removed from the scene. Cardinal Humbert died in May 1061 a few months before Nicholas II; it was probably to Berengar's advantage that, from 1057 until his death in 1072, Peter Damiani was cardinal-bishop of Ostia and a prominent Roman figure. Lanfranc did not return to the city until 1067, briefly and upon ducal business, and in 1071, as archbishop of Canterbury. From 1058/9 Hildebrand, to whom Berengar had looked for sympathy, was archdeacon at Rome, and therefore more concerned with local affairs[59]. If matters at Rome became better for Berengar, in Anjou they became worse. The death in November 1060 of Count Geoffrey *Martel* robbed him of a friendly prince. His

---

52 *DC* 415BC.
53 EF no. 87, p. 149/7.
54 *RCL* i. 1122–7, p. 67.
55 *RCL* i. 1112–27, pp. 66–7.
56 *RCL* i. 1086–9, p. 66.
57 *RCL* i. 933–41, p. 62.
58 *RCL* i. 903–12, 1112–26, pp. 61, 67.
59 For the date of Hildebrand's archidiaconate, see D. Jasper, *Das Papstwahldekret von 1059. Überlieferung und Textgestalt* (Sigmaringen, 1986), pp. 34–46.

successors, Geoffrey *le Barbu* (1060–8) and Fulk *le Réchin*
(1067/8–1109) were hostile. Berengar was for long unable to discharge his duties as archdeacon or even to enter the city of Angers[60].
Bishop Eusebius-Bruno, for so long his patron if not his leader,
found it politic to assume a posture of neutrality, if not of hostility,
towards him[61].

A little light upon the situation in Anjou is shed by an exchange of
letters between Berengar and Eusebius-Bruno after a council held at
Angers in 1062 in the chapel of Countess Hildegard, widow of Count
Fulk *Nerra*[62]. The leading figures present, besides Berengar, were
Archbishop Hugh of Besançon and Bishops Eusebius-Bruno of Angers and Vulgrin of le Mans. It seems that Count Geoffrey *le Barbu*
wished to benefit from the presence of an influential archbishop by
damping down the potentially dangerous eucharistic controversy. To
this end, no more was to be required as a public profession of faith
than an assent to New Testament passages about the eucharist as
enshrined in the canon of the Latin mass[63]. After his experience at
Rome in 1059 when he was made to throw into the flames the catena
of *prophetica, evangelica et apostolica scripta* that he had hitherto
relied upon[64], Berengar appears from a letter to Eusebius-Bruno to
have been content for the present to accept this solution. He wrote to
the bishop because, after the council, a canon of Angers named Geoffrey Martini had fallen out of line by ostentatiously propounding
Lanfranc's teaching. Berengar asked his bishop to restrain the
canon's temerity or else to arrange a debate before competent judges
in which Berengar and Geoffrey Martini could test the acceptability
by biblical standards of St Ambrose's *De sacramentis*. Berengar made
no mention of other church fathers, or of 'John the Scot'.

In reply, Eusebius-Bruno refused to sanction further discussion.
While not despising the words of the fathers, he preferred to rest
upon those of the Gospels, and he defended the ruling of the recent
council by simply citing the anodyne section *Qui pridie* of the canon
of the mass. His policy was evidently one of *quieta non movere*: the
decision taken at Angers was final; matters at issue had three times
been settled by episcopal judgement in the province concerned (he
referred to the councils at Tours in 1051/2 and 1054, and at Angers in
1062), and on a fourth occasion (at the Roman council of 1059) a
synod of the apostolic see had set it to rest.

60 EF no. 100, p. 167/18–25.
61 EF no. 100, p. 168/3–8.
62 EF no. 86, p. 147–8, *EE.*
63 Montclos, pp. 203–5.
64 *RCL* i. 850–2, 877–83, pp. 59, 60.

If the controversy was thus damped down in Anjou, at Rome Alexander II seems to have continued though with some mitigation his predecessors' tradition of antipathy to Berengar's teachings. Bernold of St Blasien later wrote of an exchange of letters in which the pope had sent Berengar a friendly but firm warning to refrain from his heresy (*secta*) and no longer to give offence to holy church; Berengar had been so bold as to send a written refusal to obey[65]. In 1072, Lanfranc, who may have discussed the Berengarian controversy with Alexander during his visit to Rome in 1071, referred to his having, as commanded, sent the pope a copy of his 'letter to the schismatic Berengar' – the *De corpore et sanguine Domini*[66]. It was, perhaps, the first copy of Lanfranc's treatise to reach Rome. Berengar's own letters suggest that Alexander nevertheless presented a personally friendly face. He had sent a verbal, though not a written, benediction through Provost Rahard of Orleans and Bishop Quiriacus of Nantes[67]. Berengar responded with alacrity to Rahard's intimation that the pope wished to send a young kinsman to study with him[68]; however, it rested upon a misunderstanding.

There is nothing to suggest that, between 1061 and 1073, Berengar's eucharistic teachings were formally considered at Rome. Whether before or after Lanfranc's visit of 1071, informal discussions may have exposed differences of view. In his Memoir of the Roman councils of 1078 and 1079, Berengar represented Pope Gregory VII as testifying publicly to Peter Damiani's having sided with Berengar's approach as against Lanfranc's, and to his own concurrence with Peter Damiani:

> He [Gregory] testified to everyone in his hearing [Berengar wrote], that Peter Damiani was not Lanfranc's inferior in the polish of his learning or the excellence of his Christian teaching. At Rome Peter Damiani had not agreed with Lanfranc's pronouncements about the sacrifice of the church [i.e. the eucharist]. He [Gregory] gave his own opinion for Peter: what Lanfranc had said should be set aside rather than what Peter had said.[69]

---

65 *De veritate corporis et sanguinis Domini*, PL cxlviii. 1456BC = Huygens, 'Bérenger', p. 382/97-100.

66 *The Letters of Lanfranc, Archbishop of Canterbury*, edd. and trans. H. Clover and M. Gibson (Oxford, 1979), no. 4, p. 56/119-21.

67 EF no. 100, p. 168/1-3.

68 EF no. 100, p. 168/14-15.

69 *Mem.* 103BC = Huygens, 'Bérenger', pp. 388/18-389/25. In his writings Peter Damiani took a realist view: *De variis miraculosis narrationibus*, Op. 34, Prol., *De castitate*, Op. 47,2, PL cxlv. 573A-C, 712B-D.

Berengar's principal known contact with the Roman church while Alexander was pope was not Hildebrand but the cardinal-priest Stephen of San Grisogono, a Burgundian and perhaps former Cluniac who had accompanied Leo IX to Rome[70]. As Alexander's legate, Stephen in 1060 held a council at Tours during which, although eucharistic teaching does not seem to have been discussed, he visited the church of Saint-Martin and may have met Berengar informally[71]. After the tribulations that followed the succession of Count Geoffrey *le Barbu*, Berengar wrote Stephen a cordial letter[72], in which he recognized him to be well disposed and the only, or at least the most appropriate, Roman person for him to approach. Berengar hoped for papal protection in a letter that he asked Stephen to procure; Berengar would reward him liberally and reimburse his expenses. No certainly genuine letter of Alexander in Berengar's favour survives, but there is a series of four letters in the pope's name that Berengar probably himself drafted – to himself, with an exhortation to steadfastness in persecution for righteousness' sake; to the archbishop of Tours and the bishop of Angers in which Berengar was said to be the pope's *confrater* whom the prelates were to urge the count not to vex; and two letters to the count himself, charging him to spare Berengar, ultimately on pain of anathema[73]. Berengar clearly set value upon papal protection when he needed it. He also continued to draft letters to the pope on behalf of others in which he did not neglect to mention his own plight.[74]. A reference to the letters in Alexander's name suggests that his compositions were sometimes written, not for dispatch, but as local, anti-comital propaganda[75]. However this may be, they add to the impression that Berengar entertained hopes of sympathy and understanding from Alexander and his Roman entourage.

---

70  Hüls, *Kardinäle, Klerus und Kirchen Roms*, pp. 169 – 70.

71  *Narratio controversiae inter capitulum S. Martini Turonensis et Radulphum eiusdem urbis archiepiscopum*, RHGF xii. 460A.

72  EF no. 100, pp. 167 – 8.

73  *EB* = JL 4546, 4588, 4547, 4601 (in probable chronological order). For their composition see C. Erdmann, 'Gregor VII. und Berengar von Tours', *Quellen und Forschungen aus italienischen Archiven und Bibliotheken*, xxviii (1937), 48 – 74, at pp. 52 – 4. However, O. Capitani, 'Per la storia dei rapporti tra Gregorio VII e Berengario di Tours', *Studi Gregoriani*, vi (1959 – 61), 99 – 145, at pp. 104 – 5, has reservations about Erdmann's conclusions.

74  For Archbishop Bartholomew of Tours: EF no. 90, pp. 155 – 7; for Bishop Eusebius-Bruno of Angers: EF no. 91, pp. 157 – 9; for Archbishop Bartholomew of Tours: EF no. 94, pp. 160 – 1.

75  EF no. 90, p. 156/30 – 1.

Whereas his predecessors maintained a straightforward and open opposition to Berengar's teachings, Pope Gregory VII (1073–85) adopted an approach that is more complex and hard to understand. It must be approached by way of his almost twenty years of sporadic concern with them since, as a young subdeacon of the Roman church, he attended the council of Tours in 1054 as Leo IX's legate. His conduct of its proceedings was characterized by dispassionate orderliness and moderation[76]. He seems to have begun by holding private talks with Berengar at which the latter expounded his views and supported them by citing many prophetic, New Testament, and patristic texts[77]. Once the council had assembled in the church of Saint-Maurice, however, there was no more general discussion[78]. In his private talks as in public session, Hildebrand's concern was to establish what Berengar's teachings were, not to pass immediate judgement upon them. He allowed the council a choice of two procedures: it might either attempt a survey of eucharistic teaching by searching the library of marked books with which he had come provided, or it might allow Berengar to state his beliefs and to pass a judgement of its own. The council opted for the second procedure, but deputed the hearing to the archbishop of Tours and the bishops of Orleans and Auxerre. They privately brought Berengar to declare that, after the eucharistic consecration, the bread and wine on the altar are truly (*revera*) the body and blood of Christ[79]. After further debate in full session, Berengar grudgingly agreed to make a written and sworn profession to this effect[80]. Hildebrand then turned to other business, having safely reached a position at which Berengar's case could be reserved for a definitive hearing at Rome[81]. But tidings of Leo's death, which terminated Hildebrand's legatine authority, enabled Berengar to evade the journey. His reason is not stated; no doubt he wished at least to be sure that the new pope was not someone of Cardinal Humbert's mind or temper.

Berengar included a retrospect of the council of Tours in a letter that he wrote to Hildebrand in 1059 in the name of Count Geoffrey *Martel.* Four points emerge about Hildebrand's conduct. First, he maintained that there must eventually be a clear doctrinal solution to the eucharistic question that could be communicated to Christians everywhere at all social and cultural levels.

---

76 *RCL* i. 590–670, pp. 52–4; EF no. 87, pp. 148–52.
77 *RCL* i. 590–606, p. 52; see Montclos, pp. 149–62.
78 EF no. 87, p. 149/23–5.
79 *RCL* i. 606–29, p. 53.
80 *RCL* i. 629–50, p. 54.
81 *RCL* i. 651–60, p. 54.

> I hear [Berengar wrote] that those who are evidently ashamed of Christ and of his words so covered over their fears when you were with us [at the council] as to say that it was no business of such an occasion to debate what a Christian should believe about the body and blood of Christ. You were then at no little pains to insist to the abbot of Saint-Aubin [of Angers] that every effort must be made to understand it, for it would run counter to the needs of Christianity if the crowd were abandoned to its error.[82]

Secondly, Hildebrand insisted that the papacy was the forum in which the question would be settled finally and certainly. 'You boasted', Berengar reminded him, 'and made it as it were your wager of battle, that your own Rome was always invincible in faith as in arms.'[83] Thirdly, to Berengar's chagrin Hildebrand had refrained from condemning his (Berengar's) opponents.

> You feared to maintain Berengar's cause and, after his adversaries had assembled, to meet him apart from the crowd. You kept absolutely aloof from excommunicating the fool who anathematized all who denied that the bread did not remain upon the Lord's table, although you perfectly well knew that he did this with impious boldness against the truth of sound doctrine.[84]

So, fourthly, although Hildebrand's arrival at Tours had been awaited as that of an angel, he had disappointed Berengar's expectation of his positive support. 'Although you learnt about the falsehood of the charge of heresy brought against [Berengar] by most evil men who unalterably blackened him with the smoke of envy and pride, you in no way brought to bear the censure of the apostolic office by championing the truth or confounding his adversaries.' Berengar castigated Hildebrand for being like Joseph of Arimathaea who was 'a disciple secretly for fear of the Jews', and like Pontius Pilate who found Christ innocent but did not use his authority to save his life[85].

There is nothing to suggest that the young Hildebrand shared or even sympathized with Berengar's eucharistic teachings as such, or that his personal credo was other than that of Leo IX. But its formulation was an open question. At Tours he kept his detachment from all points of view and did not declare his own, if indeed his mind was made up about how best to express the doctrine of the eucharistic presence. He came provided, not with any formula or vocabulary, but with an anthology of ancient authorities from which the truth might

82  EF no. 87, p. 151/18–25. On this letter, see O. Capitani, 'La lettera di Goffredo il Martello conte d'Angiò a Ildebrando (1059), *Studi Gregoriani*, v (1956), 19–31.
83  EF no. 87, p. 152/4–5.
84  EF no. 87, pp. 149/23–150/2.
85  EF no. 87, p. 149/10–23.

be sought. He may have welcomed the profession to which Berengar swore, that the bread and wine were *revera* Christ's body and blood; although ambiguous, it could be interpreted according to the mind of Leo IX. But only at Rome, and by the apostolic see itself, could the searching of traditional sources provide an authoritative statement.

Berengar's letter further establishes that, by 1059, Hildebrand had written, perhaps more than once, inviting Berengar to Nicholas II's Roman council. Its salutation foreshadowed its content: 'Count Geoffrey to Hildebrand, a venerable son of the Roman church, may he conduct himself as one not unworthy of such a mother.'[86] Berengar was insistent that, when he came to Rome, Hildebrand should be his advocate:

> Behold the acceptable time! Behold, you now have Berengar present with the pope! If you yet again defer to the error of fools, it will be crystal clear that you did not formerly [at Tours] act reasonably in deferring the matter to an acceptable time, but that from weak-mindedness and fear you wholly failed to protect the cause of the innocent. If, which heaven forbid! history repeats itself, we shall assuredly have fallen from our great hope in you, and you will certainly have committed no small offence against yourself, not to say against God. You will deservedly be judged to have been a most perverse 'dayspring from the east' which came to us in the west not 'to lighten our darkness' but rather, so far as in you lay, altogether to darken our daylight.[87]

In conclusion, Berengar followed his recollection that Hildebrand had vaunted *Roma fide et armis semper invicta* by urging him that

> you will in no small measure contradict your own boasting if, at a time when God wished you to shine forth before all others at the apostolic see, the error that is most assuredly the seedbed of heresy were to gain strength through dissimulation on your part and through the silence of papal dithering.[88]

In the event, Hildebrand's part during the hearing of Berengar's case in 1059 seems to have been marginal. As the new archdeacon, Hildebrand had other concerns[89]; Humbert took the lead against Berengar. Only as proceedings were concluded did the pope rather dismissively

---

86 EF no. 87, p. 149/5–6.
87 EF no. 87, pp. 150/32–151/9; p. 151/5–9 appears to echo the canticle *Benedictus Dominus Deus Israel*: cf. Luke 1: 78–9.
88 EF no. 87, p. 152/4–9.
89 See esp. A. Werminghoff, 'Die Beschlüsse des Aachener Concils im Jahre 816', *Neues Archiv der Gesellschaft für ältere deutsche Geschichtskunde*, xxvii (1901–2), 605–75, at pp. 669–75.

invite Berengar to consult Hildebrand [90]. It was probably no more than an invitation to seek a little balm after the bruising that Berengar received at Humbert's hands.

Gregory's continuing concern during his early years as pope to resolve Berengar's case is manifest in a letter that Berengar sent him between 1075 and 1078[91]. Berengar wrote cordially, even obsequiously: 'To Pope Gregory, to be received with all reverence in Jesus Christ, Berengar sends every possible offering of love unfeigned.'[92] Three times he addressed him as *pater optime*[93]. It transpires from the letter that, some time before, whether while still archdeacon or more probably since 1073, Gregory had charged Berengar through Durand, a subdeacon and canon of Angers, to keep strict silence whenever he was challenged about his eucharistic teachings. Berengar had complied *quantum oportebat*, a phrase implying that he had not felt bound to silence except when under challenge[94]. Gregory had twice, by Bishop Eusebius-Bruno of Angers and then by Bishop Quiriacus of Nantes, intimated to Berengar that he might soon have a chance of presenting his case personally to Gregory at Rome [95]. Berengar nevertheless expressed surprise that Gregory's dispositions had been ignored by persons who had come to France under papal authority. He perhaps had in mind Cardinal-bishop Gerald of Ostia, a sometime Cluniac who held a council at Poitiers in 1075 during which Berengar, who was apparently so rash as to call in question the orthodoxy of the local patron St Hilary, was nearly lynched; and also Bishop Hugh of Die, to whom Berengar thanked Gregory for sending a letter (since lost) in his support.[96] Berengar insisted that, when he came to Rome, he expected to meet Gregory in private audience[97]. In language that echoed his repugnance at his public treatment in 1059, he disclaimed any obligation to appear before suspect or hostile

90  *RCL* i. 1126–7, p. 67.
91  EF no. 89, pp. 154–5.
92  EF no. 89, p. 154/24–5; cf. the political prudence and pastoral tact of Berengar's letter to King Philip I of France: EF no. 82, pp. 132–6.
93  EF no. 89, pp. 154/27, 155/12, 19.
94  EF 89, p. 155/2–6, accepting Erdmann's emendation *per Durandum* for *perdurandum.*
95  EF no. 89, p. 155/5–11.
96  EF no. 89, p. 154/1–5 (EF no. 93, p. 160, may also allude to events at Poitiers); *Ex Chronico S. Maxentii quod vulgariter Malleacense dicitur, a.* 1075, RHGF xii. 401A; cf. *The Letters of Lanfranc,* edd. Clover and Gibson, no. 46, pp. 142–51. For the council of Poitiers, see R. Somerville, 'The Case against Berengar of Tours – a New Text', *Studi Gregoriani,* ix (1972), 53–75.
97  EF no. 89, p. 155/7.

judges[98]. In the event, Berengar travelled to Rome in the mid-winter of 1077-8 and stayed in the city for about one year[99].

The months after his arrival were marked by progaganda for and against his opinions. A calm and measured treatise, probably by a disciple rather than by himself, advocated them[100]. Another Berengar, perhaps Bishop Berengar of Venosa, addressed to Gregory VII an energetic rebuttal, expressing confidence that what Pope Gregory I had taught about the eucharist his namesake would, by divine purpose, confirm[101]. Bishop Bruno of Segni referred to philosophical disputes in which Berengar led his audience to impossible conclusions[102], while Peter the Deacon much later referred to his irresistable power of argument[103]. Berengar himself was to take another Cassinese monk, Alberic, to task for having at this time shared his point of view but for turning his coat in 1079[104]. Gregory himself gave Berengar's case consideration; his letter of 7 May 1078 to Abbot Hugh of Cluny reveals that, in reply to the abbot's inquiry, Gregory sent verbal information about his own opinions and intentions[105].

Much light, if from a partial source, is shed upon events at Rome in late 1078 by Berengar's Memoir - his *historia calamitatum* of the years 1078-9 that he wrote soon afterwards. It opens with a meeting of bishops in the Lateran on 1 November 1078, and so in advance of

98  EF no. 89, p. 155/12-18.

99  *Mem.* 103C = Huygens, 'Bérenger', p. 389/30-1.

100  M. Matronola, *Un testo inedito di Berengario di Tours e il concilio Romano del 1079* (Milan, 1936); for its authorship, cf. Montclos, pp. 7-8.

101  G. Morin, 'Bérenger contre Bérenger. Un document inédit des luttes théologiques du xie siècle', *Recherches de théologie ancienne et médiévale*, iv (1932), 109-33, at pp. 117-33; for the citation, see p. 124/32-5.

102  *Expositio in Leviticum*, cap. 7, PL clxiv. 404C.

103  *De viris illustribus Casinensibus opusculum*, cap. 21, PL clxxiii. 1033AB.

104  P. Meyvaert, 'Bérenger de Tours contre Albéric du Mont-Cassin', *Revue bénédictine*, lxx (1960), 324-32, text at pp. 331-2.

105  *Reg.* v. 21, p. 384/27-9. Anti-Berengarian works appear to have entered the library at Cluny at a relatively early date: see the great wall-catalogue of 570 items published by L. Delisle, *Le Cabinet des manuscrits de la Bibliothèque nationale*, 4 vols. (Paris, 1868-81), ii. 458-81, nos. 373 (the lost work of Jotsald), 433 (Lanfranc), and 565 (Guitmund). Although Delisle dated the catalogue to the time of Abbot Hugh III (1158-61), Mme Veronika von Büren has argued strongly that most of it belongs to that of Abbot Hugh I (1049-1109): paper read to the Colloquium on 'Le Gouvernement d'Hugues de Semur à Cluny', Cluny, 14-17 Sept. 1988 (to be published). For another view of the significance of *Reg.* v. 21, see M. Gibson, 'The Case of Berengar of Tours', in: *Councils and Assemblies*, edd. G.J. Cuming and D. Baker, Studies in Church History, vii (Cambridge, 1971, 61-8, at pp. 67-8.

the full November council that began on 19 November. Berengar cited a profession of faith that was prepared for the All Saintstide meeting:

I profess that, after the consecration, the bread on the altar is the true body of Christ, which was born of the Virgin, which suffered on the Cross, which is seated at the right hand of the Father, and that the wine on the altar which is afterwards consecrated is the true blood that flowed from Christ's side.[106]

While this profession was patient of an orthodox construction, it could also be taken in a sense that Berengar could accept; therefore he welcomed it. Gregory (he said) caused it to be read in ringing tones so that all present might hear, and the pope approved it though in cautious terms: it should suffice as a statement of faith, particularly for simple Christians 'to whom milk should be given rather than solid food'. He assured the assembly that Berengar was no heretic but that he based his teaching upon good written tradition. It was in this context that Gregory cited Peter Damiani's *nihil obstat* for Berengar's teachings[107].

Berengar commented that Gregory seemed thereby to have quietened the folly of those who deemed him a heretic. He claimed that Gregory did so the more effectively because, before the All Saintstide meeting, he widely canvassed amongst the regular and secular clergy of all grades a catena of excerpts from Augustine, Jerome, Ambrose, and other fathers of the church. No doubt it was the same as, or similar to, the patristic anthology that he had brought to Tours in 1054[108]. Berengar dropped names of those who went along with his own view of the eucharist (*mecum sentientes*) as drawn from these passages: Bishop John of Porto, Bishop Bruno of Segni, Bishop Ambrose of Terracina, Cardinal Atto of Milan, Cardinal Deusdedit, Peter the papal chancellor, the French clerk Fulco, the learned Tethbaldus, a monk named Bonadies, and many others[109]. It should be noticed that Berengar did not claim that Gregory or these associates fully assented to his teachings, or that there was an identity, as opposed to a compatibility, of view. Rather, in the light of the newly-prepared profession, they regarded Berengar's teachings as being intrinsically acceptable when set against the background of early Christian authorities.

According to the Memoir, at the end of the assembly Gregory offered to have Berengar confirm his profession by an oath to be

---

106 *Mem.* 103A = Huygens, 'Bérenger', p. 388/4–9.
107 *Mem.* 103A–C = Huygens, 'Bérenger', p. 388/10–389/30; see above, p. 12.
108 See above, p. 14.
109 *Mem.* 103DE = Huygens, 'Bérenger', pp. 390/38–391/47.

taken in its hearing. If the assembly wished, the oath might be supported by an ordeal by hot iron, presumably to establish his sincerity in taking it, which would be undergone by someone of his circle. But on the evening before the ordeal was to take place, Abbot Desiderius of Montecassino unexpectedly visited Berengar to tell him that the pope had cancelled both the oath and the ordeal[110]. According to Berengar, Gregory's volte face was the result of an intervention by hostile persons who urged the necessity of a more public ventilation of the eucharistic controversy in the Lent council of 1079. Berengar heaped blame and vituperation upon Bishops Ulrich of Padua and Landulf of Pisa[111].

For events at the Lent council which opened on 11 February, Berengar's Memoir must be set against the perfervidly anti-Berengarian record in Gregory's Register[112]. This record opens with a reference to a sermon on the body and blood of Christ; the preacher is not named. It is implied but not stated that it was the first act of the council. Before it was delivered, most of those present (*maxima pars*) held, with full warrant from the Greek and Latin fathers, that the bread and wine of the eucharist were changed *substantialiter* into Christ's body and blood, while others blindly (*quidam cecitate nimia et longa perculsi*) advanced a figurative view. The summary of the Berengarian view is partly erased and manifestly incomplete[113]. The words erased suggest that the scribe was making a garbled attempt to record Berengar's view that, to safeguard the Christian doctrine of the resurrection, the real presence of Christ's risen body was to be located in one place at the Father's right hand in heaven, not in innumerable scattered fragments upon earthly altars[114].

Next, offering a clearer sequence of events, the official record stated that, when Berengar's case began to be dealt with and before the council assembled for its third day (13 February), the Berengarian party 'ceased to strive against the truth (*defecit contra veritatem niti*)'. The reason given was a sudden and dramatic manifestation of the Holy Spirit[115]. This is unexplained, but it suggests some such miracu-

---

110 *Mem.* 108AB = Huygens, 'Bérenger', p. 400/257-65.

111 *Mem.* 103C-104C = Huygens, 'Bérenger', pp. 391/47-393/74.

112 *Reg.* vi. 17a, pp. 425/17-427/15.

113 'Quidam vero cecitate nimia et longa perculsi figuram tantum se et alios decipientes quibusdam cavillationibus conabantur astruere.' After *tantum* the words 'quę substantiale illud corpus in dextera patris sedens esse' are erased.

114 *PE* pp. 530-5, esp. 530/6-8, 534/76-80; EF no. 87, pp. 151/31-152/3.

115 'Nempe sancti Spiritus ignis emolumenta palearum consumens et ful-

lous vindication of the anti–Berengarian party as was later the subject of discussion, perhaps a sign at an early-morning mass which was interpreted as meaning that the adverb *substantialiter* must be adopted[116]. Whatever happened, Berengar, *huius erroris magister*, now confessed his longstanding fault, and asked and received a papal pardon. He made a profession expressing the view of the eucharist that had been so dramatically vindicated:

> I Berengar believe in my heart and confess with my lips that the bread and wine that are placed upon the altar are, by the mystery of the sacred prayer and the words of our Redeemer, substantially (*substantialiter*) changed into the true and authentic and lifegiving flesh and blood of Jesus Christ our Lord. After consecration they are the true body of Christ which was born of the Virgin and which, being offered for the salvation of the world, hung upon the Cross and is seated at the right hand of the Father, and the true blood of Christ that flowed from his side, not only through the sign and power of the sacrament but also in reality of nature and truth of substance (*non tantum per signum et virtutem sacramenti, sed in proprietate naturę et veritate substantię*).

In conclusion, Gregory charged Berengar not to teach or dispute with anyone about the body and blood of Christ, unless it were to recall to true belief those whom his teachings had led astray[117].

Not surprisingly, Berengar's Memoir presents a different picture. There is no reference to debate during the Lent council. Having described the intervention, and the subsequent ill fates, of the bishops of Padua and Pisa,[118] Berengar retailed how Gregory sank so low (*usque eo ... deiectus est*) as to permit the profession of faith prepared for All Saintstide 1078 to be expanded into that of 1079 with its use of

gore suo falsam lucem diverberando obtenebrans noctis caliginem vertit in lucem.'

116 Peter the Deacon much later retailed a story of Theodemarius, a Cassinese monk who, at a time not stated, said mass and at the consecration saw the bread become flesh; when Gregory was told, he rejoiced and compelled Berengar and his followers to renounce their heresy: *Petri Diaconi Ortus et vita iustorum cenobii Casinensis*, cap. 48, ed. R.H. Rodgers (University of California Publications: Classical Studies, 10. Berkeley, Los Angeles and London, 1972), pp. 71–2. A source hostile to Gregory, Cardinal Beno's *Gesta Romanae aecclesiae contra Hildebrandum*, i, cap. 4, wrote of Gregory's failure to procure such a miracle, perhaps with the intention of scotching a tradition that one had occurred: *MGH LdeL* ii. 370–1.

117 Cf. the version inserted as *Reg.* iii. 17a, p. 281, and that in *Mem.* 104CD = Huygens, 'Bérenger', pp. 393/78 –394/87. For its circulation, see Somerville, 'The Case against Berengar of Tours', *Studi Gregoriani*, ix (1972), p. 74, n. 84.

118 As above, n. 111.

VI

130

*substantialiter*[119]. On Gregory's behalf, Bishop Landulf of Pisa brought the revised profession to Berengar. He hoped still to equivocate, and set out his position at length [120]. In this hope he read and accepted the new profession upon oath[121]. His enemies proceeded to try to wrest from him a further declaration that he shared their interpretation of it. He silenced them by an oblique allusion to a recent interview with Gregory: the pope had summoned him and, in the presence of Bishop Peter of Porto, had assured him that not only was he himself confident that Berengar's teaching was compatible with Christian tradition but he had sought and received confirmation that this was so through a vision of the Blessed Virgin to one of his *familiares*[122]. Berengar thought that he had thus escaped, but Gregory again disappointed him by a volte face. He made the unprecedented demand that Berengar should prostrate himself and confess that hitherto he had been in error by not adding *substantialiter* to his assertions that the consecrated bread and wine were the body and blood of Christ[123]. By an admission that he retrospectively condemned as sacrilegious, Berengar confessed his error. He pleaded in mitigation that he had done so not only from fear of death but also because he had in mind an episode at a time unspecified, when Abbot Desiderius of Montecassino and a Cassinese monk, Petrus Neapolitanus, whom he greatly respected, had intimated to him Gregory's own wish that he should retreat for Gregory's lifetime to a place of quasi-imprisonment; then Gregory might be free from the allegation that he himself went along with Berengar's reading of traditional Christian texts and from the need to vindicate his own right belief[124].

119 For a comparison of texts, see Montclos, p.231. It is uncertain who introduced the adverb *substantialiter* into the business of the Lent council. It figured in the conciliar profession adopted at Poitiers in 1075: Somerville, art. cit. pp.68-9 at lines 11-12 of the text; for its prominence in the writings of Guitmund of Aversa, see ibid. pp.70-1. Peter the Deacon's story that the Cassinese monk Alberic sought a week's delay in 1079 to compose a treatise bringing together the different points of view (as above, n. 103) is improbable in the light of the compressed timetable suggested by *Reg*. vi. 17*a*. In his Memoir, Berengar surprisingly made no reference to Alberic's adoption of *substantialiter* which he blamed severely in his letter to Alberic (as above, n.104), and which parallels Gregory's own change of view.
120 *Mem*. 104E-108A = Huygens, 'Bérenger', pp.394/96-399/250.
121 *De veritate corporis et sanguinis Domini*, PL cxlviii. 1457AB = Huygens, 'Bérenger', p.383/118-28.
122 *Mem*.108B-E = Huygens, 'Bérenger', pp.400/265-401/298.
123 *Mem*. 109A = Huygens, 'Bérenger', p.401/298-402/307.
124 '... voluntatem papae in eo fuisse, si soli illi assensum praebuissem, me

What, then, may be concluded about Gregory's approach to the Berengarian problem? He manifestly adopted a more tentative and even sympathetic approach than did his predecessors from Leo IX to Alexander II. This moderation was understandable in one brought up, as they were not, at Rome with its caution and conservatism in liturgical and dogmatic matters. There is no suggestion that anyone at Rome understood Christ's words of institution otherwise than literally. But the Christian tradition as the young Hildebrand gathered it together in 1054, or as Pope Gregory canvassed it before All Saintstide 1078, provided only a catena of New Testament and patristic passages that had never been ordered and synthesized in an agreed and satisfactory formula embodying realist and excluding figurative language. In so far as the *lex orandi* indicated a *lex credendi*, the canon of the mass in its *Quam oblationem* and *Qui pridie* sections was cast in language that was settled long before medieval ways of doctrinal expression became established: 'Quam oblationem tu, Deus, in omnibus, quaesumus, benedictam ... facere digneris; ut *nobis* corpus et sanguis fiat dilectissimi Filii tui ...'. Such words Humbert and Berengar could alike gladly use, for they could be construed in either of their senses.

It may be suggested that Gregory acted towards Berengar very much as he did in several other liturgical and sacramental matters, not by trying to establish and impose a single usage but by exploring what varieties of usage were and were not acceptable in the light of traditional authorities. Some usages might be allowable, even though they differed from a familiar norm. His guiding principle was best formulated in a letter of 1075 about practices to do with ordination: 'The holy and apostolic see is accustomed to tolerate many things once their warrant has been considered, but never to depart from the concord of canonical tradition in its decrees and constitutions'[125]. His application of this principle may be illustrated from his attitude to the liturgical practices of the Christian East[126]. In 1080 it came to his

---

quamdiu viveret loco aliquo quasi carcere claudere, ut mecum sentire de scripturis minime putaretur et ita adversariis sibi complacitis, de auctoritate confirmandae veritatis minime laboraret': *Mem.* 109C = Huygens, 'Bérenger', pp. 402/323 – 403/327. With *mecum sentire*, cf. *mecum sentientibus* in *Mem.* 103D = Huygens, 'Bérenger', p. 390/38.

125 'Solet enim sancta et apostolica sedes pleraque considerata ratione tolerare, sed nunquam in suis decretis et constitutionibus a concordia canonicę traditionis discedere': *Reg.* ii. 50, to King Sancho I of Aragon, 24 Jan. 1075, p. 191/24 – 6.

126 For a fuller discussion, see H.E.J. Cowdrey, 'The Gregorian Papacy,

notice that the Armenians added the words 'Qui crucifixus es nobis' to the chant *Sanctus Deus, sanctus fortis*. Writing to an Armenian patriarch, Gregory did not concern himself with Monophysite implications; he simply cited at length the rule of faith of Pope Gregory I as based upon the early ecumenical councils, and asked for the intrusive phrase to be omitted in order to avoid scandal to others. He also referred in his letter to the Greeks' use of leavened bread in the eucharist, and defended it as a permissible, if to him unfamiliar, custom: 'while we defend our unleavened bread with arguments irresistable to God, we do not condemn or reject their leavened bread, following the Apostle's word that to the pure all things are pure.'[127] Gregory ended his letter to the Armenian patriarch with a prayer that God would more abundantly illuminate his mind by guiding him in the way of wise understanding and preserving him in the concordant unity of the faithful (*in concordi fidelium unitate*)[128]. His concern was to promote what he called *concordia*: not a uniformity of thought and statement imposed from above, but a mutual acknowledgement of different usages so long as they were severally compatible with Christian tradition.

This inquiring and conciliatory approach to liturgical and sacramental matters is not the usual modern perception of Gregory, but a study of the word *concordia* in his letters indicates that a desire to promote it in fact had a large place in his thinking. It may help to explain his patient and conciliatory dealings with Berengar. They nowhere suggest that he shared Berengar's opinions, any more than he shared the customs of the Greeks or Armenians. At no time did he express agreement with Berengar, with whom he was most cordial in 1078 when Berengar seemed likely to adopt a profession of faith that was patient of a strongly realist interpretation; even so, Gregory saw in it a profession for babes in faith rather than for adults[129]. It must not be overlooked that Berengar's eucharistic teaching is not without its merits from a Catholic point of view; Berengar derived from Augustine a new line of thinking that was to be fruitful for later scholastic theology – that of a sacrament as a *sacrum signum*[130]. Whether

Byzantium, and the First Crusade', in: *Byzantium and the West, c. 850–c.1200*, ed. J.D. Howard–Johnston (Amsterdam, 1988), pp.145–69, esp. pp.152–60.

127 *Reg.* viii. 1, to Archbishop Gregory II of Tzamandus, 6 June 1080, p. 513/16–19.

128 *ibid.*, pp.513/35–514/3.

129 See above, pp.18–19.

130 Montclos, pp.125, 133, 140, 452–3.

or not Gregory appreciated this, he was at all times up to the Lent council of 1079 concerned to examine whether Berengar's view of the eucharist, however unfamiliar, could be deemed intrinsically acceptable in the light of biblical and patristic authorities. Hence his canvassing at Tours in 1054 and at Rome in 1078 of a catena of traditional texts in order to seek a consensus as to whether Berengar's views were acceptable in the light of them[131]. Berengar's acceptance at Tours of the proposition that the bread and wine on the altar are *revera* the body and blood of Christ, and in Rome in 1078 that the bread on the altar is the true body of Christ[132], was calculated to encourage Hildebrand/Gregory to hope that, even though Berengar's opinions differed from his own and from those generally current, they might be within the limits that Christian tradition established. For his part, Berengar no doubt made too much of Gregory's preparedness, especially during the winter of 1078-9, to hear him sympathetically and to incline to his views. But that was the price of Gregory's long and patient search for *concordia* with him, which marks Gregory out as the unique figure that he was and which, after his second excommunication of Henry IV of Germany in 1080, exposed him to the allegation of his imperialist enemies that he was himself a Berengarian[133].

The most difficult question of all about Gregory remains to be put: why, during his Lent council of 1079, did he shift his ground so drastically, cease to hesitate, and insist upon the past error of Berengar's eucharistic doctrine with a demand that he adopt the adverb *substantialiter*? The meagre evidence makes it impossible to do more than pose a hypothesis. It is that, for the first time in conciliar proceedings about Berengar in which Hildebrand/Gregory was directly involved, at the Roman council of Lent 1079 the soteriological aspect of the Berengarian controversy was a central issue. It may have brought home to Gregory some implications of Berengar's teaching that he had not hitherto appreciated.

---

131 See above, pp.14, 19.
132 See above, pp.14, 18-19.
133 '... catholicam atque apostolicam fidem de corpore et sanguine domini in quęstionem ponentem, heretici Beringarii antiquum discipulum': 'Dekret der Synode zu Brixen, 1080', in: *Quellen zur Geschichte Kaiser Heinrichs IV.* (Ausgewählte Quellen zur Geschichte des Mittelalters, 12, Berlin, 1963), pp.477-83, at p.480/19-21; letter of Egilbert, bishop-elect of Trier (June 1080), in: *Udalrici Codex*, no.61, *Bibliotheca rerum Germanicarum*, ed. P. Jaffé, v: *Monumenta Bambergensia* (Berlin, 1869), pp.127-9, at p.128/23-7.

134

A novel feature of the profession that Berengar was compelled to make in 1079, in addition to the adverb *substantialiter,* was the introduction of vocabulary expressing Christ's redemptive work both in general and in the sacrament: *verba nostri Redemptoris, vivificatricem carnem, pro salute mundi oblatam*[134]. Such vocabulary had been absent from Berengar's profession of 1059 as drafted by Cardinal Humbert, from the profession of the council of Poitiers (1075) that had introduced into such formulas the word *substantialiter,* and even from the profession of All Saintstide 1078[135]. This is surprising, for Berengar had often argued that his figurative interpretation of the eucharist was necessary in order to safeguard the effectiveness of Christ's redemptive work. The bread and wine upon the altar were not changed *per absumptionem* (by the taking away of their reality) but *per assumptionem* (by their being invested with the significance of Christ's body and blood). Berengar made this distinction on the grounds that, as St Augustine repeatedly taught, after Christ became obedient to death upon the Cross his body was raised to immortality and impassibility and was seated in heaven at the Father's side. Christ's risen and glorified body could not suffer the fragmentation upon earthly altars that a realist interpretation of the eucharist required; if it did the heavenly integrity of Christ's body upon which the Christian hope of salvation depended would be destroyed. Christ's body was, indeed, set forth upon the church's altars, but it was known spiritually by the inner man.

> My case [Berengar argued in a characteristic passage], or rather that of the Christian authors, is that the bread and wine of the Lord's table are converted into the Lord's body, not according to the senses but according to the mind, not by being taken away but by being taken up, and not (against Christian authors) as into a fragment of flesh but (according to them) as into the whole body and blood of Christ.[136]

Upon the garbled evidence of Gregory VII's Register, this case seems to have been part of the Berengarian statement at the Lent council of 1079[137]. It had begun to be challenged by Berengar's oppo-

---

134 *Reg.* vi. 17*a*, pp. 426/18, 19, 427/2–3.

135 Though implications for human salvation may be present in the Roman deacon Peter's question at Vercelli: above, p. 7.

136 *PE* pp. 531–5, citation from p. 534/76–80; cf. *RCL* ii. 2708–94, 3035–81, iii. 740–65, pp. 175–7, 184–5, 210–1 *Mem.* 107C–108A = Huygens, 'Bérenger', pp. 398/223–399/250.

137 See above, p. 20. The following paragraph may be read in the light of the theological discussion of the Paschasian approach to the eucharist by G. Macy, *The Theologies of the Eucharist in the Early Scholastic Period. A Study of the Salvific Function of the Sacrament according to the Theolo-*

nents in Normandy as long ago as the 1050s. In 1055(?), a council
held at Rouen by Archbishop Maurilius drew up a confession of faith
'against the most foul opinion of Berengar and his followers' which
later councils renewed and which passed into Norman usage at episcopal consecrations. It insisted that the consecrated bread of the
eucharist is the flesh of him who died for men and their salvation,
and the wine is the blood that flowed from Christ's side for the
redemption of the world[138]. Norman writers against Berengar
enlarged upon this theme, bringing in the word *substantialiter* which
they made familiar in writings about the eucharist. The way was
pointed by Durandus of Troarn, who wrote c. 1053[139]. It was pursued
by Guitmund of Aversa who wrote between 1073 and 1078, and who
moved from Normandy to Rome in the mid-1070s. He argued that, if
men received the body and blood of Christ figuratively, they were
only figuratively saved; the truth of human salvation required that
Christ be received in the eucharist *substantialiter*[140]. In succeeding
generations, death-bed professions that leading churchmen made
before receiving the viaticum took up this thought. Prior Bruno of
Chartreuse and La Torre (†1101) professed his belief 'that what is
consecrated upon the altar is Christ's true body, and the true flesh
and blood of our Lord Jesus Christ; we ourselves receive it for the
remission of sins and in hope of eternal life.'[141] When Abbot Hugh of
Cluny died in 1109, the last question put to him was whether he
acknowledged the lifegiving (*vivificatricem*) flesh of the Lord. 'I
acknowledge and I adore it', he replied, and fortified by his last communion he left his earthly prison without fear[142]. In 1135 the Cluniac
Cardinal Matthew of Albano died after making a similar profession
of faith: 'Through this sacred body of my Saviour I believe that I am

    *gians c. 1080-c. 1220* (Oxford, 1984), esp. pp. 5-6, 44-53, 137-41. For
    material in this paragraph I am also indebted to Somerville, 'The Case
    against Berengar of Tours', *Studi Gregoriani*, ix (1972), 69-71.
138 *Observationes praeviae in sequentia concilia de multiplici Berengarii dam-
    natione*, in: *RHGF* xi. 529AB; cf. the probably eleventh-century exami-
    nation of a bishop appended to *The Benedictional of Archbishop Robert*,
    ed. H.A. Wilson (Henry Bradshaw Society, 25, London, 1903), p.
    164/3-12.
139 *Liber de corpore et sanguini Christi*, iv. 8, v. 14, vi. 19, PL cxlix. 1386B
    -1387B, 1397D-1398B, 1404D-1405B.
140 *Liber de corporis et sanguinis Christi veritate in eucharistia*, iii, PL cxlix.
    1477D-1478D.
141 *Confessio fidei Magistri Brunonis*, cap. 3, *Lettres des premiers Chartreux*, i,
    ed. by a Carthusian (Sources Chrétiennes, 88, Paris, 1962), p. 92.
142 Gilo, *Vita sancti Hugonis abbatis*, ii. 9, ed. H.E.J. Cowdrey, 'Two Studies
    in Cluniac History, 1049-1126', *Studi Gregoriani*, xi (1978), 100.

incorporated into him and made one with him so that I may have eternal life.' 'So saying', commented Abbot Peter the Venerable of Cluny, 'he was nourished before his brethren with this saving body of Christ, and by the flesh that gives everlasting life he was made meet for the eternity to come.'[143]

In the light of such evidence, occasional though powerful as it is, it may well be suspected that neither dialectic nor the examination of traditional texts destroyed Berengar, but the threat that he was seen to present to men's salvation. The Lent council of 1079 at Rome may have been the occasion when, with the confirmation of whatever miracle its official record in Gregory's Register may hint at, the connection between the unqualified reality of Christ's presence in the sacrament and the hope of human salvation was officially recognized and expressed in the widely circulated profession that Berengar was constrained to make. Not least as it was borne in upon Gregory's own mind it may have been decisive in bringing about an absolute Roman condemnation of Berengar's teaching. The Roman enforcement of the word *substantialiter* followed, not because it met the demands of dialectic but because it guaranteed the hope of salvation as eleventh- and early twelfth-century Christians widely entertained it.

In view of the developments after 1080 in Gregory VII's struggle with Henry IV of Germany, it is not surprising that there is no further record of papal dealings with Berengar. Berengar himself partly complied with Gregory's wish that he should seek a place of retreat: after the Lent council of 1079 he returned to Tours and to residence upon the nearby island of Saint-Cosme[144]. He forged for himself letters of safe-conduct and protection in Gregory's name in which the pope was made to describe him as *filius noster karissimus Berengarius sacerdos* and as *Romanae ecclesiae filius*[145]. But, until his death in 1088, he did not lie as low as Gregory wished. Besides writing *c.* 1080 the Memoir which concluded with an ardent plea for the reader's sympathy[146], two letters bear upon his attitude to the papacy[147]. One, probably to be dated 1080/1, is addressed to a *frater R.*, perhaps the Roman subdeacon Roger who had come to Tours as papal legate in

---

143 Peter the Venerable, *De miraculis libri duo*, ii. 22, ed. D. Bouthillier, *CCM* 83 (Turnhout, 1988), pp. 136-7.

144 Montclos, pp. xliii-xliv.

145 *The Epistolae vagantes of Pope Gregory VII*, ed. and trans. H.E.J. Cowdrey (Oxford, 1972), nos. †72-3, pp. 156-7.

146 *Mem.* 109DE = Huygens, 'Bérenger', p. 403/339-43.

147 I accept Erdmann's opinion that EF no. 103, pp. 171-2, refers to Count Geoffrey *Martel*, not Pope Gregory VII.

1078 while Berengar was at Rome[148]. While the letter is barren of specific details, its purpose may have been to parry a reminder from Rome of his oath to maintain silence: Berengar promised that, as a solitary, he would contradict without animosity and be contradicted without obstinacy. He evidently had no intention of simply keeping quiet. A still more problematic letter is addressed to Bishop Odo of Bayeux[149]. Berengar first offered thanks for Odo's deliverance from his enemies and opponents, an apparent reference either to events after the bishop's fall from favour in 1082 with his half-brother King William I of England, or to his release from imprisonment at Rouen upon William's death in 1087[150]. Berengar urged Odo to show himself duly grateful by repentance and love of God[151]. He next adapted to Odo a passage from a letter that he had long ago written to Pope Alexander II on behalf of Archbishop Bartholomew of Tours, in which he had prayed in exalted terms for the pope's prosperity:

> May God fulfil my joy in you by making you like an arrow in the hand of the powerful and a son of the mighty ones, most worthy indeed of the rudder that you have received to direct the church, and by ordering you, as you advance from strength to strength, to rise up to his embattled people.[152]

Berengar observed that Odo was concerned to restore his own fortunes, as well, for which he was deeply appreciative[153]. He concluded by referring to Odo's messenger whose haste to return made impossible a longer reply[154]. The reference to the messenger establishes that real and urgent negotiations were taking place. Berengar hoped to benefit further from Odo's goodwill, and it must be an open question whether Odo had not confided in him about plans to intervene at Rome during or after Gregory VII's last years that, according to some reports, included his own candidature for the papacy[155]. Berengar's

---

148 For the text, Montclos, p. 521, and for discussion, *ibid.*, pp. 521 – 30.

149 EF no. 101, pp. 168 – 9. Like Berengar's letter to *frater R.*, this letter also survives in Vorau, Stiftsbibliothek, MS 412.

150 EF no. 101, p. 169/1 – 6. Erdmann's dating should be amended to (1082 – 8).

151 EF no. 101, p. 169/6 – 9. The phrase *abyssum corruptionis* probably does not allude to a single heinous offence or evil quality of Odo, but after the manner of the eleventh-century *mépris du monde* to the general corruption of the human condition.

152 EF no. 101, p. 169/9 – 12, cf. no. 94, p. 161/3 – 9. The biblical references to Ps. 126: 4, 83: 8, and Hab. 3: 16 should be noticed.

153 EF no. 101, p. 169/13 – 14, 20 – 1.

154 EF no. 101, p. 169/22 – 3.

155 *Chronica monasterii de Hida iuxta Wintoniam*, in: *Liber monasterii de*

138

adaptation of a letter to Pope Alexander II is, at least, a pointer to Odo's having indeed entertained such an ambition, by association with which Berengar himself hoped for a measure of vindication. It seems likely that he was mindful of papal affairs to the very end of his life, and would not himself lie down.

*Hyda*, ed. E. Edwards (London: Rolls Series, 1866), p. 296; William of Malmesbury, *De gestis regum Anglorum libri quinque*, iii. 277, ed. W. Stubbs (2 vols., London: Rolls Series, 1887-9), ii. 334; *The Ecclesiastical History of Orderic Vitalis*, vii. 8, ed. M. Chibnall (6 vols., Oxford, 1969-80), iv. 40-4.

# VII

## THE GREGORIAN REFORM IN THE ANGLO-NORMAN LANDS AND IN SCANDINAVIA*

According to medieval cosmography the Anglo-Norman lands and Scandinavia had the common feature of being situated along the outer fringe of the *Europa* which, together with Africa, comprised the southern sector of the world. Beginning from the River Don this fringe ran westwards along the northern ocean to the limits of Spain.[1] As viewed from Gregory VII's Rome it was a zone of peripheral principalities that lay beyond Salian Germany, Capetian France, and the Empire of Constantinople. The location of Denmark, *in ultimis terrarum finibus positus*,[2] and so of the rest of Scandinavia,

---

* **Abbreviations.** The following abbreviations are used in the notes that follow:

ADAM OF BREMEN    MAGISTRI ADAM BREMENSIS *Gesta Hammaburgensis ecclesiae pontificum*, ed. B. SCHMEIDLER and W. TRILLMICH, in: *Quellen des 9. und 11. Jahrhunderts zur Geschichte der Hamburgischen Kirche und des Reiches*, Ausgewählte Quellen zur deutschen Geschichte des Mittelalters, 12, Darmstadt 1961.

CS    *Councils and Synods with other Documents relating to the English Church*, i: *AD 871-1204*, ed. D. WHITELOCK, M. BRETT, and C.N.L. BROOKE, 2 vols., Oxford 1981.

Dipl. Danic.    *Diplomatarium Danicum*, 1 Raekke, pt. 2: *1053-1169*, ed. N. SKYUM-NIELSEN and L. WEIBULL, Copenhagen 1963.

LANFRANC, *Epp.*    *The Letters of Lanfranc, Archbishop of Canterbury*, ed. H. CLOVER and M. GIBSON, Oxford 1979.

RS    *Rolls Series = Rerum Britannicarum medii aevi scriptores*, 99 vols., London 1858-96.

VSD    *Vitae sanctorum Danorum*, ed. M.C. GERTZ, Copenhagen 1908-12.

[1] ISIDORI HISPALENSIS EPISCOPI *Etymologiarum sive originum libri xx*, ed. W.M. LINDSAY, 2 vols., Oxford 1911, 14.2.1-3, 4.2.

[2] *Reg.* VII, 5, to King Harold Hein of Denmark, p. 464.

was defined by the route to it across the *Teutonica terra*.[3] As for Norman England, strictly speaking it was beyond the fringe altogether. From ancient times, *Brittania* with its surrounding ocean was the first of the world's islands, set over against *Europa* as an *alter orbis* beyond *Francia*.[4] But the duchy of Normandy was set up in 911 upon territory wich, in Roman times, had been part of *Gallia Lugdunensis*, and in due course it had belonged to Carolingian *Neustria*. The Norman province of Rouen belonged to the French church.[5] Nevertheless in ecclesiastical matters the exceptionally frequent councils and synods that the seventh duke, William (1035-87), held from *c.* 1040 made it clear that the Norman church was subject to his masterful authority.[6] After he seized the crown of England in 1066 the rule that he established there over the church and lay authority became still more masterful. For he had the advantage of inheriting ancient and strong institutions that Norman energy could exploit. Meanwhile his contemporary and enemy in Denmark, King Swein II Estridson (1044-74/76), began in earnest his country's transition from the Viking age to statehood. By contrast with England, its institutions were rudimentary; but there, too, the church was to be part of the fabric of royal power.

Sheer physical distance, problems of language and comprehension, and the rulers' aspirations to mastery over their lands, presented the papacy with difficulties in its dealing with such peripheral regions of Christendom. But, leaving aside the problems that Byzantium set,[7] the prolonged and bitter conflict between Gregory VII and Henry IV of Germany, together with the Capetian king Philip I's heedlessness of papal admonitions, compelled the papacy to contain disobedient rulers near the centre of Western Christendom by attempting to hold, and if possible increase, the goodwill of peripheral regions; above all it must cultivate their rulers and buttress their power. Un-

---

[3] *Reg.* II, 51, to King Swein II of Denmark, p. 192.

[4] ISIDORE OF SEVILLE (as n. 1), 14.6.2; see C. ERDMANN, *Forschungen zur politischen Ideenwelt des Frühmittelalters*, Berlin 1951, pp. 8-11, 38-43. For Pope Urban II's dictum that Archbishop Anselm of Canterbury was *velut alterius orbis apostolicu[s] et patriarcha*, see *The Life of St. Anselm Archbishop of Canterbury*, II. 29, ed. R.W. SOUTHERN, London, etc. 1962, p. 105.

[5] As was made clear in Norman *Laudes regiae* texts: H.E.J. COWDREY, *The Anglo-Norman Laudes regiae*, in: *Viator*, XII (1981), pp. 37-78, esp. pp. 68-9, 76-8, repr.: *Popes, Monks and Crusaders*, London 1984, n. VIII. For Gregory VII's view, see *Reg.* VI, 34-5, 20 Apr. 1079, pp. 447-52.

[6] R. FOREVILLE, *The Synod in the Province of Rouen in the Eleventh and Twelfth Centuries,* in: *Church and Government in the Middle Ages. Essays presented to C.R. Cheney on his 70th Birthday*, ed. C.N.L. BROOKE, D.E. LUSCOMBE, G.H. MARTIN, and D. OWEN, Cambridge 1976, pp. 19-39.

[7] See H.E.J. COWDREY, *The Gregorian Papacy, Byzantium, and the First Crusade*, in: *Byzantium and the West, c. 850 - c. 1200*, ed. J.D. HOWARD-JOHNSTON (forthcoming).

derlying this political motive was the age-long papal sense of mission to teach the way of the Lord to all peoples. It was proclaimed by Pope Gregory the Great, who understood that, especially in remote lands, the key figures were the kings.[8] Gregory VII took a similar view. The Gregorian papacy, therefore, dealt with the Anglo-Norman lands and with Scandinavia from motives that were at once pastoral and political.[9]

## I.

The objectives of the Gregorian reform in these peripheral lands may best be defined from letters which Gregory VII and his associates dispatched as events developed, and which were addressed to, or were written concerning, the kings and their families.[10] From these letters four objectives emerge.

---

[8] GREGORY I, *Ep.* XI, 37, cited by BEDE, *The Ecclesiastical History of the English People*, I, 32, ed. B. COLGRAVE and R.A.B. MYNORS, Oxford 1969, pp. 110-15. See also Pope Vitalian's letter to King Oswiu of Northumbria (664), ibid., III. 29 pp. 319-23, and Pope Nicholas I, *Ep.* 63, to King Horich I of Denmark (864), MIGNE, *PL* CXIX, 879-80.

[9] See H.E.J. COWDREY, *Pope Gregory VII and the Anglo-Norman Church and Kingdom*, in: *SGreg* IX, 1972, pp. 79-114, esp. pp. 79-80, repr.: *Popes, Monks and Crusaders*, n. IX.

[10] The following letters are here considered:

*(i)* Relating to William I, duke of Normandy (1035-87) and king of England (1066-87), and his family. *Reg.* I, 31, to Archbishop Lanfranc of Canterbury (1070-89), 20 Nov. 1073, pp. 51-2; *Reg.* I, 70 to William I, and I, 71, to Queen Matilda, 4 Apr. 1074, pp. 100-3; *Reg.* IV, 17, to William I, 31 Mar. 1077, pp. 322-3; *Reg.* V, 19, to William I, 4 Apr. 1078, pp. 382-3; *Reg.* VI, 30 to Lanfranc, 25 Mar. 1079, pp. 443-4; *Reg.* VII, 1, to the Roman sub-deacon Hubert, 23 Sept. 1079, pp. 458-60; *Reg.* VII, 23, to William I, 24 Apr. 1080, pp. 499-502; *Reg.* VII, 25, to William I, VII, 26, to Matilda, and VII, 27, to Robert their eldest son, 8 May 1080, pp. 505-8; *Reg.* IX, 5, to Bishops Hugh of Die and Amatus of Oleron, (1081), pp. 579-80; *Reg.* IX, 37, to William I, (1082/3), pp. 630-1; *Epp. vag.*, 53 to Archbishop Hugh of Lyons, (1082/3), p. 128: *Die Hannoversche Briefsammlung*. I: *Die Hildesheimer Briefe*, n. I, Bishop Anselm II of Lucca to William I, (1085), *Briefsammlungen der Zeit Heinrichs IV.*, ed. C. ERDMANN and N. FICKERMANN, *MGH, Briefe*, v, 15-17.

*(ii)* Relating to Ireland. *Epp. vag.*, 57, to Toirdhealbhach Ó Briain, king "of Ireland" and all the Irish, (1074/85), pp. 138-41.

*(iii)* Relating to Denmark. *Reg.* II, 51, to King Swein II Estridson (1047-74/6), 25 Jan. 1075, pp. 192-4; II, 75, to Swein II, 17 Apr. 1075, pp. 237-8; *Reg.* V, 10, to King Harold IX Hein (1076-80), 6 Nov. 1077, pp. 361-3; *Reg.* VII, 5, to Harold IX, 15 Oct. 1079, pp. 464-5; *Reg.* VII, 21, to Harold IX and the Danish bishops, princes, clergy, and people, 19 Apr. 1080, pp. 497-8.

*(iv)* Relating to Norway. *Reg.* VI, 13, to King Olaf III (1069-93), 15 Dec. 1078, pp. 415-18.

*(v)* Relating to Sweden. *Reg.* VIII, 11, to King Inge I (1080-1112), 4 Oct. 1080, p. 530; *Reg.* IX, 14, to Kings Inge I and Halstan and their people, (1081), pp. 592-4. (Items relating to Denmark also appear in *Dipl. Danic.*, i/2, and to Norway in *Latinske dokument til Norsk historie fram til år 1204*, ed. E. VANDVIK, Oslo 1959).

First, Gregory was concerned to guide and strengthen Christian princes who promoted the welfare of their peoples in the concerns of this world and the next. A king was entrusted by God with an office of kingship (*honor regni*) (V, 10). He exercised a stewardship and was an instrument in God's hands; his good and famous deeds were accomplished by the working of divine power (II, 51; VII, 21; Anselm of Lucca). Kings no less that priests must answer for their subjects' souls at the Day of Judgement (II, 51). They should strive for Christian righteousness (*iustitia*) in themselves and foster it among their subjects (I, 70; VI, 13; VII, 21; VIII, 11; IX, 5, 37). So Gregory looked for secure and vigorous Christian monarchs who would guarantee peace to their subjects at home and abroad, and guide them in the way of salvation.

A second, and complimentary, objective was that kingdoms should be brought to follow the admonitions of the apostolic see and should be serviceable to it. The law of the Roman pontiffs encompassed more nations than that of the ancient emperors had done (II, 75). Gregory emphasized the way of direct, personal obedience rather than of ecclesiastical structures or hierarchical order.[11] Kings should cleave to the Roman church like sons to their mother (I, 70; VII, 5). Accordingly they might become the *fideles* of the apostolic see or commend themselves and their kingdoms to St. Peter's *patrocinium* (II, 75; V, 10), or else they might be joined to it in mutual *amicitia* (IX, 37).[12] God had set the church over all the kingdoms of the earth (*Epp. vag.*, 57). The papal dignity stood to the royal as the sun to the moon: the world needed both; but the royal was subject, after God, to the supervision and direction of the papal (VII, 25). Kings should defer to papal authority, and so discharge their debt of obedience and reverence (VII, 21, 23). They should foster in their lands the knowledge and observance of the Christian faith and divine laws (II, 75; VI, 13; VIII, 11; IX, 14). And despite problems of distance, Gregory expected certain practical duties to be discharged. Where the apostolic see had a claim to Peter's Pence, kings should honour it (I, 70). When military service might advance papal interests, especially when Rome itself was threatened by papal enemies, even distant kings might be called upon to supply armed forces (II, 51; Anselm of Lucca).[13]

---

[11] A. NITSCHKE, *Die Wirksamkeit Gottes in der Welt Gregors VII.*, in: *SGreg* V, 1956, pp. 115-219, esp. pp. 136-43, 189-92, 213-19.

[12] For Gregory's use of the terms *fidelis* and *patrocinium*, see C. ERDMANN, *Die Entstehung des Kreuzzugsgedankens*, Stuttgart 1935, pp. 188-206, Eng. trans. by M.W. BALDWIN and W. GOFFART, *The Origin of the Idea of Crusade*, Princeton 1977, pp. 204-24.

[13] Gregory's request at the end of *Reg.* II, 51 to Swein of Denmark for military help that he hoped the king would make available to the Roman church *contra profanos et inimicos Dei*

Thirdly, Gregory sought to promote communication by all practicable means between the apostolic see and distant kingdoms. Kings should keep him informed about their realms by sending regular letters and such messengers as might be useful (II, 51, 75; VII, 5). He especially required them to permit archbishops and bishops to pay visits *ad limina* (VII, 1); where metropolitan authority was not established, kings should help to set it up (II, 51). If such requirements as these could not be met, kings should at least send clerks to Rome for familiarization with its aims and standards (VI, 13; IX, 14).

Fourthly, kings should protect the poor and vulnerable, and they should ensure the security and the moral discipline of the clergy. Gregory and his agents made much of the kings' charitable duty to provide for the poor, for widows, for the sick, and for orphans (V, 10; VI, 13; IX, 14; Anselm of Lucca). They should protect such groups as the clergy and the women, popularly deemed to be witches, whom Scandinavians blamed in times of storm and pestilence (VII, 21). Gregory also approved of a ruler who took part in the struggle against simony and clerical marriage (IX, 5). By such means as these he aspired by directing kings to propagate Christian charity and Christian morality amongst clergy and laity alike.

With variations of emphasis and application, Gregory pursued these objectives both in the Anglo-Norman lands and in Scandinavia. Just how he did so depended upon the state of development of ecclesiastical and secular institutions. In the lands of the king-duke William I they were old-established and comparatively elaborate, but in Scandinavia they were still rudimentary and insecure. I begin with Scandinavia where, like the kings themselves, Gregory had perforce to work with the little that was ready to hand.[14]

---

related, not to help against the South Italian Normans, but to the situation in Croatia after the death in 1074 of King Peter Krešimir IV. Peter's pro-Gregorian nominee Zwonimir was, for a time, successfully resisted by Duke Slavac of Narentani, who enjoyed wide popular support in opposing ecclesiastical reforms and especially the introduction of Latin into the liturgy: D. MANDIĆ, *Gregorio VII e l'occupazione veneta della Dalmazia nell'anno 1076*, in: *Venezia e il Levante fino al secolo XV*, ed. A. PERTUSI, I/1, Florence 1973, pp. 453-71, esp. p. 461. The Danish bishop who had informed Gregory that Swein might be prepared to make a son available, with a posse of knights, for service as *dux ac princeps et defensor christianitatis*, is unlikely to have been Rikwal of Lund in view of his canonical position; Gregory probably referred to a bishop like Rikwal's predecessor Egino who had visited Rome in Alexander II's later years: see below, pp. 327, 328-329. Gregory's hope that Swein would send a son *apostolicae aulae militandum* suggests that Gregory had in mind Scandinavian service at Constantinople in the Varangian guard. For the Lateran as *apostolica aula*, see also *Reg.* VI, 13.

[14] I am particularly indebted to the following books and articles on Scandinavian history: (i) On Scandinavia in general. W. SEEGRÜN, *Das Papsttum und Skandinavien bis zur Vollendung*

## II.

The recent background was as follows. Gregory became pope after the endeavours of Archbishop Adalbert of Hamburg-Bremen (1043-72) to develop claims of his see to jurisdiction over the North which could be traced back to the late seventh century.[15] Especially at first, King Swein II of Denmark had not been hostile to Adalbert; but he also broached a plan for a Danish archbishopric. Adalbert concurred, but he further proposed the setting up of a northern patriarchate to be centred upon Hamburg-Bremen, to which the Danish metropolis as well as the churches of Norway and Sweden would be subject. Adalbert hoped for the co-operation of pope and emperor in this plan, by which the North would become ecclesiastically subject to a German see.[16] In 1053 he received papal sanction when Pope Leo IX confirmed his authority over the Scandinavian peoples, recognizing him and his successors as apostolic legates and papal vicars.[17] But after the deaths of Leo in 1054 and of the Emperor Henry III in 1056, it became clear that Adalbert's plans were over-ambitious, in face of a papacy that became increasingly uneasy at the aggrandisement of an imperial see, and of Scandinavian peoples who aspired to build their own nationality and statehood by accepting Christianity and

---

*der nordischen Kirchenorganisation,* Neumünster 1967; E. HOFFMANN, *Die heiligen Könige bei den Angelsachsen und den skandinavischen Völkern,* Neumünster 1975. (ii) On Denmark. A.E. CHRISTENSEN, *Mellem Vikingetid og Valdemarstid. Et forsøp̊å en syntese,* in: *Historisk Tidsskrift,* 2nd ser., xii, 1966, pp. 31-56. ibid., *Archbishop Asser, the Emperor and the Pope,* in: *Scandinavian Journal of Hystory,* I (1976), pp. 25-42; N. SKYUM-NIELSEN, *Das dänische Erzbistum vor 1250,* in: *Kirche und Gesellschaft im Ostseeraum und im Norden vor der Mitte des 13. Jahrhunderts,* Acta Visbyensia, 3, Visby 1967, pp. 111-38; E. HOFFMANN, *Knut der Heilige und die Wende der dänischen Geschichte im 11. Jahrhundert,* in: *HZ* 218 (1974), pp. 529-70; ibid., *Die Einladung des Königs bei den skandinavischen Völker im Mittelalter,* in: *Medieval Scandinavia,* VIII (1975), pp. 100-39; ibid., *Königserhebung und Thronfolgeordnung in Dänemark bis zum Ausgang des Mittelalters,* Berlin and New York 1976; C. BREENGAARD, *Muren om Israels Hus. Regnum og Sacerdotium i Danmark, 1050-1170,* Copenhagen 1982. (iii) On Norway. A.O. JOHNSEN, *Biskop Bjarnhard og kirkeforholdene,* summarized in: *Excerpta historica nordica* VII (1975), pp. 135-6. (For items in Scandinavian languages I have depended on English summaries. I am grateful to Dr. E. CHRISTIANSEN for help and advice.)

[15] The fullest account of Adalbert is in ADAM OF BREMEN, IV. Besides the items in n. 14 I have used the following modern authorities: O.H. MAY, *Regesten der Erzbischöfe von Bremen,* I, Bremen 1928; H. FUHRMANN, *Studien zur Geschichte mittelalterlicher Patriarchate,* III, in: *ZRGKan* XLI (1955), pp. 95-183, at pp. 120-70;. W. SEEGRÜN, *Das Erzbistum Hamburg in seinen älteren Papsturkunden,* Cologne and Vienna 1976.

[16] ADAM OF BREMEN, III, 33, p. 368.

[17] *Ep. 77,* MIGNE, *PL* CXLIII, 701-3, *GP* VI, pp. 56-7, n. 81. Cf. ALEXANDER II's allusion to the title of patriarch in *JL* 4474, *GP* VI, p. 60, n. 88b, where he also reserved his own rights of jurisdiction.

its institutions. In the early 1060s Adalbert could not hold a reforming synod at Schleswig because Danish bishops, especially Eilbert of Fünen, refused to attend.[18] Adalbert persuaded Pope Alexander II to forbid King Swein to support Eilbert.[19] But in 1063 Adalbert thought it wise to concur in Swein's plan to increase the Danish bishoprics to nine and so strenghthen the Danish church.[20] Despite papal support, Adalbert also could not make good his authority over Norway,[21] where the desire for independence of Hamburg-Bremen cannot have escaped Danish notice. The pope, for his part, fostered such direct contacts between Rome and Scandinavia as had occasionally occurred since King Cnut I of Denmark and England's visit to Rome in 1027. Alexander urged Swein and his successors to send Peter's Pence regularly.[22] There were also moves from the Danish side. In 1072, Bishop Eilbert of Fünen, whom Adalbert had suspended, died when about to leave for Rome, while Bishop Egino of Lund died soon after returning thence.[23] It seems likely that, with papal approval, the ground was being prepared for the see of Lund to be the Danish metropolis. Perhaps in 1063/5 but probably in 1072, Swein tried to secure the Danish royal succession by sending an illegitimate son, Magnus, to Rome for consecration as king; however the boy died upon the journey.[24] All these events suggest that, by the time Gregory VII became pope, Swein was looking to Rome rather than to Hamburg-Bremen.[25] In Albert Hauck's phrase, under Alexander II the apostolic see was already acting upon Germany "like a magnet upon iron filings";[26] it was also beginning so to act upon Denmark.[27] Indeed, in letters of 1075 to Swein, Gregory himself recalled that, while he

---

[18] ADAM OF BREMEN, III, 74-7, p. 426-8, *Ep.* 4, MIGNE, *PL* CXLVI, 1281-2; *JL* 44721-4, *GP* VI, p. 60, n. 88.

[19] *JL* 4472-3; also as in the last note.

[20] ADAM OF BREMEN, III, 25, 27, IV, 2, 3, 8, 9, pp. 358, 360-2, 438-40, 444-6.

[21] Ibid., III, 17, pp. 346-50, *Ep.* 3, MIGNE, *PL* CXLVI, 1281, *GP* VI, p. 59, n. 87.

[22] *Ep.* 6, MIGNE, *PL* CXLVI, 1283. To underline the directness of Danish loyalty, Peter's Pence were to be presented, not as hitherto on the altar of St. Peter's basilica, but to the pope and his successors in person. If Alexander was seeking to establish feudal superiority, Swein and his sons did not acknowledge it.

[23] ADAM OF BREMEN, IV, 9, Schol., 115, pp. 444-7.

[24] Ibid., Schol., 72, p. 354.

[25] It is not clear whether or not Adalbert's successor Liemar (1072-1101) was made papal vicar or received a *pallium;* that he was given some such authority is suggested, but not established, by the opening phrase of *Reg.* II, 28, p. 160. See MAY (as n. 15), pp. 80-1, nos. 341-2; *GP* VI, pp. 61-2, n. 91.

[26] A. HAUCK, *Kirchengeschichte Deutschlands,* 5 vols. Leipzig 1914-20, III, 736.

[27] For the resumption by c. 1070 of relations between Rome and Norway, see JOHNSEN (as n. 14).

was still archdeacon, he and the king had been in touch by letters and messengers about the Danish metropolis and other matters; and they had exchanged promises about them (II, 51, 75). That in 1073 Gregory had high and immediate expectations of Swein is apparent from his being the sole king to whom, according to Gregory's Register, official notice of the papal election was sent.[28]

To Gregory's surprise these contacts did not at once develop, and his first two years as pope saw no further approach from Swein's realms (II, 51). It is necessary next to explain why not, and why the plan for a Danish metropolis got no further during Gregory's lifetime. In January 1075 Gregory himself wrote to Swein and recalled that he had recently sent legates to resume business that, for the honour of the Danish kingdom (*pro honorificentia regni*), had been broached under Alexander II (II, 51). The legates were probably Cardinalbishops Gerald of Ostia and Hubert of Palestrina, whom Gregory sent to Germany in March 1074 to hold a reforming council;[29] but because of the disturbed state of Germany they were compelled to cut short their journey.

A main reason why the German council was not held was the hostility of Archbishop Liemar of Bremen (1072-1101), whom in January 1075 Gregory suspended and summoned to his next Lent synod.[30] Liemar did not attend the synod; Gregory therefore excommunicated him.[31] But, for all his hostility to a legatine council in Germany, Liemar had always favoured ecclesiastical reform. Above all, he wished to secure the traditional claims of his see in the North.[32] So he tried to relax the tension between Gregory and

---

[28] *Reg.* I, 4, 28 Apr. 1073, p. 7. The political significance of Gregory's sending notice to Denmark is underlined by his not sending notice to Henry IV of Germany: G.B. BORINO, *Perché Gregorio VII non annunziò la sua elezione ad Enrico IV e non ne richiese il consenso,* in: *SGreg* V, 1956, pp. 313-43.

[29] The legates are not known to have been back in Rome until December. For their activities, see O. SCHUMANN, *Die päpstlichen Legaten in Deutschland zur Zeit Heinrichs IV. und Heinrichs V. (1056-1125),* Marburg 1912, pp. 23-8; R. HÜLS, *Kardinäle, Klerus und Kirchen Roms, 1049-1130,* Tübingen 1977, pp. 100-1, 110-11. For discussion, see C. ERDMANN, *Studien zur Briefliteratur Deutschlands im elften Jahrhundert, MGH Schriften,* I, Stuttgart 1938, pp. 244-55. In *Reg.* II, 75, the phrase *ut fere quiescentibus legationibus nostris, quoniam pene sine fructu videntur,* seems to refer to these legates.

[30] *Reg.* II, 28, to Archbishop Liemar of Bremen, 12 Dec. 1074, pp. 160-1. For Liemar's attitude to the council, see esp. his letter to Bishop Hezilo of Hildesheim: *Die Hildesheimer Briefe,* n. 15 (as n. 10), pp. 33-5.

[31] *Reg.* II, 52a, p. 196.

[32] To this end he may have prepared for submission to the papacy a dossier of six forged papal privileges underlining the claims of the archbishops of Hamburg-Bremen to be papal legates and vicars and so promoting their authority over the Scandinavian churches: SEEGRÜN (as n. 15), pp. 83-100.

the German Church. After the Lent synod he acknowledged the sentence passed upon him and sent envoys to Gregory; then he went to Rome in person to seek restoration to office.

In preparation for his journey he asked Bishop Immad of Paderborn to write to Gregory on his behalf.[33] Immad's letter helps to explain why the plan for a Danish metropolis had failed to develop. He gave an adverse account of a bishop named Rikwal, who in 1072 had succeeded Egino at Lund. Immad said that Rikwal was a clerk and sometime canon of Paderborn, who for ten years had been a wanderer and fugitive. He had contumaciously refused to return to Paderborn, so Immad had excommunicated him. He had then fled to the Danes whose lands, Immad reminded Gregory, were by ancient right subject to the see of Hamburg. Therefore Immad had written to Archbishop Adalbert, whose summons to return to Paderborn Rikwal ignored; Adalbert added his own excommunication. But now at last, Immad concluded, after so many delays — perhaps because he feared to lose his Danish bishopric — Rikwal had promised to return and make satisfaction. Immad's purpose in writing to Gregory in these terms seems clear: as Rikwal's bishop he wished to regularize his subject's position; but he wished also to convince Gregory that Liemar's own restoration to communion, and perhaps also his confirmation as papal vicar and legate in the North, were called for, in order that he might absolve Rikwal from the excommunication that his predecessor Adalbert had imposed.

It will be noticed that Immad did not seek Rikwal's deposition from the see of Lund which he retained until he died in 1089. And in the event, Immad's letter did little to help Liemar, whose ambitions for his see, so far as they depended upon Gregory's goodwill, were frustrated after 1076 by his unbroken adherence to Henry IV.[34] The principal importance of Immad's

---

[33] B. SCHMEIDLER, *Ein Brief Bishof Imads von Paderborn an Papst Gregor VII.*, in: *NA* XXXVII (1912), pp. 804-9, *Dipl. Danic.*, I/2, pp. 29-31, n. 14. Immad had already written a similar letter to Liemar, who had forwarded it to Gregory.

[34] It is possible but not certain that, as SEEGRÜN and HOFFMANN suggest, after his excommunication of Liemar of Bremen in 1080 Gregory regarded Archbishop Hartwig of Magdeburg as exercising comparable powers over Scandinavia: SEEGRÜN (as n. 14), p. 99; HOFFMANN, *Knut der Heilige* (as n. 15), p. 545. In 1082 Hartwig did, indeed, on Gregory's instructions ordain to the episcopate Bishop Gizur (1082-1118) of Skálholt in southern Iceland. But Gizur had been educated and ordained priest in Saxony (it is not known where): *Hungrvaka*, caps. 4-5, in: J. HELGASON, *Byskupa Sǫgur*, 2 vols., Copenhagen 1938-78, I, 83-90; Eng. trans. in: *Stories of the Bishops of Iceland*, ed. [M. LEITH], London 1895, pp. 45-50; cf. *Dipl. Danic.*, I/2, pp. 80-3, 91, n. 36-7, 43. The *Hungrvaka* dates from the early thirteenth century but embodies older, reliable material: see M.M. LÁRUSSON, *Hungrvaka*, in: *Kulturhistorisk Leksikon for Nordisk Middelalder fram Vikingetid til Reformationstid*, 22 vols., Copenhagen 1956-78, VII, 88-9. (I am grateful to Dr. Ursula DRONKE for help in connection with this source.)

intervention seems to have been its impact upon Gregory. His further correspondence with Swein and his successor Harold Hein yields no hint that he
blamed Swein for making Rikwal a bishop or for giving him protection. But
after hearing of Rikwal's record Gregory never again referred to a plan for
a Danish metropolitan see, which was revived only after Rikwal's, and therefore Gregory's, deaths. Only the king could provide for the day-to-day welfare of his churches, and it was now necessary to work through him directly
and regularly. So in his letter of 20 April 1075 Gregory threw open for Swein's
suggestions the ways in which co-operation might develop.[35] He praised Swein
fulsomely, and asked him to say, through his own messengers and through
Gregory's, how the authority of the Roman church might best be brought
to bear.[36]

It was after this turning-point in 1075 that the objectives of the Gregorian reform in Scandinavia were made fully apparent. In letters to kings of
Denmark, Norway, and Sweden between 1077 and 1081 Gregory sought to
impress upon them a pattern of righteousness that would foster prosperous
kingship. Royal dynasties were to recognize their sources in Christian exem-
plars, and where possibile the divisiveness of the ancient succession rights of
royal clans was to be remedied by their limitation to a single son who followed his father.

In Denmark, Gregory posthumously built up the image of Swein II as
an ideal Christian ruler. In November 1077 he praised him to his son and
successor, the peaceable but competent Harold IX, as a king who had always
and in all respects diplayed to St. Peter an unfeigned reverence through service and obedience: as a son of the Roman church he was second to almost
no other king. During his lifetime he had, indeed, been stained by grievous
carnal sins;[37] but they would be purged by his own repentance and by me-
morial prayers and alms (V, 10). In April 1080 and so only some six weeks

---

[35] Between 17 and 20 Apr. 1075 Gregory dispatched letters to the rulers of the peripheral
lands of Bohemia, Poland, Russia, and Denmark, which must be appraised as a group: *Reg.*
II, 70-5, pp. 229-38.

[36] Swein II's death is variously indicated by the sources as having occurred in 1074 or in
1076, but there are strong reasons, especially in Icelandic sources, for accepting the latter date:
see SEEGRÜN (as n. 14), p. 85 (suggesting 28 Apr. 1076), and SAXO GRAMMATICUS, *Danorum regum heroumque historia, Books X-XVI*, trans. E. CHRISTIANSEN, 3 vols., Oxford 1980-1 (with
page photographs of the edition by C. PEDERSON, Paris 1514), I, 236-7. It cannot be presumed
that Gregory dispatched *Reg.* II, 51, 75, after Swein's death: see CASPAR's annotations, *Reg.*,
pp. 7, 192, 238.

[37] For Swein's character, see ADAM OF BREMEN, III, 12, 54, pp. 338-40, 396-8; SAXO GRAM-
MATICUS, XI, 7 (as n. 36), I, 58-60.

after the second excommunication of Henry IV of Germany, Gregory carried eulogy to the limit. Omitting all reference to Swein's sins he now commended him to Harold as an immaculate model of kingly excellence. He had been second to no king of his time: "His surpassing virtues", Gregory asserted, "so shone out above all other kings that we ranked him above them all, not excepting even the Emperor Henry III who adhered so closely to the holy Roman church; and we considered that we should embrace him in an unique love" (VII, 21). From such a king Gregory wished a dynasty to descend. In the earlier letter Harold was to attend dutifully to his father's commemoration (V, 10). In the later one he was urged so to imitate his father that a royal stock should manifestly be established:... *quatinus inde possis ornamenta virtutum propagando educere, unde videris nobilissimi sanguinis lineam trahere* (VII, 21). When Gregory learnt that Harold's brothers were seeking the aid of King Olaf III of Norway to compel Harold to divide his inheritance, he summoned Olaf to procure their peaceful and honourable submission, [*ne*] *regni status labefactetur aut dignitas* (VI, 13).[38] In Sweden, to a similar end Gregory proposed that Kings Inge I and Halstan who already shared power should live in brotherly concord and love, and should look back to the good deeds and reputation of their father King Stenkil (1060-6) (IX, 14).[39]

In his attempts direcly to secure the wellbeing of the Scandinavian churches and their clergy, Gregory approached the kings of all three kingdoms. The Swedish kings were to secure respect and obedience towards priests and especially bishops (IX, 4); Harold of Norway was first to see that churches were protected, and then to ensure reverence for the priestly order (VII, 21). Gregory also wanted the kings' help in building up liturgical and pastoral zeal, and in promoting Roman standards and usages. In the short term he requested the dispatch to Rome of bishops or other mature and prudent clergy who might come with information about their kingdoms and return with written and verbal advice and commands. Thus in 1079 he asked Harold IX to send a Danish clerk (VII, 5). In October 1080 he similarly asked King Inge of Sweden for a bishop or suitable clerk; a pastoral letter to Sweden in 1081 establishes that a bishop — possibly Rodulvard of Skara[40] — made the jour-

---

[38] For the circumstances, see ibid., XI, 10, pp. 69-73.

[39] For Stenkil, see ADAM OF BREMEN, III, 15-16, 53, IV, 30, pp. 344-7, 394-7, 474-5. One should bear in mind Gregory's hopes for Henry IV of Germany, which persisted until at least Sept. 1076, that he might be induced to rule after his father Henry III's example: *Reg.* IV, 1, 3, pp. 290-1, 298; cf. II, 44 to Henry III's daughter Queen Judith of Hungary, pp. 180-1.

[40] C.J.A. OPPERMANN, *The English Missionaries in Sweden and Finland*, London 1937, pp. 128, 130, 136-7.

ney (IX, 14). To promote longer-term results, Gregory sought from the three kingdoms the dispatch of young nobles for a period of training at the Lateran palace in the Latin language and in Gregorian standards of religion and discipline (VI, 13; IX, 14).[41] In the circumstances of the 1080s it may be doubted whether any such youths were trained at Rome. But Gregory's intention shows how, after the plan for a Danish metropolis fell by the wayside, he sought to train young Scandinavians both for the present and, perhaps, against times when such plans might be revived.

Gregory's last and most important letter to Denmark (VII, 21) was written two days after the death of Harold IX, its principal addressee. Harold was succeeded by his brother, the energetic and warlike Cnut II (1080-6), who trenuously resumed his father's policies in building up royal power.[42] Cnut's reign illustrates both the affectiveness and the limitations of Gregory's impact upon Denmark. He seems to have paid some attention to Gregory's letter. His kingdom became a refuge for hard-pressed German Gregorians: in 1085 Archbishop Hartwig of Magdeburg, Bishop Burchard II of Halberstadt, and the anti-king Hermann of Salm all fled there.[43] The hagiographical tradition that rapidly grew after Cnut's murder credited him with having done much that Gregory pressed upon the Scandinavian kings. He built and endowed churches, notably at Roskilde, Dalby, and Lund.[44] He promoted reverence for Christian worship and he instituted fasts according to the general discipline of Christendom. He secured the levying and payment of tithes. He safeguarded the rights of bishops and clergy, and he cared for the vulnerable in society (*sustentabat inopes et refovebat flebiles*): the sources particularly men-

---

[41] The reference to Denmark in *Reg.* VI, 13, establishes that there was another, lost letter from Gregory to the Danish king. For the education of young men at the Lateran, see *Reg.* III, 21, IV, 11, pp. 228, 310-11. (For the last reference I am grateful to Mgr. M. MACCARRONE).

[42] For the date of Harold IX's death, see SEEGRÜN (as n. 14), p. 91, n. 283. For Cnut and his cultus the principal sources are: the *Tabula Othiniensis* (c. 1095) by an Anglo-Saxon priest: *VSD*, pp. 60-2; the *Passio sancti Kanuti regis et martyris* (c. 1095/6), by an Anglo-Saxon monk: *VSD*, pp. 62-71; the *Epitaph* (c. 1101), perhaps by the Anglo-Saxon monk Aelnoth: *VSD*, p. 76: AELMOTH *Gesta Swenomagni regis et filiorum eius et passio gloriosissimi Canuti regis et martyris* (c. 1107-11): *VSD*, pp. 77-136. (These sources are also in M.C. GERTZ, *Knud des Heiligen Martyrhistorie*, Copenhagen 1907.)

[43] *Annales Magdeburgenses, a.* 1085, *MGH SS* XVI, 178. For the political background, see HOFFMANN, *Knut der Heilige* (as n. 14), pp. 560-3.

[44] *Passio*, cap. 3, p. 65. For Cnut's arrangements for the consecration and endowment of St. Laurence's, Lund, see *Dipl. Danic.*, I/2, pp. 43-51, n. 21 (21 May 1085), a copy of which preserves the oldest surviving Danish royal charter and evidence for the earliest-known Danish ecclesiastical immunity.

tion strangers, pilgrims, and slaves.[45] In sum, his hagiographers presented Cnut as the *gloriosus rex et protomartyr Danorum* who died from zeal for the Christian religion and for his works of righteousness.[46] The opposition that built up in the nobility and the lesser ranks of society on account of his exaltation of royal power was said to have caused him to suffer "for the love of righteousness and holy religion".[47] In harmony with clerical aspirations Cnut built up the Danish church as a counterweight to the feuding nobility and to the Thing, or assembly, in which they predominated. He became the custodian of its rights and liberties, and the effect of his life and death was to criminalize violations of them.[48] Thus far the image of Christian kingship that Gregory proposed in Swein II was established in one of his sons, and the position of the church was left more secure.

Yet there were limitations. Cnut II had become king after his brother through family arrangements, not by the kind of hereditary claim that Gregory desired; for towards the end of his life Swein has secured the oaths of his leading subjects that his many sons should succeed each other in order as kings of an undivided inheritance.[49] The records of Cnut's reign and cultus do not emphasize obedience to the apostolic see or refer to the need for communication with it. The cultus, in particular, developed in the hands of Anglo-Saxon monks of insular training and outlook, especially monks from Evesham whom King William II of England dispatched in 1095 to set up a monastery at Odense where Cnut had been killed.[50] Their main inspirations were British or English martyrs like Alban, Oswald, and Edmund, and especially the Norwegian martyr-king Olaf II who had died in 1030. Their motives were domestic to Denmark. Gregory's letters record how the Danes were

---

[45] *Passio,* caps. 4, 41, pp. 64-6; *Gesta,* caps. 7, 14, pp. 93, 101.

[46] *Tabula,* p. 60; *Passio,* caps. 1, 6-9, pp. 62-3, 68-71; *Epitaph,* p. 76; *Gesta,* caps. 26-31, pp. 116-29. For the circumstances of Cnut's death, see esp. HOFFMANN, *Knut der Heilige* (as n. 14), pp. 564-7.

[47] *Passio,* cap. 6, p. 68.

[48] But cf. the less sympathetic account of Cnut II given by the *Chronicon Roskildense,* in: *Scriptores minores historiae Danicae medii aevi,* ed. M.C. GERTZ, 2 vols., Copenhagen 1917-20, I, 23-4.

[49] ... *fraternis suffragiis in regni fastigium revocatur:* SAXO GRAMMATICUS XI, 11 (as n. 36), i, 72-3. WILLIAM OF MALMESBURY recorded Swein II's final dispositions as follows: *Swanus, ad mortem veniens, omnes iuramento provinciales constrinxit ut, quia quatuordecim* [sic] *filios habebat, omnibus per ordinem regnum delegarent, quantum ipsa soboles durare posset: De gestis regum Anglorum libri V,* III, 261, ed. W. STUBBS, 2 vols., *RS,* II, 319.

[50] P. KING, *English Influence on the Church at Odense in the Early Middle Ages,* in: *JEH* XIII (1962), pp. 144-55.

apt to blame natural disasters upon the Christian clergy (VII, 21);[51] the year 1086 saw not only Cnut's murder but also grave famine. The Danish clergy needed a patron saint to offer immediate security against lay reprisals for the famine; this St. Cnut afforded. And in the long term they needed him as a guarantor of their own corporate position in society; they looked no further for their principal guarantor.

Thus, if Gregory's letters helped somewhat towards the establishment of St. Cnut as the royal patron of Denmark, the springs of his cultus lay within Danish society and its institutions. Gregory's admonitions to the Scandinavian kings yeld important evidence for his ideas and policies, but their immediate consequences in shaping eleventh-century Scandinavia in church and state were marginal.[52]

## III.

I turn to the Anglo-Norman lands, where his letters show that Gregory had similar objectives both religious and political, but where there were ancient and organized churches, and better-founded structures of royal or ducal authority.[53] More than was the case with Scandinavia, Hildebrand's archidiaconate had seen significant Anglo-Saxon and Norman contacts with the apostolic see.[54] The archbishops of Canterbury and York regularly received the *pallium*, often by travelling to Rome; in Normandy William of Poitiers held it against the deposed Archbishop Mauger of Rouen (c. 1037-54) that he neither possessed a *pallium* nor paid *ad limina* visits when summoned to do so.[55]

---

[51] For witchcraft, see also WILLIAM OF MALMESBURY, *Gesta regum*, III, 261 (as n. 49), II, 319-20; and amongst the Swedes, Aelnoth, *Gesta*, cap. 1 (as n. 42), p. 83.

[52] The limitations of Gregory's perspectives and policies are further illustrated by his apparent lack of awareness of the threat presented by Swein II and Cnut II to King William I in England. The threat became the greater after 1071 when William broke with Count Robert I of Flanders, whose daughter Cnut II married. In 1069 William had asked Archbishop Adalbert of Bremen to negotiate peace between Swein and himself: ADAM OF BREMEN, III, 54, pp. 396-7.

[53] For a fuller discussion, see COWDREY (as n. 9).

[54] See esp. F. BARLOW, *The English Church, 1000-1066*, 2nd edn., London and New York 1979, pp. 289-310.

[55] See the cases of Archbishops Robert of Jumièges (1051) and Stigand (1058: from the antipope Benedict X) of Canterbury, and Kynsige (1055) and Aldred (1061) of York, in the *Anglo-Saxon Chronicle: English Historical Documents*, II: *1042-1189*, ed. D.C. DOUGLAS and G.W. GREENAWAY, 2nd edn., London 1981, pp. 116, 133, 138, 139. For Mauger, see GUILLAUME DE POITIERS, *Histoire de Guillaume le Conquérant*, I, 53, ed. R. FOREVILLE, Paris 1952, pp. 130-2.

Papal legates came to Normandy, and letters and other forms of communication passed between the Norman and English churches and the papacy.[56] Before he became archbishop of Canterbury in 1070, Lanfranc visited Rome three times, and he secured form Pope Alexander II the juridical exemption of his abbey of St. Stephen's, Caen.[57] Most Norman and, indeed, English churchmen would have accepted William of Poitiers's assertions that the pope's primacy made him *praesulum orbis terrae caput... atque magister*, and that Alexander himself was *dignissimus cui obediret quemque consuleret ecclesia universa*.[58] Nevertheless, except for archbishops collecting the *pallium*, recourse to the apostolic see was, in practice, a matter of occasional convenience; and the initiative lay locally rather than with Rome.

The most momentous recourse to Rome was that of Duke William of Normandy when he secured approval for his bid to conquer England. Gregory VII later testified that he had given the Conquest his zealous and effective approval (VII, 23). The arguments that William caused to be presented at Rome are not known for certain, but they are likely to have concerned the need to correct King Harold of England's perjury and Archbishop Stigand of Canterbury's uncanonical position. Their impact may be judged from Alexander II's indictment of English apostasy, when he requested the victorious William to restore the annual payment of Peter's Pence.[59] It is likely that Alexander gave William a banner in token of S. Peter's patronage of his expedition.[60] After the Conquest, Alexander consistently addressed William

---

[56] For papal legates, see T. SCHIEFFER, *Die päpstlichen Legaten in Frankreich vom Vertrage von Meersen (870) bis zum Schisma von 1130*, Berlin 1935, pp. 53-4, 65-6, 79-80. For examples of correspondence with Normandy, see ALEXANDER II, *JL* 4479, *Epp.* 56-7, 70, 128, MIGNE, *PL* CXLIII, 1339-41, 1353, 1408. For England, see *CS*, pp. 521-5, 533-8, 543-5, 548-52, nos. 69-70, 72, 74-5, 77-8.

[57] Lanfranc's three visits were as follows: 1050, LANFRANC, *De corpore et sanguine Domini*, cap. 4, MIGNE, *PL* CL, 413. 1059, MILO CRISPIN, *Vita beati Lanfranci*, III, 8, MIGNE, *PL* CL, 37; NICHOLAS II, *Ep.* 30, MIGNE, *PL* CXLIII, 1349-50. 1067, *Acta archiepiscoporum Rothomagensium*, MIGNE, *PL* CXLVII, 279. For St. Stephen's, Caen, see ALEXANDER II, *Epp.* 20, 35, MIGNE, *PL* CXLVI, 1299, 1339-41.

[58] II, 3 (as n. 55), pp. 152-4.

[59] *Novit prudentia tua Anglorum regnum, ex quo nomen Christi ibi clarificatum est, sub apostolorum principis manu et tutela extitisse, donec quidam, membra mali capitis effecti, zelantes superbiam patris sui Satanae, pactum Dei abiecerunt et Anglorum populum a via veritatis averterunt... Nam, ut bene nosti, donec Angli fideles erant, piae devotionis respectu ad cognitionem religionis annuam pensionem apostolicae sedi exhibebant: Ep. 139*, MIGNE, *PL* CXLVI, 1413.

[60] The main evidence is WILLIAM OF POITIERS, II, 3, 16 (as n. 55), pp. 154-5, 184-5. C. MORTON, *Pope Alexander II and the Norman Conquest*, in: *Latomus* XXXIV (1975), pp. 362-82, exposes the limitations of the evidence for the conferring of a banner. But she is unduly dismiss-

much to criticize in William's conduct, especially his obstruction of communications between the Anglo-Norman lands and the apostolic see. For almost the whole of his pontificate he kept his complaints out of his letters to William himself. As addressed to others they began to appear only in 1079, when he blamed Archbishop Lanfranc for not visiting Rome since he became pope, stressing how blameworthy the king would be if he were preventing Lanfranc from coming (VI, 30). In the same year Gregory exposed to his legate Hubert the complaints that the holy Roman church could justly lay against William — especially that he shamelessly and irreverently prohibited prelates from visiting Rome (VII, 1). (Gregory probably had principally in mind William [1079-1110], the new archbishop of Rouen). Early in the 1080s Gregory wrote still more sternly to both archbishops about their failure to visit Rome.[67] But — one notes a certain parallel with the case of Rikwal of Lund — he never proceeded to positive sanctions, and only in 1082/3 did he address a complaint directly to the king. It concerned his imprisonment of his half-brother Bishop Odo of Bayeux: in a letter that began with expressions of friendship and praise he chided William about this, the single aberration that cast a shadow upon his many royal virtues. But the censure was mild when compared with Gregory's apparently simultaneous comments about the same matter addressed separately to his legate Archbishop Hugh of Lyons (IX, 37, *Epp. vag.*, 53).[68]

It was in letters of 1079 and 1081 to legates whom he judged to have exceeded their brief in opposing the king that Gregory spelt out his underlying attitude to William with clarity and frankness. In 1079 (VII, 1), he referred to his own forbearance but introduced a note of threatening: "If [William] does not set bounds to his blameworthy acts, he should have no doubt whatsoever that he will gravely provoke St. Peter's anger towards himself". But in 1081 (IX, 5), writing when Henry IV was again excommunicated and hostile, and when his letters of 1080 to William and his family (VII, 23, 25-7) had cleared the air, he sounded no such hostile note. He conceded that in some respects William had not behaved with the scrupulous obedience (*ita religiose*) that he would have liked to see. But he had otherwise shown himself more deserving of approval and honour than other kings. He had neither destroyed nor sold the churches of God; he had laboured for peace and right-

---

[67] *Reg.* IX, 1, to Archbishop William of Rouen, (1081), pp. 568-9; IX, 20, to Archbishop Lanfranc of Canterbury, (May/June 1082), pp. 600-1.

[68] For the later story that Odo had prepared an expedition to Rome, see *The Ecclesiastical History of Orderic Vitalis*, VII, 8, ed. M. CHIBNALL, 6 vols., Oxford 1969-80, IV, 38-45, cf. pp. XXVII-XXX.

eousness to prevail among his subjects; when "certain enemies of the cross of Christ" had incited him against the apostolic see he had refused to have dealings with them; he made priests swear to abandon their wives and laymen their tithes. Such a king and his subjects should be treated with moderation and forbearance: "It seems to us that he can much better and more easily be won for God and attracted to an unwavering love of St. Peter by amicable mildness and a show of reason than by the severity and rigour of righteousness". Of all Gregory's letters, this is the one that most authentically sets out Gregory's considered attitude to King William I.

Gregory perceived rightly that William shared his purposes only in part. William knew his place in a single hierarchy that comprehended *sacerdotium* and *regnum* in a harmonious relationship;[69] but he was no Gelasian: for him pope and king were each supreme after his own fashion. Through hard struggles before 1066 to master an unruly duchy, he had learnt the value for ducal authority of a reformed and vigorous church, functioning well in its secular and monastic aspects, but firmly subject to his control.[70] In the first years after the conquest of England, when he was establishing his authority there, he was ready and anxious to invoke papal help. The year 1070, in particular, was marked by the mission of Cardinals John and Peter together with Bishop Ermenfrid of Sion. At legatine councils at Winchester and Windsor they deposed a number of Anglo-Saxon prelates, including Archbishop Stigand of Canterbury; while in Normandy Ermenfrid convened an assembly of bishops and abbots at which a reluctant Lanfranc agreed to succeed Stigand. One source has it that the legates officiated at William's Easter crown-wearing and confirmed him as king.[71] In 1071 Lanfranc again travelled to Rome with Archbishop Thomas of York to collect their *pallia*.[72] But after these events, and so from just before Gregory became pope, with Lanfranc's fullest concurrence William exercised in England as in Normandy the masterful authority over spiritual and temporal matters to which the chronicler Eadmer later referred.[73] Eadmer noticed the barriers that William set between his lands and the papacy: no one might recognize a new pope except by his order or receive a pope's letters unless they had at first been shown to him;[74] at an arch-

---

[69] COWDREY (as n. 2), pp. 53-4, 70-1.

[70] D.C. DOUGLAS, *William the Conqueror*, London 1964, pp. 105-55.

[71] *CS*, pp. 563-85, nos. 85-9; MILO CRISPIN, *Vita beati Lanfranci*, VI, 12, MIGNE, *PL* CL, 40.

[72] For Lanfranc, Thomas, and the papacy at this time, see LANFRANC, *Epp.*, pp. 30-63, n. 1-7.

[73] EADMER, *Historia novorum in Anglia*, I, ed. M. RULE, *RS*, pp. 9-10, cf. pp. 52-3.

[74] It is unlikely that William wished to have, or did have, every incoming papal letter referred to him. For apparently unmonitored communications, see *Reg.* I, 34, to Bishop Re-

bishop of Canterbury's primatial councils nothing might be enjoined or forbidden that the king himself did not sanction and approve. Eadmer's account was composed by way of an introduction to Anselm's archiepiscopate, and it is coloured by developments after the Conqueror's death.[75] But until 1125 there were no more legatine councils in England; councils assembled under royal and primatial authority, and the drafting of their canons left no doubt that the king was master of the church in his realm.[76] In Normandy, too, ducal authority remained paramount.[77]

In England William's resolve to be master was reinforced by Lanfranc, a figure unmatched in the Scandinavian realms. Soon after he became archbishop of Canterbury, Pope Alexander II did, indeed, give him authority to decide disputes in England and to act on the pope's behalf and with his sanction.[78] In 1073 Gregory VII appeared to accept his primatial claims over the whole of the British Isles when he urged him to correct Irish matrimonial customs.[79] But Gregory's complaisance was not likely to continue; for given his hostility to over-mighty archbishops the quasi-imperial claims of Canterbury were no more congenial than those of Hamburg-Bremen. Moreover,

---

migius of Lincoln, 2 Dec. 1073, p. 55; LANFRANC, *Epp.*, pp. 114-15, n. 29; and, in Normandy, *Epp. vag.*, n. 34, to Abbot Anselm of Bec, pp. 88-91. Eadmer's account is based upon ANSELM, *Ep.* 210, S. ANSELMI CANTUARIENSIS ARCHIEPISCOPI *Opera omnia*, IV, ed. F.S. SCHMITT, Edinburgh 1949, p. 106; Eadmer significantly omits the words *nec ut epistolam ei mitterem aut ab eo missam reciperem vel decretis eius oboedirem*. For the stricter custom of Henry I's time, see HUGH THE CHANTOR, *The History of the Church of York, 1066-1127,* London etc. 1961, p. 108.

[75] As a comparison with ANSELM, *Ep.* 210 suggests.

[76] e.g., council of London (1074/5), can. 3, *CS,* p. 613, n. 92, LANFRANC, *Epp.,* pp. 76-7, n. 10, by which three transfers of episcopal sees were effected *regia munificentia et sinodali auctoritate,* while further proposals were postponed *usque ad regis audientiam.* For the ecclesiastical assemblies of William's reign, see K. SCHNITH, *Die englischen Reichskonzilien 1070-86 im Spiegel der anglonormannischen Geschichtsschreibung,* in: *AHC* XII (1980), pp. 183-97, and his comments on *CS* in: *HJ* CIII (1983), pp. 411-18.

[77] See the canons of the council of Lillebonne: ORDERIC VITALIS, V, 5 (as n. 68), III, 24-35, P. CHAPLAIS, *Henry II's Reissue of the Canons of the Council of Lillebonne of Whitsun 1080 (? 25 February 1162),* in: *Journal of the Society of Archivists,* IV (1973), pp. 627-32, repr.: *Essays in Medieval Diplomacy and Administration,* London 1981, n. XIX.

[78] *In causis autem pertractandis et diffiniendis ita sibi nostrae et apostolicae auctoritatis vicem dedimus, ut quicquid in eis iusticia dictante determinaverit, quasi in nostra presentia definitum deinceps firmum et indissolubile teneatur: Ep.* 83, MIGNE, *PL* CXLVI, 1366AB, LANFRANC, *Epp.,* p. 62, n. 7.

[79] *Epp. vag.,* n. 1, pp. 2-5, LANFRANC, *Epp.,* pp. 64-7, n. 8. Lanfranc's claims are well illustrated by the terms of episcopal professions of obedience to him: *Canterbury Professions,* ed. M. RICHTER, The Canterbury and York Society, LXVII, 1972-3, pp. 26-47, n. 26-33.

Lanfranc gradually veered away from Gregory. It seems to have weighed with him that in 1072, thanks partly to Archdeacon Hildebrand, he was not granted *in absentia* the papal privilege that would have secured him the prize of the permanent subjection of York to Canterbury.[80] Despite Gregory's chidings Lanfranc never again visited Rome.[81] In 1080 he remonstrated with Gregory that whereas his own devotion to Gregory had demonstrably increased, Gregory had lapsed from his former cordiality.[82] It is hard to see anything save Hildebrand's attitude to the primacy that Lanfranc can have had in mind. But whatever the reason for it, his sense of Gregory's coolness left him free to yield William the service that he was temperamentally suited to yield — that of "the perfect second-in-command, given a commander whom he could respect and admire".[83] Up to a point he did, nevertheless, promote papal authority. By circulating his canonical collection, an adapted version of the Pseudo-Isidorian Decrees, he gave currency in England to material that emphasized papal claims and rights.[84] He urged its study upon episcopal colleagues. "Give up your dicing, to name nothing worse, and the worldly games to which you are said to devote yourself all day long", he scolded Bishop Herfast of Thetford; "read the holy scriptures, and let your especial study be the decrees of the Roman pontiffs and the holy canons [of church councils]".[85] But all the pontiffs to whom he referred were long-since dead ones; they did not include the present vicar of St. Peter. Similarly, in the canons of Lanfranc's council of London (1074/5), the text of which is attributable to him, ancient popes and councils are cited in eight of the nine canons; yet when decisions were called for about the transfer of episcopal sees — in Gregory VII's eyes a papal prerogative — Lanfranc deferred to his master William, not to the apostolic see.[86] In Gregory's last months it was Archbishop Lanfranc, rather than King William, who was in cautious touch with a representative of the antipope Clement III.[87] (Lanfranc could be venturesome,

---

[80] LANFRANC, *Epp.*, pp. 48-59, n. 4-6.

[81] *Reg.* VI, 30, 25 May 1079, pp. 443-4, IX, 20, May-June 1082, pp. 600-1.

[82] LANFRANC, *Epp.*, pp. 130-1, n. 38.

[83] F. BARLOW, *A View of Archbishop Lanfranc*, in: *JEH* XVI (1965), pp. 163-77, at p. 175, repr.: *The Norman Conquest and Beyond*, London 1983, pp. 223-38, at p. 235.

[84] The canonical collection is now Cambridge, Trinity College, MS. B. 16.44: see Z.N. BROOKE, *The English Church and the Papacy*, Cambridge 1931, pp. 57-83. For Pseudo-Isidore in England, see H. FUHRMANN, *Einfluss und Verbreitung der pseudoisidorischen Fälschungen von ihrem Auftauchen bis in die neuere Zeit*, I, *MGH Schriften*, XXIV/1, Stuttgart 1972, pp. 229-32.

[85] LANFRANC, *Epp.*, pp. 150-3, n. 47.

[86] As n. 76; the canon should be compared with *Dictatus papae*, cap. VII, *Reg.* II, 55a, p. 203.

[87] LAFRANC, *Epp.*, pp. 164-7, n. 52. For comment upon this letter, see COWDREY (as. n. 9), pp. 109-14.

since he was free from the specifically Norman interests that had made Gregory's goodwill valuable to William).[88]

Nothing more clearly illustrates the steady transformation of William's and Lanfranc's attitude to the exercise of papal and royal authority than their dealings with regard to the abbey of Bury St. Edmunds. Its abbot, Baldwin, had come to England in 1065 as King Edward the Confessor's physician, and he continued to serve William and Lanfranc in this capacity;[89] he therefore stood close to them both. He sought to prevent the East Anglian bishop, Herfast of Elmham, from transferring his see to Bury and from exercising jurisdiction over the abbey. In 1071, with the king's permission, Baldwin travelled to Rome and presented his case to Pope Alexander II.[90] Alexander ordained him priest and he returned home with a papal privilege conferring upon his abbey the special protection of the Roman church, confirming its rights and possessions, and prohibiting any power whether secular or ecclesiastical from making it an episcopal see.[91]. On the last point Baldwin forestalled Herfast, who in 1072 moved his see to Thetford. But Baldwin's recourse to the apostolic see over the issue of exemption displeased Lanfranc, who, despite their enduring friendship, thought that he as metropolitan should oversee exempt abbeys.[92] He therefore ignored the papal privilege. In 1073, when the monks of Bury again turned to Rome, his stance came to Gregory VII's attention.[93] Gregory sent him a letter of rebuke for allowing Herfast to defy the Roman church and set at nought papal decrees. He vindicated the pope's rights to provide for the consecration of churches and clergy, and to respond to all who came to him for counsel and aid. He called on Lanfranc to act on his behalf (*vice nostra*) by restraining Herfast, and if necessary by ordering Baldwin to have his case determined at Rome (I, 31). If Lanfranc's

---

[88] See ibid., pp. 100-3.

[89] See esp. A. GRANSDEN, *Baldwin, Abbot of Bury St. Edmunds, 1065-1097*, in: *Proceedings of the Battle Conference on Anglo-Norman Studies*, IV, ed. R.A. BROWN, 1981, pp. 65-76.

[90] Baldwin travelled to Rome with Archbishops Lanfranc of Canterbury and Thomas of York: HEREMANNI ARCHIDIACONI *Miracula sancti Edmundi*, cap. 38, in: *Ungedruckte Anglo-Normannische Geschichtsquellen*, ed. F. LIEBERMANN, Strassburg 1879, pp. 249-50. (The *Miracula* also appear in *Memorials of St. Edmund's Abbey*, ed. H.R. LUARD, 3 vols., RS, I, 26-92).

[91] ALEXANDER II, *Ep.* 81, MIGNE, *PL* CXLVI, 1363-4. Alexander at one point safeguarded Lanfranc's primatial interest (*salva primatis episcopi canonica reverentia*): col. 1364A.

[92] For their continuing friendship, see LANFRANC, *Epp.*, pp. 104-5, 140-1, n. 22, 44, and for Lanfranc's attitude, EADMER, *Hist. nov.*, III (as n. 73), pp. 132-3.

[93] HEREMANNI ... *Miracula,* cap. 48 (as n. 90), p. 259, may relate to their journey.

reaction included his sending to Herfast the sharp letter about studying the decrees of Roman pontiffs that has already been cited,[94] he said not a word about the papacy of his own day or, indeed, about Bury's exemption; he was concerned to vindicate his own metropolitan authority. In the end, however, Bury was vindicated neither by the pope nor by the metropolitan, but by the king. By himself Lanfranc could not prevail: when William sent him to try the issue of exemption by a jury drawn from nine shires and he decided in Baldwin's favour, Herfast was contumacious.[95] So, in 1081, the king imposed discipline by summoning the case to his autumn court at Winchester. The outcome was a royal writ in Baldwin's favour.[96] The change over ten years was complete. Whereas in 1071 the king was content for Baldwin to procure a papal privilege, in 1081 when his regime was secure he proceeded simply by his own writ.

On the other side of the coin, however, there is also much to warrant Gregory's observation that in important respects William was more worthy than other kings of approval and honour.[97] Even in the last stages of Grego-

---

[94] LANFRANC, *Epp.*, pp. 150-3, n. 47; see above, pp. 340-341.

[95] LANFRANC, *Epp.*, pp. 136-9, n. 42; HEREMANNI ... *Miracula*, cap. 43 (as n. 90), p. 254.

[96] *Feudal Documents from the Abbey of Bury St. Edmunds*, ed. D.C. DOUGLAS, London 1932, pp. 55-6, n. 8; see also the general notification in *Regesta regum Anglo-Normannorum, 1066-1154*, I, ed. H.W.C. DAVIS, Oxford 1913, pp. 121-2. William's charter is unlikely to be genuine: *Feudal Documents*, ed. DOUGLAS, pp. 50-5, n. 7, see pp. XXXII-IV; F.E. HARMER, *Anglo-Saxon Writs*, Manchester 1952, pp. 141-5. But its account of proceedings at the king's court may be substantially historical; it apparently underlies HEREMANNI ...*Miracula*, caps. 44-7 (as n. 90), pp. 255-7. It is probably to this time that there should be ascribed the references to Bury's perpetual status as a monastery and complete liberty from episcopal authority in documents associated with Kings Cnut and Edward the Confessor, the full authenticity of which is doubtful. Cnut's charter (1021/3) provides, in its present form, *ut monasterium ... sit per omne aevum monachorum gregibus deputatum ad inhabitandum, et ab omni dominatione omnium episcoporum comitatus illius funditus liberum: Memorials* (as n. 90), I, 342-4, n. 3; for doubts as to its authenticity, see HARMER, pp. 433-4, although it is accepted by C.R. HART, *The Early Charters of Eastern England*, Leicester 1966, pp. 63-5, n. 86. Edward's writ (1042/65) provided *ut nullus espiscoporum monasterium Sancti Edmundi ullo modo sibi vendicet:* HARMER, pp. 153-4, n. 8, pp. 433-5. The passages cited are best regarded as formulated in William I's reign to establish tha Bury's liberty had its origin in royal rather than papal grants. The matter remained closed for the rest of Herfast's episcopate but revived under his successor Herbert Losinga. According to a source favourable to the bishops, after Herfast's death in ?1085 William I himself tried to make Baldwin bishop and to have him establish the see at Bury: V.H. GALBRAITH, *The East Anglian See and the Abbey of Bury St. Edmunds*, in: *EHR* XI (1925), pp. 222-8, at p. 227. See also BARLOW (as n. 66), pp. 207-8.

[97] See above, p. 338.

ry's pontificate, his kingdom maintained contacts with the apostolic see. After William of St. Carilef became bishop of Durham in 1080 he wished to establish a monastic cathedral chapter; at the king's bidding he went to Rome and returned with Gregory's authority to do so.[98] In 1085 William was exchanging letters with Gregory's most loyal followers, who believed him to be watchful and zealous in their cause (Anselm of Lucca).[99] More generally, in partnership with Lanfranc William was responsible for reorganizing the English church in ways that, especially in the long run, were consonant with some, at least, of Gregory's reforming objectives. This is above all true of the ecclesiastical councils and other gatherings that were held throughout William's reign.[100] Such high-level assemblies came to be complemented by diocesan synods; their history in Norman times is obscure, but as early as 1070 the intention of holding them regularly was announced.[101] The reorganization of cathedral chapters, both monastic and secular, provided the dioceses with much-frequented centres, not only for more dignified and popular liturgical worship, but also for the dissemination of theology and canon law.[102] The general introduction of archdeacons and rural deans, which was another subject of early legislation, gave dioceses an internal structure and facilitated the pastoral oversight of clergy and laity.[103] Lanfranc's zeal in promoting and disseminating canon law took forms which, by Gregorian standards, were

---

[98] *De iniusta vexatione Willelmi episcopi primi,* cap. 1, in: *The Historical Works of Simeon of Durham,* ed. T. ARNOLD, 2 vols., RS, I, 170-1; for its authenticity, see F. BARLOW, *The English Church, 1066-1154,* London 1979, p. 281. For the text and history of a spurious privilege of Gregory, see *Quellen und Forschungen zum Urkunden- und Kanzleiwesen Papst Gregors VII.,* I: *Urkunden. Regesten. Facsimilia,* ed. L. SANTIFALLER (Studi e testi, 190), Vatican City 1957, pp. 247-50, n. 210.

[99] *... et propter periculosa tempora, quae nunc imminent, in exequendis, quae ad partes nostras litteris mandasti et quae rescripta sunt tibi, viriliter age, caute prudenterque sollicitudinem tuam impende.* William had earlier sought information about an event in Henry IV's lands by sending an envoy to report on the deposition in 1075 of Abbot Grimald of Saint-Vanne, Verdun: HUGH OF FLAVIGNY, *Chronicon, MGH SS,* VIII, 407.

[100] For the councils, see CS, pp. 563-634. n. 85-98, with important commentary, but see SCHNITH's remarks (as n. 76).

[101] Winchester (1070), can. 13, CS, p. 576, n. 86; Windsor (1070), can. 4, CS, p. 580, n. 87.

[102] Pope Alexander II safeguarded English monastic chapters: *Epp.* 142-4, MIGNE, *PL* CXLVI, 1415-17; for Gregory VII and Durham, see above, n. 98. In general on monastic chapters, see D. KNOWLES, *The Monastic Order in England,* 2nd edn., Cambridge 1963, pp. 129-34, 619-22, and for secular chapters, K. EDWARDS, *The English Secular Cathedral in the Middle Ages,* 2nd. edn., Manchester 1967, pp. 8-22.

[103] Windsor (1070), can. 5, CS, p. 580, n. 87.

old-fashioned; yet they prepared the way for the more up-to-date collections of Ivo of Chartres and, ultimately, Gratian himself.[104] William's ordinance concerning ecclesiastical jurisdiction did not at once introduce ecclesiastical courts. But it was directed towards the recovery for the spiritual forum of matters concerning the cure of souls which had become entangled with lay pleas. It prepared the way for independent ecclesiastical jurisdiction to develop, and for the law of canonical collections and the consequential rulings of councils and synods (*canones et episcopales leges*) to be implemented.[105]

In England as in Normandy the councils of the Conqueror's day sought to implement such Gregorian demands as the collection of tithes and respect for clergy and religious,[106] as well as legislating on other matters of ecclesiastical discipline. Gregory correctly regarded William as a redoubtable foe of simony. The death-bed speech that Orderic Vitalis placed upon his lips, ascribing to him many deeds and attributes that Gregory would have approved, includes the claim that "Never did I expose ecclesiastical offices for sale, but I always hated and rejected simony". His ecclesiastical councils legislated against it, and in his own dealings he cannot be convicted of it.[107] There was also legislation in Normandy and England against clerical marriage and concubinage; although in England Lanfranc tempered the rigour of Norman canons by allowing lesser clergy who were already married to keep their wives.[108] Soon after the Conquest William introduced into England the lay investiture

---

[104] See above, pp. 340-341.

[105] *CS*, pp. 620-4, n. 94; see C. MORRIS, *William I and the Church Courts*, in: *EHR*, LXXXII (1967), pp. 449-63.

[106] Tithes: Winchester (1070), can. 14, *CS*, p. 576, n. 86; Windsor (1070), can. 10, *CS*, p. 581, n. 87; Lillebonne (1080), ORDERIC VITALIS (as n. 68), III, 26-7. Reverence to clergy: Windsor (1070), can. 13, *CS*, p. 581, n. 86; Lillebonne, p. 32-3.

[107] For William's deathbed speech, see ORDERIC VITALIS, VII, 15 (as n. 68), IV, 80-95, esp. pp. 90-1. For examples from Normandy of conciliar legislation against simony: Rouen (1050), cans. 2, 4, 6, 7, 15, 16, Rouen (1072), can. 13, Rouen (1074), can. 1, *Sacrorum conciliorum nova et amplissima collectio*, ed. J.D. MANSI, 31 vols., Florence and Venice, 1759-98, XIX, 752-3, XX, 38, 397-8; Lillebonne (1080), ORDERIC VITALIS (as n. 68), III, 28-9. For English examples, Winchester (1070), can. 1, *CS*, p. 575, n. 86; Windsor (1070), cans. 3-4, *CS*, pp. 605-6, n. 91; London (1074/5), can. 7, *CS*, p. 614, n. 92.

[108] For Norman legislation: Lisieux (1064), cans. 2-3, L. DELISLE, *Canons du concile tenu à Lisieux 1064*, in: *JS*, 1901, pp. 516-21, at p. 517; Rouen (1072), can. 15, MANSI (as n. 107), XX, 38; Lillebonne (1080), ORDERIC VITALIS (as n. 68), III, 26-7. For English legislation: Winchester (1070), can. 15, *CS*, p. 576, n. 86; ?Windsor (1070), can. 3, *CS*, p. 580, n. 87; Winchester (1076), can. 1, *CS*, p. 619, n. 93. For discussions, see esp. DOUGLAS (as n. 69), pp. 332-3; C.N.L. BROOKE, *Gregorian Reform in Action: Clerical Marriage in England, 1050-1200*, in: *CHJ* XII (1956), pp. 1-21, repr.: *Medieval Church and Society*, London 1971, pp. 69-99.

of bishops with the ring and the staff. But he did not thereby challenge the reform papacy, for legislation against it even began only in 1078.[109]

In the Anglo-Norman lands as in Denmark, during the 1070s and early 1080s the king ruled the church masterfully and in the interests of his own authority. But if Gregorian objectives were imperfectly understood and not fully shared, the results were beneficial, and in some measure compatible with them. In return Gregory was statesmanlike in honouring the rulers with whom he dealt, and in treating them with moderation and forbearance. For like the kings in Scandinavia with whom Gregory VII was contemporary, William I never abandoned his loyalty to him. Although the close dealings that marked Alexander II's reign did not continue under Gregory VII when William's authority in Normandy and England was established, pope and king found a *modus vivendi* based upon respect and mutual usefulness. It was well illustrated in 1080, when Gregory both sought William's fealty and requested that Peter's Pence be duly and regularly paid to Rome.[110] The claim for fealty William politely but firmly declined. But he acknowledged the request for Peter's Pence, and he and Lanfranc seem thereafter to have duly collected it.[111] To the end William's relations with Gregory persisted upon a basis of *amicitia.*[112] While Lanfranc ventured upon prudent and guarded communications with a partisan of the antipope Clement III,[113] William kept in touch with the zealous Gregorian Bishop Anselm II of Lucca.[114] There is nothing to suggest that king or archbishop gave the antipope any recognition, or that

---

[109] For the first reference to it in England, see *Facsimiles of English Royal Writs to A.D. 1100 presented to Vivian Hunter Galbraith,* ed. T.A.M. BISHOP and P. CHAPLAIS, Oxford 1957, Plate XIII; and for the beginnings of papal prohibition, R. SCHIEFFER, *Die Entstehung des päpstlichen Investiturverbots für den deutschen König, MGH Schriften,* XXVIII, Stuttgart 1981, pp. 132-76. In Normandy it is probable that ducal investiture was not customary: see the Rouen order for ordaining a bishop preserved in a late eleventh-century hand: *The Benedictional of Archbishop Robert,* ed. H.A. WILSON, Henry Bradshaw Society, XXIV, 1903, pp. 162-5.

[110] LANFRANC, *Epp.,* pp. 128-33, n. 38-9; see COWDREY (as n. 9), pp. 89-94.

[111] For William, see the mandate in *Calendar of the Manuscripts of the Dean and Chapter of Wells,* 2 vols., London: Historical Manuscripts Commission, 1907-14, I, 17; for Lanfranc, *The Domesday Monachorum of Christ Church, Canterbury,* ed. D.C. DOUGLAS, London 1944, p. 80. Neither document is dated, but this seems the probable context.

[112] For this *amicitia,* see also King Henry I's letter of 1101 (*recte*) to Pope Paschal II in *Foedera, conventiones, litterae, et cuiuscumque generis acta pubblica....* ed. T. RYMER and R. SANDERSON, new edn. by A. CLARKE and F. MOLBROOKE, I/1, London 1816, p. 8.

[113] LANFRANC, *Epp.,* pp. 164-7, n. 52.

[114] See above, pp. 324 and 343.

Gregory or Pope Urban II considered that their loyalty was in doubt.[115] Gregory and William knew that they needed each other and that they had everything to gain from their *amicitia*.

IV.

In a brief paper it is possible to notice only a few points about the effectiveness of the Gregorian reform in the regions under discussion after Gregory VII's death in 1085. In Denmark, which after the weakening of the claims of the see of Hamburg-Bremen to general authority over the North held the key to the ecclesiastical organization of Scandinavia, Gregory's hopes for a monarchy strong because of assured descent from generation to generation were long deferred.[116] After King Swein II died the crown passed laterally to five of his sixteen surviving sons — Harold IX (1076-80), Cnut II (1080-86), Olaf V (1086-95), Eric I (1095-1103), and Nils (1104-34). Under Nils in particular there were bitter struggles about the succession that continued through the middle of the twelfth century and were overcome only under Waldemar I (1157-82). These struggles harmed both church and state; they proved Gregory's wisdom and foresight in seeking to promote strong hereditary monarchy.

Despite them, however, the higher ecclesiastical organization of Scandinavia slowly developed as Gregory and the Danish kings had intended.[117] Ecclesiastical unity provided a basis of political unity, and by protecting the church the kings augmented their authority. The plan for a metropolitan see, which had been set back by Bishop Rikwal's succession at Lund, was revived after he died in 1089: under King Eric I Evergood, Lund was established as an archbishopric with Asser (1089-1137) as the first metropolitan. The claims of Hamburg-Bremen were not yet completely laid to rest, and they became particularly menacing in 1133. But in retrospect Saxo Grammaticus could represent Eric I's first visit to Rome, probably in 1095/6, as a critical step in freeing Denmark from the Saxon primacy.[118] Soon after the coming to Denmark in 1102/3 of the legate Alberic, cardinal-priest of San Pietro in Vincoli,

---

[115] See COWDREY (as n. 9), pp. 109-14.

[116] See above, pp. 330-331.

[117] But for contacts after 1085 between Denmark and the antipope's party, see SEEGRÜN (as n. 1·.), pp. 100-6.

[118] SAXO GRAMMATICUS, XII, 5 (as n. 36), I, 98-9.

Asser was named archbishop and received the *pallium*.[119] His area of jurisdiction included the churches of Norway and Sweden, and also Iceland.[120] Gregory VII's papal successors also sought to implement his policy of providing for the security of the church and clergy by cultivating strong monarchy. To this end they approved the cultus of King Cnut II: it was with Urban II's encouragement and with Paschal II's sanction that in 1101 Cnut received the full honours of sainthood.[121] Closer papal over-sight of the Danish church served to promote further measures associated with the Gregorian reform: a regular system of tithes, legislation for clerical celibacy, and the provision of juridical immunity for the clergy.[122] In 1104 Paschal II instructed the Danish bishops to renew the regular payment of Peter's Pence.[123] Paschal intended that there should be frequent legatine missions to Denmark and that Danish bishops should pay regular visits *ad limina*.[124] In 1139, in the presence of the papal legate Theodinus, cardinal-bishop of Santa Rufina, Archbishop Eskil of Lund (1137-77) held the first recorded metropolitan synod for the Scandinavian churches.[125]

It was in 1152-54, with the mission to Scandinavia as papal legate of the Englishman Nicholas Brakespeare, that such measures as Gregory VII envisaged had their fullest development. It is possible that the papacy had never envisaged as a permanent arrangement the placing of the Norwegian and Swedish churches under the authority of Lund, and Nicholas gave Norway its own archbishopric at Nidaros/Trondheim. At the synod of Nidaros he enacted a lengthy series of canons which implemented Gregory's reforming intentions in the light of accumulated twelffh-century experience.[126] He then

---

[119] *Dipl. Danic.*, I/2, pp. 62-7, 96-7, n. 28-30, 46; ANSELM, *Ep.* 447 (as n. 74), pp. 394-5. Partly with an eye to his own times, SAXO GRAMMATICUS commented that *Nec parum Dania Romanae benignitati debet, qua non solum libertatis ius sed etiam exterarum rerum dominium assecuta est:* XII, 6 (as n. 36), pp. 102-3.

[120] For the diplomatic preparation, see SEEGRÜN (as n. 14), pp. 116-18.

[121] AELNOTH, *Gesta*, caps. 33-5 (as n. 42), pp. 131-3.

[122] *Dipl. Danic.*, I/2, pp. 86-8, n. 41. The local organization of the Danish church came later and differed from that of most Western churches. Thus, the office of archdeacon was not introduced into Scandinavia. The equivalent there was the local *prepositus*, first attested c. 1140 in Zealand: T. DAHLERUP, *Die nordische Lokalprobstei und ihr Verhältnis zum Archidiakonat*, in: *Kirche und Gesellschaft im Ostseeraum* (as n. 14), pp. 139-45.

[123] *JL* 6335; *Dipl. Danic.*, I/2, pp. 66-7, n. 30; see above, p. 327.

[124] *Dipl. Danic.*, I/2, pp. 77-8, n. 33, cf. pp. 104-5, n. 55.

[125] Ibid., pp. 146-50, n. 77.

[126] VANDVIK (as n. 10), pp. 42-50, n. 7. See the analysis in SEEGRÜN (as n. 14), pp. 150-62.

went to Sweden, which since Gregory's letters to its kings had remained almost without contact with the papacy. Tribal rivalries were to prevent the establishment of an archbishopric until that of Uppsala was set up in 1164. But Nicholas held a reforming synod at Linköping which published in Sweden some, at least, of the measures enacted at Nidaros. He also visited Denmark, where his leaving the Swedish church for the time being under the primacy of Lund helped to reconcile Archbishop Eskil to the abridgement of his authority elsewhere in Scandinavia.[127] It was Nicholas's achievement that he confirmed the independence, under papal authority, of the Scandinavian churches and brought them into the order of Western Christendom.

In the Anglo-Norman lands as in Scandinavia, the long-term consequences of the Gregorian reform only gradually became apparent. There, too, the succession did not proceed as Gregory wished. The Conqueror's eldest son, Robert Curthose, succeeded him only in the duchy of Normandy, which he retained until 1106 when his brother Henry defeated him at the battle of Tinchebrai. In England, William I's second and third surviving sons, William II (1087-1100) and Henry I (1100-35), were even more impatient than their father became of papal intervention in their affairs. Their resistance was the stronger because as archbishop of Canterbury Anselm insisted more stringently than Lanfranc upon contact with Rome and obedience to its decrees.[128] Yet not only the kings but also Anselm himself advanced old fashioned claims to be the channel by which papal government should operate in England.[129] Apart from the extreme and aberrant notions of the so-called "Norman Anonymous",[130] there is also evidence of reaction against Gregory's later, more ambivalent views about royal authority as expressed towards Germany.[131] In a tract dedicated to Henry I of England, the French monk Hugh of Fleury attacked, though without naming Gregory, the *frivola sententia* of his second letter to Bishop Herman of Metz, that royal power had its origin in human

---

[127] SAXO GRAMMATICUS, XIV, 12 (as n. 36), II, 382-3.

[128] R.W. SOUTHERN, *St. Anselm and his Biographer,* Cambridge 1963, pp. 122-80; F. BARLOW (as n. 66), pp. 300-9, 326-34; 338-50, 373-6, 397-9.

[129] See esp. J. DEÉR, *Der Anspruch der Herrscher des 12. Jahrhunderts auf die apostolische Legation,* in: *AHP* II (1964), pp. 117-86, repr.: *Byzanz und das abendländische Herrschertum. Ausgewählte Aufsätze von Josef Deér,* ed. P. CLASSEN, Vorträge und Forschungen, XXI, Sigmaringen 1977, pp. 439-94; *CS,* pp. 646-7, n. 104; SOUTHERN (as n. 128), pp. 130-2; BARLOW (as n. 66), p. 344.

[130] *Die Texte des Normannischen Anonymus,* ed. K. PELLENS, Wiesbaden 1966.

[131] See I.S. ROBINSON, *Pope Gregory VII, the Princes, and the Pactum, 1077-1080,* in: *EHR* XCIV (1979), pp. 721-56.

pride and greed which the devil inspired: in truth, as St. Paul taught it came directly from God.[132] In practice Henry's control over the church in England remained substantial. Hught the Chantor, the historian of the church of York, correctly observed that in the struggle over investitures he lost little or nothing: "a little, indeed, of his royal dignity, but nothing at all of his power of enthroning whom he pleased".[133] In broader terms, as was already apparent in the trial for treason under William II of Bishop William of St. Carilef, the Norman work of preparing the English church to find its place in the developed Gregorian system of church government was partly offset by its firm inclusion in the post-Conquest feudal polity.[134] Moreover, the precocious development of Norman secular government, especially in the England of Henry I, has reasonably been seen as, in part, a reaction against the claims and pressures of the Gregorian church order;[135] certainly it was incongenial to them. And under Henry the sheer distance, not only physical but above all in ideas and outlook, between the Anglo-Norman church and the apostolic see still inhibited contacts and kept them infrequent.[136]

Yet during the twelfth century there was cumulatively change, and with setbacks papal aspirations for effective authority were increasingly fulfilled. This was partly the outcome of the dramatic crises that centred upon Archbishops Anselm and Thomas Becket.[137] More powerfully and fundamentally it reflected the development, decade by decade, of the machinery of papal government and especially the system of judges delegate, the greater maturity of canon law after the compilation c. 1140 of Gratian's *Decretum*, and the readiness of some later twelfth-century English bishops to promote the mor-

---

[132] HUGONIS MONACHI FLORIACENSIS *Tractatus de regia potestate et sacerdotali dignitate*, I, 1, ed. E. SACKUR, *MGH Ldl*, II, 467, cf. *Reg.* VIII, 21, p. 552.

[133] HUGH THE CHANTOR (as n. 74), pp. 13-14. For King Henry II's reign, see H. MAYR-HARTING, *Henry II and the Papacy, 1170-1189*, in: *JEH* XVI (1965), pp. 39-53.

[134] As n. 98; on the trial, see esp. BARLOW (as n. 66), pp. 75-6, 176-7. For the long-term issues, see esp. D. KNOWLES, *The Episcopal Colleagues of Archbishop Thomas Becket*, Cambridge 1951, pp. 140-56.

[135] A. BRACKMANN, *Die Ursachen der geistigen und politischen Wandlung Europas im 11. und 12. Jahrhundert*, in: *HZ* CXLIX (1934), pp. 229-39, esp. p. 235, repr.: *Gesammelte Aufsätze*, 2nd edn., Darmstadt 1967, pp. 356-66, esp. p. 362.

[136] See esp. M. BRETT, *The English Church under Henry I*, Oxford 1975, pp. 14, 34-62.

[137] See esp. Z.N. BROOKE, (as n. 84), pp. 147-229; SOUTHERN (as n. 128), pp. 122-80; C. DUGGAN, *From the Conquest to the Death of John*, in: *The English Church and the Papacy in the Middle Ages*, ed. C.H. LAWRENCE, London 1965, pp. 65-115, repr.: DUGGAN, *Canon Law in Medieval England*, London 1982, n. XV; C.R. CHENEY, *From Becket to Langton*, Manchester 1956, pp. 42-118.

al reforms that Gregory VII had demanded, especially the struggle against clerical marriage and concubinage. Two landmarks are particularly significant: the revival in England during Henry I's latter years of legatine councils at which the archbishops of Canterbury presided on account, not of their primatial authority, but of the legatine commissions that after Archbishop William of Corbeil (1123-36) they normally received;[138] and the prominence under King Henry II (1154-89) of such canonist bishops as Bartholomew of Exeter (1161-84) and Roger of Worcester (1163-79).[139] It was during the pontificate, and largely as a result of the work, of the lawyer-pope Alexander III (1159-81) that the church in the Anglo-Norman lands and especially in England began seriously and with some effectiveness to implement Gregorian demands such as the enforcement of clerical celibacy.[140]

## V.

Four main conclusions may be suggested.

First, Gregory VII's dealings with the Anglo-Norman lands and with Scandinavia, as parts of Christendom's periphery, were partly inspired by a desire to counterbalance politically the intractable rulers of Germany and France, and partly by his pastoral concern for all peoples, far as well as near. The strength of the latter motive is illustrated by his solicitude for even further-flung lands with little political significance, such as Ireland whose loyalty to Rome and obedience to righteousness he warmly sought (*Epp. vag.*, 57), and Iceland for which, in the difficult year of 1082, he arranged for the consecration to the see of Skálholt of the clerk Gizur. According to the *Hungrvaka* saga, upon his return home Gizur ruled well for more than thirty years "as both king and bishop over the land".[141]

Secondly, Gregory sought to achieve his political and pastoral ends in England and in Scandinavia by fostering strong and compliant monarchies, descending from generation to generation in established and proven Christian families, preferably from father to son. In Scandinavia, however, his in-

---

[138] *CS*, pp. 730-54, n. 129-34.

[139] A. MOREY, *Bartholomew of Exeter, Bishop and Canonist*, Cambridge 1937, esp. pp. 44-54, 75-8; M.G. CHENEY, *Roger, Bishop of Worcester, 1164-1179*, Oxford 1980, esp. pp. 113-93. More generally, see J.E. SAYERS, *Papal Judges-Delegate in the Province of Canterbury, 1198-1254*, Oxford 1971, pp. 1-15, 34-41.

[140] FOREVILLE (as n. 6), pp. 37-9.

[141] Above, n. 34.

tentions were hindered and obscured by the different succession custom that prevailed, and by kings' need to use the church as a means towards building national statehood. They were likewise hindered in England by the recalcitrance of the Norman and in due course the Angevin kings, who were intent upon retaining the church and clergy within the feudal order of their kingdom.

Thirdly, in England, given William I's strong will and purpose, Gregory was never wholly at ease in dealing with him. He needed his political support, and he genuinely valued his — upon his own terms — Christian kingship; and their *amicitia* persisted unbroken. Yet Gregory increasingly found it necessary to cajole, warn, and even threaten the king and his loyal archbishop in an endeavour to bring them to a better mind. Gregory never solved the problem of how to secure strong and effective monarchy but at the same time to promote the liberty of the church and to implement the division of spiritual and temporal powers that such liberty required. His failure to do so reduced his impact upon king, clergy, and laymen alike.

Fourthly, therefore, only when the twelfth century was well advanced did the direct results of the Gregorian reform begin markedly to establish themselves in either Scandinavia or the Anglo-Norman lands. They then did so within a Western Christendom that had undergone much development since Gregory VII's time, especially with respect to ecclesiastical government and canon law; and they remained far from complete in their implementation. But in the final analysis, the changes in the *ecclesia Romana* that Gregory did much to initiate counted for more in promoting its general authority and effectiveness than did political events of a local or national character.[142]

---

[142] I am grateful to Professor R.H.C. Davis for reading and commenting upon this paper.

# Pope Gregory VII
# and the Bishoprics of Central Italy

At a meeting in Spoleto of a European Congress of Medieval Studies, it may be appropriate to present a paper on the light that can be shed upon the pontificate of Pope Gregory VII (1073-85) by what is known of his dealings with the bishoprics of Central Italy which were in direct subjection to the jurisdiction of the pope as bishop of Rome. They numbered at least some sixty-four bishoprics, many of them small, which were situated between the provinces of Ravenna and Milan to the north and Capua and Benevento to the south. They are sometimes collectively referred to as the 'Roman ecclesiastical province', but they were not organized as such, and under so powerful and pastoral a pope as Gregory the designation obscures the active and personal concern that the pope felt for their well-being and for their loyalty.

The bishopric of Rome and its suburbicarian sees lie outside the scope of this paper; it may be useful to indicate the number, names, and locations of the bishoprics with which it is concerned (¹). Two groups of them mostly lay in the western region

---

This paper was read as a Communication at the Ier Congrès européen d'études médiévales held under the auspices of the Fédération internationale des instituts d'études médiévales (FIDEM) at Spoleto, 27-29 May 1993. The following abbreviations are used. CATALANUS: M. CATALANUS, *De ecclesia Firmana eiusque episcopis et archiepiscopis commentarius*, Fermo, 1783. *E. V.*: *The Epistolae vagantes of Pope Gregory VII*, ed. and trans. H. E. J. COWDREY, Oxford, 1972. *M.G.H.*: *Monumenta Germaniae Historica*. *Q. F.*: *Quellen und Forschungen zum Urkunden- und Kanzleiwesen Papst Gregors VII.*, I: *Quellen: Urkunden. Regesten. Facsimilia*, ed. L. SANTIFALLER, Vatican City, 1957 (Studi e testi, CXC). *Reg.*: *Das Register Gregors VII.*, ed. E. CASPAR, *M.G.H.*, Epistolae selectae, II, Berlin, 1920-3.

(1) The data in this paragraph are concerned with those bishoprics which certainly or probably existed as such in the second half of the eleventh century. They are based upon G. SCHWARTZ, *Die Besetzung der Bistümer Reichsitaliens unter den sächsischen und*

52

of Italy between Acquapendente and Terracina which in the directest sense formed the lands of St. Peter. To the south were ten bishoprics of the Roman Campagna: Alatri, Anagni, Cervetri, Ferentino, Segni, Sezze, Terracina, Tivoli, Velletri, and Veroli. To the north-west of them were thirteen bishoprics of Roman Tuscany: Bagnorea, Bieda, Castro, Città Castellana, Città Vecchia, Gallese, Massa Maritima/Populonia, Fossombrone, Gubbio, Montefeltro, Osimo, Pesaro, Rimini, Sinigaglia, Umana, and Urbino. These three groups were in regions that were recognized, for example by the Emperors Otto I in 962 and Henry II in 1020, to be papal bishoprics the disposal of which was wholly in papal hands; there must be added to this category eleven further nearby bishopries, those of Amelia, Città di Castello, Furconia, Marsi, Narni, Nocera, Perugia, Rieti, Teramo, Todi, and Valva/Salmona. Two further groups of bishoprics that were directly subject to the jurisdiction of Rome differed because they were also subject to imperial claims, notably in connection with the choosing and investing of bishops. There were eight such bishoprics in the duchy of Spoleto: Ascoli, Assisi, Camerino, Chieti, Fermo, Foligno, Penne, and Spoleto itself. A final group of ten was situated in the margraviate of Tuscany and in Liguria: Arezzo, Chiusi, Fiesole, Florence, Lucca, Luni, Pisa, Pistoia, Siena, and Volterra.

There is a dearth of surviving evidence for the history of these bishoprics, both severally and collectively, in the time of Gregory VII; the principal source is his own letters and privileges (²). Nevertheless, it has a twofold importance. First, the number and the proximity to Rome of these bishoprics and Gregory's manifest concern for them make it likely that business involving them occupied much of the time and attention of Gregory and his entourage at the Lateran. The historian should not become so preoccupied with Gregory's activities in wider connections that he overlooks the local and routine matters that were his daily concern. Secondly, many of the claims and methods that he pursued locally appear to have been the basis of his activities in more distant parts of Latin Christendom.

---

salischen Kaisern mit den Listen der Bischöfe, 951-1122, repr. with Introduction by O. Capitani, Spoleto, 1993; together with Italia Pontificia, ed. P. F. Kehr, 10 vols., Berlin and Zürich, 1906-75, vols II-IV, VI.

(2) Reg., E.V., and Q.F.

For most of his pontificate, Gregory enjoyed a remarkable degree of support or at least of complaisance from the Central Italian bishoprics. Up to the installation of Clement III as antipope in 1084, Gregory encountered little open resistance in the lands of St. Peter that were nearest to Rome. Indeed, in the Roman Campagna episcopal loyalty to the Gregorian cause persisted even after 1084, especially among bishops whose background was monastic. In Roman Tuscany, as well as in the Pentapolis and in Umbria, a number of bishoprics showed after 1084 a division of loyalties. Even before that date, Bishop Bonizo of Sutri, who after Gregory's death wrote the *Liber ad amicum* in his defence, was driven from his see upon the advance of the army of King Henry IV of Germany, and at Massa Maritima Henry could secure the election of a friendly bishop [3]. There, and still more in bishoprics to the north and east where the king had an acknowledged stake, Gregory faced a more delicate situation of which there are hints. Between 1076 and 1080, his dealings with Henry IV met with criticism to which Gregory and his supporters referred without precisely stating its source. In the winter of 1076-7, he travelled towards Germany against the counsels of almost all his advisers except Countess Matilda of Tuscany [4]. In October 1079, he told his German supporters that 'However many *Latini* there are, all but a tiny few applaud and defend Henry's cause, and accuse me of excessive harshness and mercilessness towards him'; the Swabian annalist Berthold confirmed the strength and vitality of such sentiments [5]. The criticism is likely to have come, at least in part, from the clergy and laity of Central Italy who, after 1084, showed Guibertine sympathies.

Gregory appears to have responded by showing salutary caution and moderation in his dealings with the bishops of the region and thus retaining their support for so long. An example is his dealings with Bishop Rudolf of Siena. On 1 November 1076, Gregory informed five Tuscan bishops that Rudolf had gone illicitly to the excommunicated Henry IV and had communicated with him, thus incurring an excommunication from which he had

---

(3) SCHWARTZ, p. 261.

(4) *E.V.*, nos 17 (pp. 46-49) and 19 (pp. 50-55).

(5) *Reg.*, VII, 3 (p. 462), cf. IV, 12 (pp. 312-313) and IX, 3 (p. 574); for Berthold of Reichenau's indication that there was considerable support for Henry at Gregory's Lent synod at Rome in 1079, see *Annales, s.a.* 1079 (*M.G.H., Scriptores*, V, pp. 316-317).

lightly sought release. His brother bishops were to urge him to do proper penance so that his restoration to communion might be allowed. As with German bishops in 1076, Gregory offered him a road to restoration; in the following September, he went further by employing Rudolf, together with Bishop Rainer of Florence, to oversee the canonical election of a bishop of Volterra (⁶). When dealing with an erring bishop, Gregory showed a prudent blend of firmness, canonical correctness, and moderation.

Until his breach with Henry IV in 1076, Gregory showed a comparable restraint in accommodating the king's claims and interests which, while reflecting his approach to German affairs, may also have had regard to a prevailing loyalty to Henry in Central Italy. Two examples illustrate this restraint. In 1073, the strongly reform-minded Anselm II was elected bishop of Lucca. Anselm entered into a prolonged consultation with Gregory about whether he should receive investiture at Henry's hands. Gregory's reiterated advice to the reluctant Anselm was to refrain from receiving investiture until the king had made amends for his contact with excommunicate counsellors and was restored to peace with Gregory (⁷). When Gregory's legates visited Germany in the spring of 1074, these conditions were met. According to the chronicler Hugh of Flavigny, in December 1074 Anselm came to Rome for ordination by Gregory. But messengers came from Henry, who asked Gregory to follow custom by postponing ordination until Anselm, and also Hugh, bishop-elect of Die in Henry's kingdom of Burgundy, had not only been elected bishop but had also received royal investiture. Gregory took no decision but turned to the cardinals for advice which, in Hugh of Flavigny's opinion wrongly, supported the king. Gregory accepted it to the extent of deferring Anselm's consecration until the king had invested him although he performed Hugh of Die's (⁸). In Burgundy, Henry's power was weak; in Italy as at Rome, there was sufficient recognition of Henry and his claims for Gregory prudently to allow investiture before consecration.

A second example of Gregory's countenancing of royal claims is the filling in 1074 and 1075 of the bishoprics of Fermo and

---

(6) *Reg.*, IV, 8 (pp. 306-307), V, 3 (pp. 350-351).
(7) *Reg.* I, 11, 21 (pp. 17-19, 34-35).
(8) HUGH OF FLAVIGNY, *Chronicon*, II (*M.G.H.*, *Scriptores*, VIII, pp. 411-412).

Spoleto. In December 1075, Gregory's chagrin at Henry's naming of bishops for these sees was a major factor in his sudden disenchantment with the king (9). But a year earlier, Gregory's careful provisions for filling the see of Fermo had included an express intention of consulting the king; by June 1075, a new bishop was in office, apparently by general agreement (10). When the see again became vacant and Henry high-handedly filled both it and Spoleto, Gregory did not object on the grounds that his action was in itself inadmissible; he allowed himself only the conditional aside, 'if, however, a church can be handed over or given by a man' (11). His complaint was that Henry had not returned his own courtesy of 1074: in derogation of the canonical rule that a bishop should ordain only those approved by and known to their ordainer, Henry had given the churches to clerks unknown (*ignoti*) to himself (12). As at Lucca Gregory countenanced royal investiture, so at Fermo he would allow the king a voice in the choice of a bishop, so long as the clerk who was chosen was known to him as the canons required.

Gregory's letters show that he regularly required that candidates for bishoprics should be known to him, and that this was a means by which he secured his authority over the bishops. At Lucca, Anselm was known to him as a learned and discreet man (13). At Volterra in 1077, Gregory set out fully the stages of the making of a bishop: a candidate should be established in his eyes to be *utilis et idoneus*; his election should be made by the clergy and people of his prospective church and confirmed on the pope's behalf; the duly elected candidate should come to the pope for ordination. (Gregory made no reference to the king, no doubt because, although he had been restored to communion at Canossa, the kingdom was in suspense) (14). Gregory's oversight of episcopal elections in Central Italy was calculated to foster

---

(9) *Reg.*, III, 10 (p. 264).

(10) For Bishop Peter, see CATALANUS, no. 10 (pp. 327-328).

(11) Possibly referring to the synodal letter of Popes Nicholas II and Alexander II, *Vigilantia universalis*, cap. VI: R. SCHIEFFER, *Die Entstehung des päpstlichen Investiturverbots für den deutschen König*, Stuttgart, 1981, pp. 222-223 (Schriften der *M.G.H.*, XXVIII).

(12) *Reg.*, III, 10 (p. 264). The canon-law text that Gregory probably had in mind was *Decreta Leonis papae ad Anastasium episcopum Thessalonicensem*, caps. II-V, *Decretales Pseudo-Isidorianae et Capitula Angilramni*, ed. P. HINSCHIUS, Leipzig, 1863, p. 619.

(13) *Reg.*, I, 11 (pp. 18-19); see also *Vita Anselmi episcopi Lucensis*, cap. III (*M.G.H.*, *Scriptores*, XII, pp. 12-13).

(14) *Reg.*, V, 3 (pp. 350-351).

deep and standing loyalties between the pope and the bishops. Papal ordination, in particular, was more than an exercise of jurisdiction: it established a personal bond which was cemented by the pastoral care upon which Gregory set great store [15]. His ordination in his first papal year alone of three Central Italian, as well as two Sardinian, bishops is a reminder of the bond that episcopal appointments established between Gregory and the bishoprics of his immediate jurisdiction [16].

There were other means by which Gregory's authority was promoted in Central Italy. There can be no doubt that its bishoprics usually provided a numerically predominating element in his Lent and November synods at Rome [17]. Like crownwearings in the courts of lay rulers, the synods provided occasions for regular contact between the pope and the leading figures, clerical and lay. Both formally and informally, much local business is likely to have been transacted during them [18].

Over the region at large, Gregory was active both to fulfil the pastoral commission of his office and to promote order and the resolution of disputes. He was very much concerned with the public transgressions and penance of laymen, especially as regards marriage within the prohibited degrees and homicide [19]. Especially in Tuscany, Gregory's many privileges for monasteries and houses of regular canons testify to his care for them and to his confidence in them as centres of reform and of political influence [20]. As regards local disputes, in 1076 he propounded with regard to the see of Roselle a principle that underlay his actions both locally and in the troubles of the German kingdom: it belonged to the papal office to recall to concord those who were in mutual discord. The churches of Roselle and Massa Maritima were, therefore, set a time-limit before which they were to

---

(15) *Reg.*, I, 21 (pp. 34-35); cf. *Vita Anselmi*, cap. III (p. 14).

(16) *Reg.*, I, 85a (p. 123).

(17) See, e.g., *Reg.* II. 52a (p. 196), III, 10a (p. 268), V, 14a (368), VI, 17a (p. 425), VII, 14a (p. 480).

(18) e.g. *Reg.*, III, 13 (274-275), V, 14a (7) (8) (12) (p. 371). Invaluable evidence for the impact of Gregory and his Roman synods on a local church is preserved in the *Liber officiorum* of the cathedral chapter of Volterra, caps. LVIII, LXIV, CXIV, CXXXIV, CXXXVI, CXXXVIII, CCLXII: *De sancti Hugonis actis liturgicis*, ed. M. BOCCI, Florence, 1984, pp. 79, 84, 129-130, 149, 151-152, 153, 221.

(19) *Reg.*, I, 5 (pp. 7-8), II, 48 (p. 74), V, 14a (7) (8) (p. 371).

(20) *Q.F.* nos. LXI, LXX, LXVIII, CXIII, CXXXIX, CXLIV, CXLIX, CLIV, CLXIV, CLXXXII, CXCVIII, CCXVIII (pp. 40-41, 46-49, 60-61, 108-110, 153-155, 159-161, 165-167, 176-180, 191-193, 213-214, 227-229, 265-267); cf. *E.V.* no. 2 (pp. 4-7).

agree about disputed possessions and were to respect past papal rulings ([21]).

For such routine purposes as the collection of revenues, the papacy evidently had agents at large; thus, when Gregory gave certain possessions of the Roman church at Rimini to the monastery of St. Peter and St. Paul, the annual rent of twelve pence was to be paid to the agents (*actionarii*) of the apostolic see ([22]). Gregory also pursued his ends in Central Italy by the sending of legates. His dispatch early in 1075 of the abbots of two Roman monasteries, Gepizo of SS. Bonifacio e Alessio and Maurus of S. Saba, is well documented. His commission to them included an important statement of Gregory's view of legates: the pope needed in practice to entrust his care for the whole church to trusted sons who would represent locally the fullness of his authority. Writing about their legation to the clergy and people of Montefeltre and Gubbio in the Pentapolis, he urged each church to act under the legates' oversight in electing a new bishop, and to prevent the spoliation of their churches by producing the churches' treasure and ornaments for the legates' inspection. The legates' ultimate destination was the whole of the march of Fermo. They were to recover the goods that the bishop of Pesaro had rashly alienated, and they were to settle law-suits between the bishop and his local adversaries. They were to warn Rainer, of the family of the dukes of Spoleto, to do proper penance for an act of fratricide ([23]).

By such means as these Gregory sought to establish and maintain control over the dioceses of Central Italy; for most of his pontificate he was able to do so with a remarkable degree of success. It remains to notice some of the respects in which his dealings had a wider bearing. It has already been suggested that Gregory's use of legates and his concern to promote peace and concord disclose in a relatively local context aspects of his aims and methods in the church at large. Two further elements in his activities as pope may particularly be noticed.

(21) *Reg.*, III, 13 (pp. 274-275), cf. II, 17, 57 (pp. 149-150, 210-211), and *Q.F.*, no. 140 (pp. 155-157).
(22) *Q.F.*, no. 154 (pp. 176-180).
(23) *Reg.*, II, 40-1, 46, 48, V, 14a (7) (pp. 177-178, 185-186, 188, 371). Gregory's concern for the march of Fermo is accounted for partly by its importance for controlling the Flaminian Way and partly by the disintegration of the duchy of Spoleto and the consequent increase in importance of the marches of Fermo and Camerino.

58

First, Gregory was much concerned to expand and to intensify his authority, and upon occasion he used bishops to further
his plans. He especially wished to extend the effective rule of
the apostolic see from the mainland of Central Italy to the islands
which lay to the west, such islands being deemed to belong in
proprietorship to the apostolic see by the provisions of the 'Donation of Constantine'. As early as October 1073, he wrote to the
judges of Sardinia expressing his especial care for their island (24). In November 1074, an elaborate privilege for Bishop
William of Massa Maritima/Populonia and his successors included
a provision granting to their church the island of Elba, critically
situated between the Tuscan coast and Corsica, with the express
intention of forestalling the wrongful claims of any king or mag-
nate, lay or ecclesiastical (25). In September 1077, as he passed
through Siena on his return journey to Rome from Canossa, he
sent the bishops, clergy, and consuls of Corsica an energetic assertion of papal authority over local churches. In words reminis-
cent of his commission of 1075 to the abbots who were his legates
in the march of Fermo, he observed that his multifarious commit-
ments impeded his duty himself to visit every province of the
church. He must, therefore, according to need send agents to
represent his authority and to provide for the salvation of the
people and for the common good. He commissioned Landulf,
bishop-elect of Pisa, to be the permanent vicar of the apostolic
see in Corsica, 'so that, duly pursuing the things that belong to
the good order of holy religion, according to the word of the
prophet (Jer. 1:10) he might « root out and destroy, build and
plant »' (26). From Rome he quickly followed this letter by
another to all the Corsicans, reminding them of the papal
proprietorship of their island, and also of the sacrilege and spiritual
peril of those who had withheld due subjection and obedience.
The Corsicans must repent and return. Gregory confirmed that
he was sending Landulf of Pisa as bishop and as upholder of the
rights and interests of St Peter (27). In November 1078, Gregory
confirmed matters by giving Landulf and his successors as bishops

(24) *Reg.*, I, 29 (pp. 46-47); see also I, 41, 85a (pp. 63-4, 123).
(25) *Q.F.*, no. 84 (pp. 67-69).
(26) *Reg.*, V, 2 (pp. 349-350).
(27) *Reg.*, V, 4 (pp. 351-2).

of Pisa a privilege in which he promised papal protection against the enemies of their church, recognized that Landulf had come to his see in a canonical manner with consecration at his hands, and entrusting the bishops of Pisa with a papal vicariate over Corsica (28).

In October 1080, Gregory reverted to the problem of the larger and more southerly island of Sardinia. In a letter, he praised the judge of Cagliari for having received with respect his legate, Bishop William of Massa Maritima; it was equivalent to a display of devotion to the pope and to St Peter. Gregory was concerned to enforce upon the archbishop of Cagliari and his clergy the canonical requirement that, according to the custom of the Roman church, they should shave their beards. More important, he reflected that Normans, Tuscans, Lombards, and even Germans had importuned him to sanction their incursion into Sardinia, but he had forbidden them and would continue to do so (29). Gregory did not clinch his authority in Sardinia so fully as he did in Corsica. But in the case of both islands, he worked through Tuscan bishops to advance the universal and particular claims of the papacy, and he showed his determination by all possible means to enforce his rulings and to effect his purposes.

A second aspect of Gregory's dealings with the Central Italian bishoprics which has a wider bearing, and one which is even more noteworthy, is his often repeated requirement that his directions should be implemented by the concurrent bringing to bear of the spiritual sanctions and pressures of all grades of the clergy and of physical coercion as applied by the armed force of faithful laity. Gregory's habitual reference to the mobilization of the laity calls for particular attention. In December 1074, Count Hubert and the whole clergy and people of Fermo were to support the archdeacon, to whom Gregory had committed the administration of the vacant see, and to aid him by all means (*modis... omnibus*) in recovering its despoiled property; let them so act as to be revealed as the free and faithful sons (*ingenuos et fideles... filios*) of their mother church (30). In January 1075, when Gregory com-

---

(28) *Reg.*, VI, 12 (pp. 413-415).
(29) *Reg.*, VIII, 10 (pp. 528-530).
(30) *Reg.*, II, 38 (pp. 174-175). For Gregory's vocabulary, see C. ERDMANN, *Die Entstehung des Kreuzzugsgedankens*, Stuttgart, 1935, pp. 147-148, trans. M. W. BALDWIN and W. GOFFART, *The Origin of the Idea of Crusade*, Princeton, N.J., 1977, pp. 162-163.

missioned the abbots who were his legates to the march of Fermo, he was quite explicit. In order to right the wrongs of the church of Pesaro, he insisted that all possible force should be brought to bear upon wrongdoers. 'Resolutely commanding the bishops, the counts, and all the faithful of St Peter, call upon them faithfully to help the bishop of Pesaro to defeat them by bringing spiritual and secular aid according to necessity (*Quatenus episcopo Pensauriensi ad eos expugnandum spirituali et seculari auxilio, prout necesse fuerit, fideliter subveniant*). Above all, you are most sternly to chastise (*acerrime corrigatis*) those who after payment of money do not fear to continue holding land in violence and pride; you are to intervene and restore the church's goods to the bishop' (³¹). On the same day, in a letter to laity both named and unnamed in the county of Chiusi, Gregory ended by reminding them that help in expelling the perjurer and adulterer Provost Guy from his church of S. Mustiola and in restoring their church to its pristine condition would win them salvation and forgiveness of sins (³²).

In connection with the islands of Corsica and Sardinia, Gregory made remarkable claims to dispose of secular arms. In 1077, he told the Corsicans whom he exhorted to repent and return that they should not be mistrustful or doubting, 'for, if only your purpose remains firm and your faith towards St Peter unmoved, we have in Tuscany by God's mercy large forces of counts and valiant men who stand ready, should need arise, for your help and defence (*quoniam... habemus per misericordiam Dei in Tuscia multas comitum et nobilium virorum copias ad vestrum adiutorium, si necesse fuerit, defensionemque paratas*)' (³³). When telling the judge of Cagliari on 5 October 1080 that he had hitherto warded off the approaches of Normans and others who coveted his island, Gregory promised that, so long as the judge continued in the obedience to St Peter that he had exhibited in welcoming his legate, not only would Gregory give licence to no one to enter his land by force but further, if anyone should attempt to do so, Gregory would forbid and repulse him by both secular and spiritual means (*si quis atemptaverit, et seculariter et spiritualiter prohibebitur a no-*

---

(31) *Reg.*, II, 46 (pp. 185-186).
(32) *Reg.*, II, 47 (pp. 186-187).
(33) *Reg.*, V, 4 (pp. 351-352).

bis ac repulsabitur) (³⁴). No doubt Gregory again had in mind the availability of military forces from the mainland.

Sardinia was only one of three destinations which, in 1080, Gregory threatened with sanctions both spiritual and military. Late in June, a sudden crisis in the Spanish kingdom of León-Castile led him to give warning that he would himself come to Spain and lead a military campaign (*dura et aspera moliri*) against King Alphonso VI as an enemy of the Christian religion (³⁵). A third, and the most important, threat to combine military with spiritual action, and one that involved the bishops of Central Italy, arose from King Henry IV's proceedings at the synod of Brixen, which on 25 June chose Archbishop Guibert of Ravenna to be anti-pope. Twenty-eight bishops subscribed the decree of the synod, but only one of them, Hugh, bishop-elect of Fermo, was associated with a Central Italian bishopric. He may not have established himself there, for in 1081 Gregory commissioned a Bishop W. of Fermo — probably not the Wolfgang whom Gregory excommunicated in 1079 *sine spe recuperationis* but an Ulcendinus who is also attested in charters of 1086 — together with Archbishop Urso of Bari and a legate W. to investigate whether the bishop of Mileto should be ordained by the archbishop of Reggio/Calabria (³⁶). Gregory was in South Italy when tidings of the synod of Brixen reached him. He at once turned for military help to the South Italian bishops and to the Normans, Robert Guiscard, duke of Apulia and Jordan, prince of Capua. He claimed that the Normans promised to rally to the aid of St Peter, and of the Roman church and of himself. Furthermore, the lay leaders of Central Italy had also made such promises (*Id ipsum quoque nobis et qui circa Urbem longe lateque sunt et in Tuscia ceterisque regionibus principes firmiter pollicentur*). He summoned all the faithful of St Peter to a campaign which would assemble after 1 September, when the weather was cooler, to seize the church of Ravenna from the hands of the ungodly and to restore

---

(34) *Reg.*, VIII, 10 (pp. 528-530).

(35) *Reg.*, VIII, 2-3 (pp. 517-520). The first of these letters was addressed to Abbot Hugh of Cluny; in the phrase quoted, Gregory adapted the language of *Regula Benedicti*, cap. LVIII, 8.

(36) For the decree, see *M.G.H., Constitutiones et acta publica*, I, no. 70 (pp. 118-120). For Bishop W. (? Ulcendinus), see *Reg.*, IX, 25 (p. 608), and CATALANUS, no. 15 (p. 329). For Bishop Wolfgang, see CATALANUS, no. 14 (pp. 328-329) and pp. 124-126; and for Hugh, CATALANUS, no. 16 (pp. 329-330) and p. 129.

it by armed force (*armata manu*) to St Peter ([37]). In 1080, Gregory was sanguine about the prospect of support from Central Italy.

It is certain that the Normans at this time played no active part on Gregory's behalf, and it is unlikely that any expedition assembled. Gregory, none the less, retained hopes of mobilizing the clergy and laity of the dioceses directly subject to him. In two letters of 15 October, he made a new initiative which disregarded the Normans. He first wrote to all the bishops, abbots, clergy, and laity in the marches of Tuscany and Fermo, as well as in the exarchate of Ravenna, 'who obey the holy Roman church as Christian should'. He reaffirmed his purpose of seizing the church of Ravenna from the hands of the wicked and of bringing about the election of a new archbishop; all his hearers should help him. A second letter charged the Ravennese to bring about an election ([38]). By 11 December, Gregory could write of a new archbishop, named Richard, who had just (*nuperrime*) received the see of Ravenna from the Roman church. He made an impassioned call for support from all the bishops and abbots, counts and knights, in the bishopric of Ravenna, the Pentapolis, the march of Fermo, and the duchy of Spoleto, who were not excommunicated, urging them to support Richard against Guibert 'by all means (*modis omnibus*)' ([39]). Nothing further is known of Archbishop Richard, and there was no known response or sequel to Gregory's summonses. They illustrate both Gregory's persistent expectation of clerical and lay support throughout the bishoprics of Central Italy and the lack of practical response when Gregory called for aid on a large scale.

It is not easy to appraise the significance for the general history of Gregory's pontificate of his claims upon the sanctions which the clergy and laity of Central Italy might provide. It will not have escaped notice that some of the evidence for their exercise in Central Italy synchronizes with his threats of coercion elsewhere. Thus, the records in his Register of the legatine mission of the two Roman abbots early in 1075 followed closely upon his envisaging the deliverance by all means (*modis omnibus*) of the French kingdom from the ungodly rule of King Philip I and upon

---

(37) *Reg.*, VIII, 5, 7 (pp. 521-523, 524-525).
(38) *Reg.*, VIII, 12-13 (pp. 531-534).
(39) *Reg.*, VIII, 14 (pp. 534-535).

his urging the French episcopate to proceed against the king's butler *spiritualibus et secularibus armis* if he did not free a captive clerk ([40]), as well as upon his encouragement in Germany of lay sanctions against simoniac clergy ([41]). In 1080, Gregory's plans for a campaign against Archbishop Guibert of Ravenna followed hot upon his bizarre threat to lead a campaign against King Alphonso VI of León-Castile. Gregory's measures in Central Italy might be interpreted as one facet of a warlikeness, apparent also in France, Germany, and Spain, which was a distinguishing feature of his years as pope. Yet Gregory's measures to promote the moral and material well-being of the churches of Fermo, Pesaro, and Chiusi seem more like a continuation of means of control that had for some time been employed in churches directly subject to Roman jurisdiction. If so, Gregory as pope was less an innovator than a ruler who extended to Christendom at large methods which had already been practised in those churches.

There is much to suggest that, before 1073 as Archdeacon Hildebrand, Gregory had himself developed the military and judicial resources of the apostolic see in Central Italy in order to promote the order and reform of its churches and to extend papal authority. After his death, publicists like Wenric of Trier and Guy of Ferrara made much of his activity before and after his becoming pope. Wenric attributed his promotion as archdeacon to his exceptional personal gifts, even remarking that his discharge of his duties won him general favour and love. Guy made much of the band of knights that he recruited; he established peace and order in the lands of St Peter and he protected the poor and defenceless. However, both writers were, on balance, critical. Wenric placarded his high-handed and arrogant dealings with archbishops and bishops, declaring him to be excessively given to the employment of money and military might; his personal image was tarnished by the parade and practice of warfare. Guy, too, dwelt upon his dedication to arms: from boyhood, he had been skilled in their use, and in adult life he had virtually a private army ([42]).

---

(40) *Reg.*, II, 5 (pp. 129-133), cf. II, 18 (pp. 150-151).
(41) *Reg.*, II, 11 (pp. 142-143).
(42) WENRIC OF TRIER, *Epistola sub Theoderici episcopi Virdunensis nomine composita*, caps I-II (*M.G.H., Libelli de Lite*, I, pp. 285-287); GUY OF FERRARA, *De scismate Hildebrandi*, I, 2, II (*M.G.H., Libelli de Lite*, I, pp. 534-535, 554-555).

64

Archdeacon Hildebrand's involvement with doing justice, giving protection to the vulnerable, and using both spiritual and secular sanctions, is well documented. Three examples will serve to illustrate it. At Pope Alexander II's post-Easter council of 1067, a plea by Bishop William of Sinigaglia against Bishop Benedict of Fossombrone about the possession of a church was heard by Alexander at the Lateran; he did so in the presence of a large group of bishops and others, of whom Hildebrand was named first [43]. In 1069, Alexander dispatched Hildebrand to the monastery of Subiaco, where he was to put an end to vexations by neighbouring lay magnates and to restore internal discipline. Accompanied by Abbot Desiderius of Montecassino, Hildebrand took a band of clerks and knights. He addressed the monks in chapter about the reasons for his coming, received the abbot's resignation, and supervised the election of his successor whom he invested with his pastoral staff [44]. In 1072, he heard a plea arising from a long-standing dispute between the abbey of Farfa and the Roman monastery of SS. Cosma e Damiano in *Mica Aurea* about the possession of a church and its appurtenances. According to the record of the case, he 'appointed a day upon which the abbots of both monasteries should be present to plead their case before him, acting on the pope's behalf in the Lateran palace, the bishops and cardinal-priests, the prefect with the judges and elders of Rome sitting with him' [45]. The interventions and pleas in which Hildebrand is known to have taken part are likely to have been only a few of many in which he was involved. He came to the papal office with a widespread familiarity with the persons and problems of the regions of Central Italy. An experience of the concurrent application of spiritual and secular sanctions which he gained as archdeacon of Rome and in the parts of Italy subject to immediate papal jurisdiction was there built upon by him as pope, and developed by him in his own distinctive way when he dealt with other parts of Christendom.

---

(43) *Sacrorum conciliorum nova et amplissima collectio*. ed. J. D. MANSI, 31 vols., Florence and Venice, 1759-1798, XIX, cols. 997-998.

(44) *Chronicon Sublacense*, ed. R. MORGHEN (*Rerum Italicarum Scriptores*, N.S., XXIV/6, pp. 10-12).

(45) *Il Regesto di Farfa*, edd. I. GIORGI and U. BALZANI, 5 vols., Rome, 1914, no. 1010 (vol. V, pp. 9-11), cf. no. 1012 (vol. V, pp. 16-17).

# IX

# Death-bed Testaments

Historians have devoted only occasional attention to the death-bed testaments by which leading figures in the period of the reform papacy between the Emperor Henry III's Roman expedition of 1046 and the Anacletan schism of 1130–9 made pronouncements, admonitions, and dispositions which their followers and contemporaries recorded and circulated*. Their principal importance in connection with medieval forgery is that they offer insight into the mental outlook that made what a modern observer might deem to be falsifications (Fälschungen), that is, the pious modification of events or documents, in the eyes of contemporaries morally acceptable and, indeed, compatible with the objective, divinely sustained order of the world[1]. Only seldom do death-bed testaments involve forgery as a culpable Verfälschung which would bring them under St Augustine's definition of a lie: *mendacium est ... falsa significatio cum voluntate fallendi*[2]. A death-bed is, after all, not a prudent context for mendacium, whether on the part of a testator or of his witnesses. It is likely to be found only in material prepared at a distance by persons with a tendentious or hostile purpose. In the period under consideration, death was a sacred and solemn occasion, marked out by rituals and conventions which are best illustrated from monastic customaries[3]. They gave death its place in the divine scheme of heaven and earth; death-bed testaments must be understood within this setting.

The testaments most rewarding for study are those of three popes (Leo IX, Gregory VII, and Victor III), two monastic superiors (St Bruno, founder of the

---

*) I gratefully acknowledge the help on particular matters of Professors R. H. C. Davis and K. J. Leyser, and of Dr C. J. Wells.

1) On the subject of forgery in general, see esp. H. FUHRMANN, Die Fälschungen im Mittelalter, HZ 197 (1963) p. 529–554, and ID., Einfluß und Verbreitung der pseudoisidorischen Fälschungen 1 (Schriften der MGH 24, 1, 1972) p. 65–136.

2) Contra mendacium, c. 12, CSEL 41 p. 507, see FUHRMANN, Einfluß p. 81.

3) E.g. Liber tramitis aevi Odilonis abbatis II 33, ed. P. DINTER, Corpus consuetudinum monasticarum 10 (1980) p. 272–278; Udalrici Cluniacensis monachi Antiquiores consuetudines Cluniacensis monasterii III 28–33, MIGNE PL 149 col. 770–778; Guigues 1er, Coutumes de Chartreuse, c. 13–14, ed. a Carthusian, Sources chrétiennes 313 (1984) p. 188–197.

Carthusian order, and Abbot Hugh of Cluny), and two English kings (Edward the Confessor and William the Conqueror). The genre has an age-long background. In law, there was a tradition of attaching especial significance to men's verba novissima[4]. The Bible yields examples of death-bed testaments like those of Jacob (Gen. 49) and Moses (Deut. 33); in the New Testament, besides Christ's own last discourses (John 14–17), St Paul's address to the elders of Ephesus who grieved *quoniam amplius faciem eius non essent visuri* (Acts 20, 17–38), had the ring of a testament. From Socrates onwards, the exitus illustrium virorum both pagan and Christian were often recorded, with explicit or implicit testaments to posterity[5]. One of the most familiar was that of the monk-bishop St Martin of Tours (died 397) in his Life by Sulpicius Severus[6]. For it filled a major gap in the medieval pattern of a holy life: the Rule of St Benedict gave no special prescriptions for a monk's terminal sickness and death, whereas the Life of St Martin afforded guidance both in general and in detail. For example, Martin's last prolonged utterance had the form of a prayer addressed to Christ; he contrasted the vanities of life with the realities of death by insisting that he die upon a 'noble couch' of sackcloth and ashes; and his last words are recorded: they included the statement, *Non decet ... christianum nisi in cinere mori.*

I

The epoch-making significance of Pope Leo IX's death on 19 April 1054 strikes the eye in the catalogue of popes: not since Leo IV (847–55) had a pope been canonized. The written record of his last three days which is complemented by a description of his death and first miracles represents a first step toward an acknowledgement that the Roman church had once again been ruled by a saint who should be honoured as both a strength and an example[7]. It was written by

---

4) M. M. SHEEHAN, The Will in Medieval England (1963) p. 5–106.

5) A. RONCONI, Exitus illustrium virorum, in: Reallexikon für Antike und Christentum 6 (1966) col. 1258–1268. For comment on Merovingian bishops, see G. SCHEIBELREITER, Der Bischof in merowingischer Zeit (1983) p. 242–251.

6) Sulpice Sévère, Vie de Saint Martin, ed. J. FONTAINE, 3 vols., Sources chrétiennes 133–135 (1967–1969). For Martin's sickness and death, see Ep. 3.9–16, I 338–342.

7) BHL 4819; for the text, MIGNE PL 143 col. 525–531. The account circulated widely; cf. the text of most of the first five chapters in A. PONCELET, Vie et miracles du pape S. Léon IX, Analecta Bollandiana 25 (1906) p. 258–297, at p. 288–292. The Latinity is poor, particularly in Poncelet's text, which seems to be nearer the original; it is

a bishop of Cervia, near Ravenna, probably John (attested in charters between 1040 and 1053). He was in Rome with members of his flock during Leo's last days, of whose events he claimed to be an eye witness; he wrote soon after returning to his see[8].

As the bishop presented it, Leo's death-bed testament is divided among five papal discourses in oratio recta. The first was delivered on the evening of 17 April to bishops whom Leo summoned to his presence[9]. He announced his imminent death, and described a vision of the next world that he had experienced the previous night: he had seen men who had fallen *in Apuliam,* that is, at the Norman defeat of the papally assembled army at Civitate on 18 June 1053[10], as martyrs now in glory; they called on him to join them, which one of their number said that he would do in three days. Leo authenticated the vision by declaring that it would be proved true if he did so die. By relating it, the bishop established upon Leo's own testimony that the Roman church had again received a saint – indeed, a martyr-saint, like the popes of the ideal days of the pre-Constantinian church[11].

Leo's second discourse was delivered next morning (18 April) in St Peter's, to a crowd of the faithful[12]. He charged them to continue in good deeds, while they had the light to do so. The bishop of Cervia made it clear that Leo was particularly concerned to protect papal property from spoliation. He introduced Leo's discourse by an account of how the pope had his sarcophagus brought into St Peter's, whereupon the Romans made for the Lateran palace to despoil it 'as their custom was'; but Leo's *meritum et virtus* were such that no one could enter it[13]. Leo forbade anyone to seize church property: *Precipio vobis ut rebus*

---

here cited when available. For the textual problems, see, besides Poncelet, H. TRITZ, Die hagiographischen Quellen zur Geschichte Papst Leos IX., Studi Gregoriani 4 (1952) p. 191–364, esp. p. 300–321; W. WATTENBACH and R. HOLTZMANN, Deutschlands Geschichtsquellen im Mittelalter 3, new edn. by F.-J. SCHMALE (1971) p. 848–850.

8) C. 10, PONCELET p. 295.

9) C. 2, PONCELET p. 289–290.

10) E. STEINDORFF, Jahrbücher des Deutschen Reichs unter Heinrich III. 2 (1881) p. 243–250.

11) For the early popes as martyrs, see H. E. J. COWDREY, Martyrdom and the First Crusade, in: Crusade and Settlement, ed. by P. W. EDBURY (1985) p. 46–56, at p. 46.

12) C. 3–4, PONCELET (as n. 7) p. 290–292.

13) For Leo's concern over the spoliation of episcopal goods, see Die Briefe des Petrus Damiani, ed. K. REINDEL, 1, MGH Die Briefe der Deutschen Kaiserzeit 4, 1 (1983) no. 35, p. 336–339. For the problem at Rome, see R. ELZE, Sic transit gloria mundi. Zum Tode des Papstes im Mittelalter, DA 34 (1978) p. 1–18.

*ecclesiae nec vineae* (!), *nec terras, nec castella, nec mansionibus* (!), *nec aliquam rem nullus iniuste per possessionem contentionem faciat.* He urged men not to swear oaths and so risk perjury, not to commit incest, not to withhold tithes, and not to obstruct pilgrims to St Peter's. Next, like St Martin, he addressed a prayer to Christ. In effect he recapitulated and confirmed the acts of his pontificate. He prayed for the church universal remembering especially those slain in the church's defence – another allusion to Civitate, then for the confounding of all faithless and heretics, next for the conversion of all whom he had excommunicated, and finally for a blessing both spiritual and material upon all whom in his papal travels he had visited and blessed.

Thirdly, Leo addressed the evil of simony, linking it with the Tusculan family which had dominated the papacy before 1046[14], and which immediately after his own death would try to recover the papal throne[15]. He again prayed to Christ, who through his apostles Peter and Paul had brought about Simon Magus' defeat[16], that he would convert Theophylact (Pope Benedict IX) and his brothers Count Gregory II of Tusculum and Peter, *qui in toto pene mundo symoniacam heresim solidaverunt.* Leo finally reverted to a theme familiar from St Martin's death-bed, by contrasting the circumstances of life and death: he blessed his tomb and compared a pope's lifetime honours and riches with the *parva et vilissima mansiuncula* where he would soon repose.

Leo's fourth discourse, on the evening of 18 April, was a further prayer to God that God's word as uttered through his lips might prevail: *concede, ut praedicatio tua non vacua sit omnibus audientibus eam, sed ostende veritatem tuam in nobis*[17]. Finally, on the morning of 19 April, the bishop of Cervia referred to another, unrecorded utterance, followed by Leo's last words: *Audite propter Dominum, habete silentium, forsitan possem propter modicum accipere somnum.* After a fifteen-minute sleep, Leo peacefully died[18].

In thus presenting Leo's death-bed testament, the bishop undoubtedly availed himself of the liberty employed by ancient and medieval writers to compose for their subjects such statements as they deemed appropriate. The record of

---

14) C. 5, PONCELET (as n. 7) p. 299, MIGNE PL 143 col. 529–530.

15) Benonis aliorumque cardinalium schismaticorum contra Gregorium VII et Urbanum II scripta II 10, ed. K. FRANCKE, MGH Ldl 2 (1892) p. 379.

16) For eleventh-century legends concerning Simon Magus, see H. E. J. COWDREY, The Age of Abbot Desiderius. Montecassino, the Papacy and the Normans in the Eleventh and Early Twelfth Centuries (1983) p. 83–87.

17) C. 6, MIGNE PL 143 col. 530.

18) C. 7, MIGNE PL 143 col. 530–531.

Leo's last words, at least, is likely to be close to what the pope actually said: they have no religious or political overtones but relate only to his personal wish for sleep and a quiet death; they appear to be recorded in deference to a convention that last words should be faithfully preserved. But the earlier discourses had a different purpose. They are so framed as to give Leo and his pontificate their due place in an eternal, divinely willed order of righteousness. He was a martyr-saint, who had witnessed heroically for the faith. His preaching was God's own preaching which proclaimed God's eternal truth to the world. The acts of his five-and-a-half year pontificate were validated sub specie aeternitatis. At the same time, his last dispositions guarded against two threats to the Roman church after his death: the spoliation of the Lateran, and a Tusculan restoration. The bishop of Cervia so presented Leo's affairs in life and in death as to make them part of an unchanging divine order which events at Rome since 1046 had vindicated. He introduced no subject that the dying pope is unlikely to have touched upon. But he piously modified the pope's words by presenting them as both an expression of divine wisdom upon the lips of a saint and a protection for the Roman church against the misfortunes that might accompany his death.

The fullest text of Pope Gregory VII's death-bed testament, spoken before he died at Salerno on 25 May 1085, is preserved in the Hildesheim portion of the so-called Hannover letter-collection[19]. In form it is a brief memorandum, with no opening address and greeting or closing attestation. It records, first, Gregory's pronouncements in reply to questions of Roman bishops and cardinals concerning whom he recommended as his successor in the papal office, and the correct treatment of excommunicated adherents of the party of King Henry IV of Germany and the antipope Clement III; next comes Gregory's precept to them, which is said to be one of many which were otherwise unrecorded, that the next pope should be canonically elected; finally Gregory's last words are given: *Dilexi iustitiam et odivi iniquitatem, propterea morior in exilio.*

---

19) Die Hannoversche Briefsammlung: 1. Die Hildesheimer Briefe, no. 35, in: Briefsammlungen der Zeit Heinrichs IV., ed. C. ERDMANN – N. FICKERMANN, MGH Die Briefe der Deutschen Kaiserzeit 5 (1950) p. 75 – 76; for the date, see C. ERDMANN, Studien zur Briefliteratur Deutschlands im elften Jahrhundert (Schriften der MGH 1, 1938) p. 171, and P. E. HÜBINGER, Die letzten Worte Papst Gregors VII. (Rheinisch-Westfälische Akademie der Wissenschaften. Vorträge G 185, 1973) p. 79 – 82. For discussion, COWDREY (as n. 16) p. 181 – 185.

Like Leo IX's testament, Gregory's was probably delivered verbally over a period of time which may have been longer than Leo's three days: according to Paul of Bernried, Gregory's biographer, Gregory's illness was long-heralded although its final crisis was quite brief[20]; and the statements that Gregory summoned the bishops and cardinals at Salerno *cum … gravi teneretur infirmitate, unde postea ipse obiit* and spoke his last words *ubi vero in extremo positus est* may suggest the lapse of a significant time. The memorandum was not drawn up by any of the Roman bishops and cardinals, who are referred to in the third person. But the opening reference to Gregory as *domnus noster* indicates a loyal source close to him; the statement by Bishop Anselm II of Lucca's biographer that he learned of Gregory's last words *ab ipsius capellanis religiosis* suggests that the pope's chaplains may have been that source[21]. Its preservation among the Hildesheim letters, which include items connected with Countess Matilda of Tuscany and Bishop Anselm of Lucca[22], indicates that it may have been directed to, or even composed amongst, their circle soon after Gregory died by papal chaplains who were in touch with it[23].

There is little or no hint that it has been materially falsified, even by such pious modification as Leo IX's death-bed dicta have undergone. Gregory's first provision, in which he recommended for election whichever of the three figures, Bishop Anselm of Lucca, Bishop Odo of Ostia, or Archbishop Hugh of Lyons, the bishops and cardinals could procure, appears to reflect Gregory's predilection for Anselm; it was evidently current among his followers in South Italy until Abbot Desiderius of Montecassino first emerged as a candidate in

---

20) Gregorii P. P. VII vita a Paulo Bernriedensi conscripta c. 108, in: Pontificum Romanorum … vitae, ed. J. B. M. WATTERICH, 1 (1862) p. 538–539; Paul wrote his Life in 1128. According to him, Gregory knew at the beginning of 1085 that he would die by about the beginning of June. A Cassinese tradition recorded that Gregory made his pronouncement about the succession *ante diem tertium obitus sui,* i.e. on 23 May: Chronica monasterii Casinensis III 65, ed. H. HOFFMANN, MGH SS 34 (1980) p. 447; but its account is falsified: see below, p. 711. Paul of Bernried gave no precise indication of the date of the pronouncement: c. 109 WATTERICH, p. 539.

21) The biographer referred to Gregory, *quem pauperem et in exilio novimus defunctum, qui etiam in extremis suis, sicut ab ipsius capellanis didicimus religiosis, 'post omnia', inquit, 'dilexi iustitiam et odio habui iniquitatem, idcirco morior in exilio':* Vita Anselmi Lucensis, c. 38, ed. R. WILMANS, MGH SS 12 (1856) p. 24.

22) Matilda: no. 43, Anselm: nos. 1, 21: ERDMANN–FICKERMANN, Briefsammlungen (as n. 19) p. 86–87, 15–17, 50–52.

23) For evidence of contact, see Chronica monasterii Casinensis III 65, HOFFMANN (as n. 20) p. 447–448.

1086[24]. The second provision, *de excommunicatis,* embodies a milder attitude to Gregory's opponents than he had shown in 1084 at the council of Salerno and than Pope Urban II would later adopt[25]. But it has a parallel in Leo IX's seeking the conversion of his Tusculan opponents; it probably likewise expresses Gregory's death-bed forgiveness, and it resumes the attitude whereby, after his first and second excommunications of Henry IV, he had sought the repentance and reconciliation of the king and his followers[26]. Gregory's third dictum, which recorded in general terms the need for a papal election to proceed canonically, is in line with his previous outlook[27].

When compared with Paul of Bernried's account of Gregory's illness and death[28], the authenticity of the record of the pope's last words raises more difficulties. Paul cited the last words verbatim as in the final testament (c. 110), but he had already cited the opening phrase from Ps. 44 (Vg.), 8 (c. 108): at the onset of the crisis of Gregory's illness, the bishops and cardinals who were present blessed him for the labours (*labores*) of his holy life and teaching; he replied, *Ego, fratres mei dilectissimi, nullos labores meos alicuius momenti facio, in hoc uno solummodo confidens, quod semper dilexi iustitiam et odio habui iniquitatem*[29]. Paul's two citations have been discussed by P. E. Hübinger. So far as it goes, his conclusion that they do not express bitterness and disillusion but Gregory's confidence that he shared the blessedness which, in the Beatitudes, Christ associated with suffering for righteousness' sake, is soundly based[30]. But Hübinger's argument is open to criticism in two respects. First, having rightly affirmed the authenticity of Gregory's utterance as Paul records it in c. 108[31], he casts doubt upon that in c. 110, because „nur eine von ihnen kann wohl authentisch sein"[32]. But there is no reason why Ps. 44, 8 should not have been much in Gregory's mind during his last days, or why he should not

---

24) Cowdrey (as n. 16) p. 182–184.

25) Ibid.

26) Gregorii VII Registrum III 10 a, VII 14 a, ed E. Caspar, MGH Epp. sel. 2 (1920–1923) p. 268–269, 487; The Epistolae vagantes of Pope Gregory VII, ed. H. E. J. Cowdrey (1972) no. 14, p. 40.

27) P. Schmid, Der Begriff der kanonischen Wahl in den Anfängen des Investiturstreits (1926) p. 171–199, 202–204.

28) C. 108–110, Watterich (as n. 20), p. 538–540.

29) Cited from Admont, Stiftsbibliothek, MS 24, f. 141ᵛ–142ʳ; the verbal echo of Acts 24, 21 is to be noted.

30) Hübinger (as n. 19) p. 65–74.

31) Ibid. p. 54, 56–57.

32) Ibid. p. 65, cf. p. 101.

have developed it in both the ways to which Paul alludes. Secondly, Gregory's last words may have a further level meaning that Hübinger does not notice. St Martin and Leo IX both dwelt upon the humble circumstance to which death brought them: Martin reflected that *non decet ... christianum nisi in cinere mori,* while Leo referred to the *parva et vilissima mansiuncula* of his tomb. Gregory's substitution of *propterea morior in exilio* for the Psalmist's *propterea unxit te Deus, Deus tuus oleo laetitiae prae consortibus tuis,* which was associated with the glories of episcopal and royal anointings[33], shows a similar concentration upon the straitened circumstances of death. Martin's and Leo's convention of thought, if not their actual words, may have been in Gregory's mind. Since a similar version of Gregory's last words, which minor verbal variants show to be independent, has the authority of transmission to Anselm of Lucca's biographer by Gregory's chaplains[34], their authenticity may be regarded as virtually certain.

As a posthumous selection of Gregory's utterances, Gregory's final testament as preserved in the Hannover letter-collection has every claim to be considered authentic.

To judge by what is known of its circulation both north and south of the Alps, the final testament was used as a propaganda broadsheet to further the Gregorian cause and to provide guidance for the Gregorian party[35]. Other surviving texts give it in a reduced form. The Gregorian chronicler Hugh of Flavigny inserted into the autograph manuscript of his Chronicle a scrap of parchment upon which he had copied its first two dispositions[36]. He introduced it with the words, *Dixit Urbanus papa in quadam epistola sua.* No such papal letter is known, but Urban II's Register is lost; he may have circulated it as Cardinal Odo of Ostia, perhaps before Bishop Anselm of Lucca's death on 18 March 1086. Hugh of Flavigny's partial citation establishes that part, at least, of Gregory's final testament circulated in its authentic form. It appears, too, in a much curtailed form in the German letter-collection known as the Codex Udalrici, the first part of which was compiled by 1125[37]. The Codex tended, in general, to neutralize partisan documents, especially those of a papalist

---

33) HÜBINGER (as n. 19) p. 57–60.

34) Above, n. 21.

35) Cf. HÜBINGER (as n. 19) p. 93.

36) Hugh of Flavigny, Chronicon, ed. G. H. PERTZ MGH SS 8 (1848) p. 466.

37) Udalrici Codex no. 71, in: Monumenta Bambergensia, ed. P. JAFFÉ, Bibliotheca rerum Germanicarum 5 (1869) p. 143–144.

character; this may account for the omission of Gregory's reference to a free papal election, as well as to the replacement of the opening words *Domnus papa noster* by the more conventional formula *Piae memoriae domnus Gregorius papa septimus*. Nevertheless the substance of what the Codex Udalrici retained was not materially altered or falsified.

For the manifest falsification of the tradition, if not the text, of Gregory's final testament, one may look to Gregorian circles concerned with the succession to the papacy in 1086 of Abbot Desiderius of Montecassino (Pope Victor III). The Montecassino Chronicle gives a long account of his election, which seems to be a conflation of pre-existing sources[38]. So far as the tradition at Montecassino of Gregory's disposition about the succession is concerned, there seems to have been a three-stage development. First, in a narrative of events of June 1085 immediately after Gregory's death, Desiderius told Cardinal-bishop Hubert of Sabina and one Gratian, whom he met on their way from Rome, of a discussion Gregory had had with him about the succession. He urged the cardinals to consider electing a pope with all speed, and to request Countess Matilda of Tuscany to direct to Rome Gregory's three episcopal nominees and others whom she saw fit. There was no mention of Desiderius as a candidate; he was the executor of Gregory's wishes, not their beneficiary. Secondly, only in 1086, when Gregorians at Rome sought to make Desiderius pope, did a passage in the Chronicle for the first time refer to a *iudicium* of Gregory in Desiderius' favour. Thirdly, what seems like a later redactional introduction, perhaps by the monk Guido who was Leo of Ostia's successor as compiler of the Chronicle, conflated the two stories by alleging that Gregory himself first named Desiderius; only if he were insuperably reluctant should the first to hand of the bishops of the final testament be chosen. The redactor's language suggests that he had to hand a version of Gregory's first disposition that was similar to or identical with that of the authentic final testament[39]. The Cassinese tradition sought to warrant Desiderius' election by bringing it within the terms of Gregory's disposition but by there giving it priority.

Forty years after Gregory's death, Paul of Bernried dealt similarly with the problem of the succession. When writing of Gregory's sickness and death, he used a text of the final testament that, as is clear from the second, third, and fourth pronouncements which he cited, was similar to but not verbally iden-

---

38) See COWDREY (as n. 16) p. 185–201, 251–256.
39) Ibid. p. 251 n. 1.

tical with that in the Hannover letter-collection[40]. Paul made much of Desiderius/Victor, whose pontificate he regarded as indeed a victorious one for the Gregorian cause[41]. He précised the introduction to Gregory's first pronouncement by giving it a violently anti-Guibertine tone. He then represented Gregory's reply as omitting Anselm of Lucca, whose death had early removed him from consideration, and as giving the Roman church an option amongst three figures – Desiderius, Odo of Ostia, and Hugh of Lyons.

Both the Montecassino Chronicle and Paul of Bernried illustrate how the tradition of a death-bed testament might be modified by partisans of a prominent figure – in this case Desiderius/Victor, in order to accommodate and warrant developments seen as beneficial and as furthering the testator's cause.

Such beneficial falsification is unlikely to have been thought to involve mendacium. But Gregory's death-bed pronouncements were also the subject of a forgery certainly undertaken to deceive. A widely circulated Henrician manifesto of 1085/88 purported to record how, on his death-bed, Gregory called to himself *unum de XII. cardinalibus quem multum diligebat pre cęteris,* to whom he confessed that he had sinned against his pastoral duties at the devil's prompting by stirring up hatred and wrath against mankind. Gregory next made an apparent reference to his second excommunication of Henry IV in 1080, which he said that he had broadcast to the world. He now sent his confessor to Henry and to the whole church in order to beg forgiveness. He absolved all Henry's followers and the whole Christian people, and he ordered his Roman supporters to surrender the Castel Sant'Angelo to Henry's party[42]. In face of the high degree of reliability that must be accorded to Gregory's final testament as in the Hannover letter-collection, this document, which bears the attestation of Archbishop Wezilo of Mainz (1084–88), Henry's imperial chancellor, must be dismissed as a blatant forgery. It was contrived to recruit support for Henry and to secure the capture of a strategically critical fortress. Like the genuine document, it shows the propaganda value of death-bed testaments; but it takes to the length of mendacium the processes by which they might be adapted or concocted to meet changing circumstances.

Like most of the reform popes after 1046, Desiderius/Victor III retained

---

40) C. 110, WATTERICH (as n. 20) p. 539–540.

41) C. 109, WATTERICH p. 539; see COWDREY (as n. 16) p. 212–213.

42) Ibid. p. 250. The Manifesto also appears in two manuscripts of Beno (as n. 15): IX, p. 422.

until his death his previous office – that of abbot of Montecassino[43]. His last dispositions before his death at Montecassino on 16 September 1087 are recorded in a part of the Montecassino Chronicle usually assigned to the monk Guido[44]. They were made after his hasty return, as a mortally sick man, c. 29 August from the council of Benevento, and mostly if not entirely on the third day before his death (14 September). He made a number of dispositions concerning the abbey: no future abbot was to sell or alienate its possessions; no monk was to prepare a charter or other instrument without his abbot's knowledge; all Montecassino's dependent houses were to furnish it with an annual *prandium*. The latter disposition must be read in the light of Desiderius' extant statute of 1080/87 requiring a list of named *monasteria* and other dependencies to furnish the mother house with yearly *prandia*[45]. By comparison, the Chronicle's summary *omnia monasteria* and its use of the singular *prandium* are imprecise, and it is unlikely to allude to more than a death-bed confirmation of the earlier statute. But there are no grounds for doubting that Victor may have made such a confirmation. At the same meeting of the monastic chapter, he solemnly designated the abbey's *prepositus*, Oderisius I, to succeed him as abbot.

He thereafter called to himself the bishops and cardinals, perhaps apart from the chapter, and spoke of the papal succession. Alluding to Gregory VII's disposition about it, he charged them to elect Bishop Odo of Ostia as quickly as they could. He took Odo's hand and delivered it to the other bishops, telling them to take him and appoint him to the Roman church: *Accipite eum et in Romanam ecclesiam ordinate* ... He further charged them in the meantime to act in his own stead so far as they could: ... *meamque vicem in omnibus, quousque id facere possitis, habete.* Victor evidently thereby attempted to remedy a weakness that was for long to beset the medieval papacy: a pope's authority died with him, and did not revive until his successor was duly elected[46]. Victor's resourceful and urgent provision that sede vacante the Roman bishops should exercise apostolic authority is consistent with his energy immediately after Gregory VII's death in pursuing the interests of the Roman church.

---

43) W. GOEZ, Papa qui et episcopus. Zum Selbstverständnis des Reformpapsttums im 11. Jahrhundert, Archivum Historiae Pontificiae 8 (1970) p. 27–59.

44) Chronica monasterii Casinensis III 73, HOFFMANN (as n. 20) p. 455–456; see also Annales Casinenses, a. 1087, ed. G. SMIDT, MGH SS 30, 2 (1934) p. 1424–1425.

45) H. DORMEIER, Montecassino und die Laien im 11. und 12. Jahrhundert (Schriften der MGH 27, 1979) p. 250–252 no. 5, cf. p. 4–5.

46) See ELZE (as n. 13).

Urban II's letters leave no doubt that he followed Gregory in designating Urban as his successor[47].

There are no grounds for suspecting the hand of a deliberate falsifier in the account of Victor's final testament, which ended with his making arrangements for the construction of his tomb in the chapter house at Montecassino.

## II

Exclusively monastic death-bed testaments are best illustrated by St Bruno, founder of the Carthusian order (†1101), and Abbot Hugo I of Cluny (†1109). Bruno died at his Calabrian foundation of Santa Maria della Torre. His final testament survives only in sixteenth- and seventeenth-century copies[48]. But the letter of the hermits of La Torre which introduces Bruno's strictly contemporary Mortuary Roll confirms that, on the eve of his death, he summoned his brethren and reviewed the stages of his life. He then declared and expounded his faith, first in the Trinity and then in the sacraments and especially in the reality of Christ's presence in the eucharistic bread and wine[49]. Such death-bed professions of faith, as testaments made to God in the presence of human witnesses, are otherwise known amongst monastic and episcopal figures[50]. Those who recorded Bruno's declared its purpose: *scriptam curavimus servare, eo quod satis intime rogaret, ut fidei illius coram Deo testes essemus*[51]. The pious duty of witnessing before God to so personal a statement may well have favoured authenticity and the avoidance of mendacium. Nevertheless, Bruno's profession raises a problem. It opens with a Trinitarian declaration affirming

---

47) See COWDREY (as n. 16) p. 216 n. 9.

48) For Bruno's career, see Lettres des premiers Chartreux, 1: Bruno, Guigues, S. Anthelme, ed. a Carthusian, Sources Chrétiennes 88 (1962) p. 9–27. For comment upon and the text of the Profession, see ibid. p. 37–41, 90–93 no. 3.

49) MIGNE PL 152 col. 554 AB.

50) E.g. Archbishop Gervase of Reims (†1067): Gallia Christiana 9 (1751) col. 70; John Gualbertus, founder of Vallombrosa (†1073): Vita Iohannis Gualberti auctore Andrea abbate Strumensi, c. 79–82, ed. F. BAETHGEN, MGH SS 30, 2 (1934) p. 1100–1102; Bishop Hugh of Lisieux (†1077): The Ecclesiastical History of Orderic Vitalis V 3, ed. M. CHIBNALL, 6 vols. (1969–1980) 3, p. 14–17; Cardinal-bishop Matthew of Albano (†1135): Peter the Venerable, De miraculis II 22, MIGNE PL 189 col. 933–934. None of these raises problems of falsification.

51) Prologus, p. 90.

the double procession of the Holy Spirit[52], and its penultimate clause includes
a eucharistic profession which, with verbal differences, repeats what the Mortuary Roll declares to have stood as its conclusion[53]. But it proceeds to a further
Trinitarian declaration which is closely modelled upon one of the sixteenth
council of Toledo (675): it makes no reference to the double procession but
declares the Father to be *fons ipse ... et origio totius divinitatis*[54] – a formula
calculated to reassure those in an Eastern theological tradition. There are three
possibilities. First, in view of the statement in the Mortuary Roll that Bruno
*fidem suam de Trinitate protracto et profundo sermone exposuit*[55], he may have
eirenically alluded to various Trinitarian formulations current in South Italy,
with its many Eastern ecclesiastical connections. Secondly, it may have been
added by his followers in good faith, to satisfy Eastern-minded monks that,
despite Bruno's Western profession, he safeguarded the faith as Easterns held
it; if so, it may have been added so that it expressed what both Western- and
Eastern-minded monks could testify before the Lord. Or, thirdly, it may have
been added later, in order to assure Eastern objectors that Bruno had held the
same faith as they. All three possibilities remain open. But if the profession was
posthumously altered, care was taken to avoid expressly contradicting Western
formulas, and also to avoid any form of words which Bruno could not have
used without serious self-contradiction.

The terminal illness of the eighty-five-year-old Abbot Hugh of Cluny was
brief, and towards the end he seems to have been too weak for extended utterances[56]. But before this occurred he made at least two extended dispositions
which were placed on written record. In the earlier, he charged those who succeeded to his authority to take especial care of the house for nuns which he had
established at Marcigny[57]. His longstanding concern for his nuns makes its
authenticity highly probable[58]. In the second, which dates from very late in-

---

52) C. 1, p. 90.
53) C. 3, p. 92, cf. MIGNE PL 152 col. 554 AB.
54) C. 4, p. 92; for the council of Toledo's formula, see MIGNE PL 84 col.
452 D – 453 A.
55) MIGNE PL 152 col. 554 A.
56) The main source is Gilo, Vita sancti Hugonis abbatis II 7 – 13, in: Two Studies in
Cluniac History, ed. H. E. J. COWDREY, Studi Gregoriani 11 (1978) p. 97 – 104.
57) Miscellanea 8, ed. H. E. J. COWDREY, Studi Gregoriani 11 (1978) p. 170 – 172.
Hugh said that he spoke when *nativitatis et vite tempora iam peregi et ad ultimam sortem
deveni:* p. 171.
58) See Gilo I 12, COWDREY (as n. 56) p. 61 – 63; Miscellanea 7, COWDREY, p. 168 – 170.

deed in his life, and which is in effect his final testament to his own monks at Cluny, he ranged more widely[59]. Like Bruno he reviewed his life's work, pointing out both his transgressions and his endeavours as abbot of Cluny, and providing for his own post mortem commemoration. He besought his successors to care for Marcigny and to cherish his monks at Cluny. He desired that the whole document should be read aloud to all his monks there by his successor as abbot as soon as he had taken office. But he refrained from designating a successor, thereby following the example of his predecessor Abbot Odilo, who in 1048 had declined to propose a name but had left the matter to a small circle of leading and worthy monks[60]. This document, too, gives no ground for suspecting falsification but seems to record Abbot Hugh's authentic dispositions.

## III

The evidence for the last testaments of the pre- and post-Norman Conquest kings of England, Edward the Confessor and William the Conqueror, is deeply coloured by problems relating to the succession to the crown. Edward's final dispositions are alluded to in the literary evidence of his Life, written by an anonymous monastic biographer before 1075[61], and in the visual evidence of the Bayeux Tapestry, embroidered almost certainly by English needlewomen working under the patronage of Bishop Odo of Bayeux before his imprisonment in 1082[62]. Edward's biographer told how, on 4/5 January 1066, the king recovered consciousness and summoned to himself a group which included Queen Edith, her brother Earl Harold Godwinson, the king's stewart Robert fitzWimarch, and Archbishop Stigand of Canterbury. Edward recounted a vision in which he had been forewarned of the punishment that would in-

---

59) Miscellanea 9, Cowdrey (as n. 56) p. 172–175.

60) Udalricus Cluniacensis monachus, Antiquiores consuetudines Cluniacensis monasterii III 1, Migne PL 149 col. 732 BC; see also Jotsald, De vita et virtutibus sancti Odilonis abbatis I 14, Migne PL 142 col. 911 C, and Gilo II 15, Cowdrey (as n. 56) p. 105.

61) The Life of King Edward the Confessor, ed. and trans. F. Barlow (1962); for Edward's final dispositions, see Bk. II, p. 74–81. For the problems of date and authorship, see also A. Gransden, Historical Writing in England, c. 550–c. 1307 (1974) p. 60–66. For Edward's death, F. Barlow, Edward the Confessor (1970) p. 247–255.

62) The Bayeux Tapestry, ed. D. Wilson (1985); references are to the Plates of this edition.

evitably overcome his people because of its lay and clerical magnates' sins. He asked those present for their prayers, and he prayed for the queen, committing her to Harold whom he described as his protector (*nutricius*) and her brother: *'Hanc,'* inquit, *'cum omni regno tutandam tibi commendo'*. He likewise commended to Harold his servants from overseas, asking that they be allowed either to attach themselves to Harold's protection and service by a bond of fealty, or to have safe conduct home with such property as they had acquired under Edward. Finally the king provided for his burial in Westminster Abbey and for the prompt public announcement of his death.

The account was deeply coloured by the author's commitment to Queen Edith who was still alive when he wrote, and by his hostility to Archbishop Stigand. About Harold he was studiously evasive. Other literary sources reported that, on his death-bed, the childless Edward disregarded any promise he may have given to Duke William of Normandy that he should be his heir and designated Harold as his successor[63]. Edward's biographer did not make a clear statement to this effect. The king's words to Queen Edith leave open for how long and upon what terms he commended the kingdom to Harold, although the provision for the transfer of his vassals' fealty to Harold suggests a fairly permanent arrangement. In a passage written during the Conqueror's reign, the author left Edward's intentions obscure, and was content to fulfill his didactic purpose of pointing out the consequences of the English magnates' sins[64].

The representation in the Bayeux Tapestry of Edward the Confessor as he made his death-bed testament has widely and correctly been held to bear a close relationship to the account in the Life[65]. But it is impossible to be sure which

---

63) Anglo-Saxon Chronicle, E Version, a. 1066, in: English Historical Documents, 1042–1189, ed. D. C. DOUGLAS and G. W. GREENAWAY (²1981) p. 144; Guillaume de Poitiers, Histoire de Guillaume le Conquérant II 11, 25, ed. R. FOREVILLE (1952) p. 172–174, 206–207; Florence of Worcester, Chronicon ex chronicis, a. 1066, ed. B. THORPE (English Historical Society 1848–49) 1, p. 224; Eadmer, Historia novorum in Anglia 1, ed. M. RULE (Rolls Series 81, 1884) p. 8.

64) Cf. BARLOW, Edward the Confessor (as n. 61) p. 251.

65) BARLOW, Life of King Edward (as n. 61) p. 74 n. 5; N. P. BROOKS and H. E. WALKER, The Authority and Interpretation of the Bayeux Tapestry, in: Proceedings of the Battle Abbey Conference on Anglo-Norman Studies 1, ed. by R. A. BROWN (1978) p. 1–34 at p. 11–12; WILSON, Bayeux Tapestry (as n. 62) p. 198. The clerical figures in Pl. 30 (right) and 31 probably all represent Stigand, as the Tapestry shows little consistency in depicting individuals. The figure with a crosier in Pl. 30 (left) is perhaps Abbot Edwine of Westminster.

is the earlier in date, whether either depends directly upon the other, or whether both independently follow a common source or tradition. However, the Tapestry sets events in sharper focus than the Life. It is above all concerned to placard Harold's perjury in accepting the English crown as an affront to divine order and to the workings of fortune. Harold's oath to Duke William was given emphasis[66], and the upper and lower borders of the Tapestry were made to comment upon his sins ands the risks attendant upon his service[67]. The depiction of the Confessor's death and burial are part of a sequence of events deliberately placed out of historical order to heighten the dramatic effect: the king's burial in his newly consecrated abbey church precedes his death[68]. In the upper half of the death scene, Edward addresses a group of *fideles* who seem to correspond to the named figures in the Life; in the lower half he is shown as dead.

From this scene up to that in which Harold comes under the influence of the comet[69], particular emphasis is placed upon the left hand – from classical times the symbol of the adverse, baleful, and perverted[70]. As the king utters his last words, the female figure at the foot of the bed whom the Life identifies with Queen Edith points ominously to an emphasised left forearm and hand which her veil half shrouds. The king, who is crowned, extends his right hand to touch that of a lay figure whom the Life suggests to be Harold; another lay figure behind the king (Robert fitzWimarch?) gestures with his left hand towards this symbol of the king's laying a charge upon Harold. At the same time, Harold and the clerk behind him – probably Stigand – gesture with emphasised left hands towards the king's crown. A confident interpretation of this scene is not possible. But it conveys a strong propagandist suggestion that, on the side of rightness, Edward made a death-bed disposition in which he held

---

66) Pl. 25 – 26.

67) E.g. cunning, Pl. 3, and lust, Pl. 14. Pl. 27, where Harold returns to England, has a marginal reference to the fable of the fox and the crane with its moral that it is unwise to serve the wicked: see M. PARISSE, La Tapisserie de Bayeux (1983) p. 129.

68) Pl. 28 – 31; Edward's final testament, with the legend *Hic Eadwardus rex in lecto alloquitur fideles,* appears in Pl. 30. For the historical inversion, see PARISSE (as n. 67) p. 76 – 77.

69) Pl. 32.

70) The interpretation of the Tapestry is complicated by the fact that the need to impart a powerful forward momentum to events in any case frequently leads to the emphasis of the left arm, in many instances where no pejorative meaning is conveyed, e.g. Pl. 10, 16, 34 – 35. But the emphasis in Pl. 30 – 32, introduced by the figure of the queen, is exceptional.

to an earlier promise that the crown should pass to William and, with his right hand, charged Harold to bring this about. Meanwhile, on the side of falsity, Harold conspired with Stigand to seize the crown for himself.

Such, at least, was the development of events as the Tapestry seems to have presented it. In the next episode, a figure offers Harold the crown with his left hand. Harold is then shown enthroned and crowned; he is *rex Anglorum,* but his authority is flawed: a retainer holds a sword upright but in his left hand, while Archbishop Stigand, now named, clasps in his left hand, according to the older liturgical manner, a maniple that gives it emphasis[71]. Immediately two groups of men point to the comet with their left hands. Then Harold – *rex* no longer though still wearing a crown, his sceptre exchanged for a javelin – slumps in weakness; while his swordbearer retains the sword in his left hand but pointing downwards, in token of the military defeat that fortune is preparing and that a fleet of ships in the lower border foreshadows. Harold's spiritual supporter Stigand has disappeared[72].

Upon such an interpretation, the Bayeux Tapestry forcibly depicts Edward as the good king whose testamentary intentions were honourable in holding to his promise that William should be his successor. They were deceitfully falsified by Harold and Stigand, whose iniquities were speedily punished by powerlessness and defeat. The handling in the Tapestry of Edward's death-bed dispositions is, in a sense, the reverse of the bishop of Cervia's handling of Pope Leo IX's. The bishop built upon Leo's last speeches to show how just and fitting they were as part of the objective divine purpose for the reformed papacy. In the Tapestry, events surrounding the righteous king were false, and in particular Harold's plot with Stigand to secure the crown for himself. It was part of the order of things that nemesis should overtake such machinations. The facts are not likely to have been so simple as the Tapestry suggested. The evidence for Edward's making Harold a death-bed bequest of the crown is

---

71) Pl. 31. The sword should be compared with that to which, in Pl. 48, Duke William points in confidence that he wields it justly; Stigand's maniple – a vestment assumed liturgically *ad abstergendam omnem maculam immundam* – may likewise refer ironically to the archbishop's notoriously irregular rule: Harold's seeming glory as *rex* is false, for the powers of regnum and sacerdotium are both compromised. Pl. 31 perhaps presents an icon of Harold's false kingship rather than his actual coronation at which Archbishop Aldred of York, rather than Stigand, may have officiated: Florence of Worcester (as n. 63) p. 224; however William of Poitiers named Stigand as consecrator: II 1, cf. II 30 (as n. 63) p. 146, 220.

72) Pl. 32.

strong, even from the Norman side[73]. It is likely that, upon his death-bed, the Confessor uttered verba novissima to this effect which conflicted with an earlier valid gift of the crown to Duke William that, in Norman if not English law, not even verba novissima could reverse[74]. If so, when the Confessor died on 5 January 1066, both William and Harold had a case. But the Tapestry suggests how, during the 1070s and 1080s, the events of Edward's last hours were so interpreted as to vindicate the final Norman view that Harold was a perjurer, while William had an unanswerable claim to the crown. Where the Life of the Confessor concealed the issue, the Tapestry blatantly falsified.

The death-bed of William the Conqueror is presented in two sources, the so-called De obitu Willelmi ducis Normannorum regisque Anglorum qui sanctam ecclesiam in pace vivere fecit[75], and Orderic Vitalis' Ecclesiastical History[76]. At first sight, the former of these affords a circumstantial account of William's death, followed by an authentic description of his personal appearance. Those present at his death are listed, his last testamentary dispositions, which included his permission that his regalia should pass to his second son William, and his pardon for his eldest son Robert Curthose, to whom he granted the duchy of Normandy. The De obitu was for long accorded high authority as the work of a monk of Saint-Étienne, Caen, who wrote soon after the event. But just as the description of William that follows has for some years been recognized as a sequence of phrases culled from Einhard's Life of Charlemagne, so now the account of his death has been shown to be a lightly modified abridgement of the so-called Astronomer's description of Louis the Pious's death in his Vita Hludowici imperatoris[77]. Comparison with a charter of King William II for Saint-Étienne, Caen, of 1096/98, granting it a Somerset manor in exchange for regalia which his father had given it suggests that the De obitu was written in

---

73) As above, n. 63.

74) A. WILLIAMS, Some Notes and Considerations on Problems connected with the English Royal Succession, 860–1066, in: Proceedings of the Battle Conference 1 (1979) p. 144–167, at p. 165–166. For legal aspects, see SHEEHAN (as n. 4) p. 107–119.

75) L. J. ENGELS, De obitu Willelmi ducis Normannorum regisque Anglorum: Texte, modèles, valeur et origine, in: Mélanges offerts à Mlle Christine Mohrmann (1973) p. 209–255 (text at p. 223–230); E. M. C. VAN HOUTS, Gesta Normannorum ducum (1982) p. 98–106. For the date, see also A. SAPIR and B. SPEET, De obitu Willelmi (Historisch Seminarium van de Universiteit van Amsterdam, Werkschrift 10, 1976) p. 30–34, 56–57.

76) VII 14–16, ed. CHIBNALL (as n. 50) 4, p. 79–103.

77) For the use of these models, see ENGELS (as n. 75).

England soon afterwards to justify his claim about them[78]. For the most part, however, the author borrowed from the Astronomer such material as was appropriate to William; he was, no doubt, anxious to praise William I *qui sanctam ecclesiam in pace vivere fecit* by exhibiting him in Carolingian terms. On the issue of the regalia, he used a lightly but significantly adapted phrase of the Astronomer to give ex post facto warrant for William's claiming of regalia, the use of which was consistent with his inheritance of his father's kingdom[79].

William's death-bed speech as presented by Orderic Vitalis is probably the historian's own free composition which, although comprising material which Orderic deemed appropriate upon William's lips, is deeply coloured by Orderic's own outlook as he wrote many years later. It has been noticed that Orderic, half-English by birth, expressed in the speech something of the bitterness of dispossessed Englishmen and of their horror at William's harrying of the North[80]. He also put into the king's mouth a similar blend of praise and blame, of self-justification and self-accusation, to that which he elsewhere exhibited[81]. As the example of Abbot Hugh of Cluny illustrates, it was an established convention for a dying man to review at length, in the presence of leading subjects, the course of his life and to include self-justification and self-accusation. It was no less a matter of convention that, at the end of his discourse, William should turn to the matter of the succession. He acknowledged that, because he had invested his first-born son Robert with the duchy even before 1066, Robert must succeed him there despite the misfortunes that the Conqueror foresaw in his rule. As for England, the king's sins were such that he dared not entrust the *fasces ... huius regni* to any man; he entrusted it to God alone, hoping that his second son William would reign there *feliciter* if God so willed. The words *fasces huius regni* may refer to the king's death-bed donation of his regalia to Saint-Étienne, Caen; if so, they impart a significant note of historicity to the end of the discourse[82]. Nevertheless, the

---

78) Les Actes de Guillaume le Conquérant et de la reine Mathilde pour les abbayes caennaises, ed. L. MUSSET (Mémoires de la Société des Antiquaires de Normandie 37, 1967) p. 132–134 no. 24.

79) For the probable suggestion that William II, and afterwards Henry I, secured only the right to borrow the regalia for crown-wearings in Normandy, see F. BARLOW, William Rufus (1983) p. 50 n. 200.

80) M. CHIBNALL, The World of Orderic Vitalis (1984) p. 184–186.

81) K. SCHNITH, Normannentum und Mönchtum bei Ordericus Vitalis, in: Secundum regulam vivere. Festschrift für P. Norbert Backmund O. Praem., ed. by G. MELVILLE (1978) p. 105–119, esp. p. 115–117.

82) CHIBNALL, Orderic Vitalis (as no. 80) p. 186–187.

immediate sequel as Orderic presents it is not quite in harmony with it. The king told his youngest son Henry, not mentioned in the address, that he would receive 5000 marks of silver; but he also prophesied that Henry would in due course rule prosperously over the whole Anglo-Norman realm, as was to be the case from 1106[83]. The king further foresaw, though he did not enjoin, that his second son William would be king in England, whither he dispatched him with a letter to Archbishop Lanfranc of Canterbury *de constituendo rege*. It is likely that the Conqueror's true wish was to hand down an undivided inheritance but that this proved impossible because of his relationships with his eldest son[84]. Orderic himself certainly regarded Henry I's rule as king-duke with admiration[85]. The difference regarding the succession in William I's discourse and in the sequel suggest that Orderic incorporated a discourse which he had written at an earlier time. His concern throughout was to exhibit all that had happened since the Conqueror's death as a working out of the divine purpose for the Anglo-Norman realms; he gradually adjusted his record of William's last testament the better to reflect what actually happened. His purpose was to justify the course of events, not to falsify it. As a final detail, his graphic description of the plundering of King William's possessions immediately upon his death illustrates, as does the account of Pope Leo IX's death-bed, the importance of august death-bed testaments to counterbalance in both the short and the long term by an impressive statement of the ruler's authority and will the lawlessness to which post mortem spoliation might give rise[86].

The evidence that has been considered illustrates the variety of material to be found in eleventh- and twelfth-century accounts of the death-bed testaments of the great. Behind them lay a centuries-long tradition of what was appropriate in them; it guided the dying in what they said, and also those who immediately or subsequently recorded it. Some elements, at least, of that tradition are present in each of the accounts. Thus, at least among clerics, it was not uncommon

---

83) *Pacifice patere ut maiores fratres tui precedant te. Robertus habebit Normanniam et Guillelmus Angliam. Tu autem tempore tuo totum honorem quem ego nactus sum habebis, et fratribus tuis divitiis et potestate prestabis:* VII 16, CHIBNALL (as n. 50) 4, p. 94–96.

84) J. LE PATOUREL, The Norman Succession, 996–1135, English Historical Review 86 (1971) p. 225–250; ID., The Norman Empire (1976) p. 180–187.

85) CHIBNALL, World of Orderic Vitalis (as n. 80) p. 188–190, 196, 198–200.

86) VII 16, CHIBNALL (as n. 50) 4, p. 100–103.

for a dying figure to testify, with witnesses, before God as to his right belief, especially in the Trinity and in the Eucharist[87]. More often, a dying man reviewed the course of his life with much self-accusation and self-commendation. It was a widespread custom to comment on the succession to one's office and to make special admonitions to a successor, whether named or not. Advice or directions were sometimes given about the affairs of particular churches, monasteries, or realms, and (in the case of a pope) about the church at large. A dying man sometimes related visions or dreams that he had recently experienced, often with a didactic import; especial importance was attached to the precise preservation of last words, even if their content was personal or trivial. The dying often made arrangements for their burial.

A critical review of the material suggest that, in some instances, records of last testaments may have a high degree of authenticity, whether because they seem to have been written down at dictation or under close supervision (Abbot Hugh of Cluny) or because they were drawn up soon after death by loyal clerks concerned to preserve a great man's words (Pope Gregory VII's final testament). At the other extreme, there may be blatant forgery designed to deceive (the Henrician Manifesto about Gregory VII's death). In between, there is a broad spectrum of falsification, much of it from a pious motive, designed perhaps to heighten the effect of a dead man's words and to establish his sanctity against a background of eternal divine purposes (Pope Leo IX), perhaps to provide subsequent events, in a weighty matter like a royal succession possibly developing over several decades, with justification in a dead man's dispositions (Orderic Vitalis on King William I), or perhaps to give a propagandist justification to an interpretation of events at odds with what really happened that had both became current with lapse of time and was deemed to represent the divine purpose and human propriety (the Bayeux Tapestry). The greatest value to the historian of death-bed testaments is that they illustrate how, in the interests of upholding an underlying and permanent moral order,

---

87) Here, Cardinal Matthew of Albano's testament before men who were to be his witnesses *hic et in aeternum* is particularly significant: *Confiteor hoc sacrum Salvatoris mei corpus, illud vere et essentialiter esse, quod de sancta Virgine ab ipso sumptum est ... Per ipsum credo incorporari ei, et fieri unum cum ipso, et habere vitam aeternam*: as n. 50. It was not a matter only of dogma but also of salvation: only the reception of the Eucharist as *vere et essentialiter* the body of Christ could guarantee incorporation in him; a merely figurative belief could not save. The importance for salvation of a right Eucharistic faith, especially at death, goes far to explain the universal concern that the Berengarian controversy had engendered.

a death-bed testament might be adapted in its substance or in its circumstances. Such adaptation might serve the interests of hagiography and the promotion of what ought to be (Pope Leo IX), or it might display how actions like those of the perjurer King Harold of England in allegedly frustrating the testament of King Edward the Confessor belonged to a self-destructive world of objective evil (the Bayeux Tapestry).

From motives such as these, a large part of medieval 'forgery' was undertaken.

# X

## Lanfranc, the Papacy, and the See of Canterbury

The purpose of this study is to examine Lanfranc's relations with the popes of his time with whom he is known to have had dealings or who had dealings with him—Leo IX, Nicholas II, Alexander II, Gregory VII, Urban II, and the antipope Clement III *. His dealings with Alexander II be-

\* The following abbreviations are used:

CLOVER/GIBSON *The Letters of Lanfranc, Archbishop of Canterbury*, edd. and trans. H. CLOVER and M. GIBSON, Oxford 1979.

CS *Councils and Synods with Other Documents relating to the English Church*, i: *A.D. 871-1204*, edd. D. WHITELOCK, M. BRETT, and C. N.L. BROOKE; part i: *871-1066*; part ii: *1066-1204*; Oxford 1981.

DC LANFRANC, *De corpore et sanguine Domini, PL* col. 307-342.

HBS The Henry Bradshaw Society.

JE, JL *Regesta pontificum Romanorum*, ed. P. JAFFÉ, 2nd edn. by W. WATTENBACH et al., 2 vols., Leipzig 1885-1888.

MGH *Monumenta Germaniae Historica*.

—— BDK *Die Briefe der Deutschen Kaiserzeit*.

—— Const. *Constitutiones et acta publica*.

—— Epp. sel. *Epistolae selectae*.

—— L de L *Libelli de lite imperatorum et pontificum*.

—— Schriften *Schriften der MGH*.

PL J. P. MIGNE, *Patrologiae cursus completus*.

OV *The Ecclesiastical History of Orderic Vitalis*, ed. and trans. M. CHIBNALL, 6 vols., Oxford 1969-1980.

Reg. *Gregorii VII Registrum*, ed. E. CASPAR, 2 vols., *MGH Epp. sel.* ii.

RS *Rolls Series*.

VH *Vita Herluini*, in: *The Works of Gilbert Crispin*, edd. A. S. ABULAFIA and G. R. EVANS, London 1986, p. 183-212.

VL *Vita Lanfranci, PL* 150, col. 29-58 (see below, p. 659-715).

WILLIAM OF POITIERS GUILLAUME DE POITIERS, *Histoire de Guillaume le Conquérant*, ed. and trans. R. FOREVILLE, Paris 1952.

I am most grateful to Dr Margaret Gibson and to Mr Mark Philpott for their criticisms of a draft of this study, and also to Dr Martin Brett for some long discussions and invaluable information and guidance. Responsibility for errors of fact and judgement remains entirely my own.

tween his accession to the see of Canterbury in 1070 and Alexander's death in 1073 demand especial attention, for upon them turns one of several paradoxes that mark his career: to the aims and measures of the early reformed popes from Leo IX to Alexander II he seems to have become deeply and lastingly committed, yet his relationship with Gregory VII as pope became strained and distant while his commitment to King William I became ever closer and, indeed, overriding. It is this change of attitude to the papacy that an attempt will be made to explore and to explain.

The depth and durability of Lanfranc's commitment to the early reform papacy were almost certainly greater than has been appreciated. His early career was as follows: he was perhaps born c.1010 and left Italy c.1030 to establish himself as a teacher at Avranches c.1039; in 1042 he entered le Bec as a monk, becoming prior three years later; in 1063 he became abbot of Duke William II of Normandy's new foundation of Saint-Étienne, Caen[1]. He left Italy a decade and a half before the Emperor Henry III in 1046 set in train the process of serious papal reform; by that time he had embarked upon his years of monastic responsibility at le Bec. It has too readily been assumed that he therefore never strongly experienced or responded to the initiatives of the reform popes. The duchy of Normandy was distant from Rome in space and in sentiment; under Duke William and especially in the 1060s, the monastic and secular churches there were undergoing reform and reorganization while simony was not a major problem; under a vigorous lay ruler well supported by energetic bishops and abbots the spiritual needs of society were provided for. Against this background, Lanfranc's commitment to and contacts with the papacy have appeared occasional and even distant. It would be wrong to go to the opposite extreme. Nevertheless, there are reasons for thinking that, while a monk in Normandy,

---

[1] For these dates I follow M. GIBSON, *Lanfranc of Bec*, Oxford 1978.

Lanfranc became closely identified with the persons, aims, and methods of the reform papacy, in decades when, like other parts of Latin Christendom, Normandy was not infrequently being drawn to seek from Rome the exercise of an authority that the popes were actively concerned to display [2].

The popes themselves suggested this in two of their letters. Writing to Lanfranc very early in 1059, Nicholas II expressed his strong desire that he should visit Rome. He had heard of Lanfranc's serviceableness in papal affairs (« quem in Romanis et apostolicis servitiis satis opportunum audivimus »). Nicholas understood that a visit to Rome would not at present be easy, and he wished that Lanfranc's activities in Normandy might be fruitful for the pope and the Roman church. Nicholas certainly saw these activities as extending beyond the cloister, the schools, and theological writing. For he urged Lanfranc to be a faithful adviser of the pope's friend the duke of Normandy, and also to bring forth such fruit as he could amongst the clergy and the rude people of the duchy [3]. The evidence of Nicholas's letter to Lanfranc is complemented by the retrospective implications of Alexander II's to William as king of England in October 1071. Alexander exhorted William willingly to follow the admonitions of his 'brother' Archbishop Lanfranc. « We are sorry, » he wrote, « that he is not constantly (*assidue*) joined to us as one of the foremost sons of the Roman church »; there is a strong suggestion here that Alexander would have liked Lanfranc to have become based upon Rome as Cardinals Humbert and Peter Damiani had been. « But », the pope continued, « we take comfort for his absence from the fruit that he brings to the church in your kingdom » [4].

---

[2] For the papacy and Germany, see A. HAUCK, *Kirchengeschichte Deutschlands*, 5 vols., Leipzig 1914-1920, iii, p. 736-752, and for the extent of its influence in immediately pre-Conquest England, F. BARLOW, *The English Church, 1000-1066*, London-New York 1979², p. 289-310. For Normandy, see D. BATES, *Normandy before 1066*, London-New York 1982, p. 198-204.

[3] *PL* 148, col. 1349-1350, *Ep.* 30; now, better, R. W. SOUTHERN, *Saint Anselm: a Portrait in a Landscape*, Cambridge 1990, p. 32-33; cf. p. 20-22.

[4] CLOVER/GIBSON, p. 60-61, no. 7, 25-9.

Lanfranc's standings as a counsellor and confidant of the papacy as of the duke of Normandy should clearly not be underestimated[5].

As for Lanfranc's own direct contact with the popes and their leading supporters at Rome, it was occasional but cordial and fruitful. Given his responsibilities as prior at le Bec, his possibly year-long association with Leo IX was surprisingly protracted. It probably began at the council of Reims (3-5 October 1049), at which, in Dr Gibson's judicious words, « it is a fair guess, but only a guess, that Lanfranc was present ». A letter from Berengar of Tours which seemed to implicate him in Berengar's heresy fell into the hands of a clerk of Reims, probably as a result of his attendance[6]. Moreover, since the business of the council certainly included a papal prohibition of Count Baldwin V of Flanders's giving his daughter Matilda in marriage to Duke William of Normandy and of William's marrying her[7], Lanfranc may have had a brief to watch over William's interests[8]. If he were at Reims, Lanfranc would have witnessed, not only perhaps the consecration of the abbey church of Saint-Rémi, but also a council at which Leo deployed the full powers of papal authority as he undertook to wield it. The assembled bishops acknowledged that the pontiff of the Roman see alone is primate and pope of the church universal,

---

[5] Cf. S. N. VAUGHN, *Lanfranc of Bec: a Reinterpretation*, « Albion », 17 (1985), p. 135-148; also Lanfranc's own plea: CLOVER/GIBSON, p. 32-33, no. 1, 41-43.

[6] GIBSON, *Lanfranc*, p. 66-67.

[7] ANSELM, *Historia dedicationis ecclesiae s. Remigii apud Remos*, PL 142, col. 1415-1440, at col. 1437C.

[8] See BATES, *Normandy*, p. 200-201, although Leo's sentence (*interdixit*) was more than a threat. Stories that Lanfranc was almost banished from the duchy for disapproving of the marriage, that he negotiated about it with Nicholas II at Rome in 1059, and that William and Matilda founded the twin abbeys of Saint-Étienne and la Trinité at Caen in penance for their marriage depend upon twelfth-century evidence of more than dubious value: *VL* (date c. 1140-1156), cap. 3, col. 34-37 (see below, p. 675-678). Cf. *VH* (date 1109-1117/1118), cap. 64-68, p. 197-198; ORDERIC VITALIS's interpolation in GUILLAUME DE JUMIÈGES, *Gesta Normannorum ducum*, cap. 36, ed. J. MARX, Rouen-Paris 1914, p. 181-182.

while the faults of the French church were arraigned, many bishops and abbots purged their simony, and reforming canons were enacted [9].

Leo travelled by way of Mainz where he held another council in the presence of the German Emperor Henry III; Lanfranc may have witnessed pope and emperor jointly promoting reform. At Remiremont, in the Vosges, Lanfranc was certainly present on 14 November when Leo consecrated the church of Saint-Pierre des Dames, for Lanfranc later referred to his observation of papal usage as regards liturgical vesture [10]. Leo and his party were back in Rome for a council in the Lateran which began on 29 April 1050 [11]. In Berengar's absence, the clerk of Reims who brought to Rome the letter that embarrassed Lanfranc read it out. After Berengar's position as expressed in it had been condemned, Leo called upon Lanfranc to purge himself from the stain of the false accusation. This he did to the satisfaction of all present, appealing (as he said) to sacred authorities rather than to arguments. Having established his orthodoxy in a manner appropriate to a Roman gathering, Lanfranc was asked by the pope to remain in the papal entourage until a further inquiry into Berengar's teaching had taken place at the council of Vercelli in the following September [12].

The audience at Rome that Lanfranc thus satisfied comprised not only the pope but also those whom he had brought with him from north of the Alps for the service of the Roman church. To the young clerk Hildebrand, returning from exile, it will be necessary to revert later. A more immediately dominant figure was Humbert, monk of Moyenmoutier. Leo almost at once ordained him as archbishop of Sicily so that he might preach to that as yet unreconquered island. Like Lan-

---

[9] ANSELM, *Historia*, gives a full account.

[10] CLOVER/GIBSON, p. 84-85, no. 14, 28-31. Lanfranc's instancing of the papal consecration of Remiremont rather than Saint-Rémi, Reims, somewhat weakens the case for his presence at the latter, which immediately preceded the council.

[11] Leo's itinerary is indicated by JL, p. 531-538.

[12] *DC*, cap. 4, col. 413BC; *VL*, cap. 3, col. 35-36 (see below, p. 676-678).

franc, he was at the Lateran council of spring 1050. Thereafter
Leo appointed him to the cardinal-bishopric of Silva Candida,
which he held until his death in 1061 [13]. Lanfranc's own references to Humbert leave no doubt about the high and lasting
regard in which he held him, both for his life and for his
teachings. In view of its extremely limited circulation, Lanfranc may not have ever read Humbert's *Libri iii adversus
simoniacos*, probably written in 1057 or 1058, with its high
teaching about *sacerdotium* and *regnum* [14]. But no reader of
Lanfranc's *Liber de corpore et sanguine Domini*, which he
composed at Caen between 1063 and 1070, can fail to observe
the memory that he cultivated of Humbert's career while they
were together. He castigated Berengar for calling Humbert a
Burgundian when Leo had recruited him in Lorraine. As for
Humbert's years as cardinal-bishop, Lanfranc regarded them in
terms of eulogy:

> When established in this office, he so lived and taught that not
> the slightest breath of suspicion arose about his faith and doctrine.
> Witness to this is borne by practically all of Latin Christendom
> which, given the pre-eminence of the apostolic see in whose coun-
> cils and counsels he was always present and predominant, could not
> fail to regard them [15].

Both for what he was and for what he taught, Cardinal Humbert must be accounted a major and a direct influence upon
Lanfranc in his middle years.

Whether Lanfranc came to Rome during the pontificate
of Nicholas II, when Humbert's career was at its apogee, it
is difficult to be sure. The twelfth-century *Vita Lanfranci* is
categorical that he did so, and that he attended the momentous

---

[13] For Humbert, see R. Hüls, *Kardinäle, Klerus und Kirchen Roms, 1049-
1130*, Tübingen 1977 (Bibliothek des Deutschen Historischen Instituts in Rom,
48), p. 131-134.

[14] See the comments of R. Schieffer, *Die Entstehung des päpstlichen Investiturverbots für den deutschen König, MGH Schriften*, 28, Stuttgart 1931,
p. 36-47.

[15] *DC*, cap. 2, col. 409B-410B.

Lateran Council of 1059 when Berengar was again condemned [16]. Nicholas II's only surviving letter to Lanfranc makes it
clear that, if Lanfranc came to Rome, he may have done so
early in the new pontificate [17]. His main concern may have
been to resolve the issue of Duke William's marriage; he
may have been an admiring spectator of Humbert's dealings
with Berengar [18]. It is true that Lanfranc's *Liber de corpore
et sanguine Domini* may be scanned in vain for the slightest
pointer to whether he did or did not come to Rome before
Nicholas and Humbert died in 1061. But in his treatise against
Berengar, the references to Berengar's hearing and condemnation are informed and vivid; for all its theological crudity,
the profession and oath that Humbert drew up had binding
authority [19]. Lest anyone ignorant of the Roman council should
carry away a false impression, Lanfranc cited it in full [20].
Moreover, Lanfranc preserved with remarkable deliberateness
the documents of Nicholas II's reign as additions to his text of
the canonical collection, now Trinity College, Cambridge, MS
B 16 44 (405), that he caused to be brought over from le
Bec for his use in England [21]: besides Berengar's oath of 1059
(p. 210) and Nicholas II's letter to Lanfranc (p. 211) [22], there
appear the encyclical letter *Vigilantia universalis* that Nicholas

---

[16] *VL*, cap. 3, col. 35D (see infra, p 676).

[17] As note 3; cf. BERENGERIUS TURONENSIS, *Rescriptum contra Lanfran-
num*, 1, 10-16, ed. R. B. C. HUYGENS, Turnhout 1988 (*CCCM* 84), p. 35.

[18] But cf. BATES, *Normandy*, p. 201.

[19] *DC*, cap. 1, 2, 5, col. 407-412, 414-415.

[20] *DC*, cap. 2, col. 411BC. It should be noticed that the material based
upon the Protocol of Gregory VII's Lent council of 1079, including Berengar's
oath as then taken (*Reg.* vi. 17a, p. 425-7), in printed editions of *DC, ibid.*,
is devoid of manuscript authority: R. B. C. HUYGENS, *Bérenger de Tours, Lanfranc et Bernold de Constance*, « Sacris Erudiri », 16 (1965), p. 355-403, at
p. 359 and 367.

[21] For the *Collectio Lanfranci*, see esp. Z. N. BROOKE, *The English Church
and the Papacy*, Cambridge 1931, p. 57-83 and 231-235; H. FUHRMANN, *Einfluß und Verbreitung der pseudoisidorischen Fälschungen*, MGH *Schriften*,
24/1-3, Stuttgart 1972-4, ii, p. 419-422. I am grateful to Mr Mark Philpott for
help and advice.

[22] As note 3.

wrote to publicize the decrees of the Lateran council of 1059 (p. 209) [23] and his decrees about simony and papal elections of probably the same date (p. 209-210) [24]. It is arresting that Lanfranc should have been careful to preserve Nicholas's encyclical letter. Not only does it summarize the decree about papal elections but it imposes a strict duty of celibacy and common life upon all in major orders, requires that no clerk should in any wise receive a church from laymen whether gratis or for a price, proscribes simony, and makes stringent moral demands of clergy and laymen alike. No comparable document from before Gregory VII's pontificate so largely embodies the programme of the reform papacy.

Lanfranc may have gained his knowledge of Nicholas II's pontificate at second hand from others who were present, and the texts in the *Collectio Lanfranci* may have been taken from material that Nicholas circulated. But the sources suggest no intermediary, and the sharp impression created upon Lanfranc suggests, though it does not prove, a visit to Rome during which he met Nicholas and in the course of which he discussed his work. In any case, Lanfranc's *De corpore et sanguine Domini* proves that Nicholas's pontificate confirmed him in the impression that he had formed at Rome in 1049-1050. Nicholas was « of blessed memory », and « supreme pontiff of the whole Christian profession » [25]. Lanfranc countered Berengar's disparagement of Humbert by protesting that all who knew him whether at first or at second hand bore witness to him as a man of religion, most assiduously distinguished for his Christian faith and most holy works, and eminently learned in religious and secular studies [26]. When Berengar called the Roman church « a church of the malignant, a council of vanities, and the seat

---

[23] Best edited by SCHIEFFER, *Die Entstehung*, p. 208-225.

[24] *MGH Const.*, I, p. 549-551, no. 386, caps. 1-4. For the date, see SCHIEFFER, *Die Entstehung*, p. 64-66.

[25] *DC*, cap. 1, col. 409B.

[26] *DC*, cap. 2, col. 409D-410B.

X

of Satan », Lanfranc expostulated that others, however far they had strayed from the faith, had never uttered such words:

They have splendidly honoured the see of St Peter the Apostle, and have not presumed to speak or to write any such blasphemy against it. ... Christ himself spoke of it in the Gospels [Lanfranc cited Mt. 16,18-19]; even if these words [he commented] are held to have been spoken of the pastors of the church as some Catholics expound them, yet the sacred canons and the decrees of the pontiffs testify that they are especially to be understood of the Roman church [27].

Once more, Lanfranc expressed his deep commitment to the reform papacy. It comes out again at the head of his commentary upon the Epistle to the Romans, when he declared that « this Epistle is placed first to honour the city in which God willed the primacy of the entire holy church to be » [28].

Under Alexander II, Lanfranc was not sent to Rome during Duke William's preparations for the Norman conquest of England in 1066, but in 1067 he paid a further visit. William wished to fill the vacant see of Rouen by translating Bishop John of Avranches; in canon law a translation demanded papal sanction. Lanfranc presented William's plea to Alexander in concert with Bishop Ermenfrid of Sion, several times papal legate in Normandy and England; Alexander gave his ready permission [29]. Lanfranc's good standing with Alexander was further illustrated in 1068, when he conferred upon the abbey of Saint-Étienne, Caen, a carefully drafted privilege conferring exemption from the authority of the bishop of Bayeux [30].

---

[27] DC, cap. 16, col. 426BD.

[28] Best edition of the passage in question by M. GIBSON, Lanfranc's « Commentary on the Pauline Epistles », « The Journal of Theological Studies », NS, 22 (1971), p. 86-112, at p. 108.

[29] Acta archiepiscoporum Rothomagensium, PL 147, col. 279-280; Alexander's letter to John of Avranches is printed in PL 146, col. 1339, Ep. 56. For Ermenfrid, see H. E. J. COWDREY, Bishop Ermenfrid of Sion and the Penitential Ordinance following the Battle of Hastings, « Journal of Ecclesiastical History », 20 (1969), p. 225-542.

[30] PL 146, col. 1339-341, Ep. 57.

There was a further dimension to Lanfranc's good standing with the popes. His fame as a teacher, which probably made le Bec a centre of international fame throughout the 1050s as well as in the 1060s [31], led Nicholas II and Alexander II to direct pupils to him. In his letter to Lanfranc, Nicholas said that he was sending both imperial and papal chaplains for instruction in dialectic and rhetoric [32]. Probably after Lanfranc moved to Caen, Alexander wrote to him commenting upon the fame of his learning and urgently seeking to send to him a kinsman (*fratruelis*) who was competent in grammar and had some knowledge of dialectic; probably Lanfranc was to instruct him in theology [33]. Both letters were copied into the *Collectio Lanfranci* with marginalia indicating that he received them at le Bec and Caen respectively [34]. Lanfranc was evidently proud to have been the tutor of papal clerks [35].

No doubt one must beware of giving Lanfranc's dealings with the papacy and his high regard for its personnel and authority too strong an emphasis. He was a monk first and

---

[31] See VAUGHN, *Lanfranc of Bec*. That le Bec's fame was long-standing is suggested by GUITMUND OF AVERSA, *De corporis et sanguinis Christi veritate in eucharistia*, I, *PL* 149, col. 1428; *The 'Expositio in Cantica Canticorum' of Williram Abbot of Ebersberg, 1048-1085*, ed. E. H. BARTELMEZ, Philadelphia 1967, P15-22, p. 1.

[32] As note 3.

[33] *PL* 146, col. 1353, *Ep.* 70; cf. CLOVER/GIBSON, p. 32, no. 1, 37-43. The identity of the kinsman cannot be ascertained; there is no positive evidence that it was the future Bishop Anselm II of Lucca: T. SCHMIDT, *Alexander II. und die Römische Reformgruppe seiner Zeit*, Stuttgart 1977 (Päpste und Papsttum, 11), p. 20-1 and 26-30.

[34] Cf. GIBSON, *Lanfranc of Bec*, p. 205 note 3; it should, however, be noticed that Alexander did not address Lanfranc as abbot.

[35] It remains unproven that Alexander himself was Lanfranc's pupil at le Bec, in view of the lateness of all the evidence: EADMER, *Historia novorum in Anglia*, I (written by 1109/1115), ed. M. RULE, London 1884 (*RS* 81), p. 11; WILLIAM OF MALMESBURY, *Vita Wulfstani*, II, 1 (written after *c.* 1124), ed. R. R. DARLINGTON, Camden Society, 3rd ser. 40 (1928), p. 24-5, and *De gestis pontificum Anglorum*, I, 42 (written 1125), ed. N. E. S. A. HAMILTON, London 1870 (*RS* 52), p. 65; *VL*, cap. 11, col. 49A (see below, p. 697). Lanfranc's omission of a reference to Alexander as a pupil in CLOVER/GIBSON, p. 32, no. 1, 37-43, makes it unlikely that he had been one.

foremost, and secondarily a scholar; only thereafter was he a participant in papal and ducal affairs. Nevertheless, his participation in them was an integral element in what he was and did. He was far from being at a distance in sympathy or involvement from developments at Rome since 1046. He was committed to collaboration with the popes, their agents, and especially Cardinal Humbert. His continuing commitment is clear because Nicholas II's encyclical *Vigilantia universalis* was copied into the *Collectio Lanfranci* and therefore disseminated later in the century throughout the Anglo-Norman lands [36].

Lanfranc was nominated archbishop of Canterbury on 15 August 1070 and consecrated on 29 August; almost four years had elapsed since the battle of Hastings on 14 October 1066. During these years, the stage was set for Lanfranc's dealings as archbishop with Alexander II up to the latter's death on 21 April 1073. To understand Lanfranc's problems and actions during his early years as archbishop, it is necessary to digress at some length to consider papal relations with the Norman king-duke in the aftermath of the Conquest when Lanfranc was not at the centre of the stage.

There can be no doubt about Alexander's strong support of William's invasion of England. According to Orderic Vitalis, William prepared the way by dispatching to Rome Gilbert, archdeacon of Lisieux; the pope charged the duke boldly to take up arms against the perjurer Harold and sent him a « vexillum sancti Petri »; the early testimony of William of Poitiers confirms the sending of a papal banner [37]. The papal household was divided about this sponsoring of bloodshed, but upon his own later testimony Archdeacon Hildebrand, the future Pope

---

[36] For its dissemination, see SCHIEFFER (as n. 14), p. 61-66, 208-210.
[37] OV, II, p. 142-143; WILLIAM OF POITIERS, II, 3, p. 154-155. C. MORTON, *Pope Alexander II and the Norman Conquest*, « Latomus », 34 (1975), p. 362-382, demonstrates how largely the sending of the banner depends on William of Poitiers's testimony but too readily dismisses his value as evidence.

Gregory VII, strenuously upheld the pope's position [38]. After the Conquest, a succession of papal letters implied warm recognition of William's kingship; Alexander's approval found its fullest expression in a letter of October 1071 to his « dearest son » William, applauding his exemplary piety, his repression of simony, and his zeal for the customs and practices of catholic liberty [39]. The legatine activity that had for some years been manifest in ducal Normandy and Anglo-Saxon England was resumed. Bishop Ermenfrid of Sion, who confirmed the penitential ordinance of the Norman bishops after the battle of Hastings [40], attended the councils of Winchester and Windsor at Easter and Pentecost 1070, and consecrated Bishop Walkelin of Winchester [41]. Then he crossed to Normandy where, in concert with the Roman subdeacon Hubert, he was to the fore at the meeting of Norman bishops and abbots at which Lanfranc was urged to accept the see of Canterbury [42]. Hubert attended the council of Winchester at Easter 1072 [43], and was thereafter occasionally active in the Anglo-Norman lands until his death at le Bec in 1080 [44].

[38] *Reg.* VII, 23, p. 499,31-500,11; cf. *Wenrici scolastici Trevirensis Epistola,* cap. 6, ed. K. FRANCKE, *MGH, L de L,* I, p. 294,19-24.

[39] To John of Avranches (1068), « ex electione principis tui dilectissimi filii nostri Guillelmi regis Anglorum »: *PL* 146, col. 1339, *Ep.* 56; privilege for Saint-Étienne, Caen (1068), « a glorioso Willelmo principe Normannorum et victoriosissimo rege Anglorum »: *ibid.,* col. 1339-1341, *Ep.* 57; privilege for Bury St Edmunds (1071/1072), « necnon charissimi filii nostri Willelmi regis benignae interpellationis vota attendentes »: *PL* 146, col. 1363D, *Ep.* 81; CLOVER/GIBSON, p. 60-61, no. 7,1-9.

[40] *CS,* II, p. 581-584, no. 88.

[41] FLORENCE OF WORCESTER, *Chronicon ex chronicis,* ed. B. THORPE, 2 vols., London 1848-1849, II, p. 5-7.

[42] CLOVER/GIBSON, p. 30-31, no. 1,9-17.

[43] *CS,* p. 601-604, no. 91/III.

[44] For legates in France, see T. SCHIEFFER, *Die päpstlichen Legaten in Frankreich vom Vertrage von Meersen (870) bis zum Schisma von 1130,* Berlin 1935 (Historische Studien, 263) p. 53-55, 65-66, 79-80, 107-107, 125-126; H. TILMANN, *Die päpstlichen Legaten in England bis zur Beendigung der Legation Gualas (1218),* Bonn 1926, p. 11-18. A further indication of legatine activity in England during the early 1070s may be provided by the discovery at Lincoln in 1985 of a mutilated seal matrix, perhaps that of Hubert: T. A. HESLOP, *A*

Such papal letters and such legatine activities were the everyday business of the reform papacy. More striking is the especial concern that Alexander seems to have had for England in the aftermath of the Norman Conquest. Whether on the basis of Norman propagandist reports in 1066 or of independent Roman judgements on the irregular position of Archbishop Stigand of Canterbury [45], or perhaps of both, the pope wrote to King William at a date after the Conquest that is uncertain a letter in which he requested the due payment of Peter's pence [46]. He introduced his request with a reminder that, from its late sixth-century beginnings, the English kingdom had enjoyed special papal protection (« sub apostolorum principis manu et tutela extitisse »). But this had latterly been ignored; Alexander clearly related the offence to the recent non-payment of Peter's pence and commented strongly that « some who were made the members of an evil head and who were inflamed by the pride of Satan their father cast off the covenant of God and turned the English people from the way of truth ». In Italy, Alexander had recent experience of the Cadalan schism (1061-1064), and he transferred the language of virtual schism to Stigand, who alone matches the designation *mali caput*, a divider of the church. If three further letters in Alexander's name which refer to attempts to replace monastic cathedral chapters at Canterbury and Winchester by secular clerks are genuine, Alexander II was at great pains in response to apply to the church in early Norman England the precedents of the Gregorian

*Walrus Ivory Seal Matrix from Lincoln*, « The Antiquaries Journal », 66 (1986), p. 371-372, 396-397 and pl. LXIII*bc*.

[45] For papal dealings with England after Stigand became archbishop, see *CS*, p. 543-555, nos. 74-80. Under Kings Edward the Confessor and Harold, Stigand performed few if any major public duties and in particular consecrated no bishops and abbots; in 1061 Bishops Giso of Wells and Walter of Hereford were consecrated at Rome by Pope Nicholas II.

[46] *PL* 146, col. 1413, *Ep*. 139. Its authenticity is likely since it is preserved by the Roman cardinal-priest DEUSDEDIT: *Collectio canonum*, III, 269, *Die Kanonessammlung des Kardinals Deusdedit*, ed. V. WULF VON GLANVELL, I, Paderborn 1905, p. 378.

mission of 597; if, as is probable, they are near-contemporary forgeries, they may reflect his known frame of mind [47]. It is, in any case, illustrated by an unimpeachable document connected with his sending from Rome in 1070 of two further legates, Cardinals Peter and John Minutus [48]. From Alexander's viewpoint their authority took precedence over that of Bishop Ermenfrid of Sion with whom they worked. Summonses to the council of Winchester that the three legates held at Easter 1070 were issued in their names alone; although only Ermenfrid was at the council held at Windsor the following Pentecost, Alexander himself wrote as if his legatine authority at it derived from that of Peter and John (« a suppositis legatorum nostrorum ») [49].

The two legates' writ of summons to Winchester as addressed to Bishop Wulfstan II of Worcester was programmatic. It expressly alludes to Alexander's intention to renew the Christianity of a people that Pope Gregory I's mission had permanently set in a particularly close relationship to the Roman church:

Although the Roman church should be vigilant to correct all Christians, it is especially concerned to examine your customs and way of life, and to renew by diligent visitation the Christian religion in which it at first instructed you.

Accordingly, in 1070 Alexander's two legates acted on an impressive scale. According to the late testimony of Orderic Vitalis which is however credible since Archbishop Aldred of York was dead and Stigand, archbishop of Canterbury and bishop of Winchester, was about to be deposed, it was the legates who officiated at King William's Easter crownwear-

---

[47] PL 146, col. 1415-1417, Epp. 142-144. For discussion, see Appended Note A, below.

[48] CS, p. 563-576, nos. 85-86; TILLMANN, Die päpstliche Legaten, p. 12-15. For chroniclers' views, CS, p. 569-572, no. 86/II-VI.

[49] CS, p. 568, no. 86/1; CLOVER/GIBSON, p. 62-63, no. 7,30-4.

ing [50]. « Florence of Worcester » records Stigand's deposition on the three charges of pluralism, of usurping Archbishop Robert of Jumièges's see and pallium, and of receiving his own pallium from the excommunicated and simoniacal antipope Benedict X. Other bishops and abbots were deposed [51]. At both legatine councils, stringent canons were enacted in line with the aspirations and legislation of the reform papacy. They included the proscription of episcopal pluralism and simony and a stringent requirement of clerical celibacy. Reform was to be perpetuated by the holding of regular episcopal synods and by the introduction of archdeacons and other such ministers [52]. The scope of the legates' action indicates a resolute purpose to implement their task as set out in the writ of summons to the bishop of Worcester: as ministers of St Peter and on behalf of Pope Alexander to prune out the evils that had multiplied in the Lord's vineyard and to plant things healthful for soul and body [53].

As for the king, despite Alexander's praise William did not go more than half way during the years 1066-1070 towards matching the pope's concern for his kingdom by adopting his outlook and measures. Up to a point he was at pains to do so, particularly in his public image. This is reflected in his panegyrist William of Poitiers's expressions of deference to the pope as « head and master of the bishops of the world », and to Alexander himself as one « most worthy to be obeyed and consulted by the whole church » [54]. Similar right thinking

---

[50] OV, II, p. 236-237.

[51] FLORENCE OF WORCESTER, *Chronicon*, ed. THORPE, II, p. 5-6.

[52] *CS*, p. 574-575, 580-581, nos. 86/IX, 87/III. The editorial comment at p 566-568 and 577-578, should be noted.

[53] As note 49.

[54] WILLIAM OF POITIERS, II, 3, p. 152-154. For fuller discussions of William's ecclesiastical dealings, see H. E. J. COWDREY, *Pope Gregory VII and the Anglo-Norman Church and Kingdom*, « Studi Gregoriani », 9 (1972), p. 79-114, repr. in ID., *Popes, Monks and Crusaders*, London 1984, no. IX; and ID., *The Gregorian Reform in the Anglo-Norman Lands and in Scandinavia*, « Studi Gregoriani », 13 (1989), p. 321-352.

marked the *Laudes regiae* compiled for the queen's coronation in 1068 [55]. When William needed papal sanction to reinforce his provisions for a newly conquered realm, as by the coming of the papal legates in 1070, he was prepared (in Orderic Vitalis's words) « to hear and honour them as angels of God » [56].

On the other hand, even in 1066 it can hardly have escaped attention at Rome that William's deference would go no further than his political advantage dictated, and that he aimed at mastery over his own lordship. His dealings during the early 1060s with regard to the abbots of Saint-Évroult which brought the abbey's affairs to the direct notice of both Nicholas II and Alexander II must have made the papacy well aware that William could be masterful and recalcitrant, as when in violent anger he declared that he would gladly receive the legates of the pope, the common father of all, in matters of Christian faith and religion; but if a monk of his land ventured to bring a plea against him, he would hang him by his cowl from the nearest oak [57]. After 1066, William's treatment of Archbishop Stigand was far from being consistent with Alexander's stigmatiation of him as *mali caput*. William was, indeed, too circumspect for himself or his queen to be crowned by such an archbishop, and called upon Archbishop Aldred of York. But, with his massive pre-Conquest territorial holdings in East Anglia and elsewhere, Stigand remained a powerful figure, « cuius inter Anglos auctoritas erat summa », William of Poitiers commented [58]. In December 1066 he had done homage and fealty

[55] See H. E. J. Cowdrey, *The Anglo-Norman 'Laudes regiae'*, « Viator », 12 (1981), p. 37-78, repr. in Id., *Popes, Monks and Crusaders*, no. VIII, at p. 70; and cf. p. 53-55.

[56] OV, II, p. 7.

[57] Cf. OV, II, p. 90-101 and 107-115; citation at p. 94.

[58] Stigand's landed wealth before 1066 may best be seen in *Domesday Book*, using the index of H. Ellis, *A General Introduction to Domesday Book*, 2 vols., London 1833, II, p. 229-230. For William of Poitiers's comments, see II, 28 and 33, p. 214-215 and 234-235. Stigand's career is well summarized by N. P. Brooks, *The Early History of the Church of Canterbury*, Leicester 984, p. 304-310.

to William at Wallingford before Aldred followed suit at Berk-
hamstead[59]. For the next three years he loomed surprisingly
large. His attestations of William's early diplomas makes it
clear that he had an honourable place at court with precedence over Archbishop Aldred[60]. Most remarkable of all, in
1067 he consecrated the only bishop to be appointed between
1066 and 1070, Remigius, monk of Fécamp, who became bishop
of Dorchester[61]. Under William, Stigand enjoyed a recognition that the two previous kings had withheld. Only with
Aldred's death on 11 September 1069 did the breakdown of
the uneasy balance between the two Anglo-Saxon archbishops
necessitate the first steps on William's part to replace Stigand
in the see of Canterbury; until then he had disregarded the
pope's stigmatization of him.

It should further be noticed that, at the legatine councils
of 1070, William's deference to papal legates as angels of God
was much qualified when it suited his secular interests. Not
one of the English documents, whether records or chronicles,
reflects Alexander II's construction of events as a papal initiative
to renew through his Roman legates John and Peter a church
with an especial and ancient debt to the papacy; Bishop Ermenfrid of Sion was invariably referred to as though he were the
senior or the sole legate[62]. William's propaganda at Rome in
1066 may have worked all too well in eliciting Alexander's
reforming zeal, so that William preferred the familiar Ermenfrid
to Alexander's newly briefed cardinals. According to « Florence
of Worcester » he made cunning use of the council of Winchester to further his political position. English abbots were
got rid of so that Normans could be substituted in order to

[59] WILLIAM OF POITIERS, II, 28, p. 216-217; Anglo-Saxon Chronicle, D
version, a.1066. For the alleged terms of William's recognition of Stigand, see
WILLIAM OF MALMESBURY, De gest. pont. Angl., I, 23, ed. HAMILTON, p. 36.
[60] COWDREY, The Anglo-Norman 'Laudes regiae', p. 52 and note.
[61] CS, p. 573-574, no. 86/VIII; Canterbury Professions, ed. RICHTER,
« The Canterbury and York Society », 67 (1973), p. 27, no. 32.
[62] CS, p. 569-575 and 578-581, nos. 86/II-V,IX and 87/I,II.

secure his newly acquired kingdom; apart from Stigand and his brother Bishop Ethelmar of Elmham, abbots and bishops were disposed of and imprisoned for life not for transgressing church canons or secular laws but upon suspicion of political unreliability [63]. Like William's long-standing attitude towards Stigand, whom he seemed at Winchester somewhat unscrupulously to drop [64], the councils of 1070 showed that, if papal and royal aims and policies overlapped, they were very far indeed from coinciding.

The difference between pope and king which confronted Lanfranc in August 1070 is clear. Alexander was guided by his sense of special responsibility for a people whose conversion had been initiated by Pope Gregory the Great. His judgement on Stigand as *mali caput* was in the harsh terms appropriate to a sponsor of virtual apostasy, and his legatine mission of 1070 was intended to effect an energetic reform of the church and its members by papal initiative. William enjoyed Alexander's respect and favour, and he declared himself to be deferential to papal authority in matters of religion. But he was overridingly concerned for his precarious mastery of his new kingdom and ruthlessly used the church and churchmen to secure this mastery. Up to 1070 it was expedient for him to retain Stigand in a position of honour and activity, ecclesiastical as well as political, which he had not enjoyed before 1066. Papal legates came to advise, not to direct matters. Nothing might challenge William's political mastery, either in theory or in practice.

To return to Lanfranc. His succession was manifestly the result of co-operation between pope and king. To Alexander he was eminently *persona grata*; William had for long seen him as a suitable candidate for an archbishopric, for in 1067 he had

---

[63] FLORENCE OF WORCESTER, *Chronicon ex chronicis*, ed. THORPE, II, p. 5-6.
[64] WILLIAM OF MALMESBURY, *De gestis pontificum Anglorum*, I, 23, ed. HAMILTON, p. 37.

been willing to approve the promotion to Rouen that Lanfranc declined[65]. Lanfranc himself wrote of William's pressure upon him to become archbishop of Canterbury, to which he yielded only when Alexander's legates Ermenfrid and Hubert commanded him by authority of the apostolic see[66]. So much the elements of agreement between Alexander and William achieved. But having assumed office, Lanfranc professed a canonical obedience to Alexander which he saw as his ruling motive[67]. Given the points of difference between Alexander and William, a period of contrast and accommodation between William and Lanfranc was virtually inevitable. Lanfranc's attitude to Stigand and his acts since 1066 was a touchstone. He turned his back entirely upon William's partial recognition of Stigand and totally rejected him: for Lanfranc it was as though his archiepiscopate had never been. His judgement is reflected in the professions of obedience that survive from those which he exacted from all bishops who had been consecrated by Stigand, by other archbishops, or by the pope since Stigand had usurped the see[68]. In the profession of Remigius of Dorchester, it is expressly stated that, when Remigius travelled to Rome with Lanfranc in 1071-1072, the pope excluded Stigand from the succession of archbishops, saying that he was not Lanfranc's predecessor or Lanfranc his successor. Remigius had received the pope's pardon for his consecration by Stigand. In the three professions that survive—those of Wulfstan II of Worcester and Herfast of Elmham as well as Remigius—

[65] VL, cap. 5, col. 40A (see below, p. 682); for William's high regard for Lanfranc, see WILLIAM OF POITIERS, I, 52, p. 126-129.

[66] CLOVER/GIBSON, p. 30-33, 38-39, 130-131, nos. 1,3-21; 3,1-5; 38,8-10. Cf. FLORENCE OF WORCESTER, Chronicon, ed. THORPE, II, p. 7.

[67] CLOVER/GIBSON, p. 30-31, 38-39, 48-49: nos. 1,1-2; 2,44-7; 4,3-4.

[68] WILLIAM OF MALMESBURY, De gestis pontificum Anglorum, I, 25, ed. HAMILTON, p. 40; for the professions, see RICHTER, Canterbury Professions, p. 26-28, nos. 31-33. The relative brevity and restraint of Herfast of Elmham's profession may be because Elmham was the former see of Stigand (1043, 1044-1047), and then of his deposed brother Ethelmar (1047-1070), and local sensibilities had to be considered in a region where the family was deeply rooted and powerful.

Stigand's offences were condemned in the strongest terms. In Wulfstan's and Remigius's professions it was asserted that five popes—Leo IX, Victor II, Stephen IX, Nicholas II, and Alexander II—had cited, excommunicated, and condemned him, and had sent legates to England who commanded that no one should show him reverence or be ordained by him. There is no other evidence to confirm these measures against Stigand and the gravest suspicion must attach to the record of them. They are manifestly couched in the language that Lanfranc wished to hear. They stand in contrast to the positive but relatively mild and occasional steps taken at Rome until Alexander II's letter after the Norman conquest in which he described Stigand as *mali caput* [69]; Wulfstan of Worcester may have suppressed his true opinion, since after Lanfranc's death he referred to Stigand without irony in a letter to Archbishop Anselm as the latter's predecessor [70]. It is indeed astonishing that, upon arriving in England, Lanfranc should have so radically contradicted the attitude to Stigand that King William took in the first three years of his reign, and should have adopted with an exaggeration that apparently amounted to invention the standpoint of Alexander II after 1066. Fortunately, with Stigand virtually imprisoned at Winchester, William could and did afford to tolerate Lanfranc's rigour without demur.

For the remainder of Alexander's pontificate, Lanfranc enjoyed a relationship of unique trust with the pope. He sought and received advice and favour from a pope who regarded him as a trusted intermediary with William I and the English

---

[69] As note 46.

[70] *Epp.* 170-171, in *S. Anselmi Cantuariensis archiepiscopi Opera omnia*, ed. F. S. SCHMITT, 6 vols., Edinburgh 1946-1961, IV, p. 51-53; EADMER, *Hist. nov.*, ed. RULE, p. 46; see BARLOW, *The English Church*, p. 304-307. In 1062, and so before Alexander II's post-Norman Conquest stigmatization of Stigand as *mali caput*, Stigand had supported two papal legates, one of them Ermenfrid of Sion, in commending Wulfstan to be bishop of Worcester, although Aldred of York was his consecrator: WILLIAM OF MALMESBURY, *Vita Wulfstani*, I, 11, ed. DARLINGTON, p. 18; FLORENCE OF WORCESTER, *Chronicon*, ed. THORPE, I, p. 220-221.

church. Lanfranc's own words make this clear. In the spring of 1072 he wrote to the pope:

At my intercession, you have promptly granted to everyone for whom I stood advocate whatever they rightly and profitably asked for, to say nothing of many other things which in this respect are in no way different, and which so agreeably bring me the remembrance of your name whenever I do anything that is good [71].

Alexander expressed to the king his own trust in Lanfranc later in the year when Lanfranc arrived in Rome:

We would have committed to writing many more things than we have set down in this letter, if we had not entrusted them for oral communication to Lanfranc, our most beloved brother who is also most faithful to you, so that you can hear more fully from his own lips the warmth of our love and can attend the more earnestly to the remainder of our messages [72].

The long letter of consultation that Lanfranc wrote to Alexander in the summer of 1071 shows how dependent he felt upon papal guidance. His immediate business was so urgent that he could not await the return of earlier messengers whom he had sent. He sought papal direction about two bishops— Herman of Ramsbury who wished to become a monk because, Lanfranc said, of his old age and infirmity, and Leofwine of Lichfield who wished to return to his former monastery at Coventry, having shown himself contumacious to Alexander's legates of 1070 when accused before them of his marriage. As regards both bishops, Lanfranc sought urgent guidance from the apostolic see; he would not proceed, or allow others to do so, until Alexander himself had given instructions [73]. At Rome later in the year, Eadmer claimed that Lanfranc successfully interceded with Alexander on behalf of Archbishop Thomas of York and Bishop Remigius of Dorchester when they were

[71] CLOVER/GIBSON, p. 56-57, no. 4,114-118.
[72] Ibid. p. 62-63, no. 7,44-48.
[73] Ibid. p. 34-38, no. 2.

accused of being uncanonically promoted because they were the sons of priests, and of simony. Remigius's profession to Lanfranc stated that it was in response to Lanfranc's petition that Alexander pardoned his consecration by Stigand [74].

In his letter of October 1071 to King William, Alexander informed him of matters which he had entrusted to Lanfranc for settlement in England. Lanfranc was to examine more fully, with the possibility of his reversing a legatine decision, the case of Bishop Ethelric of Chichester which the legate Ermenfrid had left unresolved at Windsor in 1070. He was also to deal with the long-standing dispute between the sees of York and Dorchester about jurisdiction over certain lands south of the River Humber [75]. Alexander went on to disclose to the king that he had given Lanfranc a personal authority that made him virtually a standing papal legate:

In hearing and settling cases we have given him such a delegation of our own and apostolic authority (*nostrae et apostolicae auctoritatis vicem*) that whatever he shall decide in accordance with righteousness shall thereafter be held to be as valid and binding as if it were settled in our own presence [76].

It was a demonstration of Alexander's regard and confidence, and a reminder of how close to Alexander Lanfranc was.

The major issue of Lanfranc's early years as archbishop was, however, his dispute with Archbishop Thomas of York about the primacy of the see of Canterbury. It was to expose the strains latent in Lanfranc's relationships first with the king

---

[74] EADMER, *Hist. nov.*, ed. RULE, I, p. 11; RICHTER, *Canterbury Professions*, p. 27, no. 32. For the charge of simony against Remigius, see E. M. C. VAN HOUTS, *The Ship List of William the Conqueror*, « Anglo-Norman Studies », 10 (1988), p. 159-183, esp. p. 167-169 and 176. Remigius was almoner of Fécamp; a decade later its abbot, John, complained to King William about the abbey's still unrequited losses in 1066: *Ep.* 1, ed. J. MABILLON, *Vetera analecta*, Paris 1732², p. 450-451.

[75] For the origins of this limited dispute, which did not involve the question of the primacy, see *CS*, p. 538-543 and 550-552, nos. 74 and 78.

[76] CLOVER/GIBSON, p. 62-63, no. 7,30-34.

and ultimately with the papacy. William had nominated Thomas, a clerk of Bayeux and royal chaplain, on 23 May, but his consecration was delayed until the see of Canterbury was filled. There is nothing in the evidence for the year 1070 to suggest that Lanfranc then looked further than to the king for the vindication of his superiority. According to the account in Lanfranc's letter collection [77], when Thomas came to Canterbury for consecration, Lanfranc « maintaining the custom of his predecessors » demanded from him a written profession of his obedience reinforced by an oath. Thomas declared himself dissatisfied by the evidence by which Lanfranc justified his demand— not surprisingly, since so far as is known no recent written professions could be cited [78], and it is hard to know what precedent Lanfranc can have claimed for exacting an oath. At a subsequent audience with the king, Lanfranc, for whom the support of English witnesses was alleged, was able to persuade the king and the Normans of the justice of his claim. By royal edict Thomas was ordered to return to Canterbury and make a profession in which he promised to obey Lanfranc absolutely and without condition in all matters of the Christian religion. This he did, and Lanfranc consecrated him.

The tentative and deeply unsatisfactory character of this settlement from Lanfranc's point of view must be fully appreciated. First, to begin with the king had been gravely displeased, thinking that Lanfranc was trying to get more than his due. Lanfranc appeased his anger, but the king clearly maintained some degree of judicial detachment as between the archbishops and was not committed to Lanfranc's cause [79]. Secondly, although the text of Thomas's first profession was lost—one suspects not accidentally—when he made his second in April

---

[77] CLOVER/GIBSON, p. 40-43, no. 3(i),13-46.

[78] See RICHTER, Canterbury Professions, p. lvi and, for surviving professions, p. 1-26, nos. 1-30.

[68] Cf. William's unwillingness to prejudge the dispute between the sees of Worcester and York before the latter church had an archbishop to defend its rights: FLORENCE OF WORCESTER, Chronicon, ed. THORPE, II, p. 6.

1072, the later profession recorded that, while he had promised to obey Lanfranc without condition, he promised to obey his successors conditionally[80]. The profession of 1070 was not more than provisional. Thirdly, although Lanfranc claimed to have produced decisive evidence for his interpretation of the primacy, the question of Thomas's obedience to Lanfranc's successors was remitted for further consideration before either the king or an episcopal council, and it was clear that Lanfranc would be expected to make a yet stronger case. Finally and most seriously, Lanfranc had wanted from Thomas a written profession of obedience reinforced by an oath[81]. He had good reason: a profession embodying even Lanfranc's fullest demands would, by itself, be insecure. Dr. Richter has pointed out that the breach of a profession canonically involved only *mendacium* punishable by excommunication, while the breach of an oath involved *periurium* punishable by deposition. The royal edict of 1070 was silent about an oath, so that Lanfranc was denied the protection of its severer sanction[82]. William's reason for not countenancing an oath is nowhere stated, but as the circumstances of Thomas's second profession tend to confirm[83], his face seemed set against an episcopal tenant-in-chief's taking an oath to any subject, even to a trusted archbishop of Canterbury. It should be recognized that, from the very start, Lanfranc's failure to get his way about how his superiority was to be secured seems, in part, to have been owing to the king himself, and that this presented a difference between Lanfranc and the king that had gradually to be resolved in the complex developments from October 1071 to the spring of 1073.

Until October 1071, Lanfranc may have hoped that the favour in which Pope Alexander held him, culminating in the

---

[80] RICHTER, *Canterbury Professions*, p. 28, no. 34; CLOVER/GIBSON, p. 44-45, no. 3(iii),94-96; cfr. *ibid.*, p. 40-43, no. 3(i),40-42.

[81] CLOVER/GIBSON, p. 40-43, no. 3(i),40-46.

[82] *Ibid.*, p. 40-41, no. 3(i),15-16, cf. 35-40; RICHTER, *Canterbury Professions*, p. xix-xx.

[83] See below, p. 470-471.

delegation to him of comprehensive power to settle matters in the English church, might enable him to establish his overall authority quietly and discreetly. The king, too, stood high in the pope's good opinion, and Thomas of York was by temperament a compliant man who could be expected to conform to a pattern of authority upheld by pope, king, and archbishop of Canterbury. For such correspondence as survives makes no reference to the issue of Canterbury and York [84]. In October the appearance of amity was sustained when the two archbishops travelled together to Rome in order to collect their *pallia*, thereby maintaining the custom of their reputable pre-Conquest predecessors [85]. Alexander received Lanfranc with conspicuous favour and affection; not only did Lanfranc take his *pallium* as was customary from the high altar of St Peter's, but Alexander presented him with a second *pallium* which he himself had worn at mass. He was gracious in granting Lanfranc's petitions on behalf of others, and he asked to be sent a copy of Lanfranc's anti-Berengarian letter, the *Liber de corpore et sanguine Domini* [86]. He hoped that Lanfranc would return to Rome at Christmastide 1072 for at least a three months stay in the Lateran palace [87]; among other things he may have wished Lanfranc to offer its perplexed members his guidance about the eucharistic question.

According to the Canterbury account, it was Thomas of York who, in the pope's presence, advanced his claim (*calumniam movit*) against the primacy of Canterbury and also about whether the sees of Dorchester/Lincoln, Worcester, and Lichfield/

---

[84] CLOVER/GIBSON, p. 34-39, 60-63, nos. 2, 7; for Thomas's character, see p. 40-41, no. 3(i),21-24, also the relationship of the two archbishops as later expressed at p. 78-81, 104-107, 110-111, nos. 12, 23, 26.

[85] For recent examples, see *Anglo-Saxon Chronicle*, DEF, *a.* 1022 (Ethelnoth, Canterbury); A, *a.* 1040, where Eadsig of Canterbury may have received the *pallium* on his visit to Rome; CDE, *a.* 1051 (Robert of Jumièges, Canterbury); D, *a.* 1055 (Cynesig, York); D, *a.* 1061 (Aldred, York). Benedict X, an antipope, sent Stigand's: DE, *a.* 1058.

[86] CLOVER/GIBSON, p. 42-43 and 54-57, nos. 3(ii), 51-55 and 4, 108-121.

[87] *Ibid.*, p. 32-35, no. 1, 57-61.

Chester were rightly subject to Canterbury or to York. Thomas
founded his case about the primacy on the letter of Pope
Gregory the Great, cited by Bede, which made the two English
metropolitans equal to each other. Lanfranc's principal rejoinder was that Gregory wrote, not of York and Canterbury,
but of York and London. After long debate upon both issues,
Alexander remitted the case to be heard in England. Lanfranc's own jurisdiction on the pope's behalf was not appropriate
in a case to which he was a party; the matter was to be settled
by the witness and judgement of the bishops and abbots of
the whole kingdom [88]. As Lanfranc returned to England, the
insufficiency of Thomas's profession of obedience in 1070
seems to have been uppermost in his mind: he could bind
Thomas only for his own lifetime, and in the interest of his
successors must attempt to secure the primacy of Canterbury in
perpetuity [89]. By itself, no profession by Thomas, however
skilfully drafted, could suffice, since professions had only limited sanction. On the side of the English kingdom—the king
and his major subjects both ecclesiastical and lay, Lanfranc needed a binding statement of his case; on that of the ecclesiastical
order—the canonical structure of archbishops and bishops, he
needed either an oath to himself from Thomas to reinforce
his profession or else a papal privilege. Best of all would be
the whole of this. The guiding thread through the negotiations
that follow is that, from the ecclesiastical side, he found no
satisfaction: thanks to the king, no oath from Thomas; thanks
to Archdeacon Hildebrand at Rome, no papal privilege. But
within the English kingdom, he secured with the king's goodwill a constitution about the primacy that brought him great
advantage.

In England, the matters at issue were discussed during

---

[88] *Ibid.*, pp. 42-45, 50-51, nos. 3(ii), 55-57, 4, 4-16. For Gregory's letter,
*Gregorii magni Registrum Epistularum*, XI, 39, ed. D. NORBERG, Turnhout 1982
(CCSL 140, 140A) II, 934-935; BEDE's *Ecclesiastical History of the English
People*, I, 29, edd. B. COLGRAVE and R. A. B. MYNORS, Oxford 1969, p. 104-107.
[89] CLOVER/GIBSON, p. 44-45, no. 3(ii), 72-75.

the meetings of the royal court at Easter and Pentecost 1072. At both meetings, the legate Hubert was present but not prominent; it is not even clear whether he travelled to England with the two archbishops or had come separately. The principal relevant documents are as follows:

(i) The conclusion of the account of Lanfranc's visit to Rome;
(ii) Lanfranc's account to Alexander II, written between Easter and Pentecost 1072, of events between his return to England and the council of Winchester, with which he enclosed (iii) but not, of course, (iv), and also not (v);
(iii) The constitution regarding the primacy drawn up at Winchester about Easter (8 April) 1072;
(iv) The slightly revised version of (iii) ratified and published at Windsor about Pentecost (27 May) 1072;
(v) Archbishop Thomas of York's second profession to Lanfranc, made soon after Easter 1072 [90].

The council of Winchester met in the chapel of the royal castle. Nevertheless, according to Lanfranc's account which the wording of the constitution supports, those who assembled did so under the dual sanction of their obedience under papal authority and of their sworn fealty to the king. They agreed to bring the matters of the primacy and of jurisdiction over the three disputed bishoprics to a sure and right conclusion (« ad certum rectumque finem ») [91]. Such a result, with all ends neatly tied in, was undoubtedly what Lanfranc hoped for. He told Alexander about the arguments by which he developed his case as stated at Rome. To the modern historian they seem weak. He began by ransacking Bede's *Ecclesiastical History*, tendentiously calling its author a priest of the church of York, for

---

[90] All five documents occur in Lanfranc's letter collection: CLOVER/GIBSON, p. 44-45, nos. 3(ii), 75-82 (iii), (iv), 4, 1-104. See also *CS*, II, p. 591-607, no. 91; and for (iii) and especially (iv), *Facsimiles of English Royal Writs to A.D. 1100 presented to V. H. Galbraith*, edd. T. A. M. BISHOP and P. CHAPLAIS, Oxford 1957, plate XXIX.

[91] CLOVER/GIBSON, p. 50-51, no. 4, 20-26; cf. *ibid.*, p. 44-45, no. 3(iv), 100-101.

examples from the first 140 or so years of its history of the exercise of Canterbury's primacy over York, neglecting the plain fact the see was then not fully established. He cited later councils and disputed elections which he claimed to illustrate the primacy, and episcopal professions of obedience that supported his case about the disputed bishoprics. The professions were fair evidence for this, but the argument about the primacy was a novelty. A story of an unnamed Northumbrian king whom an archbishop of Canterbury excommunicated after he disposed simoniacally of the see of York has never been corroborated. Finally, as « the heart and foundation of our case », Lanfranc appealed to the privileges and letters of a catena of eight popes, beginning with Gregory the Great and ending with Leo IX. He did no more than name names, but historians have related the middle six of them to the so-called Canterbury forgeries—the forged privileges, produced at Canterbury in the late eleventh or early twelfth century, which were used at Rome in 1123 to support Canterbury's primacy. Either Lanfranc referred to some or all of these forgeries but wisely did not quote them, or his list was the basis upon which they were later made [92]. If the first, he could not quote them because Roman eyes would have detected forgery; if the latter it was because he was bluffing without having plausible texts.

Lanfranc's case may, however, have seemed cogent to his audience. It can be read as mainly depending on the addresses,

---

[92] For the text of the forgeries, H. Böhmer, *Die Fälschungen Erzbischof Lanfranks von Canterbury*, Leipzig 1902, p. 147-161, nos. II-X. For recent discussions, see esp. R. W. Southern, *The Canterbury Forgeries*, « The English Historical Review », 73 (1958), p. 193-226; Gibson, *Lanfranc of Bec*, p. 53 n. 7 and 231-237. Apart from arguments in the text, several other considerations tell against a reference to the forgeries: (i) they contain no items of Gregory the Great or Leo IX; (ii) of the remaining six, four are, indeed, addressed to archbishops of Canterbury but none strictly to *Anglorum reges*; (iii) if the words *data* and *transmissa* distinguish between items given to present and absent recipients, it is hard to justify from Böhmer's texts the word *data*; (iv) the supporting documents that Lanfranc sent to Alexander (Clover/Gibson, p. 54-55, no. 4, 101-105) need not have included any of these items; excerpts from Bede, for example, would have sufficed if reinforced by a few later documents.

not the contents, of whatever letters he had in mind; for he set
them aside as a miscellany in date and subject-matter alike
(« aliis atque aliis temporibus variis de causis sunt data aut
transmissa »).   His key point concerned to whom the letters
were addressed: archbishops of the church of Canterbury and
kings of the English.   Popes had always addressed the former
as sole leaders of the English church and the latter as rulers of
a single English people.   Thus, he could insist that there had
been many more such documents, originals and copies, until
the Canterbury fire of 1067 destroyed them.   On such a line
of argument, Lanfranc could cite even Pope Gregory the Great.
For he addressed Ethelbert of Kent as *rex Anglorum*; Augustine
was never, in so many words, bishop of London, but normally
*episcopus Anglorum*.   It can scarcely have escaped Lanfranc's
eye that, in Gregory's *Responsiones* as recorded by Bede,
Augustine was *episcopus Cantuariorum ecclesiae*—not so good
as *Cantuariae* or *Doroberniae*, but a useful pointer [93].   Lanfranc's concentration upon titles gave him a debating point
against Archbishop Thomas's main counter-argument, that
Gregory the Great had ordained an equality of London and
York: Lanfranc was not bishop of London, and five and a
half centuries of papal usage as regards addresses showed that
the church of London had nothing to do with matters presently
at issue.   According to Lanfranc, his verbal victory was enough
to persuade the king to rebuke Thomas for the weakness of
his case.

Once Lanfranc gained this success, the way was open for
the English kingdom, on its side, to give him in the constitution
that was drawn up exactly the permanently binding statement
that he needed, and even to enhance his claims for his see.   It
recognized that he was pleading the rights, not just of himself,
but of his church over that of York: the church of York should

---

[93] For the opening of the *Responsiones*, see BEDE, *Ecclesiastical History
of the English People*, I, 27, ed. COLGRAVE-MYNORS, p. 78-79.   For Gregory's use
of titles, see esp. *Registrum*, XI, 36-37 and 39, ed. NORBERG, p. 925-932 and
934-935.

permanently be subject to Canterbury and obey its archbishop in all matters concerning the Christian religion. It was specifically provided that, if the archbishop of Canterbury—the reference is to the officer, not just to an individual—should die, the archbishop of York should consecrate his successor at Canterbury as his own primate; if the archbishop of York died, his successor was to be consecrated by the archbishop of Canterbury in the latter's see or wherever he might appoint. By these provisions, Canterbury's primacy was permanently assured[94].

The question of the respective jurisdiction of the two archbishops was amicably and decisively settled. The archbishop of Canterbury confirmed to his brother of York jurisdiction over the bishop of Durham and all regions *usque ad extremos Scotiae fines* from the northern border of the see of Lichfield and the River Humber, together with a few uncontested land further to the south. Lanfranc was left with the three contested dioceses, but the archbishop of York was given a potentially viable province to the north as his *quid pro quo*[95]. It should not be forgotten that the year 1072 was later to see King Malcolm of Scotland becoming King William's vassal at Abernethy.

With this extension of the English church and kingdom, Lanfranc was able not only to secure his earlier claims but to enhance them. The constitution drafted at Winchester is the first surviving document to refer to the archbishop of Canterbury as *primas totius Britanniae*[96]. This was a title that Lanfranc may have thought to be warranted by Bede, most significantly in the description of Augustine's successor Laurentius, who « not only had the oversight of the new church that was gathered from the English, but also bestowed his

[94] CLOVER/GIBSON, p. 44-47, no. 3(iv), 102-110 and 128-134.

[95] *Ibid.*, p. 46-47, no. 3(iv), 111-117.

[96] *Ibid.*, p. 46-47, no. 3(iv), 109. Only with the profession of Osbern fitzOsbern, elect of Exeter, also made between Easter and Pentecost 1072, does a Canterbury profession yield a similar phrase: see RICHTER, *Canterbury Professions*, p. 28-29, no. 35.

pastoral care upon the older inhabitants of Britain (*Brittania*) and on the Irish (*Scotti*) who inhabited Ireland, an island close to Britain » [97]. The extension of his subordinate archbishop's jurisdiction *ad extremos Scotiae fines* gave Lanfranc his opportunity to advance a similar claim. It is not clear whether Lanfranc had canvassed his authority over the whole of Britain while he was in Rome. But he referred to it in wide terms in his report to Alexander II, and a year later Pope Gregory VII, no less, assumed his active jurisdiction over the whole of the British Isles [98]. Tacitly, at least, the papacy accepted the phraseology of the constitution.

Thus far, Lanfranc won a resounding victory for his see, and it appears to have been complete at Winchester. The reissue of the constitution at Windsor involved no change to the substance of his claim, and such formal changes as were made are explicable on diplomatic grounds. As was commonly the case, the constitution was drafted after the assembly at Winchester had mainly dispersed. It therefore received only the autograph signa of the king and queen, the legate, the two archbishops, and four bishops. At Windsor, the constitution was issued in multiplicate and in an officially ratified and published form [99]. This time it bore the autograph signa of only the king and queen. But, as well as by the legate and the archbishops (the priority now accorded to the legate should be noted), it was subscribed by thirteen bishops and twelve abbots. This looks like a deliberate conformity with Alexander II's direction that matters at issue between Canterbury and York should be settled in England « by the witness and judgement of the bishops and abbots of the whole kingdom » [100].

[97] *Ecclesiastical History of the English People*, ii. 4 (as n. 88), p. 144-147, cfr. i. 29, p. 104-105. Lanfranc's source for the title *primas* remains unknown.

[98] CLOVER/GIBSON, p. 50-51 and 64-67, nos. 4, 32-34 and 8, 30-39.

[99] See *Facsimiles*, ed. BISHOP-CHAPLAIS, plate XXIX.

[100] CLOVER/GIBSON, p. 42-45, no. 3(ii), 71-72. Such an association of bishops and abbots was, of course, in itself standard current practice: e.g. *CS*, p. 568-569 and 612, nos. 86/i, ii, 92.

470

Within the context of the English kingdom Lanfranc was well secured by a constitution which was massively attested and preserved in all major archives; but when it came to securities within the ecclesiastical order he was left dangerously vulnerable. Archbishop Thomas soon made a second profession of obedience to him [101]. In the light of the constitution agreed at Winchester, in all save its last sentence it, too, gave Lanfranc what he wanted. Thomas alluded to the debate at Winchester (*auditis cognitisque rationibus*) and made his absolute profession of canonical obedience to Lanfranc and to his successors. It could be anticipated that, under the constitution, future archbishops of York would do the same. But the last sentence damagingly weakened the effect of what went before, and it is hard to know why Lanfranc permitted it to be added: perhaps there had to be some explanation of a second profession. Thomas recalled that, when he first sought consecration, he was uncertain about his canonical subjection to Canterbury, and therefore had promised obedience to Lanfranc unconditionally but to his successors conditionally. He said that he had been uncertain (*dubius*), not that he had been wrong. It was, therefore, open to him, or to his successors, to become persuaded that his first thoughts had been his better thoughts, and so to reopen the issue. Given the weakness of Lanfranc's case at Winchester, that could be dangerous.

Worse still, as in 1070 so in 1072, Lanfranc failed to underpin the fragile sanction of a profession with an oath to himself. A sentence of the Winchester constitution in which one suspects his drafting makes clear his purpose of doing so, He demonstrated, or so it was claimed, that by the ancient right of his predecessors the archbishop of York should profess obedience to the archbishop of Canterbury by a public oath. But « out of love for the king », Lanfranc waived the oath and accepted only a written profession. Two considerations suggest that this was a euphemism for his having again had to give

---

[101] CLOVER/GIBSON, p. 44-45, no. 3(iii).

way to the king's refusal to permit the taking of an oath by a tenant-in-chief to anyone but himself. First, Lanfranc yielded without prejudice to his successors, leaving the way open for them to secure an oath if a king were ever compliant. In fact, they were able to do so only from the mid-thirteenth century [102]. Secondly, in his letter to the pope Lanfranc's oblique reference to his having from charity conceded to Thomas—not the king— some things that were his by right is eloquent of his embarrassment at the king's refusal [103]. It is highly likely that Lanfranc's failure to secure his position completely in relation to the archbishop of York was partly the result of the king's insistence on sole mastery of the feudal order so that he disallowed an oath.

Denied by the king the sanction of an oath to underpin Thomas's loyalty, he turned to Rome for the only alternative— a papal privilege. He did so in haste, and did not wait for the final form of the constitution of 1072 which complied with papal specifications about those who should warrant it. He was patently anxious: his letter to Alexander II is the longest in his letter collection, and the note of importunate urgency upon which it ended verged upon tactlessness. From the accompanying dossier, it said, Alexander

might clearly know from the practice of your predecessors what you should concede to me and to the church of Christ which I have undertaken to govern. I ask for this in due form (*honeste*) and without delay through the granting of a privilege by the apostolic see... [104].

Lanfranc also wrote a supporting letter to Hildebrand, archdeacon of the Roman church, who was well known to be

---

[102] *Ibid.*, p. 46-47, no. 3(iv), 121-128; for the history of the oath, see RICHTER, *Canterbury Professions*, p. lxxviii-lxxix.

[103] CLOVER/GIBSON, p. 54-55, no. 4, 92-93. For the king's command of the sworn fealty of his subjects, ecclesiastical and lay, see *ibid.*, p. 50-51, no. 4, 21-22.

[104] *Ibid.*, p. 48-57, no. 4, esp. lines 99-108. The letter occupies 125 printed lines.

powerful in its counsels [105]. It is surprising that this letter is the first recorded contact between Lanfranc and Hildebrand, for they are likely to have met during Lanfranc's visits to Rome and both were concerned with Berengar of Tours [106]. Lanfranc's letter was brief, formal, and unwontedly fulsome in style; it was not as one would write to someone with whom one was at ease. But Lanfranc felt that he needed Hildebrand's help, and he ended with a request that he read the letter he had sent to the pope:

I ask and beg you to read it with due attention, so that you will securely grasp what the apostolic see should grant and confirm by its privilege to me and to my church [107].

Lanfranc did not explain the haste and urgency with which he wrote. He was probably anxious to get matters settled before Archbishop Thomas could also write, and before the pope learnt of the terms of his profession. That would have created a danger that the debate might be reopened at Rome. There is no evidence that Alexander sent a reply. But Hildebrand wrote a curt letter regretting that no such privilege could be granted unless Lanfranc came to Rome in person, which Hildebrand urged him to do for the discussion of this and other matters [108]. Hildebrand gave no reason why Lanfranc must come in person, but the demand would have been unusual unless his request were thought at Rome to be for a novel right. Hildebrand's letter thus had the implication that Lanfranc was not seen, as he claimed, to be requesting the

---

[105] As illustrated, for example, by PETER DAMIANI's well-known epigrams: L'opera poetica di S. Pier Damiani, ed. M. LOKRANTZ, Stockholm-Göteborg-Uppsala 1964, p. 55 and 68, nos. 17-18 and 78-79.

[106] Gregory wrote in 1079 of a « prisci amoris memoria »: Reg., VI, 30, p. 443. For the popes and Berengar, see H. E. J. COWDREY, The Papacy and the Berengarian Controversy, in Auctoritas und Ratio: Studien zu Berengar von Tours, edd. P. GANZ - R. B. C. HUYGENS - F. NIEWÖHNER, Wiesbaden 1990, p. 109-138.

[107] CLOVER/GIBSON, p. 56-59, no. 5, esp. lines 17-21.

[108] Ibid., p. 58-59, no. 6.

confirmation of ancient and established custom; at very least, his claims as so far presented had not carried conviction. In the event, Lanfranc never travelled to Rome although Hildebrand made it clear that the door was open; he never, therefore, received a privilege. And in April 1073 the instrument of his rebuff, Archdeacon Hildebrand, became Pope Gregory VII.

Meanwhile, probably after Christmas 1072, Lanfranc sent Alexander a lengthy plea that he be allowed to resign his see and revert to the life of a simple monk [109]. It has recently been argued that the letter was « an irritated, politically motivated response to the papal stand on Lanfranc's attempt to establish the Canterbury primacy » [110]. This is almost certainly an over-simplification of Lanfranc's complex caracter and motives. Such letters by monk-bishops were far from infrequent; in 1098 Anselm of Canterbury was to write to Pope Urban II in very similar terms [111]; he and Lanfranc had more in common than is generally credited. The main reason that he gave Alexander, that no spiritual benefit had come to England either by or through him, probably represents his true feelings. He began his letter with an expression of canonical obedience to the supreme pastor of the church. The concluding sentences show that he expected to be made to carry on, and there is no need to doubt the genuineness of his expressed wish to visit the holy apostles, Alexander himself, and the Roman church. What is lacking is any political statement or undertone; the note, rather, was a weary acceptance of the world as Lanfranc found it. The road to a papal underwriting of his claims in England was barred. No sentence in Lanfranc's letters is more revealing than that with which he closed. He urged Alexander to pray for the long life of the king, for his military security, and for the increase of his love for the church. In William there was a ray of hope: « while he lives we have peace of a

[109] *Ibid.*, p. 30-35, no. 1.
[110] M. RUUD, *Episcopal Reluctance: Lanfranc's Resignation Reconsidered,* « Albion », 29 (1987), p. 163-175, citation from p. 164.
[111] ANSELM, *Ep.* 206, ed. SCHMITT, IV, p. 99-101.

kind; after his death we can hope neither for peace nor for anything that is good » [112]. Since Lanfranc had made progress over the primacy only in the context of the English kingdom and since the king was ruling with increasing effect, it was through loyalty to the English king in his feudal kingdom that the best hope for the future rested.

By the spring of 1073, Lanfranc's attitude during the rest of his archiepiscopate seems to have become settled in his mind. Hitherto his dealings with the king had not always been those of men who saw eye to eye: their attitudes to Stigand were very different; the king withheld from Lanfranc the oath of the archbishop of York that he urgently needed; the king's stance had been a key factor in his failure completely to resolve the matter of the primacy. But the limitations of papal action had been revealed: as was canonically warranted, Alexander remitted for settlement in England and in royal gatherings the major questions about the sees of Canterbury and York that he lacked the means to resolve at Rome. Lanfranc had received an object lesson in where power was, and in the constitution of 1072 he had derived great benefit from the action of the English kingdom—an agreed and favourable statement of his primatial rights over York, and the recognition of Canterbury as the primatial see in the whole British Isles. It was not the kingdom but the ecclesiastical structure that failed him, by leaving the archbishop of York with a potential loophole on the primacy issue and above all by denying him the papal privilege that would have guarded him against contradiction. There was a clear lesson that the king was near but the papacy far away and not to be counted on when help was most needed. Although there were limits to what the king would concede when his interests were at stake, he alone was strong and dependable enough to offer peace and order to church and lay society alike. The somewhat uneasy *modus vi-*

---

[112] CLOVER/GIBSON, p. 30 and 34-35, no. 1, 1-2 and 65-74; cf. p. 96-97, no. 18, 3-13.

*vendi* of Lanfranc's early years as archbishop could ripen into mutual respect and, on Lanfranc's part, loyal collaboration and partnership.

With Lanfranc's dealings with the popes after the events of 1072-1073 it will be possible to deal more briefly, since they have been discussed by the present writer in two earlier studies [113]. His relations with Gregory VII remained cold and distant. To begin with, Gregory tried to be conciliatory. While still archdeacon he had ended his letter declining to send Lanfranc the privilege that he so urgently desired upon a note of regard: Lanfranc was a man of habitual charity, who might be expected to receive Hildebrand's verbal messages « as befits a most dear son of the holy Roman church and a godly bishop » [114]. As pope, Gregory's first letter to Lanfranc, which is preserved only in the latter's letter collection, greeted him as a most dear brother in Christ and, by urging him with papal authority to correct lax marriage customs not only among the Irish but also throughout « the island of the English », implicitly acknowledged his authority over all the British Isles. In November 1073 Gregory hoped that Lanfranc would support Abbot Baldwin of Bury St Edmunds against Bishop Herfast of Elmham and urge the king to do likewise [115].

But nothing could gainsay Gregory's action as archdeacon in denying Lanfranc the privilege that would have secured his title to a permanent primacy over the see of York. Moreover, Lanfranc is likely to have been further distanced from Gregory by the pope's dealings with Berengar of Tours, against whom Lanfranc continued to write after his coming to Canterbury [116]. As lately as 1072, Lanfranc had answered Alexander II's request by sending to Rome a copy of his treatise against Beren-

---

[113] See above, note 54.

[114] CLOVER/GIBSON, p. 58-59, no. 6, 12-15.

[115] *Ibid.*, p. 64-67, no. 8, 1-2 and 35-39; *Reg.*, I, 31, p. 51-52.

[116] CLOVER/GIBSON, p. 142-151, no. 46. For further discussion, see COWDREY, *The Papacy and the Berengarian Controversy*.

gar [117]. If it arrived, Gregory seems to have disregarded it; his own dealings may be searched in vain for even a hint of a debt to Lanfranc or to his treatise. Neither as archdeacon nor as pope did Gregory accept as decisive the eucharistic statement drafted by Cardinal Humbert that Lanfranc so highly regarded and preserved in his treatise and in his canon-law collection. Whereas Lanfranc had found in the ancient authorities that he marshalled a clear refutation of Berengar, Gregory never found in such authorities more than a body of material to consider and debate [118]. Gregory was sure of the inerrancy of the Roman church [119], but with regard to Berengar he looked for guidance in its exercise, not to authorities or to dialectic, but to a direct divine manifestation through vision or miracle. It seems clear that he never consulted Lanfranc or made use of his work; so far as events at Rome in 1078-1079 were concerned, it might as well not have been written. For his part, Lanfranc left no trace of having noticed the anti-Berengarian formula of the Lateran council of 1079 [120]. In the later stages of the Berengarian controversy, there was nothing to draw pope and archbishop together; instead, they seem to have drifted further apart.

If there was no meeting of minds between Gregory and Lanfranc about Berengar and the eucharist, it is also generally the case that Lanfranc was not conspicuous for forming the bonds of friendship (*amicitia*) that joined so many of his reforming contemporaries to a wide circle of their superiors, peers,

[117] See above, p. 463.

[118] See esp. BERENGAR, *Rescriptum*, 1, 651-656, ed. HUYGENS, p. 54, and his Memoir on the Roman councils of 1078-1079: HUYGENS, *Bérenger de Tours*, p. 390, 38-391, 47.

[119] *Dictatus papae*, XXII, in *Reg.*, II, 55a, p. 207.

[120] See above, note 20. The text of Gregory's council of 1079 up to Berengar's oath is included after the Decretals in two early copies of Lanfranc's canonical collection, Cambridge, Peterhouse, MS 74 and Cambridge, Corpus Christi College, MS 130, which may derive from a copy made at Canterbury in Lanfranc's lifetime; but when and at whose direction the insertion was made remains uncertain: see BROOKE, *The English Church*, p. 231-233.

and juniors [121]. Such bonds presupposed and fostered a strong element of common purpose, facilitated the circulation of ideas, and established common sympathies. At Canterbury, Anselm, Lanfranc's successor, was rich in such friendships, which included such elder statesmen of the papal reform as Pope Urban II, Abbot Hugh of Cluny, and Archbishop Hugh of Lyons [122]. Lanfranc's only strong bond of friendship in this sense was with Anselm while he was abbot of le Bec; their correspondence, though frequent, was mainly about monastic subjects [123]. Lanfranc was not by temperament a man of all-round friedships; he preferred to concentrate his loyalty upon a single superior who was close at hand. As Professor Barlow has admirably expressed it, « Lanfranc was the perfect second-in-command, given a commander whom he could respect and admire » [124]. As a monk at le Bec he found such a commander in his abbot, Herluin, for whom he retained a deep devotion until the latter's death [125]. At least from 1073 though perhaps not before, he found such a commander in King William, and accommodated himself to the king's masterful ways.

By 1073, William had effectively completed his conquest of England and could proceed to establish his mastery by way of colonization and consolidation. Henceforth Lanfranc could look to him for better peace as well as for a more effective devotion to the church as part of the Anglo-Norman kingdom

---

[121] For *amicitia*, see esp. I. S. ROBINSON, *The Friendship Network of Gregory VII*, « History », 63 (1978), p. 1-22; R. W. SOUTHERN, *Saint Anselm and his Biographer*, Cambridge 1963, p. 67-72, and ID., *Saint Anselm: a Portrait in a Landscape*, p. 139-142, 155-165.

[122] For an illustration, see H. E. J. COWDREY, *Cluny and the First Crusade*, « Revue bénédictine », 83 (1973), p. 285-311, repr. in ID., *Popes, Monks and Crusaders*, no. XV, at p. 304-309.

[123] See esp. ANSELM, *Ep.* 1, ed. SCHMITT, III, p. 97-98. Of Anselm's first 124 letters in Schmitt's edition, sixteen are addressed to Lanfranc. For Lanfranc, see CLOVER/GIBSON, p. 96-99, no. 18.

[124] F. BARLOW, *A View of Archbishop Lanfranc*, « Journal of Ecclesiastical History », 16 (1965), p. 163-177, repr. in ID., *The Norman Conquest and Beyond*, London 1983, p. 223-238; for the quotation, see p. 235 of the reprint.

[125] *VL*, cap. 8, col. 44-46 (see below, p. 690-692).

than he could envisage in the winter of 1072-1073 [126]. If the king had denied him the oath of the archbishop of York, he had also concurred in the constitution of 1072 with its unequivocal statement of his right to hold primatial councils in England [127]. Henceforth, general councils as envisaged by the constitution of 1072 were the principal expression of Lanfranc's primacy. They made possible a confident partnership with a king who was now in firm political control. The records of Lanfranc's councils may be searched in vain for references to contemporary papal authority [128]. There is a contrast here with Norman councils; at the council of Rouen (1074), for example, the king and archbishop were declared to have made a decision *auctoritate domini papae Gregorii et regia potestate*, while the decrees of the council of Lillebonne (1080) were dated by Gregory's regnal year [129]. The difference between England and Normandy is likely to have been owing to Lanfranc, not to the king-duke who was present at councils held on both sides of the English Channel.

It is not the case that Lanfranc did not defer to the rulings of popes: the canonical collection that he caused to be sent over from le Bec and that he circulated in England was a modified version of the Forged Decretals, and therefore full of them. But, for the most part, the collection was of the decretals of popes in a distant past. When Lanfranc cited papal precedents, whether in his letters or in the canons of

---

[126] CLOVER/GIBSON, p. 34-35, no. 1, 68-74.

[127] *Ibid.*, p. 46-47, no. 3(iv), 117-120.

[128] *Acta Lanfranci*, in: *Two of the Saxon Chronicles Parallel with Supplementary Extracts from the Others*, ed. C. PLUMMER, 2 vols., Oxford 1892, I, 287-292; CS, p. 607-634, nos. 92-93, 95, 97-98.

[129] Rouen: *Gallia christiana*, 16 vols., Paris 1715-1865, XI, Instr. 16-17, no. 12; Lillebonne: P. CHAPLAIS, *Henry II's Reissue of the Canons of the Council of Lillebonne of Whitsun 1080 (?25 February 1162)*, « Journal of the Society of Archivists », 4 (1973), p. 627-632, repr. in ID., *Essays in Medieval Diplomacy and Administration*, London 1981, at p. 629; cf. OV, III, p. 24-25. For Lanfranc's councils, see K. SCHNITH, *Wesen und Wandlungen des Anglonormannischen Concilium Generale*, in *Gesellschaftsgeschichte. Festschrift für Karl Bosl zum 80. Geburtstag*, ed. F. SEIBT, 2 vols., Munich 1988, II, p. 22-36.

his councils, it was to popes long dead that he appealed [130]. The collection also contained a few items of Pope Nicholas II, and so testifies to Lanfranc's continuing respect for the early reform papacy of his years in Normandy. But, unlike the legatine councils of 1070, Lanfranc's councils showed little concern to translate a papal programme into action. With regard to clerical celibacy, for example, Lanfranc tempered the severity of papal and other reforming demands by allowing parochial clergy who were already married to keep their wives. He acted in the spirit, and probably with the example in mind, of Nicholas II's concessions to those tainted by simony that were cited in his canonical collection. But it was characteristic of Lanfranc as archbishop that he should follow Nicholas, not to enforce the rigour of contemporary papal demands, but to give a colour of justification to a relaxation that Gregory VII would probably not have approved [131]. In practice, he assumed the position of a good second-in-command and accepted the leadership of the king. At the council of London (1075), for example, the transfer of further episcopal sees from villages to towns, which strictly speaking required papal sanction, was postponed *usque ad regis audientiam* [132].

Lanfranc's deference to the king fitted William's own ecclesiastical policy, which has sometimes been described as one of erecting a ring-fence about England which would exclude papal authority and intervention. The later summary of it by Eadmer has been adduced in support of this view:

---

[130] CLOVER/GIBSON, p. 108-109 and 152-153, nos. 24, 8-9 and 47, 16-41; *CS*, p. 612-614, no. 22. A St Albans tradition said that Lanfranc secured papal approval for his monastic constitutions (1079/1089) but named no pope: *Gesta abbatum monasterii sancti Albani, a Thoma Walsingham ... compilata*, ed. H. T. RILEY, 3 vols., London 1867-1869 (*RS*, 28d), I, p. 52.

[131] Council of Winchester, can. 1, *CS*, p. 619, no. 93; cf. Nicholas II's decrees of 1059 in *MGH Const.*, I, p. 550, no. 386, cap. 2.

[132] Council of London, can. 3, *CS*, p. 613, no. 92, cf. the pre-Conquest evidence of *ibid.*, p. 524-533, nos. 70-71. For similar deference to the king in Lanfranc's letters, see CLOVER/GIBSON, p. 94-95, 132-133, 166-167, 172-173; nos. 17, 19-21; 40, 13-16; 53, 13; 57, 5-7. See also EADMER's comments: *Historia novorum*, I, ed. RULE, p. 9-10.

All things divine and human depended upon his will. ... No one in all his dominions might accept a bishop of Rome as pope unless by his order, nor might anyone in any wise receive his letters unless they were at first shown to him [133].

Comparison with a letter of St Anselm which Eadmer was following suggests that Eadmer wrote these words in the light of events after the Conqueror's death [134]. In any case, under William I the ring-fence was far from complete [135]; it should be borne in mind that the concentration of ecclesiastical authority in the see of Canterbury was made possible by Alexander II's concessions to Lanfranc which Anselm was later to seize upon and augment [136]. William I is best to be regarded as collaborating with a willing Lanfranc to advance towards, but not yet fully to realise, the power in the church that Henry I was to claim in the early years of his reign.

It was in events that probably are to be located in the year 1080 that the limits of tolerance between the papacy and the Norman kingdom of England were most searchingly tested. Through his legate Hubert, Gregory VII called upon the king to do fealty to him and to his successors; he also reminded him about the regular payment of Peter's Pence. In a letter preserved in Lanfranc's letter collection which seems to bear the stamp of Lanfranc's mind, William firmly refused fealty but agreed that, in his own absence from the country, Peter's Pence had lately been carelessly collected. Hubert would bring Gregory some of the arrears; in due course, messengers from Lanfranc who was significantly described as the king's *fidelis* would bring the rest. The king's letter began and ended upon a note of friendship: « Greetings with friendship. ... Pray for

---

[133] *Ibid.* The translation « at first », rather than « first », is intended to suggest that the requirement probably related to a pope's initial letter announcing his accession.

[134] ANSELM, *Ep.* 210, 14-31, ed. SCHMITT, IV, p. 106.

[135] See COWDREY, *Pope Gregory VII*, esp. p. 82-83 and 104-106.

[136] CLOVER/GIBSON, p. 62-63, no. 7, 41-44; SOUTHERN, *Saint Anselm and his Biographer*, p. 130-132.

us and for the welfare of our kingdom; for we loved your predecessors, and we wish to love you sincerely and to hear you obediently above all men ». There is evidence that Lanfranc took steps to collect Peter's Pence in his own lands [137].

At about the same time there came into the open the coolness that had developed between Gregory and Lanfranc. The first sign to survive of Gregory's displeasure is a letter of 25 May 1079, in which Gregory rebuked his dilatoriness in coming to Rome since he had become pope. Whether the reason was Lanfranc's fear of the king or his own reluctance to come, there was a danger of a crisis in which the king might be involved. Lanfranc should forestall it by suitably advising the king, and by himself coming to Rome in order to confer with Gregory [138]. In 1080 Hubert brought either this letter or an expanded version to Lanfranc. In his reply Lanfranc gave no undertaking that he would come to Rome, and in words verging upon the contumacious he suggested that it was Gregory, not himself, who had shown coolness:

My own mind is in everything and by everything obedient to your precepts according to those of the canons. If by God's help I could talk to you face to face, I could demonstrate not so much by words as by very deeds how my own love has increased; but you, if you will excuse my saying so, have in no small measure declined from your « former love » [139].

Gregory's severest letter on the subject of Lanfranc's coming to Rome dates from the early summer of 1082. He reminded Lanfranc of his many earlier summonses to Rome; it was by his

---

[137] CLOVER/GIBSON, p. 130-133, nos. 38, 41-4 and 39. For the date and further discussion, see COWDREY, *Pope Gregory VII*, p. 89-94. For Lanfranc and Peter's Pence, see, D. C. DOUGLAS, *The Domesday Monachorum of Christ Church, Canterbury*, London 1944, p. 14-15 and 80.

[138] *Reg.*, VI, 30, p. 443-444.

[139] CLOVER/GIBSON, p. 128-131, no. 38. With the phrase « a pristino amore » (line 19), cf. Gregory's « prisci amoris memoria » in *Reg.*, VI, 30, p. 443, 25. The lapse of time and lines 8-10 of Lanfranc's letter suggest that Hubert brought a different and more strongly worded letter than *Reg.*, VI, 30.

own pride or negligence—Gregory, significantly, no longer mentioned the king—that he had abused Gregory's patience by failing to come. He had no valid excuse and must establish his obedience by coming to Rome before the next All Saints' Tide (1 November) to purge his disobedience on pain of suspension from his episcopal office [140]. The sequel is not known, but there is no reason for thinking that Lanfranc complied. Nor does Gregory seem to have implemented his threat; in the circumstances of Gregory's latter years as pope, his good relations with the Anglo-Norman kingdom were too precious to be set at risk.

Gregory's circumstances became increasingly difficult between the council of Brixen in 1080 and his own death at Salerno on 25 May 1085. At Brixen, King Henry IV of Germany designated Archbishop Guibert of Ravenna as antipope, and four months later Henry's cause was helped by the death in battle of his rival, the antiking Rudolf of Swabia. After Roman expeditions in 1081, 1082, and 1083-1084, in 1084 Guibert became the antipope Clement III (24 March). and Henry received imperial coronation at his hands (31 March). The result was schism in the western church. That Gregory and his close supporters throughout these events cherished and remained confident of King William I's loyalty is indicated by a cordial and confident letter which Bishop Anselm II of Lucca wrote to him, probably early in 1085, seeking his military help for the Roman church [141]. The scanty surviving evidence for Gregory's last years suggests that Lanfranc's attitude to the schism was more ambiguous than his master's, but that he did not act contrary to him. His letter collection includes a masterpiece of non-committal circumspection which he wrote between Clement's consecration and Gregory's death. It is addressed « Lanfrancus Hu. », which suggests that the scribe of the letter

---

[140] *Reg.*, IX, 20, p. 600-601.
[141] *Die Hannoverische Briefsammlung*, I: *Die Hildesheimer Briefe*, no. 1, in: *Briefsammlungen der Zeit Heinrichs IV.*, edd. C. ERDMANN and N. FICKERMANN, MGH BDK, V, p. 15-17; see COWDREY, *Pope Gregory VII*, p. 109.

collection was at pains to abbreviate the beginning of the letter and so play down Lanfranc's semi-official contact with Clement's party. « Hu. » was probably Hugh Candidus, cardinal-priest of San Clemente [142], and the letter was in reply to a lost letter that answered at length an earlier letter of Lanfranc, also lost. Lanfranc found much in « Hu. »'s letter of which to disapprove: he called Pope Gregory « Hildebrand », and was abusive about his legates, calling them *spinosuli*—prickly and obstinate hedge-hogs; moreover, he lavished excessive praise upon Clement. Lanfranc's use of papal names is significant: he would not renounce Gregory whom he called « pope », and he conceded Clement's papal name but without prefixing the title. He went far towards an acceptance of Henry IV of Germany: though twice excommunicated he was « gloriosus imperator », and Lanfranc observed that he would not have embarked upon his Roman expedition without good cause, nor would he have won such a victory without great help from God. But when it came to practicalities, Lanfranc was wholly non-commital. He told « Hu. » that

> I do not approve that you should come to England, unless you first receive leave to come from the king of the English. For our island has not rejected the former pope that you mention or come to a decision whether to obey the latter. When the pleas on both sides have been heard, if this should happen, it will be possible to see more clearly what should be done.

Lanfranc declared himself the partisan of neither side, but he was not willing to accept the arguments of the Clementines alone: both sides must be heard. In any case, it was for the king to decide what approaches might be countenanced [143].

After Gregory's death, Clement dispatched three substantial letters to Lanfranc in an attempt to win him over to his

[142] See HÜLS, *Kardinäle, Klerus und Kirchen Roms*, p. 158-160.
[143] CLOVER/GIBSON, p. 164-167, no. 52; see COWDREY, *Pope Gregory VII*, p. 109-111.

cause [144]. They survive because they were copied into Lanfranc's master copy of his canonical collection. But they follow the note about Lanfranc's having caused the collection to be sent over from le Bec [145]. There is no means of knowing whether or not they were copied during his lifetime or with his knowledge, and no conclusion either for or against his approval of them can be drawn from the fact of their having been thus copied. As regards their content, however, the fulsomeness of praise for Lanfranc and the prolixity are such that, since he had demurred to «Hu.»'s excessive praise of Clement [146], Lanfranc may not have been favourably impressed. His contact with Gregorian partisans, and their continuing regard for him, render it unlikely that at any time up to his death in 1089 Lanfranc earned general notoriety as a temporizer, let alone as someone who favoured Clement III [147]. In all likelihood, Lanfranc persisted in the caution of his letter to « Hu. ».

Urban II, who was elected pope on 12 March 1088, was himself confident of Lanfranc's loyalty. On 10 August he wrote to him from Terracina, describing the straitened circumstances of the church and informing him of his election. He asked Lanfranc to urge King William II to help the Roman church in its dangers and necessities, and he called for the sending of Peter's Pence either by Roger, cardinal-subdeacon of the Roman church, or by a faithful messenger of the king [148].

In England, however, the matter of which pope to recognize—Urban II or Clement III—remained in suspense. After the Conqueror's death on 9 September 1087, the duchy of Normandy passed to his eldest son Robert Curthose but the kingdom of England to his next son William II. Urban's

---

[144] F. LIEBERMANN, Lanfranc and the Antipope, « The English Historical Review », 16 (1901), 328-332, at p. 330-332.

[145] Cambridge, Trinity College, MS B 16 44, p. 405-406.

[146] CLOVER/GIBSON, p. 164-165, no. 52, 5-6.

[147] COWDREY, Pope Gregory VII, p. 112-114.

[148] Ep. 3, PL 151, col. 286-287. For Roger, see HÜLS, Kardinäle, Klerus und Kirchen Roms, p. 253.

recognition by the French, and therefore by the Norman, church did not bind England, and William II was in no hurry to make up his mind. There may have been churchmen who, as individuals, made their own decisions; at least, Bishop Geoffrey of Chichester, who died on 25 September 1088, secured papal absolution, but unfortunately it is not clear from which pope, although there may have been a connection with Urban's legate Roger [149]. Likewise, William of St Carilef, bishop of Durham, in 1088 adopted the tactic of appealing to Rome when he stood trial for treason before the king's court, but the account of his trial gives no certain clue about which pope he envisaged although there is a probability that it was Urban [150]. There is no reason to suppose that either the English kingdom or Lanfranc himself made or implied a positive commitment to Urban or to Clement during Lanfranc's lifetime [151].

For the purpose of this study, the most significant detail in Lanfranc's closing years comes from William of St Carilef's riposte at his trial to Lanfranc's contention that he must stand to justice wholly and without appeal as a feudatory in the king's court:

« It is not right », Lanfranc said, « that a royal plea or judgement should go any further on account of an objection. Whenever justice is debated in the king's court, it must be granted or withheld there. So you must either accept our judgement in this place, or else you must refuse it in this place and show good reason ».

The bishop replied, « I certainly do refuse it in this place; I intend to maintain my objection at Rome where it is right that I should do so and where justice not violence is the order of the

[149] See H. MAYR-HARTING, The Bishops of Chichester, 1075-1207. Bibliographical Notes and Problems, Chichester 1963, plate IV and p. 1-2, 21.

[150] De iniusta vexatione Willelmi episcopi primi, in: The Historical Works of Simeon of Durham, ed. T. ARNOLD, 2 vols., London 1882-1885 (RS 75), I, p. 170-195, see esp. p. 184-185. Cf. URBAN's letter in S. LOEWENFELD, Epistolae pontificum Romanorum ineditae, Leipzig 1885, p. 63, no. 129.

[151] Although the somewhat unusual invocation of St Clement after St Peter on behalf of the pope, who was not named, in a Canterbury Laudes regiae text of the later eleventh century should be noted: see COWDREY, The Anglo-Norman 'Laudes regiae', p. 72, D/6-7.

day. Since none of you when passing judgement or bearing witness dares to say what might offend the king, and I have no other witnesses, I call to witness the Christian law (*Christianam legem*), which I am holding in my hand, that I can rightly go to Rome and that the final sentence in my case should come from the autho- rity of the Roman pontiff » [152].

The irony of the situation was that he was almost certainly holding in his hand his copy of Lanfranc's own canonical collection when he rebutted the archbishop's claim that he must accept trial under feudal law in the king's court.

Twenty-two years of Norman rule had introduced into the English polity two deeply contrasting tendencies which are here thrown into relief. On the one hand, William I and Lan- franc had, more profoundly than they intended or understood, equipped the English church for Gregorianization and for gradual inclusion in the developed structure of the central medieval church. Lanfranc's widely circulated canonical col- lection in respect of mental preparation and his primatial councils and their work in matters of practical reform and reorganization foreshadowed the separateness of the spiritual order and its accessibility to papal authority. On the other hand, the Normans introduced into England a new impetus towards feudalization which, under masterful kings, included ecclesiastical as well as lay society, bishops and abbots as well as earls and barons. All alike were tenants-in-chief of the crown with common rights and obligations. Loyal to his master the king, whether it were William I or his less godly son William II, Lanfranc hoped to reconcile the obligations of churchman and feudatory in a single polity where strong kings gave church and lay society alike the peace that they needed. His coolness towards Gregory VII, especially in view of the effective denial of a papal privilege to settle the question of the primacy, made him the more prepared after 1073 to be

[152] *De iniusta vexatione*, p. 187-188.

« the perfect second-in-command » in all public matters. But the contradiction in Lanfranc's position was soon apparent: the church and the feudal order were not in the harmony that he desired. William I's insistence in 1070-1072 upon a monopoly of the oaths of all tenants-in-chief, ecclesiastical and lay alike, had also contributed to leaving the Canterbury-York dispute imperfectly resolved. From the start the king's feudal claims militated against the ecclesiastical order and harmony for which Lanfranc strove. During Lanfranc's lifetime, the appointment and investiture of bishops and abbots was never a serious issue, either in the Anglo-Norman lands or between their leaders and the papacy [153]; the bone of contention became their imprisonment. In the very early years of his reign, William I was quick to imprison bishops against whom he had a political grievance. In 1082 his imprisonment of his half-brother, Bishop Odo of Bayeux, deeply angered Gregory VII and compelled Lanfranc to take up the uncomfortable stand on the kings' feudal behalf that he was to adopt on William II's behalf in the case of William of St Carilef [154].

After his rebuff by the papacy in 1073, Lanfranc had decided that, in the power structure of the Norman kingdom of England, it was prudent to acknowledge the leadership of a powerful and essentially well disposed king; he became distanced from an incongenial and in his terms unsupportive pope. The trial of William of St Carilef showed how deep a gulf had opened between the claims of ecclesiastical and feudal loyalty and order. The relative simplicities of his days as scholar and monk, when he had been able to identify himself to a remarkable extent with the early reform papacy, were at an end. In the constitution of 1072, which had the sanction of both pope

---

[153] See below, Appended Note B.

[154] For early imprisonments, see below, Appended Note A. For Gregory and Odo's imprisonment, *Reg.*, IX, 37, p. 630-631; *The Epistolae vagantes of Pope Gregory VII*, ed. and trans. H. E. J. COWDREY, Oxford, 1972, p. 128-129, no. 53; for comment, COWDREY, *Pope Gregory VII*, p. 108-109. For Lanfranc's attitude, *De iniusta vexatione*, p. 184-185.

and king, it had seemed that this might not be so. But neither the papacy nor the king had fully supported him in his quest to make his primacy permanent, and he had to seek the best terms that he could from the one or the other. Given the position that the constitution secured for him, it was with the king that he almost inevitably came to terms. To both his royal masters his loyalty became paramount. The contradictory pressures, ecclesiastical and feudal, within the polity that they established drew him increasingly to the king's side. In the longer run, the same pressures were certain to invite a renewal of the claims of the *sacerdotium* and to make the rights of the king and the duties of the archbishop of Canterbury a matter of fundamental debate. Hence there ensued the conflicts of later Norman and Angevin times that were centred upon Anselm and Thomas Becket.

APPENDED NOTE A

## The Papacy, Lanfranc, and the English Cathedral Monasteries

At two junctures in Lanfranc's archiepiscopate, sources survive which purport to reveal papal support for the preservation, or extension, of monastic chapters in English cathedrals. This note is intended to list and to appraise these sources.

I. *Pope Alexander II, Lanfranc, and the chapters of Canterbury and Winchester, 1070-1073*

Three of Alexander's letters are involved. While they have never been the subject of full critical examination, their authenticity has been widely but not universally accepted [155]. If authentic, they would add strong support to the argument above, pp. 451-452, that Alexander drew heavily upon documents relating to Pope Gregory I's mission to England of Archbishop Augustine of Canterbury when forming his attitude to the Norman Conquest of 1066 and to Lanfranc's authority as archbishop of Canterbury. There must, however, be serious doubts as to their genuineness; accordingly, no use has been made of them in the foregoing study.

(i) *Ep. 142, PL 146,* col. 1415-1416 (JL 4761). This is a letter from Alexander to Lanfranc. Alexander has heard rumours that certain clerks, supported by the secular power, are trying to expel the monks from Christ Church, Canterbury, and to replace them with clerks. The same assailants are trying to extirpate monks from other cathedrals. Alexander has instituted a search at Rome for privileges and cites material from Popes Gregory I and Boniface

---

[155] The most telling questioning has been that of H. CLOVER, *Alexander II's Letter 'Accepimus a quibusdam' and its Relationship with the Canterbury Forgeries,* in *La Normandie bénédictine au temps de Guillaume le Conquérant (xiᵉ siècle),* Lille 1967, p. 417-442, esp. p. 430-439; the extent of forgery at Canterbury *c.* 1070 is brought out by S. E. KELLY, *Some Forgeries in the Archive of St Augustine's Abbey, Canterbury,* in *Fälschungen im Mittelalter. Internationaler Kongreß der Monumenta Germaniae Historica, München, 16.-19. September 1986,* IV: *Diplomatische Fälschungen (II), MGH Schriften,* 33/4, Hanover 1988, p. 347-369, esp. p. 369. The principal sources for early Norman designs upon monastic chapters are EADMER, *Historia novorum,* I, ed. RULE, p. 18-21, and WILLIAM OF MALMESBURY, *De gestis pontificum,* I, 44, ed. HAMILTON, p. 71-72.

IV (608-15) about the institution of monks at Christ Church. Alexander confirms these privileges.

Manuscript tradition: see CLOVER/GIBSON, p. 183, note 4. The letter is fully cited, with discussion, by EADMER, *Hist. nov.*, I, ed. RULE, p. 19-21.

Comments on date: while this letter might prima facie date from any time between Lanfranc's consecration on 29 Aug. 1070 and Alexander's death on 21 Apr. 1073, its drafting reflects a situation in late 1070 or in 1071 before Lanfranc's autumn departure for Rome: (*a*) Alexander received information, not from Lanfranc, but from unnamed visitors from England (col. 1415B). Such a channel of information would be improbable after Lanfranc had set out for Rome or when he was subsequently in communication with Alexander; it reflects the situation of his early months as archbishop. (*b*) Measures against the monks of Christ Church by « quidam clerici, associato sibi terrenae potestatis, laicorum videlicet, auxilio » (col. 1415B), especially if there is implied reference to Bishop Odo of Bayeux and the king, are not likely to relate to events long after Lanfranc became archbishop but to those before, or within two years after, his arrival.

If genuine, the letter would probably be of 1070-1071. If a forgery that looks back to this period, it may have been written within the next two years: (*a*) the detail is circumstantial. (*b*) Once Lanfranc was established, the monastic order at Christ Church became less threatened. (*c*) The account of the trial at Penenden Heath (?1072) refers, perhaps tendentiously, to general pressure upon Christ Church before Lanfranc arrived; the trial did much to make good its security [156]. However it is possible to envisage a forgery during any juncture at which the Christ Church monks felt under threat between Lanfranc's death in 1089 and its citation by Eadmer in the earlier of his *Historia novorum* (1109/1115) [157].

The following points raise serious doubts about the letter's authenticity: (*a*) the statement that Alexander received information from « quidam clerici » followed by the assertion that he instituted

---

[156] J. LE PATOUREL, *The Reports of the Trial on Penenden Heath*, in *Studies in Medieval History presented to Frederick Maurice Powicke*, edd. R. W. HUNT, W. A. PANTIN and R. W. SOUTHERN, Oxford 1948, p. 15-26, esp. p. 21-24. The opening sentences of Document A, as of the letter at present under discussion, should, however, be read in the light of D. R. BATES, *The Land Pleas of William I's Reign: Penenden Heath Revisited*, « Bulletin of the Institute of Historical Research », 51 (1978), p. 1-19, esp. p. 14-18.

[157] EADMER, *Historia novorum*, I, ed. RULE, p. 19-21.

a search at Rome for privileges, and the phrase « Dorobernia, quae est metropolis totius Britanniae » (col. 1415B) which Lanfranc never used, make it improbable that the pope used material that Lanfranc supplied[158]. (*b*) The phrase just cited is highly suspect in a papal letter, especially if the actual or purported date is early; such phrases do not appear either in England or at Rome before the constitution of 1072 (see above, p. 468), and at Rome it would have gone far towards conceding the Canterbury claim upon which Alexander was unwilling to pronounce. (*b*) The letter asserts that Alexander instituted an inquiry, evidently at Rome, *de privilegiis ecclesiarum* (col. 1415C). As a result, he made two citations. The first was from the beginning of Pope Gregory the Great's *Libellus responsionum* to Augustine of Canterbury (col. 1415C)[159]. The derivation and use of the citation are both of importance. As regard derivation, it is not in Gregory's Register and in 735 there was no copy of it in the Roman archives[160]. Bede preserved the citation in three places, but in the 1070s there is no evidence that his version was available at Rome. A version in the Pseudo-Isidorian Decrees was, however, almost certainly to hand there. At Canterbury, Bede's version was undoubtedly available; an unabridged version of Pseudo-Isidore may also have been available at least from the early twelfth century[161]. If the citation can be shown to follow Bede it is far more likely to have been made in England than at Rome; if it follows Pseudo-Isidore, citation at Rome becomes conceivable, although citation in England remains probable once an unabridged text was to hand. On the basis of the printed versions, the comparison is as follows:

[158] As was suggested by W. LEVISON, *England and the Continent in the Eighth Century*, Oxford 1946, p. 201-204.

[159] BEDE, *Ecclesiastical History of the English People*, I, 27, ed. COLGRAVE-MYNORS, p. 80-81, for the passage excerpted in the letter see also *Vita sancti Cuthberti*, cap. 16, in *Two Lives of Saint Cuthbert*, ed. and trans. B. COLGRAVE, Cambridge 1940, p. 208-209, and the citation in the account of Cuthbert in *Ecclesiastical History of the English People*, IV, 27, p. 434-435; *Decretales Pseudo-Isidorianae et Capitula Angilramni*, ed. P. HINSCHIUS, Leipzig 1863, p. 738.

[160] See BONIFACE's letter to Archbishop Nothelm of Canterbury, *Briefe des Bonifatius. Willibalds Leben von Bonifatius*, edd. M. TANGL, W. LEVISON, and R. RAU, Darmstadt 1968, *Ep.* 33, p. 108-112, at p. 110, 1-9.

[161] The date depends mainly upon the earliest known unabridged texts in England of Pseudo-Isidore—the Canterbury text in London, British Library, MS Cotton Claudius E V, and the Exeter text, Eton College, MS 97: see BROOKE, *The English Church*, p. 84-88 and 236-237.

## JL 4761 (A)

Quia tua fraternitas monasterii
regulis erudita,                in ecclesia
Anglorum, quae *nuper, auctore Deo,*
    ad fidem perducta est,
debet *conversationem instituere* quae
*in* initio nascentis ecclesiae fuit
patribus nostris, in quibus nullus
eorum ex *iis* quae possidebant
aliquid suum esse dicebat, sed
erant *illi*[s] *omnia* communia.

5

10

## Bede, *Eccles. Hist.*, I, 27 (B)

Quia tua fraternitas monasterii
regulis erudita *seorsum* fieri *non*
*debet a clericis suis* in ecclesia
Anglorum, quae *auctore Deo nuper*
    *adhuc* ad fidem perducta est, hanc
debet *conversationem instituere,* quae
    initio nascentis ecclesiae fuit
patribus nostris; in quibus nullus
eorum ex *bis* quae possidebant
aliquid suum esse dicebat, sed
erant *eis* omnia communia.

lines 4-5: IV, 27 *reads* nuper
auctore Deo *and omits* adhuc,
*as do some MSS of the Life*
*of Cuthbert*

## Pseudo-Isidore (P)

Quia tua fraternitas monasterii
regulis erudita *seorsum* vivere *non*
*debet a clericis suis* in ecclesia
Anglorum, quae *auctore Deo nuper*
    ad fidem perducta est, hanc
debet *instituere conversationem,* quae
*in* initio nascentis ecclesiae fuit
patribus nostris, in quibus nullus
eorum ex *bis* quae possidebant
aliquid suum esse dicebat, sed
erant *illis* omnia communia.

The following differences are apparent: (*a*) A agrees with B against P in the word order *conversationem instituere* (line 6); (*b*) A agrees with P against B in omitting *adhuc* (line 5), in the reading *in initio* (line 7), and in using *illis* rather than *eis* (line 11); (*c*) B and P agree against A in the word order *auctore Deo nuper* (line 4) and in reading his not *iis* (line 9). Particularly if the variants among Bede's three citations are taken into account, these differences do not decisively settle whether A followed B or P, although the number of agreements perhaps establishes a slight presumption that it was P. The use of the citation is of much greater significance than its derivation. The critical factor is the omission in A of the words « seorsum fieri non debet a clericis suis » (lines 3-4). It has the effect of changing the point of Gregory's response from a requirement that a bishop live in community with his clerks to one that cathedral clerks themselves live a common life; this change is reinforced by the comment in Alexander's letter, « That this rule of common life is pre-eminently appropriate to the monastic order, none can doubt ». On the test of *Cui bono?* the tendentious abridgement of Gregory's reply is more likely to have originated in England to justify the case of the Canterbury monastic community than in Rome after the searching of papal privileges. The second citation in Alexander's letter (col. 1415D-1416A) was from Pope Boniface IV's letter to King Ethelbert of Kent which William of Malmesbury also reproduced. The italicized words in the introduction to the letter, « Hinc habetur epistola Bonifacii, qui *quartus a beato Gregoria* ecclesiae *Romanae ...* praefuit », appear to be taken from Bede. All this material can be more easily explained in terms of composition in England from material there known and available than of composition in Rome.

(ii) *Ep. 143, PL* 144, col. 1416 (JL 4762). This is another letter from Alexander to Lanfranc. Alexander has heard that the monks of the Old Minster (the cathedral monastery) at Winchester are under threat of ejection, and he charges Lanfranc to protect them. He also refers to a captive bishop, chiding Lanfranc for not having fulfilled his command to procure his release; he further commends to Lanfranc's favour a plea of the messenger.

Manuscript tradition: see CLOVER/GIBSON, p. 183, note 5.

Comments on date: the absolute date range is as for (i). But a relatively early date is indicated by the reference to the attempt by Walkelin, bishop of Winchester (consecrated 30 May 1070), to replace the monks by secular clerks which Lanfranc upon arrival was quick to resist [162]. A further indication of date is the captivity of the unnamed bishop, about whose identity there exist the following possibilities: (a) Stigand, archbishop of Canterbury and bishop of Winchester, deposed c. 11 Apr. 1070 and imprisoned at Winchester until his death on 21/22 Feb. 1072 [163]. The designation *episcopus* and the relatively mild tone tell against this identification. (b) Bishop Ethelric of Selsey, deposed May 1070 by a legatine sentence about which Alexander expressed disquiet in a letter to the king and said that he had referred the matter to Lanfranc for re-examination. Florence of Worcester wrote of his imprisonment [164]. This is a possible identification which, in view of Lanfranc's stated delay in acting, would indicate a date after Alexander's letter to the king and so in late 1071 or 1072. (c) Bishop Ethelric of Durham, who resigned his see in 1056 but was imprisoned by William I at Easter 1070 [165]. The lapse of time since his resignation makes him a less likely person than (b) or (d). (d) Ethelric's brother Bishop Ethelwine to whom he resigned the see of Durham in 1056; William I deposed him in 1071 and subjected him to rigorous imprisonment at Abingdon until his death in the winter of 1071-1072 [166]. The notoriety of Ethelwine's revolt and the severity of his punishment make him a strong possibility; if so, his death provides a *tempus ante quem* for the letter. 1071-1072 emerges as a likely date.

In view of the specific matters dealt with in the last two sentences of the letter, this part of it may be genuine; if so, it further illustrates the close contact at this time between Alexander and Lanfranc: see above, p. 458-460. But the first two sentences

---

[162] EADMER, *Historia novorum*, I, ed. RULE, p. 18-19; WILLIAM OF MALMESBURY, *De gestis pontificum*, I, 44, ed. HAMILTON, p. 71-72; *Annales de Wintonia*, a. 1098, in *Annales monastici*, ed. H. R. LUARD, 5 vols., London 1864-1869 (RS, 36), II, p. 39-40.

[163] *Annales de Wintonia*, a. 1072, *ibid.*, p. 29-30; WILLIAM OF MALMESBURY, *De gestis pontificum*, I, 23, ed. HAMILTON, p. 37.

[164] CLOVER/GIBSON, p. 62-63, no. 7, 30-36; FLORENCE OF WORCESTER, *Chronicon*, ed. THORPE, II, p. 6.

[165] *Anglo-Saxon Chronicle*, DE versions, aa. 1069-1072; FLORENCE OF WORCESTER, *Chronicon*, ed. THORPE, II, p. 9-10; WILLIAM OF MALMESBURY, *De gestis pontificum*, III, 131, ed. HAMILTON, p. 271; SIMEON OF DURHAM, *Historia Dunelmensis ecclesiae*, III, 9, ed. ARNOLD, I, p. 92.

[166] *Anglo-Saxon Chronicle*, DE versions, aa. 1069-1071; FLORENCE OF WORCESTER, *Chronicon*, ed. THORPE, II, p. 8-9; *Chronicon monasterii de Abingdon*, II, ed. J. STEVENSON, 2 vols., London 1858 (RS, 2), I, p. 485-486; SIMEON OF DURHAM, *Historia Dunelmensis ecclesiae*, III, 17, ARNOLD, I, p. 105.

which relate to the Old Minster are evidently closely related to the suspect letter (iii): (a) the source of the rumour that Alexander has heard according to (ii) is identified in (iii) as his legates at the council of Winchester (1070). (b) The supposed (« ut dicitur »: col. 1416C) dispositions of St Augustine of Canterbury about monastic cathedrals—which, according to (i), col 1415C, were exactly traced by Alexander—are further elaborated without the ascription of a precise authority (col. 1417A). While it is possible that the legates reported to Alexander about the threat to the Winchester monks, the imprecise references to Augustine create a suspicion of drafting in England, perhaps at Winchester itself, by a writer with an insecure knowledge of the canonical tradition.

(iii) *Ep. 144, PL* 144, col. 1416-1417 (JL 4763). This is a letter from Alexander to the monks of the Old Minster at Winchester. Alexander relates that his legates of 1070, the cardinal-priests John and Peter (see above, p. 452-453) have assured Alexander about the ancient monastic constitution at Winchester, which may be traced back to St Augustine's arrangements for almost all (*fere omnes*) the greater English churches. Alexander confirms the monastic constitution of the Old Minster, urging its monks to zeal and devotion.

Manuscript tradition: London, British Library, MS Harley 633, fo. 58ᵛ; Cambridge, University Library, MS Kk 46, fo. 278.

Comments on date: closely related to the final form of (ii).

Alexander is most unlikely to have referred to Augustine as « legatus beatissimi papae Gregorii » (col. 1417A): the term *legatus* has no warrant in ancient or contemporary sources, and was not at this time applied to the archbishop of Canterbury in papal or other sources [167]. Nor is the excessive statement of Augustine's arrangements likely in a genuine papal statement.

II. *Pope Gregory VII, Lanfranc, and the monastic chapter at Durham, 1080-1083*

When William of St Carilef succeeded to the see of Durham in Dec. 1080, he planned to establish a monastic chapter in his cathedral [168]. According to the Durham historical tradition, William

---

[167] For Alexander's own definition of Lanfranc's position *nostrae et apostolicae auctoritatis vice*, see CLOVER/GIBSON, p. 62-63, no. 7, 41-44.

[168] SIMEON OF DURHAM, *Historia Dunelmensis ecclesiae*, III, 22 and V, 1, ed. ARNOLD, I, p. 113 and 119-120. See D. ROLLASON, *Symeon of Durham and the Community of Durham in the Eleventh Century*, in: *England in the Eleventh Century*, ed. C. HICKS, Stamford 1992, p. 183-197.

went to Rome at the king's bidding and secured Pope Gregory VII's sanction for his plan [169]. This is probably true, but the plan gave rise to a number of forgeries of which the following may be noted: (i) a spurious charter of Bishop William, dated 1082, according to which the bishop was advised by the king, the queen, and Archbishop Lanfranc before going to Rome. The witness list of the charter establishes its spuriousness [170]. (ii) The *narratio* of (i) is reproduced and extended in a lengthy entry in the *Liber vitae ecclesiae Dunelmensis* where Bishop William writes in the first person. It adds a statement that Gregory VII sent letters by the hands of the bishop to the king and to Lanfranc in which he bestowed his blessing upon them and upon all who furthered the bishop's plan [171]. (iii) Simeon of Durham gave an account of the introduction of monks to Durham Cathedral which reproduced (ii) almost verbatim up to the recital of the property that Bishop William secured for the cathedral monastery [172]. (iv) A spurious diploma of Pope Gregory VII, dated 6 Jan. 1083 at Benevento, in favour of Bishop William, approved the setting up of the cathedral monastery, confirmed its right of electing the prior, safeguarded its possessions, and took the monks into papal protection. Gregory was said to have acted « tam commemorabilis regiae maiestatis quam specialis filii nostri Lanfranci archiepiscopi et fraternitatis tuae iustis postulationibus inclinati » [173].

These documents are without value for a discussion of relations between Gregory and Lanfranc, save in so far as they are based upon a presumption of Lanfranc's continuing loyalty to Gregory.

---

[169] *De iniusta vexatione*, I, p. 171; for the problem of its substantial authenticity, which is accepted in this paper, see A. GRANSDEN, *Historical Writing in England, c. 550-c. 1307*, London 1974, p. 122-123.

[170] *Historiae Dunelmensis scriptores tres*, ed. J. RAINE, Durham-London 1839 (Surtees Society, 9), Appendix I, p. i-v; *Regesta regum Anglo-Normannorum, 1066-1154*, I: *Regesta Willelmi Conquestoris et Willelmi Rufi, 1066-1100*, ed. H. W. C. DAVIS, Oxford 1913, p. 40-41, no. 148.

[171] *Liber vitae ecclesiae Dunelmensis*, I, ed. A. HAMILTON THOMPSON, Durham-London 1923 (Surtees Society, 136), p. xx-xxi, facsimile of f. 45r-50r.

[172] SIMEON OF DURHAM, *Historia Dunelmensis ecclesiae*, IV, 2 ed. ARNOLD, I, p. 120-121.

[173] *Quellen und Forschungen zum Urkunden- und Kanzleiwesen Papst Gregors VII.*, i: *Quellen: Urkunden, Regesten, Facsimilia*, ed. L. SANTIFALLER, Città del Vaticano (Studi e testi, 190), p. 247-250, no. 210. For the grounds for rejecting it and for the date of its forgery, see p. 247.

APPENDED NOTE B

## The Appointment and Investiture of Bishops and Abbots in the Anglo-Norman Lands

A comment may be useful on the circumstance that, during Lanfranc's career in Normandy and England, the appointment and investiture of bishops and abbots was never a controversial issue, either within the Anglo-Norman lands or between the papacy and the spiritual and lay leaders of those lands.

A starting-point for the study of this topic in Normandy is its treatment by Orderic Vitalis, who, although he wrote a considerable way into the twelfth century, was well aware of how matters stood in Lanfranc's time [174]. According to Orderic, Duke William exercised a firm control of appointments, which was clear from his dealings with the monastery of Saint-Evroult. In 1050 he delegated to the founding family of Grandmesnil the right to select its first abbot, Thierry, but Thierry was forthwith duly presented to the duke [175]. In 1059, the monks elected Robert of Grandmesnil and at once took him to the duke who approved his election. In 1061, at a time of political crisis, Duke William intruded Osbern without the monks' knowledge or consent. In 1066, the monks requested him to provide a new abbot; he chose Mainer with the counsel of his magnates. It was the duke's custom to invest the new abbot by handing him a pastoral staff (*baculus, cambuta*), thus admitting him to his abbacy: « ille [the duke] veneratione congrua eum [Thierry] suscepit, datoque baculo pastorali sicut moris est Uticensi aecclesiae praefecit ». An abbot who wished to resign expected similarly to return his pastoral staff to the duke: « Willelmo duci Normannorum pastoralem baculum cum tota abbatia [Thierry] reddere voluit ». Orderic drew a distinction between the *abbatia* which Thierry wished to resign to the duke and the *cura animarum*: « Luxovium adiit, et Hugoni episcopo ... curam animarum reddidit » [176].

Orderic consistently maintained this distinction in writing of abbatial appointments at Saint-Evroult: « Dux ... praefato viro [Robert of Grandmesnil] qui electus erat per cambutam Ivonis

[174] E.g. OV, II, p. 16-19; iv, p. 254-255.
[175] Orderic's principal references to the appointment of the early abbots of Saint-Evroult are: Thierry (1050), *ibid.*, II, p. 16-19; Robert of Grandmesnil (1059), II, p. 74-75; Osbern (1061), II, p. 90-93; Mainer (1066), II, p. 144-147.
[176] OV, II, p. 66-69.

episcopi Sagiensis exteriorem abbatiae potestatem tradidit; Willelmus vero Ebroicensis episcopus interiorem animarum curam per pontificalem benedictionem ... spiritualiter commendavit »; « Hortatu Hugonis episcopi [of Lisieux] aliorumque sapientium [Duke William] Mainerium priorem elegit, eique per pastoralem baculum exteriorem curam tradidit, et praedicto antistiti ut ea quae sibi de spirituali cura competebat suppleret praecepit ». In the case of Robert, as also of Osbern, it is noteworthy that ducal investiture was effected, not by means of the previous abbot's staff, but by that of a bystander bishop. No doubt the symbolism was that of conferring seisin of the abbacy by ducal act, but the staff did not become a permanent pledge of such seisin. In Normandy the distinction between the *exteriora cura* that the duke conferred and the *spiritualis cura* that the bishop conferred seems to have been drawn with exceptional clearness. It would be anachronistic to conclude that the twelfth-century distinction between *spiritualia* and *temporalia* was already in effect drawn, if only because of the association of the *abbatia* with the ducal gift. Nevertheless, Peter Damiani's question of 1061/1069, posed in a letter to Pope Alexander II: « Sane cum baculum ille tuis manibus tradidit, dicitur, 'Accipe terras atque divitias illius ecclesiae', an potius, 'Accipe ecclesiam'? » would have lost something of its force in Normandy, where cure of souls was expressly excluded [177].

Episcopal elections in ducal Normandy yield no such vivid evidence for current views, though there can be no doubt of Duke William's firm control [178]. But it should be remembered that, in Normandy as elsewhere, the *baculus* was not only, or even principally, a lay symbol in the making of bishops and abbots. Contemporary pontificals both featured the bishop who consecrated bishops and blessed abbots as the conferrer of the *cura pastoralis* and made the *baculus* the instrument by which it was conferred. This may primarily be illustrated from the Romano-Germanic Pontifical, first compiled at Mainz *c*.960, and by a century later known in Normandy and England. According to it, the bishop received his staff in token of his pastoral authority:

> *Cum datur baculus episcopalis, dicat ordinator*:
> Accipe baculum pastoralis officii et sis in corrigendis

---

[177] PETER DAMIANI, *Ep.*, 1, 13, *PL* 144, col. 221A. For investiture in Germany and Italy, see SCHIEFFER, *Die Entstehung*, p. 7-47 and 95-107.

[178] See, e.g., WILLIAM OF POITIERS's account of the election of Archbishop Maurilius of Rouen: I, 54, p. 132-133.

vitiis pie seviens, iudicium sine ira tenens, in fovendis
virtutibus auditorum animos demulcens, in tranquillitate
severitatis censuram non deserens.

The abbot, too, received it as pastor:
*Tunc [episcopus] tradat ei baculum, dicens*:
    Accipe baculum pastoralitatis, quem praeferas catervae
tibi commissae ad exemplum iustae severitatis et correptio-
nis [179].

Similar formulas appear in Norman and English pontificals of
the eleventh century [180]. Contemporaries must have seen in the
conferring of the staff a spiritual significance that contrasted sharply
with the temporal; in Normandy, at least, the solemn formulas
of the pontificals must have seemed more significant than the somewhat casual practice of ducal investiture which went before, and
have made current practice acceptable. Thus, it is not surprising
that the making and investing of bishops and abbots was not, in
Lanfranc's time, a problem in ducal Normandy. Nor is it surprising that a reforming pope like Alexander II should have no qualms
in writing that the preferment of Bishop John of Avranches to
Rouen in 1067 took place *ex electione principis* [181].
    In the England of King Edward the Confessor there is no
evidence of the royal investiture of bishops and abbots by means
of the pastoral staff, and it is more than unlikely to have been
practised. Royal control of appointments was no less strong than
in ducal Normandy, and the king was recorded as « granting »
ecclesiastical offices. But grants were announced by vernacular
royal writs, the authority and permanence of which are likely to
have rendered otiose a further investiture [182]. After the Conquest,
however, the Conqueror does not appear to have used writs for
this purpose. In a more feudalized polity he may have wished for

---

[179] *Le Pontifical Romano-Germanique du dixième siècle*, sect. 12 and 41-42,
ed. C. VOGEL and R. ELZE, 3 vols., Città del Vaticano 1963-1972 (Studi e testi,
226-227, 269), I, p. 66 and 221-222; for the ring and the staff, see sect. 38-45,
*ibid.*, I, p. 220-223.

[180] For a Norman example, see *The Benedictional of Archbishop Robert*,
ed. H. A. WILSON, London 1903 (HBS 24), p. 165, and for English examples,
*The Lanalet Pontifical*, in: *Two Anglo-Saxon Pontificals*, ed. H. M. J. BANTING,
London 1989 (HBS 104), p. 11 and 146.

[181] As note 29.

[182] See references in the *Anglo-Saxon Chronicle*, CDE versions, *aa*. 1045,
1047, 1050, and, for writs, *CS*, p. 545-550, 552-555, 560-562, nos. 68, 76-77,
79-80, 83-84.

a personal bond of loyalty to himself, expressed partly in his unwillingness to share the oaths of his episcopal tenants-in-chief, but also in the introduction of investiture as it was practised in the duchy. The evidence for the promotion of Remigius to the see of Dorchester in 1067 indicates the use of Norman forms as described by Orderic Vitalis: in his later profession to Lanfranc, Remigius referred to his having received the *cura episcopalis* from Stigand when he had consecrated him; while in the so-called « Foundation Charter of the See of Lincoln » (*c.*1072), William referred to property « quod sibi [Remigius] olim cum episcopali baculo concesseram »[183]. Although this is the only reference to lay investiture in a document of William I's reign, it appears that he introduced the custom which he had for some years practised in the duchy. Since Lanfranc was familiar with it there, he is unlikely to have objected to it in England. Nor did Alexander II jib at William's changes in so far as he knew of them. In a letter to Lanfranc he assumed that a bishop who resigned would return his bishopric to the king; writing to William himself, Alexander was glad that he had acted to confirm the standards and usages of catholic liberty (« catholicae libertatis usus et officia confirmando »)[184].

Nor did Gregory VII challenge William on the issues of appointment and investiture, either in England or in Normandy. William's exchange of letters with Abbot John of Fécamp about the preferment of his subject Vitalis in 1076 to the abbacy of Westminster and that of Vitalis's brother Osbern to Bernay shows that he could proceed with diplomacy in securing the concurrence of reforming churchmen[185]. As regards lay investiture, it is improbable that Gregory published a general decree against it in 1075, and his legislation of 1078-1080 does not seem ever to have directed against the Anglo-Norman lands[186]. Gregory knew well the advantage of tempering his demands in order to retain King William's loyalty and collaboration[187]. The sustained unwillingness of the English and Norman archbishops to travel to Rome rankled severely[188]. But the nomination and investiture of bishops and abbots never emerged as a matter of open contention. The milder practice of the Anglo-Norman lands made it unlikely that it would do so.

[183] RICHTER, *Canterbury Professions*, p. 27, no. 32; *Facsimiles*, ed. BISHOP-CHAPLAIS, plate XIII.
[184] CLOVER/GIBSON, p. 36-37 and 60-61, nos. 2, 9-10 and 7, 7-8.
[185] MABILLON, *Vetera analecta*, p. 450-451.
[186] See SCHIEFFER, *Die Entstehung*, esp. p. 114-176.
[187] *Reg.*, IX, 5, p. 579-580.
[188] *Reg.*, VI, 30, p. 443-444; VIII, 1, p. 458-460; IX, I, p. 568-569.

# The Enigma of Archbishop Lanfranc

By contrast with Anselm of Aosta, his successor as archbishop of Canterbury, Lanfranc of Pavia appears to have followed a straightforward and even a largely untroubled career. There seem to be few open questions about him. As a scholar, he excelled in the liberal arts, especially grammar and dialectic. His Lombard origin left him with some knowledge of secular, that is Lombard, law. But, during his monastic years, he turned increasingly to biblical commentary and to eucharistic theology. He identified himself with the monastic life at Bec; he was before all else a dutiful prior to his revered abbot Herluin until he left to become abbot of Saint-Étienne at Caen. As archbishop, he worked in loyal harmony with King William the Conqueror, under whom as under Herluin he was `the perfect second-in-command, given a master whom he could respect and admire' and `the perfect subordinate to carry out the ecclesiastical policy of a reforming prince.'[1] Even under the Conqueror's differently disposed son William Rufus, Lanfranc, perhaps from loyalty to his old master, was a lion under the throne. This paper has a twofold purpose. The first is to suggest that Lanfranc's career presents more problems and was at times more tense and fraught than is always realized. The second is to see whether light cannot sometimes be shed upon these problems by setting them more fully than hitherto in the context of events and situations outside the Anglo-Norman lands and of Canon Law as eleventh-century churchmen interpreted it. The enigma of Archbishop Lanfranc's attitude to popes and kings may thus be presented and in part accounted for.

An initial problem in studying Lanfranc is whether, and if so how deeply, he was a student or practicioner of Lombard law. The only considerable amount of evidence for Lanfranc's early years in Italy is the Bec tradition which, as now preserved, took shape only in the twelfth century. If Lanfranc was born c. 1010 and left Italy soon after 1030, this was a hundred years or so after the events described. The most noteworthy writings are Gilbert Crispin's *Life of Herluin*, first abbot of Bec, written at Westminster between 1093 and 1117, and the *Life of Lanfranc*,

---

[1] Frank Barlow, `A View of Archbishop Lanfranc,' *The Journal of Ecclesiastical History* 16 (1965): 1751; repr. in *The Norman Conquest and Beyond* (London, 1983), 12, 235.

written at Bec after 1136, maybe by its precentor, Milo Crispin.[2] The *Life of Lanfranc* contains not one but two accounts of Lanfranc's early years. The second contains a tradition well known to Orderic Vitalis which may depend upon the lost ending of William of Poitiers' *Deeds of William the Conqueror* and, if so, upon material current in 1073/74.[3] According to it, Lanfranc was educated from childhood both in the liberal arts and in the secular law of his country. As a lawyer, he did well: as an advocate, he often floored senior opponents in legal proceedings; he also passed wise judgements which expert Pavian lawyers and judges were glad to receive. Whether the comment that `Pavia recalls these things (*meminit horum Papia*)' refers to a genuine historical recollection or is merely a rhetorical flourish is not clear. At all events, only after he left Pavia did his mind turn to the true wisdom and to the monastic life. All this is in sharp contrast to what appears in the opening paragraph of the *Life of Lanfranc*.[4] It begins with six lines of rather rhetorical introduction from the *Life of Herluin*: Lanfranc is eulogized as an Italian whose own pioneering endeavours comprehensively restored Latin culture (*Latinitas*) to its former excellence, while (in an unexplained phrase) his disciples won admiration in Greece, mistress of the nations in liberal studies. There is then inserted, from a hearsay tradition, comment upon his Pavian origins. He was now no forensic prodigy; instead, he may from the start have shunned the study and practice of the law. There is circumstantial detail.[5] His parents were prominent and respected citizens, and his father `belonged to the rank of those who watched over the rights and laws of the city (*de ordine istorum qui iura et leges civitatis asservabant fuit*).' His father was evidently one of the *iudices* or *causidici* who were not so much professional lawyers as citizen assessors in legal cases.[6] But Lanfranc's father died while he was a small child. When Lanfranc became of age to

---

2   *Vita Herluini*, in *The Works of Gilbert Crispin Abbot of Westminster*, eds. A.S. Abulafia and G.R. Evans (London, 1986), 183–212; hereafter cited as *VH*; and Milo Crispin, *Vita beati Lanfranci Cantuariensium archiepiscopi*, *PL*, 150: 29–58; hereafter cited as *VL*.

3   *VL* 5.11, col. 39AB, Orderic, 2: 248–51. For Orderic's debt to Poitiers, see Orderic, 2: xviii, xx–xxi, xxiii, xxxiii.

4   *VL* 1.1, col. 29BC; *VH* cap. 55, p. 195.

5   It must be observed that the Latin of *VL* 1.1 allows of different translations which are contradictory. The translation here adopted is that `Lanfranc was bereaved of his father at a very tender age. *When he should have* succeeded him in office and rank, he *instead* left the city and from love of learning turned to the study of letters. When he had remained away for a very long time and was fully steeped in all secular knowledge, he returned. Then he left his own country and crossed the Alps.' The alternative is that `. . . *since he must succeed* him in office and rank, he *therefore* left the city and from love of learning turned to the study of letters. . . .' Against the second interpretation, it can be urged that it would have been strange for Lanfranc to have left Pavia at a critical point of early adult life for a very long time if he had wished to establish himself in its public affairs, that it leaves little time for Lanfranc to have had a public career before his second departure, and that the first interpretation offers a more consistent and credible sequence of events.

6   For the Pavian legal system in action during Lanfranc's early years, see *I placiti del `Regnum Italiae*,' ed. C. Manaresi, 2 pt. 2, *Fonti per la storia d'Italia* 96 (Rome, 1958), 527–38, 599–605, nos. 282–83, 301. For legal personnel, see J. Fried, *Die Entstehung des Juristenstandes im 12. Jahrhundert* (Cologne and Vienna, 1974), 9–44.

succeed to his public responsibilities, he preferred to leave Pavia; from love of learning he embarked elsewhere upon the study of the arts (*ad studia litterarum perrexit*). His absence was prolonged; he returned only when fully instructed in them. There is no mention of the study, let alone the practice, of law as such. Early in the reign of the Capetian king Henry I (1031–60), he left Pavia for France. The *Life of Lanfranc* thus offers two, contradictory accounts of its subject's early years: according to the second, he was an enthusiastic and eminent student and practitioner of Lombard law; according to the first, he seems to have set his face against it and to have avoided its practice. Which account is the more probable?

One may best try to answer by working back from the developed Bec position. According to this, Lanfranc after leaving Italy turned his back upon the secular law of his Lombard homeland. In its eulogies of his learning, the *Life of Lanfranc* studiously avoided referring to legal skills.[7] But did the real Lanfranc himself at Bec shun legal studies and affairs? There is a presumption that he did. In the Bec tradition, when Lanfranc was with Herluin at Bec, it was Herluin, not Lanfranc, who was learned in the law and his monastery's skilful vindicator in legal disputes; Lanfranc remained in the cloister, pursuing sacred study and spiritual compunction.[8] When Pope Nicholas II wished to send clerks to Lanfranc for instruction in dialectic and rhetoric, he thought that Lanfranc's preoccupation with biblical commentary might preclude the liberal arts, let alone legal studies.[9] As archbishop of Canterbury, Lanfranc refused to deal with matters of secular learning (*quaestiones secularium litterarum*); long ago he had frittered his youth in them, but when he came to pastoral responsibility – whether at Bec or Canterbury – he had decided that they should be renounced.[10]

When did Lanfranc turn from the law: only upon leaving Italy, or at the very start of his education? In favour of his having studied law in Italy, it would have been a natural progression for a strand in the Bec tradition to move from his turning his back on it after leaving Italy[11] to his being the model monk who, like St. Bernard who refused his mother's breast in infancy, foreshadowed the future by shunning the law from the start.[12] By the same token, a Bec tradition concerned to show that the mature Lanfranc eschewed the law is unlikely to have gratuitously introduced the story that he was an expert pleader. If the *Life of Lanfranc* followed the lost ending of William of Poitiers, there was independent and relatively early testimony to his legal expertise. Yet the alternative story contains circumstantial detail, such as his father's early death. There is no definitive independent evidence

---

7  Esp. *VL* 1.2, col. 31A; 2.4, col. 32BC (from *VH* cap. 62, p. 197); 6.13, cols 41B–42B; 15.36, col. 55BC. Other, earlier sources made no references to Lanfranc the lawyer, e.g. Poitiers, 126–7; Florence of Worcester, *Chronica ex chronicis*, ed. B. Thorpe, English Historical Society, 2 vols. (London, 1848–49), 2: 7.

8  *VH* caps. 59–61, pp. 196–97, whence *VL* 1.3, cols. 31C–32B.

9  R.W. Southern, *Saint Anselm: a Portrait in a Landscape* (Cambridge, 1990), 32–33.

10  *The Letters of Lanfranc Archbishop of Canterbury*, eds. and trans. H. Clover and M. Gibson (Oxford, 1979), no. 49, pp. 158–61.

11  Supra, n. 3.

12  Supra, n. 4.

that Lanfranc studied or practised law at Pavia,[13] and it should be remembered that if he studied elsewhere, little is now left of the view that in his early days there were law schools at which he might have studied in Ravenna or Bologna.[14] Lanfranc's writings of all kinds – letters, commentaries, treatises – are virtually barren of secure evidence that he ever studied Lombard law.[15] As archbishop of Canterbury, he was much concerned with feudal lawsuits and proceedings in England, but the records yield no hint that his acknowledged skills were otherwise based than those of the Anglo-Norman episcopate in general.[16] It would have been consistent with Lanfranc's attitudes and development after leaving Italy if he had avoided legal learning from the outset of his career.[17]

The arguments for and against Lanfranc's early education and practical skill in Lombard law are pretty evenly balanced, and the question is best left open. It certainly cannot be presumed that he left Italy with special legal knowledge or experience, or that he had not, indeed, deliberately eschewed it. Possibly he never studied or practised Lombard law.

A second, more weighty problem about Lanfranc is that of the depth of his acquaintance with, and commitment, to the ecclesiastical as well as to the moral objectives of the early reform papacy, especially under Popes Leo IX (1049–54), Nicholas II (1058–61), and Alexander II (1061–73).[18] Historians have minimized Lanfranc's commitment to it. In the Italy of his youth, the papacy was in the hands of the local Roman family of Tusculum; if Popes Benedict VIII (1012–24) and John XIX (1024–32) so ruled that the Tusculan papacy was not always so black as it has been painted on account of Benedict IX (1032–45/46), it was still weak and fitful in what it did. Lanfranc left Lombardy long before, in 1046, the Emperor Henry III visited Rome and set in train the reform and renewal of papal authority and prestige. Lanfranc's travels ended in a Normandy where he became mainly concerned with an austere form of the monastic life and with study and teaching.

---

13  The reference in the apparatus to the legal code known as the *Expositiones* to an `Archbishop Lanfranc' who put a legal question on inheritance to a *iudex* but was corrected in discussion may be of early twelfth-century drafting and may confuse two Lanfrancs: *Leges Langobardorum Papiae: leges Widonis imperatoris*, 6.23, *MGH Leges Langobardorum* 4, eds. Friedrich Bluhme and Alfred Boretius (Leipzig, 1868), 566–67; see M. Gibson, *Lanfranc of Bec* (Oxford, 1978), 6–8.

14  For the study of law at Ravenna, see I. Heidrich, *Ravenna unter Erzbischof Wibert (1073–1100)* (Sigmaringen, 1984), 148–50; at Bologna, see Fried, *Die Entstehung des Juristenstandes*, 45–46, 139–40.

15  For such evidence as there is, see R.W. Southern, `Lanfranc of Bec and Berengar of Tours,' in *Studies in Medieval History Presented to Frederick Maurice Powicke*, eds. R.W. Hunt, W.A. Pantin, and R.W. Southern (Oxford, 1948), 28–29; Gibson, *Lanfranc of Bec*, 9–11.

16  See the material in *Lawsuits*, 1, pp. 2–107. Lanfranc's pre-eminent skills were acknowledged, e.g., in Eadmer, *Historia novorum in Anglia*, ed. M. Rule, R. S. 81 (London, 1884), 17–18, 25.

17  This does not exclude the likelihood that Lanfranc absorbed some law both from his early surroundings and in the course of other studies.

18  For a fuller discussion, see H.E.J. Cowdrey, `Lanfranc, the Papacy, and the See of Canterbury,' in *Lanfranco di Pavia e l'Europa del Secolo XI nel IX Centenario della Morte (1089–1989)*, ed. G. D'Onofrio (Rome, 1993), 439–500.

In so far as he took part in external church affairs, it was primarily as the trusted adviser of a duke, the young William II, who was dutiful to the papacy in principle but who was in practice the masterful ruler of the church in his duchy.[19] Lanfranc visited Rome more than once, but there was little depth to his attitude towards it. 'As a monk in an austere house, he had wholehearted sympathy for the papacy's moral crusade. At the same time, there is not a shred of evidence that he welcomed more than moral guidance from Rome.'[20]

However, there are reasons for questioning the accepted view of Lanfranc and the papacy before 1073. If one should guard against exaggerating his contacts with Rome and the papal household, they should not be understated. It is particularly necessary to take due note of Lanfranc's almost year-long association with Leo IX in 1049–50, for this remarkably long absence from Bec of its then prior was not highlighted in the Bec historical tradition. The association began at, or soon after, Leo's council of Reims in October 1049. Lanfranc thereafter shared Leo's journey to Rome which he reached for a council at the Lateran in April 1050.[21] Leo asked Lanfranc to remain in his household until the Council of Vercelli in the following September.[22] Lanfranc was thus the close associate of one of the most active and respected of medieval popes throughout the most significant twelve months of his pontificate. In future years, the balance of probability is that Lanfranc again came to Rome in 1059, the year in which Nicholas II held an epoch-making council there which passed various measures, including the papal Election Decree, which were designed to reduce lay influence over the church.[23] Under Alexander II, Lanfranc certainly visited Rome in 1067 when he dealt with the translation of Bishop John of Avranches to the metropolitan see of Rouen, which in Canon Law required papal sanction.[24] When himself archbishop of Canterbury, Lanfranc travelled to Rome in the autumn of 1071 to receive his pallium and to transact other business to which it will be necessary to return.[25] Lanfranc thus made three, and probably four, well spaced visits to Rome. Some of them were timed to impress upon him the leading popes and the leading papal occasions of the early reform period.

That does not necessarily mean that Lanfranc responded to Roman aims and methods, as opposed to moral aspirations, or that they made any real impression upon him. Here again, however, there are grounds for thinking that Lanfranc may

---

[19] For Lanfranc as William's adviser in Normandy before 1066, see William of Poitiers, *Gesta Guillelmi ducis Normannorum et regis Anglorum*, ed. R. Foreville (Paris, 1952), 126–28, and *VH* cap. 64, p. 197, whence *VL* 3.7, col. 34D.

[20] Barlow, 'A View of Archbishop Lanfranc,' 171, repr., 231.

[21] For Leo's itinerary, see *Regesta pontificum Romanorum*, ed. P. Jaffé, 2nd ed. by W. Wattenbach et al., 2 vols. (Leipzig, 1885–8), 1: 531–38.

[22] Lanfranc, *De corpore et sanguine Domini*, cap. 4, *PL*, 150: 413BC; *VL* 3.8, cols. 35D–36B.

[23] Lanfranc's presence is asserted by *VL* 3.8, cols. 35D–36C. The arguments for and against are examined by Southern, *Saint Anselm*, 25–28.

[24] *Acta archiepiscoporum Rothomagensium*, *PL*, 147: 279–80.

[25] For the sources and discussion, see Cowdrey, 'Lanfranc, the Papacy, and the See of Canterbury,' 457, 462–64.

134

have fallen in with the intentions of the early reform papacy more considerably than has been appreciated. His travels in 1049–50 with Leo IX must have compelled him to reflect upon that energetic pope's program. Whether he was present or not, he must have become familiar with what happened at the Council of Reims, when the pope exercised his powers to correct errors in the French church and when the assembled bishops acknowledged the Roman pontiff alone to be primate and pope of the church universal.[26] A council soon afterwards at Mainz demonstrated how pope and emperor could work in harmony to demonstrate their respective authority and to legislate about simony, clerical marriage, and church discipline.[27] No less important was the company in which Lanfranc travelled, for it almost certainly included Humbert, the future cardinal-bishop of Silva Candida, whom Leo brought to Rome from his monastery at Remiremont.

In words which are near to those used at Reims, Lanfranc showed the imprint which Rome and its primacy left upon his mind when he began his commentary on the Epistle to the Romans by observing that `This Epistle is placed first because of the dignity of the city in which it was God's will for the primacy over his whole church to reside.'[28] When Berengar of Tours called the Roman church a church of the malignant and a seat of Satan, Lanfranc rejoined that others who had erred from the faith had refrained from such blasphemy against St. Peter, and he was at pains to defend the good name and prerogatives of the Roman church; he cited Matt. 16: 18–19 as the title-deeds of its authority.[29] It has been insufficently observed that the figure at Rome of whom Lanfranc wrote most warmly was Cardinal Humbert of Silva Candida, an extreme advocate of papal prerogatives in theory and in practice. Lanfranc wrote in terms of admiration which looked further than Humbert's right-thinking about the Eucharist: as cardinal-bishop,

he so lived and taught that not the slightest breath of suspicion arose about his faith and doctrine. Witness to this is borne by practically all of Latin Christendom which, given the pre-eminence of the apostolic see in whose councils and counsels he was always present and predominant, could not disregard him.[30]

Lanfranc was Humbert's warm admirer and eulogist.

The insertion of letters of Nicholas II in the *Collectio Lanfranci*, the Canon Law

---

[26] For the Council of Reims, see Anselm, *Dedicatio ecclesiae beati Remigii Remensis*, ed. J. Hourlier, *La Champagne Bénédictine: Contribution à l'année Saint-Benoît (480–1980)*, Travaux de l'Académie nationale de Reims 160 (Reims, 1981), 179–297; for its recognition of papal authority, see cap. 26, p. 240.

[27] *MGH Constitudines et acta publica imperatorum et regum inde ab a. DCCCCXI usque ad a. MCXCVII (911–1197)*, 1, ed. Ludwig Weiland (Hanover, 1893), no. 51, pp. 97–100.

[28] M. Gibson, `Lanfranc's Commentary on the Pauline Epistles,' *The Journal of Theological Studies*, n.s. 22 (1971): 108, repr. `*Artes' and Bible in the Medieval West* (Aldershot, 1993), no. XII, p. 108.

[29] Lanfranc, *De corpore*, cap. 16, col. 426BD.

[30] Lanfranc, *De corpore*, cap. 2, cols. 409B–410B. Berengar's confession of faith in 1059, for the drafting of which Humbert was responsible, is copied in the *Collectio Lanfranci*: Cambridge, Trinity College MS. B.16.44 (405), p. 210.

collection that Lanfranc brought to England, is also eloquent of Lanfranc's regard for the papacy of c. 1060. Nicholas wrote to Lanfranc as a mentor of the papacy in terms of more than formal compliment. The pope desired Lanfranc's company and counsels in ecclesiastical concerns, for he was reputedly very serviceable (*satis opportunum*) in Roman and papal business.[31] Nicholas's program for the rehabilitation of the church in head and members was set out in his encyclical *Vigilantia universalis* which followed his Roman synod of 1059. Its programmatic opening dwelt upon the pope's duty of overseeing all Christians with a vigilance that befitted his universal dignity and office. It went beyond moral exhortation by summarizing the recent Election Decree, by rigorously prohibiting simony and clerical concubinage and by prescribing instead a common form of clerical life, by prohibiting lay possession of tithes, and by forbidding clerks to receive a church from lay hands. This was the most comprehensive papal program to be formulated up to 1073. A critical element in its manuscript transmission is its being copied into the *Collectio Lanfranci* and thence into some twenty manuscripts in the Anglo-Norman lands.[32] It is an arresting fact that its being thus copied should play so large a part in its survival. Whatever Lanfranc may have thought of some of its details, he seems to have regarded it as of high authority and worthy of record; he disseminated papal principles and not just papal morality.

Under Alexander II Lanfranc's attachment to the early reform papacy was at its most cordial and fruitful. There was personal warmth between the two men which found expression in terms that were more than conventional. In October 1071 Alexander urged King William I to follow the admonitions and advice of his (the pope's) brother Lanfranc, who was a most beloved member and an elder son of the Roman church.[33] Next Spring Lanfranc recalled to Alexander how, during his recent visit to Rome, the pope had granted all favours for others which Lanfranc had sought and which were right and profitable; the remembrance of the pope's name came to his mind whenever he did anything good.[34] Lanfranc sought Alexander's direction with respect to current problems. In 1071, he sought from Alexander as supreme ruler of the whole church of Christ detailed advice about how to deal with problem bishops – Herman of Ramsbury who, pleading old age and infirmity, wished to return to the cloister, and the carnally incontinent Leofwine of Lichfield, who had actually returned. About both bishops Lanfranc sought urgent guidance from the pope; he would not proceed until Alexander had given precise instructions.[35] Such was Alexander's trust for Lanfranc that in October 1071 he wrote to the king that he had given him a personal authority like that of a papal vicar:

---

31 Supra, n. 9.
32 For a text of the encyclical and for its MS. tradition, see R. Schieffer, *Die Entstehung des päpstlichen Investiturverbots für den deutschen König*, Schriften der MGH 28 (Stuttgart, 1981), 63–67, 208–24.
33 *The Letters of Archbishop Lanfranc*, no. 7, p. 60.
34 Ibid., no. 4, p. 56.
35 Ibid., no. 2, pp. 34–38.

In hearing and settling cases, we have given him such a delegation of our own and apostolic authority (*nostrae et apostolicae auctoritatis vicem*) that whatever he shall decide in accordance with righteousness shall thereafter be held to be as valid and binding as if it were settled in our own presence.[36]

At Rome in 1071, Alexander accorded Lanfranc the rare honour of bestowing a second pallium as a mark of personal favour.[37] From popes like Nicholas II and Alexander II, Lanfranc looked for more than moral guidance. He received and recorded their program, and he looked to a friendly pope for detailed guidance as he went about his task as metropolitan.

Lanfranc's cordial relations with Alexander II until the latter's death in 1073 point to a further problem for discussion. Undoubtedly after the succession of Pope Gregory VII (1073–85), Lanfranc settled down to a close working relationship with King William I as 'the perfect second-in-command,' thereby renewing his former serviceableness to William in the Norman duchy.[38] But it should not be assumed that between 1070 and 1073 relations between archbishop and king were not subject to stress. Lanfranc's last letter to Alexander shows signs of considerable stress. Lanfranc wrote to the pope about his own *calamitates* and pleaded to be allowed to return to the monastic life. He gave some reasons, but he hinted at more than he spelt out; for he ended his letter with a distinctly 'half a loaf is better than no bread at all' comment upon the king:

> I ask you to beseech a merciful God . . . to prick (*quatinus . . . compungat*) his heart always to love him and his holy church with godly devotion. For so long as he lives we have peace of a kind, but after his death we expect to have neither peace nor anything good.[39]

There is an implication that William might study more what Lanfranc saw as the good of the church. Two areas of friction between Lanfranc and the king may be suggested.[40]

The first is the problem presented by Stigand, the archbishop whom papal legates deposed in 1070 to make room for Lanfranc at Canterbury. In the eyes of Alexander II, Stigand was a source of evil in the English church and the cause of virtual apostasy; it was the pope's duty to act in the spirit of Pope Gregory the Great, the apostle of the English, to renew Christianity among them.[41] In and after 1070, Lanfranc adopted and acted upon the papal appraisal. This is apparent in the

---

[36] Ibid., no. 7, p. 62.

[37] Ibid., no. 4, pp. 54–56, cf. *VL* 11.24, cols. 48D–49A.

[38] Supra, n. 19.

[39] *The Letters of Archbishop Lanfranc*, no. 1, p. 34.

[40] For a fuller discussion, see Cowdrey, 'Lanfranc, the Papacy, and the See of Canterbury,' 451–58, 460–62, 470–71.

[41] See Alexander II, Ep. 139, in *PL*, 146: 1413; also his legates' summons of an English bishop to the Council of Winchester, 1070, in *Councils and Synods with Other Documents relating to the English Church*, 1: *A.D. 871–1204*, eds. D. Whitelock, M. Brett, and C.N.L. Brooke, pt. 2: *1066–1204* (Oxford, 1981), no. 86/1, p. 568.

profession of obedience which, probably in 1072, Lanfranc required from Re-
migius, bishop of Dorchester, whom Stigand had consecrated in ?1067. When
Lanfranc and Remigius visited Rome in 1071, Alexander made clear his view that
it was as though Stigand's pontificate had never been. With Lanfranc's mediation,
Remigius had besought and received Alexander's pardon for his consecration by
Stigand. In other professions, Lanfranc exhibited Stigand as an invader of his see;
until Lanfranc was consecrated, it was destitute of a pastor.[42] The construction of
Stigand's position that Lanfranc shared with Alexander II contrasted with that
upon which William had acted since the Conquest. William enjoyed and needed to
preserve Alexander's goodwill. But Stigand's wealth and influence rendered it
expedient in the confused aftermath of the Conquest for the king to accord him a
position of honour that he had not enjoyed before 1066. Ecclesiastically he was
allowed to consecrate Remigius, a monk of Fécamp, for the see of Dorchester, and
politically he was prominent in the king's court, attesting charters before all other
bishops including Archbishop Aldred of York. But when Aldred died in 1069,
William had little choice but to dispense with Stigand in order to secure unexcep-
tionably consecrated archbishops in the metropolises of the kingdom who could
expect to receive their pallia from Alexander. Given Lanfranc's rigorous insistence
upon Alexander's estimate of Stigand his relations with the king can scarcely have
been without strain. Lanfranc in effect publicly dissociated himself from the king's
tolerance of Stigand and called in question his public conduct since the Conquest
in respect of the principal English see.

A second occasion of friction arose from Lanfranc's determination to clinch his
view of the primacy in England of his see of Canterbury. When in 1071 he raised
the issue at Rome before the pope, Alexander II had remitted it for settlement in
England.[43] This left Lanfranc with the need to secure from Archbishop Thomas of
York not only a more stringent profession of obedience that he had already made in
1070, but also an oath to himself by which the profession might be underpinned;
for breach of a profession canonically constituted only a *mendacium* punishable by
excommunication, whereas breach of an oath was a *periurium* which merited the
graver sentence of deposition.[44] In 1070 Lanfranc had already sought an oath
which would reinforce Thomas's profession. Thomas had rejected Lanfranc's argument that he must take it and had departed unconsecrated. Lanfranc seems to have
acted without prior consultation with the king, who heard about the incident only
later. When he did, he took it badly and considered that Lanfranc was asking more

---

[42] *Canterbury Professions*, ed. M. Richter, The Canterbury and York Society 67 (1973), nos. 31
(Wulfstan of Worcester), 32 (Remigius of Dorchester), 33 (Herfast of Elmham), pp. 26–28. The
king's physician, Abbot Baldwin of Bury St Edmunds (1065–97/8), who had received his abbatial
blessing from Stigand at an unknown date, was probably similarly pardoned in 1071 before
Alexander II ordained him priest: Herman the Archdeacon, *De miraculis sancti Eadmundi*, caps.
28, 66, in *Memorials of St Edmund's Abbey*, ed. T. Arnold, R.S., 96, 3 vols. (London, 1890–96), 1:
61, 66; also *Lawsuits*, no. 9, pp. 24–25, 28.

[43] *The Letters of Lanfranc*, no. 3(ii), pp. 42–44.

[44] See Richter's comments in *Canterbury Professions*, xix–xx.

than was his due. After discussion at court, Lanfranc acceded to a compromise: Thomas made his profession to Lanfranc and was consecrated, but the question of an oath was left unsettled.[45]

It was once more at issue in 1072, when the question of the primacy was publicly considered and determined. During the Eastertide council of Winchester, Lanfranc demanded that, in accordance with a tradition for which it is hard to see a basis, the archbishop of York should profess obedience to the archbishop of Canterbury with an accompanying oath. Once again, the king demurred; `out of love for the king' Lanfranc had to waive, if without prejudice to his successors' right, his claim to an oath, and Thomas made only a profession.[46] The phrase `out of love for the king' has the ring of a euphemism for Lanfranc's having perforce to give way to the king, who would not allow a tenant-in-chief, like the archbishop of York, to take an oath of such weight to anyone but himself. Despite his claims, Lanfranc had to yield.[47] His preparedness to do so paved the way for his close collaboration with the king during the remainder of their joint lives. But it was also a setback in Lanfranc's struggle to tie in all loose ends of the primacy dispute. It was the king's implacable resistance to Thomas's oath of obedience that caused the setback.

It is apparent that, between 1070 and 1073, Lanfranc's hostility to Stigand in which he followed the pope and prevailed over the king, and his determination to secure an oath of obedience to himself from Thomas of York despite which the king prevailed over him, made relations between Lanfranc and King William less than easy or harmonious. Such tensions are likely to have contributed to his experiencing these years as a time of *calamitates*.[48]

If Lanfranc may thus have been more aware of and committed to the early reform papacy and especially Alexander II, and if his initial relations as archbishop with William I may have been more difficult, than has been appreciated, the problem of his uneasy dealings with Gregory VII is correspondingly intensified. Several considerations may be suggested. In general, other metropolitans who were by no means unworthy men nor lacking in commitment to reforming principles also reacted against Gregory. The basic reason was their unpreparedness to accept Gregory's rigorous theory and exercise of the prerogatives of the apostolic see of Rome. Among those to whom Gregory sent individual tidings of his election and from whom he sought collaboration were Archbishops Guibert of Ravenna, the future anti-pope Clement III, and Manasses of Reims;[49] both were in some degree reform-minded but turned strongly against him. Amongst the German archbishops, Liemar of Bremen was opposed to him, but he was no enemy of the

---

45 *The Letters of Lanfranc*, no. 3(i), pp. 40–42.
46 Ibid., no. 3(iii), p. 44.
47 Ibid., no. 3(iv), p. 46.
48 Supra, n. 39.
49 *Gregorii VII Registrum*, 1.3–4, ed. E. Caspar, *MGH Epistolae Selectae* 2 (Berlin, 1920), 5–7; see the comments of I.S. Robinson, `The Friendship Network of Gregory VII,' *History* 63 (1978): 15–18.

moral reform of the church.[50] Udo of Trier begged Gregory never again to set him such a task as the correction of Bishop Pibo of Toul.[51] At an episcopal level, Alexander II's energetic legate to the Anglo-Norman lands, Ermenfrid of Sion, ended his career in the company of King Henry IV of Germany.[52] Gregory VII was a pope who divided even good men: some became devoted supporters, others fierce opponents, others again preferred to detach themselves as much as they could. Lanfranc was not alone in distancing himself from Gregory.

Lanfranc's stance after 1073 was no doubt also determined by a recognition that in the Canterbury-York dispute the large measure of success that he achieved was the result of a constitution of 1072 settled at the Council of Winchester and circulated after the Council of Windsor; it enshrined a decision taken within the English kingdom, with the assent of a papal legate, but essentially by a king with his bishops and abbots.[53] After the meeting at Winchester, Lanfranc hastened by writing a long letter to Alexander II to seek from Rome a papal privilege which would underpin his success.[54] To accompany it, he addressed a brief letter to Archdeacon Hildebrand, so that Hildebrand might understand what Lanfranc needed. No answer from the pope survives; Hildebrand sent a curt but polite refusal to countenance the issuing of a privilege unless Lanfranc returned to Rome in person.[55] He gave no reason; the likeliest explanation is that Hildebrand discounted Lanfranc's claim to be defending ancient usage and believed him to be seeking a novel right that might be just but needed to be further tested. At all events, Hildebrand's reply withheld from Lanfranc the papal underwriting of his claims which was the more desirable since the king had not allowed him to exact an oath of obedience from Thomas of York. Soon after becoming pope as Gregory VII, Hildebrand offered Lanfranc the kind of goodwill gesture that he was extending to other archbishops: addressing him as his dearest brother in Christ, he charged him with pastoral measures towards the Irish which implied recognition of his claim to primacy over the British Isles.[56] But Hildebrand's raising of difficulties over the papal privilege is likely to have rankled in the years to come in spite of the olive branch.

Hildebrand/Gregory's attitude to Lanfranc's adversary Berengar of Tours may have been no less decisive in making Lanfranc wary of him. Whereas Lanfranc had

---

[50]  Bernold, *De damnatione scismaticorum*, 2, ed. F. Thaner, *MGH Libelli de lite imperatorum et pontificum*, 2 (Hanover, 1892), 43; *Weitere Briefe Meinhards von Bamberg*, no. 41, in *Briefsammlungen der Zeit Heinrichs IV.*, eds. C. Erdmann and N. Fickermann, *MGH Die Briefe der Deutschen Kaiserzeit* 5 (Weimar, 1950), 243.

[51]  *Hildesheimer Briefe*, no. 17, *Briefsammlungen*, 38–41.

[52]  H.E.J. Cowdrey, 'Bishop Ermenfrid of Sion and the Penitential Ordinance following the Battle of Hastings,' *The Journal of Ecclesiastical History* 20 (1969): 232–33.

[53]  *The Letters of Lanfranc*, no. 3(iv), pp. 44–46; cf. Cowdrey, 'Lanfranc, the Papacy, and the See of Canterbury,' 464–70.

[54]  *The Letters of Lanfranc*, no. 4, pp. 48–56.

[55]  Ibid., nos. 5–6, pp. 56–58.

[56]  Ibid., no. 8, pp. 64–66.

welcomed and cited Cardinal Humbert's intransigent condemnation of Berengar's eucharistic teaching in 1059 and whereas, while abbot of Saint-Étienne at Caen, Lanfranc had written his *Liber de corpore et sanguine Domini*, Hildebrand had in effect suspended judgement upon Berengar's doctrine; he had merely carried round a catena of passages of the fathers which might help to reveal the truth.[57] If, in 1072, Lanfranc responded to Alexander II's request that he send to Rome a copy of his treatise to the schismatic Berengar (*Beringerio scismatico*), there is no evidence that Gregory VII ever paid it any attention.[58] While archbishop of Canterbury, Lanfranc did not abate his hostility to the teaching of *scismaticus ille*, Berengar.[59] But, until almost the last minute before his condemnation of Berengar's teaching at his Lent synod in 1079, Gregory continued to be restrained in his dealings about Berengar. When he condemned him, he did so for reasons which seem to have less to do with the authorities and arguments in which Lanfranc dealt than with what he regarded as a sign from Heaven.[60] To Lanfranc Gregory must have seemed to have been culpably unsure and temporizing in his dealings with a hardened *scismaticus*. Nor, if it reached him, does Gregory's sentence of 1079 seem to have satisfied him. In 1080/81 he could declare that St. Augustine of Hippo did not deny the true and authentic presence of Christ's flesh and blood, as many schismatics had thought and had still not ceased to think; the allusion to Berengar is transparent.[61] About Berengar there seems always to have been between Lanfranc and Gregory a barrier of incomprehension and divergence of approach which inhibited their relationship.

For whatever reasons, their letters disclose, albeit in guarded terms, a gap of comprehension and sympathy which was never overcome.[62]

How far did Lanfranc's distance from Gregory lead him towards Archbishop Guibert of Ravenna after, in 1080, he was chosen to be anti-pope at Henry IV's Synod of Brixen and, more especially, since Eastertide 1084, when he was installed at Rome as Clement III?[63] It must be remembered that Guibert himself was in many respects a worthy man and a moderately reforming archbishop.[64] Lanfranc certainly received and preserved three letters from him between 1085 and 1089; if letters from Nicholas II and Alexander II were copied into the *Collectio Lanfranci*, so too were Clement's letters. They were cordial in tone and twice invited Lanfranc to come to Rome.[65] The letters did not come to Lanfranc unheralded, for even before

---

57  H.E.J. Cowdrey, 'The Papacy and the Berengarian Controversy,' in *Auctoritas et Ratio: Studien zu Berengar von Tours*, eds. P. Ganz, R.B.C. Huygens, and F. Niewöhner (Wiesbaden, 1990), 122–24.

58  *The Letters of Lanfranc*, no. 4, p. 56.

59  Ibid., nos. 46, 49, pp. 144, 156–58.

60  Cowdrey, 'The Papacy and the Berengarian Controversy,' 125–33.

61  *The Letters to Lanfranc*, no. 49, p. 158.

62  See esp. *Gregorii VII Registrum*, 6.30, pp. 443–44; *The Letters of Lanfranc*, no. 38, pp. 128–30.

63  See H.E.J. Cowdrey, *The Age of Abbot Desiderius* (Oxford, 1983), 140–42.

64  For recent estimates of Guibert, see Heidrich, *Ravenna*, 157–64, J. Ziese, *Wibert von Ravenna: Der Gegenpapst Clemens III. (1084–1100)*, Päpste und Papsttum 20 (Stuttgart, 1982), 275–79.

65  For the letters, see F. Liebermann, 'Lanfranc and the Antipope,' *EHR* 16 (1901): 330–32; they

Gregory VII died on 25 May 1085, Lanfranc exchanged letters with one of Clement's partisans, a `Hu.' who may have been the virulent anti-Gregorian Hugh Candidus.[66] Lanfranc seems to have initiated the exchange. In so far as his purpose can be inferred, he seems to have been keeping his options open by remaining poised between the two sides in the papal schism, without irrevocably backing either. Lanfranc's surviving letter is a masterpiece of noncommittal. He criticized the terms in which `Hu.' wrote to him: `Hu.' presumptuously vituperated Gregory and his legates but prematurely eulogized Clement. The victory at Rome of Henry IV, whom Lanfranc called *gloriosus imperator*, was perhaps a sign of God's favor. But `Hu.' might not come to England without King William's leave. So far as England was concerned, matters at issue between Gregory and Clement were not yet sufficently clarified that a decision about what should be done was possible.

There is no evidence, and a minimal likelihood, that William I wavered in his loyalty to Gregory, whose ardent supporter, Bishop Anselm II of Lucca, was confident of William's serviceableness to the end.[67] After William I's death, the English kingdom made no overt commitment to either pope – Clement III or Urban II. This, no doubt, encouraged Clement to send his three letters to Lanfranc. There is no reason to suppose that Lanfranc or anyone else responded to them. Lanfranc kept in touch with continental churchmen who were far from supporting Clement. They included the Gregorian-minded Abbot Rodolf of Saint-Vanne at Verdun[68] and Lanfranc's longstanding correspondent, Anselm, at Bec who, with the rest of the Norman church, recognized Urban II from the beginning of his pontificate in 1088.[69] On 10 April 1088, Urban himself announced his succession to Lanfranc and urged him to help and honour the afflicted Roman church by his counsel and solace.[70] Urban gave no hint of doubting Lanfranc's loyalty. The indications are that, until he died in 1089, Lanfranc maintained his position as in his letter to `Hu.' of some five years before: he remained open to contacts from both sides, but he did nothing to compromise publicly his loyalty to Gregory VII and then Urban II.

A final question that may be posed about Lanfranc is, how did he stand in English domestic affairs between the death on 9 September 1087 of his old master William I and his own death on 28 May 1089, given that the new king William II

are copied into Trinity College, Cambridge, MS. B.16.44, pp. 405–6. It is not clear when the letters were copied or whether it was during Lanfranc's lifetime. For further discussion of Lanfranc and Clement, see H.E.J. Cowdrey, `Pope Gregory VII and the Anglo-Norman Church and Kingdom,' *Studi Gregoriani 9 (1972): 109–14*, repr. *Popes, Monks and Crusaders* (London, 1984), no. IX, pp. 109–14.

[66] *The Letters of Lanfranc*, no. 52, pp. 164–66; it is not likely to date from before 24 Mar. 1084, since Guibert did not use the name Clement before his consecration.

[67] *Hildesheimer Briefe*, no. 1, *Briefsammlungen*, 15–17.

[68] Ep. 66, in *Beati Lanfranci archiepiscopi Cantuariensis Opera quae supersunt omnia*, ed. J.A. Giles, 2 vols. (Oxford and Paris, 1844), 1: 80–81.

[69] Ep. 124, in *S. Anselmi Cantuariensis archiepiscopi Opera omnia*, ed. F.S. Schmitt, 6 vols. (Edinburgh and London, 1940–61), 3: 264–65.

[70] Ep. 3, *PL*, 151: 286–87.

144

*Collectio Lanfranci.*[76] It applied mainly, but not only, to bishops and combined the legal principle that penalty should not precede judgement with a recognition that an accused person should not face judgement without the benefit of his own resources and powers; a Pseudo-Isidorian text made the last point in words that a Norman audience would appreciate: unarmed men cannot fight on fair terms with armed ones.[77] For the rule to be invoked, spoilation must be substantial and debilitating. The effects were that a despoiled bishop should not be compelled to

[76] References to the *exceptio spolii* appear in the canonical collections as follows; the list is based upon that in Ruffini, *L'actio spolii*, 183–84:

| | Source in Ps.-Isid. | *Decretales Pseudo-Isidor-ianae*, ed. P. Hinschius (Leipzig, 1863) | *Collectio Lanfranci* Camb. Trin. Coll. MS. pp. | Camb. Peterhouse MS. fos. |
|---|---|---|---|---|
| 1. | Isidori Praef., cap. 6 | 18–19 | – | – |
| 2. | Sixtus I, Ep. 2, cap. 6 | 108–9 | 28–29 | 18r |
| 3. | Zephyrinus, Ep. 2, caps. 11–12 | 133 | 35 | 22r |
| 4. | Fabian, Ep. 2, cap. 20 | 165 | – | – |
| 5. | Stephen I, Ep. 2, cap. 6 | 184 | 46–47 A | 28v |
| 6. | Sixtus II, Ep. 2, cap. 6 | 192 | 49 | 30r |
| 7. | Felix I, Ep. 2, cap. 10 | 201 | 50–51 | 31r–31v |
| 8. | Gaius, Ep. cap. 4 | 214–15 | – | – |
| 9. | Marcellus, Ep. 2, cap. 8 | 227 | 52–53 | 32r |
| 10. | Eusebius, Ep. 2, caps. 11–13 | 237–38 | 53–54 | 32v |
| 11. | Julius I, Ep. 2, caps. 12, 19 | 468, 473 | 67, 69 | 41v, 43r |
| 12. | Athanasius ep., *Ep. Felici papae directa*, cap. 3 | 480 | – | – |
| 13. | Felix II, Ep. 2, cap. 12.4, 5, 9 | 485–86 | 74–75 | 45r–45v ? |
| 14. | Stephen abp, *Ep. ad Damasum papam* | 501 | 78 | 47v |
| 15. | Damasus, Ep. 2, caps. 12–13 | 503–4 | 79–80 | 48r |
| 16. | *Actio V^{ae} synodi sub Symmacho* | 676 | 176–77 | 100v–101r |
| 17. | John I, *Decreta* | 694 | 180–81 | 102v–103r |
| 18. | Pelagius II, *Decreta ad omnes episcopos per Campaniae et Italiae provincias* | 730–31 | 191 A | 108r |

In this note and in note 79, the symbols A and ? indicate the presence of such symbols in the margin of the respective MSS. For their possible significance, see Brooke, *The English Church and the Papacy*, 68.

[77] Hinschius, 503: 'Scimus enim homines inermes non posse cum armatis rite pugnare, sic nec illi qui eiecti vel suis bonis sunt expoliati cum illis qui in suo stant statu et suis fruuntur amicis atque bonis, litigare rite non possunt.'

answer a charge until his goods were completely restored and that before proceeding with a case a judicial authority should see to such restoration.

The bishop's second line of legal defence was a corollary to the *exceptio spolii*, less because there was a close substantial connection than because many of its proof-texts in Pseudo-Isidore and derivative collections came close to it on the written page. The bishop claimed that by reason of his holy orders one of his rank should be subject neither to the accusation nor to the judgement of lay authorities.[78] If Bishop William appeared in the king's court, it could be only before its spiritual members; if this were not allowed, he would do no more than purge himself by swearing to his own innocence, perhaps with bishops as witnesses of his purgation (*DIV*, 92–93, 102). His third line of defence also found warrant on much the same canonical pages: it was that a bishop who could not secure justice in his own province had a right of appeal to the apostolic see so that his case might be heard by the pope.[79] The bishop's reading of Canon Law led him to combine these three lines of legal defence in a closely knit argument.[80]

---

[78] Some examples of proof-texts are:

| Source in Ps.-Isid. | Hinschius | *Collectio Lanfranci* Camb. Trin. Coll. MS pp. | Camb. Peterhouse MS fos |
|---|---|---|---|
| 1. Stephen I, Ep. 2, cap. 10 | 185-86 | 47 | 29r |
| 2. Julius I, Ep. 2, cap. 12 | 469 | 67 | 41v |
| 3. Felix II, Ep. 2, cap. 12.1 | 485 | 74 | 45r |
| 4. Damasus, Ep. 2, cap. 13 | 503-4 | 79-80 | 48r |

[79] Some examples of proof-texts are:

| Source in Ps.-Isid. | Hinschius | *Collectio Lanfranci* Camb. Trin. Coll. MS. pp. | Camb. Peterhouse MS. fos. |
|---|---|---|---|
| 1. Sixtus I, Ep. 2, cap. 5 | 108 | 29 | 18r |
| 2. Stephen I, Ep. 2, cap. 10 | 185-86 | 47-48 | 29r |
| 3. Sixtus II, Ep. 1, cap. 2 | 190 | 48 | 29v ? |
| 4. Julius I, Ep. 2, cap. 12 | 469 | 67 | 41v |
| 5. Stephen abp, *Ep. ad Damasum papam* | 501 | 78 | 47rv ? |

[80] See esp. the bishop's speech at *DIV*, 98–99: 'Iudicium quod hic dictum est respuo, quia contra canones et contra legem nostram factum est, neque enim canonice vocatus sum, sed coactus vi regalis exercitus adsum, et dispoliatus episcopio extra provinciam meam, absentibus omnibus comprovincialibus meis, in laicali conventu causam meam dicere compellor, et inimici mei, qui mihi consilium et colloquium suum et pacis osculum denegant, postpositis dictis meis de his quae non dixi me iudicant, et accusatores sunt simul et iudices, et in lege nostra prohibitum invenio, ne talem iudicium suscipiam. Quod si ex fatuitate mea vellem suscipere, archiepiscopus et primas

Historians have commonly seen in the situation, so far as Lanfranc is concerned, an example of 'the sport to have the enginer hoist with this own petar': at his Salisbury trial, William discomfited Lanfranc by citing against him his own Canon Law collection. There is clearly a good deal of truth in this so far as it goes. But it may be suggested that, to a remarkable extent, Lanfranc remained the master of events and was able at Salisbury to turn the tables on the bishop, both politically and in Canon Law.

Politically, first. During the trial at Salisbury, Lanfranc had the advantage of support from the lay, as well as from the clerical, part of the *curia regis*; the laity saw him as the protagonist and spokesman of their view of things (*DIV*, 96). This was dramatically apparent when Lanfranc advised the king that he might arrest the bishop if he persisted in refusing to surrender his castle of Durham, and all the laity agreed: 'Arrest him, arrest him, for this *vetulus ligaminarius* – translate, perhaps, this old dog-handler, this master of the hunting-field – says well' (*DIV*, 100). The laity applauded Lanfranc's preparedness to let slip the dogs of arrest against a recalcitrant and isolated evader of rightful judgement.[81] There were more sophisticated reasons for Lanfranc's command of lay and clerical support. The bishop's case, however capably argued, was built upon Canon Law texts which were assembled in the mid-ninth century and which were actually or purportedly gathered from popes and councils under the ancient Roman Empire. They were, no doubt, part of the material upon which the reform papacy was also drawing in order to give substance and effect to the prerogatives that it claimed. But their antiquity left them imperfectly adapted to the strong feudal polity of the early Norman kings of England, in which the bishops had a double loyalty: they were at once churchmen who owed canonical obedience within an ecclesiastical hierarchy which culminated in the apostolic see and tenants-in-chief of the crown who, just like their lay peers, owed fealty to the king, suit to the *curia regis*, and acceptance of feudal law.

meus dei ordinisque respectu ab huiusmodi praesumptione me deberent caritative compescere. Et quia per regis odium vos omnes adversarios sentio, apostolicam sedem, Romanam scilicet ecclesiam, et beatum Petrum eiusque vicarium appello, ut ipsius ordinatione negotii mei iustam sententiam suscipere merear; cuius dispositioni maiores causas ecclesiasticas et episcoporum iudicia antiqua apostolorum eorumque successorum atque canonum auctoritas reservavit.'

[81] The word *ligaminarius*, which is known only here in all classical and medieval Latin writings, defies translation. It is evidently derived from the noun *ligamen*, a fastening, tie, or string: see *Oxford Latin Dictionary*, ed. R.G.W. Glare (Oxford, 1982), s.v. *ligamen* a. Dr Gibson concludes that it refers to the bloodhound who is held by the leash: *Lanfranc of Bec*, 161. But nouns ending in -*arius* usually refer to men. At an assembly which the *DIV* declared to have included huntsmen (*DIV*, 98) and in the context of cries of *Capite, capite*, it may reasonably be understood of a man who holds a *ligamen*. A credible image of a *ligaminarius* is the huntsman in the margin of the Bayeux Tapestry who holds at leash two hounds straining to be after their prey: D.M. Wilson, *The Bayeux Tapestry* (London, 1985), Plate 12, lower right. The earliest reference in an English source to a bloodhound (*canis sanguinarius*) seems to be Walter Map, *De nugis curialium*, 1.11, *Walter Map, De nugis curialium: Courtiers' Trifles*, ed. and trans. M.R. James, revised by C.N.L. Brooke and R.A.B. Mynors (Oxford, 1983), 28.

Not only did the bishop of Durham appeal to Canon Law texts which were too ancient to match the feudal law and obligation of Norman England, but in the course of his troubles he was so ill-advised as to adopt a position that ran counter to these laws and obligations as they were generally accepted. It was no part of his submission that he did not, as a bishop, owe the king secular loyalty and services in respect of his lands; indeed, he always professed readiness to discharge them. But he rejected the notion that his lands could be collectively designated by the word *feodum*. This he claimed was appropriate only to the lands of a lay tenant-in-chief; to admit it would subject him to the judgement of the whole body of his peers, both lay and spiritual. By a vocabulary that he seems to have adopted only after the drafting of the letters at the beginning of the *DIV* (*DIV*, 91–94), he sought to appropriate to his lands the terms *episcopatus* and *episcopium*, which he opposed to the *feodum* of a lay tenant-in-chief; by this means he sought to establish the claim that as a bishop he might be tried only by his spiritual peers.[82] Lanfranc would have none of this idiosyncratic rejection of the term *feodum* and restriction of the terms *episcopatus* and *episcopium*.[83] The Norman magnates, lay and ecclesiastical alike, also dismissed it as an unacceptable novelty; for them as for Lanfranc, the terms *episcopatus* and *episcopium* embraced the whole of a bishop's public duties and responsibilities – his offices as well as his lands.[84] Most certainly, a bishop's lands were his *feodum*, which gave rise to a feudal as well as to an ecclesiastical capacity; he was, therefore, justifiable before the whole *curia regis*. As

---

[82] In *DIV*, Bishop William's identification of his *episcopatus* with his lands is on p. 96, e.g. `... qui ex praecepto regis me dissaisivit de toto episcopatu meo quem habeo in Eboracensi comitatu.' There are further instances on each of pp. 97–101; on p. 101, William distinguishes between his *episcopatus* and his *sedes*. For his rejection of the term *feodum*, see pp. 98, 99. For the use on the Continent of the words *episcopatus* and *episcopium* to designate the estates and profitable rights belonging to a bishopric, see J.F. Niermeyer, *Mediae Latinitatis Lexicon Minus* (Leiden, 1976), s.vv. *episcopatus* 7, *episcopium* 9. In England, the use of these terms by c. 1090 seems to have been more restricted to the bishop's office or diocese: *Dictionary of Medieval Latin from British Sources*, fasc. III D–E (London, 1986) s.vv. *episcopatus*, *episcopium*. Most of Bishop William's life had been spent in Maine and Normandy.

[83] As in the following exchange (*DIV*, 99): `Et episcopus ait: ``Domine archiepiscope, ego nullam feci hodie feodi mentionem vel feodum habere me dixi, sed de episcopii mei dissaisitione conquestus sum et conqueror." Et archiepiscopus, ``Si nunquam," inquit, ``audiam, te loqui de feodo, scio te tamen magnum feodum habuisse, et inde te iudicavimus." ' Lanfranc's use of *episcopatus* on p. 99 expresses the Norman view of the ecclesiastical aspect of a bishop's double capacity as churchman and feudatory; on pp. 96 and 101 he adopts ad hominem the bishop's usage in dialogue with him.

[84] E.g. Archbishop Thomas of York (*DIV*, 98): `Thomas Eboracensis archiepiscopus ait: ``Domine episcope, dominus noster archiepiscopus, et curia regis, vobis iudicat quod rectitudinem regi facere debetis antequam de vestro feodo revestiat." Et episcopus respondit: ``Investituram episcopatus mei mihi reddi precatus sum; dispoliatus sum enim sine omni vocatione et iudicio, et de episcopatu iudicandus, exivi domum istam, et inde requiro iudicium; quod nullus mihi hodie, vel ego alicui, de feodo feci verbum." ' So, too, Hugh (?Henry) de Beaumont (*DIV*, 99): ` ``Domine episcope, regis curia et barones isti vobis pro iusto iudicant, quoniam sibi vos respondere non vultis de his de quibus vos per me appellavit, sed de placito suo invitatis eum Romam quod vos feodum vestrum inde forisfacitis." '

Lanfranc pointed out with reference to the trial in 1082 of Bishop Odo of Bayeux, according to the accepted usage of the Norman kingdom, a bishop's *episcopium* or spiritual capacity was distinct from his *feodum* or temporal endowment (*DIV*, 99); different rules of justice applied to them. After the Domesday Survey, which treated lay and ecclesiastical tenants-in-chief similarly in respect of their holdings and obligations, it is surprising that the bishop of Durham should have tried to distinguish between them as he did.[85] It was a self-defeating move, for it enabled Lanfranc to oppose him as leader and guardian of the Norman order of things in England, with its lay and clerical leaders solidly behind him. At the outset of proceedings at Salisbury, he was able to brush aside the bishop of Durham's question to the two archbishops whether he should not plead his cause ecclesiastically robed before only judges who were similarly robed with the rejoinder, 'We can very well discuss the king's business and yours dressed as we are, for clothes do not hinder truth' (*DIV*, 95–96). With general approval, Lanfranc insisted that Bishop William's trial must take place before the whole *curia regis*, and there should be no prior restoration of his confiscated property (*DIV*, 96, 101; cf. Archbishop Thomas of York's advice, *DIV*, 98).

Lanfranc played his cards against the bishop no less skillfully on issues of Canon Law, and especially of the *exceptio spolii*. To appreciate his skill, it should be remembered that the *exceptio spolii*, which figured prominently in the Pseudo-Isidorian tradition, was familiar to Popes Alexander II, Gregory VII, and Urban II, for whose purposes it was valuable because it helped to promote separate ecclesiastical jurisdiction and the authority of the apostolic see of Rome. Lanfranc had reason to be aware of this. A letter of Alexander II to him in 1071, when their co-operation was at its closest, referred to how, a year earlier, underlings of Alexander's legates had deposed Bishop Ethelric of Chichester. The pope was not satisfied that he had been properly tried. 'As decreed by the canons' – the reference is clearly to the *exceptio spolii*, Ethelric was to be fully restored to his see, as the necessary preliminary to Lanfranc's hearing the case properly according to Canon Law.[86] Gregory VII's letters yield a number of references to the *exceptio spolii*.[87] While there is no direct evidence, the circumstances of the proceedings of King William I's royal court in 1082 against Bishop Odo of Bayeux suggest that they were prudently managed to leave Odo with no grounds for invoking the *exceptio spolii*.[88] This is the likeliest explanation for the circumstance that, although Odo

---

[85] It is the more surprising if P. Chaplais's attractive suggestion be followed that William of St. Calais played a key role in carrying out the Domesday Survey: 'William of St. Calais and the Domesday Survey,' in *Domesday Studies*, ed. J.C. Holt (Woodbridge and Wolfeboro, 1987), 65–77. Or did the omission of the northern shires from Domesday Book lead the bishop into the misapprehension that his lands, wherever situated, were exceptions to the usual Norman rules in England?

[86] *The Letters of Lanfranc*, no. 7, pp. 62–63; for Alexander and the *exceptio spolii*, see also his Ep. 40, *PL*, 146: 1319.

[87] It is referred to or implied in *Gregorii VII Registrum*, 1.44–45, 2.6, 5.17, 6.24–25, 9.29, 33, 34, pp. 67–69, 134, 380, 436–38, 613, 620–22; *The Epistolae Vagantes of Pope Gregory*, ed. and trans. H.E.J. Cowdrey (Oxford, 1972), no. 31, pp. 82–85.

[88] The principal sources for Odo's trial in 1082, details of which are obscure, are William of

was imprisoned, his lands were not forfeited so that, in Domesday, he remained, after the king, the largest landholder in England. By such prudence, Gregory VII's adverse reaction was kept within bounds.[89] However this may be, during William of St. Calais's trial, Lanfranc's reaction to his claim to take advantage of the *exceptio spolii* seems certainly to have been adroit. When the trial began, Lanfranc resisted this claim by rejoining that, for the rule to apply, a bishop's despoliation must be complete or substantial and also the outcome of a judgement. This was legally correct.[90] Only some of the bishop's lands had been seized – mainly those in Yorkshire and Lincolnshire, and William played into Lanfranc's hands when he protested that he was still willing to do services for the king: if he had the wherewithal he was far from destitute. He further played into Lanfranc's hands when he complained to the king that he had taken his *episcopatus* (that is, the lands that he had seized) *sine iudicio*. Lanfranc could then intervene on the king's behalf by saying that the king and his officers had taken no part of his *episcopatus* and no writ of disseisin had formally disseised him.[91] Thus, the bishop could not invoke the *exceptio spolii*; he must do right in the king's court, and do so before, not after, his lands were restored (*DIV*, 96). In the final stages of the trial, Lanfranc was no less adroit. The upshot of the trial was that by judgement of the whole *curia regis* the bishop forfeited all his property, including his castle at Durham (*DIV*, 99, 103).[92] Once this happened, Lanfranc, who throughout had urged William to place

Malmesbury, *De gestis regum Anglorum libri quinque*, ed. William Stubbs, R.S., 2 vols. (London, 1889) 2: 334; Orderic, 7.8, vol. 4: 40–45. The caution shown in 1082 is the more explicable if the *DIV* correctly makes Lanfranc Odo's judge (*DIV*, 99), thus following the precedent of Bishop Ethelric of Chichester's case in 1071. The differences, as well as the similarities, between Odo's trial in 1082 and William of St. Calais's in 1088 are important, not least as regards Odo's position in 1088. Whereas in 1082 Odo was probably tried for attempting to divert knights from England to a foreign adventure, in 1088 he had led a revolt in England itself. Hence the critical importance for the king of Odo's castle of Rochester: see *Anglo-Saxon Chronicle*, ed. Dorothy Whitelock et al. (London, 1961) a. 1088 (1087). At William's trial (*DIV*, 103) the king said of it that there, Odo taught him a hard lesson (*me castigavit*) about castles; hence his concern, which Lanfranc is likely to have shared, to secure William of St. Calais's castle at Durham.

[89]  Gregory's reaction to Odo's arrest and imprisonment was expressed in strong terms to Archbishop Hugh of Lyons: *The Epistolae Vagantes*, no. 53, pp. 128–29, but with restraint to King William I himself: *Gregorii VII Registrum*, 9.37, pp. 630–31, where the citation of ancient models of kingship should be noted. Gregory also had political reasons for restraint towards William: Cowdrey, 'Pope Gregory VII and the Anglo-Norman Church and Kingdom,' 106–9. Whether the journey to Rome which William of St. Calais is said to have made, probably in 1082 (*DIV*, 91), took place before or after Odo's trial and whether pope and bishop discussed it are uncertain, but the possibility should not be overlooked.

[90]  For the effectiveness of the *exceptio spolii* only when a bishop was despoiled of all or most of his property, see Ruffini, *L'actio spolii*, 100–1. But note the ambiguity about judgement in Urban II's mind: see infra, n. 98.

[91]  'Episcopus ergo surgens precatus est regem, ut episcopatum suum quem iamdiu sine iudicio abstulerat sibi redderet. Lanfrancus vero, rege tacente, dixit: "Rex de episcopatu tuo nihil tibi abstulit, vel aliquis per eum, neque breve suum vidisti per quod te de episcopatu tuo dissaisiret vel dissaisiri praeciperet" ' (*DIV*, 96).

[92]  See Hugh de Beaumont's speech: supra, n. 84; and the record in *DIV* that 'Acceperunt ergo Yvo

himself *in misericordia regis* (*DIV*, 102), readily conceded that the *exceptio spolii* now applied: the king could no longer implead the bishop since he had ceased to hold anything of him and was completely despoiled. He must now have the safe conduct that he desired in order to seek justice from Pope Urban II.[93]

This was Lanfranc's master stroke, for at the end of the Salisbury trial, William of St. Calais was in effect checkmated. By the terms of the *exceptio spolii*, the pope could not proceed to judge his case until his possessions had been restored; Urban II had neither the power nor, in view of the schism and the danger of impelling William II into recognition of the anti-pope, the purpose to secure their restoration. Lanfranc must have known full well that, given the terms of the *exceptio spolii*, the bishop, therefore, had no hope of an effective exercise of papal jurisdiction. Once across the sea, he would face the alternative of an indefinite stay in Normandy as a propertyless client of Duke Robert or of a return to England and perhaps restoration to his see upon whatever terms he could secure from King William. It is of course hard to decide how far the bishop's harping upon the *exceptio spolii* and upon an appeal to the apostolic see was an expression of active belief in these things or how far it had been a ploy to evade the king's judgement. On the one side, it appears that Bishop William valued papal authority, for when he introduced monks at Durham cathedral he secured King William I's permission to go to Rome and gain Pope Gregory VII's support (*DIV*, 91), and he had a right at his trial to the protection that Canon Law offered. On the other side, upon reaching the Continent, he did not go to Rome but attached himself to the king's brother and rival, Duke Robert (*DIV*, 105);[94] after three years he was reconciled to the king and restored to his see, and in 1095 at the council of Rockingham he was Archbishop Anselm's bitter opponent when Anselm wished to travel to Rome.[95] In either case, it is easy to understand why, at the end of Bishop William's trial, Lanfranc conceded the operation of the *exceptio spolii* with evident willingness and viewed the bishop's departure with equanimity.

The bishop's immediate fortunes developed with the inevitability of a Greek tragedy. A letter of Pope Urban to King William II, which may be dated to the first half of 1089 when Urban was at Rome, survives in the *Collectio Britannica*.[96] The pope acted on a hearsay report of the bishop's predicament, thus making it clear that the bishop had not gone to Rome in person; either he had sent a messenger or

---

Taillesbosc et Ernesius de Burone castellum Dunelmi in manus regis, et dissaisiverunt episcopum de ecclesia et de castello et de omni terra sua xviii. kal. Decembr.' (*DIV*, 103).

[93] `Et rex ait: ``Videant barones isti, si ego iuste possum implacitare episcopum." Et Lanfrancus archiepiscopus ait: ``Iniustum esset si amplius implacitaretis eum, cum de vobis nihil teneat, et securum conductum habere debeat" ' (*DIV*, 103).

[94] The words *totius Normanniae curam suscepit* should be translated 'took charge of all Normandy,' i.e. assisted the duke in its rule: see C.W. David, *Robert Curthose, Duke of Normandy* (Cambridge, Mass., 1920), 214–15.

[95] Eadmer, *Historia novorum*, 59–62.

[96] S. Loewenfeld, *Epistolae pontificum Romanorum ineditae* (Leipzig, 1885), no. 129, p. 63. For Urban's itinerary, see Jaffé, *Regesta pontificum Romanorum*, 1: 659–63.

he had communicated through the pope's legate Roger, who had been active in Anglo-Norman affairs.[97] Urban's letter demonstrated his own familiarity with the law of the *exceptio spolii*; this was to be expected, not only because of his association with Gregory VII, but also because, as Cardinal Odo of Ostia and Gregory's legate in Germany during the winter of 1084–85, he had warded off an attempt by Henry IV's supporters to adapt the *exceptio spolii* for this king's benefit.[98] Urban wrote to King William II in the bishop of Durham's strong support and in terms which reflected the presentation of his case in the *DIV*,[99] placing strong emphasis upon the *exceptio spolii*. He requested and required the king first fully to restore the bishop to his see and thereafter to allow him to come with his accusers for his case to be determined by the pope. Urban's directions were legally correct but politically impracticable; it is not surprising that, so far as is known, his letter had no effect. If it reached England, it is likely to have done so after Lanfranc's death. Had he seen it, he would doubtless have recognized that, legally correct though it was, from the point of view of the bishop of Durham it represented a cul-de-sac; it could not be implemented, and the bishop had little alternative in the long term but to make his peace with the king on the king's terms and to be for the future his loyal subject.

At no time in Lanfranc's life were his forensic skill and mastery more apparent than in his exploitation of the *exceptio spolii* at the trial of William of St Calais. First, when the bishop had been disseised partly and without a judgement, Lanfranc was able to use the rule to frustrate the bishop's ill-advised use of it to evade judgement in the *curia regis*. But, when the *curia regis* had formally sentenced him to complete forfeiture, Lanfranc supported the bishop's contention that he must appeal to Rome, knowing that the operation of the *exceptio spolii* was certain to frustrate such an appeal. At all stages, Lanfranc carried the support of the king and of both the spiritual and lay figures who were involved.

It is difficult to see that Lanfranc's command of the legal and political situation owed any specific debt to an early training and apprenticeship in Lombardy. His

---

[97] For Roger, see Urban's Epp. 4, 23, *PL*, 151: 287D–288E, 305CD.

[98] *Die Regensburger rhetorischen Briefe, Anhang*, no. 5, *Briefsammlungen*, 377–79; for the circumstances, see H. Fuhrmann, 'Pseudoisidor, Otto von Ostia (Urban II.) und der Zitatenkampf von Gerstungen (1085),' *Zeitschrift der Savigny-Stiftung für Rechtsgeschichte, kanonistische Abteilung*, 68 (1982): 52–69, esp. 54–57. For another letter of Urban which refers to the *exceptio spolii*, see P. Ewald, 'Die Papstbriefe der Brittischen Sammlung,' *Neues Archiv der Gesellschaft für ältere deutsche Geschichtskunde*, 5 (1879): 356–57, no. 15; the date is 1088. The letter concerned the disputed rights of the archbishop of Naples over the church af Aversa. Urban told its bishop, Guitmund, that he would restore to the archbishop the 'possessionis . . . investituram cui eam, non iudiciario ordine sed potestate auctoritatis Romane propter suam negligentiam, iustitia dictante ademeramus. Alias quippe ad iudicium revocari canonice non valerat nisi ei tot iam annis habita possessio redderetur.' See also Urban's letter to the clergy and people of Santiago de Compostela (1088) in Loewenfeld, *Epistolae pontificum Romanorum*, no. 123, p. 60.

[99] There is no reason to suppose that the *DIV* was sent to Urban. But Urban's letter and the *DIV* take a similar view of the king's proceedings against the bishop and of the bishop's own position.

greatness as an archbishop lay in his ability to respond to fresh situations as they developed. His adaptability and his stature were never more apparent than in the events of his last years, when he seems to have served his new master William II as willingly and as well as he had come to serve his old master William I.

# INDEX

This Index does not include an entry for Pope Gregory VII, who is a major subject throughout this volume, nor does it include entries for persons or topics where they are the subject of articles expressly concerned with them. The following abbreviations are used: a. = abbey; ab. = abbot; abp. = archbishop; akg. = anti-king; ap. = anti-pope; b. = battle; bp. = bishop; c. = council; ct. = count; card. = cardinal; css. = countess; d. = duke, e. = eastern; emp. = emperor; emps. = empress; kg.= king; m. = monk; mon. = monastery; p. = pope; pat. = patriarch; pr. = prior; pt. = priest; q. = queen; St = Saint.